The Ancient Near East
in Pictures

THE ANCIENT NEAR EAST
IN PICTURES

Relating to the Old Testament

BY JAMES B. PRITCHARD

PRINCETON · NEW JERSEY

PRINCETON UNIVERSITY PRESS

1954

PRINTED IN THE UNITED STATES OF AMERICA

BY PRINCETON UNIVERSITY PRESS, PRINCETON, N.J.

ILLUSTRATIONS BY THE MERIDEN GRAVURE COMPANY, MERIDEN, CONN.

Contents

CONTENTS

Introduction

THE PEOPLES of the ancient Near East left two types of records of themselves and their pursuits: literature, documents, and other writings; and the more graphic record in monument, building, and artifact, which often reveals much taken for granted by those who wrote. A picture of the life of these peoples as it has been preserved in writings was made available four years ago by eleven scholars in cooperation with the writer, who served as editor, in *Ancient Near Eastern Texts Relating to the Old Testament*, which was published by Princeton University Press. The present volume is intended to enlarge upon and to illustrate the picture one gets of the past from texts, by providing in photograph and drawing the remains of monuments fashioned purposely for record, as well as of those common, but often more revealing, objects of daily life which have come from scores of archaeological expeditions. The purpose here, as it was in *Ancient Near Eastern Texts*, is to present the primary materials themselves in such a form that the average reader and the scholar may use them.

As suggested by the subtitle "Relating to the Old Testament," the selection of illustrations has been made from a particular point of interest. The designation of the people of the ancient biblical world as a point of reference aims at a dual purpose. On the one hand it provides a canon for choice from a mass of material which otherwise would be unmanageable within the reasonable limits of a single volume; on the other, the adoption of this criterion will, it is hoped, enhance the general usefulness of the book by reference to material which is widely studied and generally known. An interest in the Hebrew Bible has long been the core of studies dealing with the ancient Near East, providing in many cases the initial impetus which led to the discovery of objects pictured here. Serious students of this document, basic both to Judaism and to Christianity and the culture once associated with them, have been led eventually into the areas adjacent to Palestine to study their several peoples, some of whom were the ancestors of the inhabitants of biblical Palestine, while others were important either as friends and allies or as bitter enemies.

Although a definite criterion of selection has been adopted, relevance has been defined broadly. In addition to those illustrations which are obviously relevant to the history, daily life, and religion of Palestine during the span of biblical times, there have been given some of the most important objects which illustrate these subjects in adjacent and related cultures and from times earlier than the biblical period. This wider interpretation of relevance rests upon the observation of a certain cultural unity which prevailed throughout the ancient Near East and in which the peoples of Palestine participated. It is hoped that the generous definition of relationship which underlies the selection of material may serve to make the volume of use to students whose primary interest is more general and who are concerned with the history and culture of the entire area of the ancient Near Eastern world.

The selection of pictures and the arrangement in which they have been placed are new. However, the author is deeply indebted to the judgment of others who have compiled handbooks of this nature. Similar in purpose was that made almost three decades ago by H. Gressmann in his *Altorientalische Bilder zum alten Testament*, 1927, which was a second, revised edition of a work that appeared first in 1909. C. Watzinger's *Denkmäler Palästinas*, completed in 1935, and K. Galling's *Biblisches Reallexikon*, 1937, have been useful as earlier collections of Palestinian and biblical materials. The four volumes of G. Contenau, *Manuel d'archéologie orientale*, 1927-1947, and the two volumes of H. Th. Bossert, *Altanatolien*, 1942, and *Altsyrien*, 1951, have been sources of constant reference. Use has been made also of the excellently reproduced photographs in H. Schäfer and W. Andrae, *Die Kunst des alten Orients*, 1925. Many references to illustrations in these volumes have been entered in the bibliographies of the catalogue in order to provide ready access to the valuable comments and descriptions in these sources, as well as for the convenience of those who are already familiar with these earlier works.

In order to have as complete a selection as possible of relevant illustrations the author asked the following scholars, each an authority on the archaeological remains of one or more of the areas to be covered, to serve as an advisory committee for the selection of material: W. F. Albright, Johns Hopkins University; Étienne Drioton, Ex-Directeur Général, Service des Antiquités, Cairo; C. J. Gadd, Keeper of the Department of Egyptian and Assyrian Antiquities, British Museum; André Parrot, Conservateur en chef des Musées Nationaux, France; E. A. Speiser, University of Pennsylvania; and John A. Wilson, University of Chicago. Each has read over the tentative list and contributed valuable suggestions as to the general organization and the specific content. A particular service was rendered by E. A. Speiser in his careful reading of the rough draft of the catalogue and in many helpful notations. For their interest in the project, criticisms, and suggestions which members of the committee have given, as well as for many courtesies in obtaining original photographs of objects, the author is grateful.

Aided by a grant from the American Philosophical Society in Philadelphia the author visited twenty-four museums in the Near East, Europe, and America for the purpose of studying at firsthand the materials and obtaining photographs suitable for reproduction. Acknowledgment is here made of courtesies on the part of the following institutions and members of their respective staffs: Ashmolean Museum, Oxford; British Museum, London; Brooklyn Museum; Cairo Museum; Cincinnati Art Museum; Cleveland Museum of Art; Collection de Clercq, Paris; Louisville Presbyterian Theological Seminary, Lemon Bible Lands Museum; Metropolitan Museum of Art, New York; Musée du Louvre, Paris; Museum of the Ancient Orient, Istanbul; Museum of Fine Arts, Boston; Museum Section, Department of Antiquities, Jerusalem, Israel; National Museum, Aleppo; National Museum, Beirut; Oriental Institute, University of Chicago; Palestine Archaeological Museum, Jerusalem, Jordan; Rijksmuseum van Oudheden, Leiden; Semitic Museum, Harvard University, Cambridge, Mass.; Toledo Museum of Art; University Museum, University of Pennsylvania, Philadelphia; Walters Art Gallery, Baltimore; William Rockhill Nelson Gallery of Art, Kansas City; Yale Babylonian Collection, Yale University, New Haven.

Although this collection gives the widest selection of illustrative material relating to the

Old Testament yet published, it is far from exhausting the rich field of possibility. Some illustrations long standard in books of this sort have been replaced by photographs of objects which have more recently been discovered—some of them not previously published. It has been considered appropriate to include whenever possible objects from museums in America, to replace some of the more familiar pieces from European museums appearing in the older handbooks. This departure may serve not only to acquaint Europeans with the less familiar American collections, but also to point the American student to collections near at hand, where the objects themselves may be seen and studied. The author is well aware that any selection from such a vast field is subjective, but it is hoped that a balance has been achieved between the older familiar objects which many will wish to have and the newer and less familiar pieces which illustrate important features of ancient Near Eastern culture.

In order to present within the available space the greatest number of photographs in a size which shows details with a clarity sufficient for use by the serious student, it has become necessary to condense the comments and accompanying text. As suggested by its position after the plates of photographs, the catalogue has been prepared as a work of reference dealing with the individual photographs and not as a running commentary on the topics dealt with in the various sections. In many points of relationship and development the pictures and their arrangement must speak for themselves. Since those who approach for the first time the study of the culture of the ancient Near East will find general works of introduction useful, suggested references to these sources have frequently been provided in the introductory paragraphs to sections or subdivisions of the catalogue. These references, it is hoped, will aid the reader who seeks for connective interpretation, which could not because of lack of space be included in this volume designed primarily to present pictures.

The descriptive catalogue is intended to give in concise notation the significant details of each picture and those references which may serve the reader who wishes to pursue them. The second paragraph (in smaller type) of each entry gives, when available, the following information: present location of the object and its museum number, where this is readily accessible or could be secured without the hazard of confusion or error;[1] the provenience, and the date of discovery (all dates here are A.D.); material of which the object is made; size or indication of scale; date to which it is attributed, either from archaeological context or on the basis of style (all dates, unless otherwise marked, are B.C.); references to publication, significant or convenient references to other publications or discussions; and the source of the photograph used in this volume. In the interest of brevity details which are given in the second paragraph of smaller type are generally omitted from the descriptive paragraph above. In general the spellings of proper names have followed the pattern used in *Ancient Near Eastern Texts*.

The pictures have been arranged in nine general sections. Within most of the sections further arrangement has been made along the lines of topics, geographical areas, or chronological divisions. Since some photographs defy classification in that they illustrate several different features and could justifiably be placed in any one of several sections, cross refer-

[1] Listing of objects formerly in the Berlin Museum is according to the prewar inventory. See R. Anthes' report on the Egyptian Museum from 1939-1950, *ZDMG*, vol. 27, NF, 1952, pt. 1.

ences have been given to direct the user to other examples of a particular feature or object which may be reproduced outside the main section dealing with the subject. In addition to the cross references the index will be of service in locating representations which may be widely scattered. A glossary of the more technical terms has been combined with the index.

In the first section, "Peoples and Their Dress," are representations of some of the peoples of the ancient Near East on paintings (particularly those on the walls of Egyptian tombs at Thebes), in bas-relief or other carving, and in statuary. Here attention has been directed primarily to the appearance and costume of the less prominent, but more representative people among the ethnic and national groups. The more prominent figures of the ancient world are pictured elsewhere, particularly in the sections dealing with "Scenes from History and Monuments," and "Royalty and Dignitaries." Among the geographical areas, that of Syria, understood in the broader sense to include both Syria and Palestine, has been most fully illustrated, not only because the particular reference of this collection is to Palestine, but also because the peripheral areas of Egypt and Mesopotamia are amply documented in the other sections of the volume.

Within the section on "Daily Life" an attempt has been made to recreate, as far as it is possible from archaeological remains, the every-day activities of people—their occupations, crafts, trade, commerce, and diversions. Here the arrangement is topical, with illustrations drawn whenever available from Palestinian excavations and supplemented by scenes and objects from the richer cultural areas of Mesopotamia and Egypt. The justification for this assembling of material into topical groupings, with apparent disregard for chronological, geographical, and cultural divisions, lies in an observed unity in the ways of making and doing things throughout the many parts of the ancient, as well as of the modern, Near East. Further, the well-attested cultural contacts between the various members of this segment of the ancient world, from as early as the beginning of the third millennium onward, lend support for this procedure and strengthen the accuracy of the general picture.

Since written documents are, without doubt, the most important remains which have come from excavations in the Near East, an attempt has been made in the section on "Writing" to illustrate how writing was done, the scripts which were employed in the various areas and during the different periods within these areas, the materials on which scribes wrote, and some of the inscribed pieces of stone and clay which have been of pivotal importance in decipherment and in the writing of history. The illustrations offered are, however, highly selective and cannot within the space available give an impression of the vast quantities of written documents which have been handed down from the past.

The illustrations in "Scenes from History and Monuments" have been arranged chronologically—or roughly so—except for slight irregularities due to the demands for a satisfactory arrangement into plates. Included are the pictorial records of certain decisive events in the early histories of Egypt and Mesopotamia that were memorialized by those who thought them important and which contain representations of cultural features of significance to the student of the ancient world. The larger part of this section is composed of scenes from the conquests of Egyptian and Assyrian kings in Palestine and Syria, sources for the political history of Palestine as well as for a knowledge of innumerable cultural details which were meticulously recorded by the artists for their victorious royal patrons.

The portraits of "Royalty and Dignitaries" have been arranged according to general areas, and chronologically within these subdivisions. An attempt has been made to include especially those kings of Egypt and of Assyria who are known to have made expeditions to Palestine and Syria, as well as a few others, who because of their prominence could not well be omitted.

Material evidence for the religions of the ancient Near East is presented in three sections. In "Gods and Their Emblems" the arrangement of the deities is according to the three general areas of Syria, Mesopotamia and Anatolia, and Egypt. For the latter, with its almost inexhaustible wealth of material, a selection has been made on the basis of the gods and goddesses which figure prominently in the religious texts translated in *Ancient Near Eastern Texts*, with some attempt to suggest diversity in the type of representation for deities—such as animal and human form, for example—and to indicate the forms of statuary, painting, and bas-relief used in the portrayals. The cult, its paraphernalia, and its functionaries are illustrated in the section "The Practice of Religion." Here the emphasis has been placed on the remains of the practice of religion in Canaan and in the more influential area of Mesopotamia. Some Egyptian funerary scenes and practices have been illustrated in the subdivision dealing with religious practices for the dead. Cylinder seals impressions have, with but few exceptions, been placed together in the section on "Myth, Legend, and Ritual." The selection here presented, from a very great circle of possibility, seeks to reproduce from each of the major periods of seal engraving in Mesopotamia those seals which tell a story, even though the interpretation of the scene cannot as yet be fully grasped. What seems relatively certain is that the meaning of these scenes was religious in the sense that the portrayal was intended to suggest a myth, a legend, or a ritual act.

The final section on "Views and Plans of Excavations" is composed primarily of illustrations from the excavations in Palestine and is intended to exhibit representative examples of city walls, gates, fortifications, houses, temples, and other public buildings. In addition there have been included some plans and buildings from the contiguous area of Mesopotamia, drawn from sites which are of interest because of association with Old Testament history. To go farther afield into the involved and rich areas of architecture in Egypt, Anatolia, and Syria would have required more space than that available in a single volume of this purpose.

The general agreement on the dates for the Assyrian kings of the first millennium has been strengthened by A. Poebel's publication of the Assyrian king list from Khorsabad,[2] and the area of virtual certainty for the dates of the Assyrian kings has been extended back to the fifteenth century. In general, the dates computed by Poebel from this list have been utilized in the catalogue, as they were in *Ancient Near Eastern Texts*.

While the general relative chronology for the period from Sargon of Akkad to the end

---

[2] A. Poebel, *JNES*, vol. 1, 1942, pp. 247-306, 460-492; vol. 2, 1943, pp. 56-90. See also E. Weidner, *AfO*, vol. 15, 1945-1951, pp. 98-102.

of the First Dynasty of Babylon is agreed upon, the absolute dates within this period are still the subject of debate. Different views upon the dating of kings and periods in this span are reflected in the following dates ascribed to the reign of Hammurabi, the sixth king of the First Dynasty of Babylon.[3]

D. Sidersky[4]	1848-1806
A. Ungnad[5]	1801-1759
S. Smith[6]	1792-1750
W. F. Albright[7] and F. Cornelius[8] (working independently)	
	1728-1686
K. Schubert[9] and E. Weidner[10]	1704-1662

In the catalogue have been given when possible the designation of the period or the name of the particular king, followed by the dates of the Albright-Cornelius school of chronology.[11] Dates may easily be adjusted to conform to the higher or the lower chronologies.

The greatest area of uncertainty as to date lies in those historical and cultural periods which are earlier than Sargon of Akkad.[12] For these, the commonly accepted designation for the period has been given, followed by an approximation of the century or millennium. It should be borne in mind that at present the dates are far from determined, but these rough approximations are given that the reader may grasp more readily the relative order of the cultural and historical periods. Convenient charts and tables which illustrate the common agreement within certain limits are those of W. F. Albright in *BASOR*, no. 88, 1942, p. 32, A. Moortgat in A. Scharff and A. Moortgat, *Ägypten und Vorderasien im Altertum*, Munich, 1950, pp. 490-503, E. Porada in *Corpus*, end of text volume, and A. L. Perkins, *The Comparative Archeology of Early Mesopotamia*, *SAOC*, 25, Chicago, 1949, tables 1-3, who does not suggest dates, but lists the sequence of the earlier periods of culture.

In order that adjustments can be made readily to other systems of chronology listed below are the chronological designations and their suggested dates as employed in the catalogue for objects from Mesopotamia:

Obeid period (fourth millennium)
Uruk (or Warka) period (end of fourth millennium)
Jemdet Nasr period (around 3000)
Early Dynastic period (first half of third millennium)[13]

[3] For discussion of the problems of chronology and tables of views of various scholars see A. Parrot, *Archéologie mésopotamienne, Technique et problèmes*, Paris, 1953, pp. 332-445.

[4] *RA*, vol. 37, 1940, p. 52; A. Goetze, *BASOR*, no. 122, 1951, pp. 18-25, prefers this system of chronology.

[5] *AfO*, vol. 13, 1940, pp. 145-146.

[6] *Alalakh and Chronology*, London, 1940, p. 29.

[7] *BASOR*, no. 88, 1942, p. 32.

[8] *Klio*, vol. 35, 1942, pp. 1-16. Others who follow the chronology of Albright and Cornelius are: B. L. van der Waerden, *Ex Oriente Lux*, no. 10, 1945-1948, pp. 414-424; M. B. Rowton, *Iraq*, vol. 8, 1946, pp. 94-110.

[9] *Wiener Zeitschrift für die Kunde des Morgenlandes*, vol. 51, 1948, pp. 21-33.

[10] *AfO*, vol. 15, 1945-1951, p. 99.

[11] *BASOR*, no. 88, 1942, p. 32, with slight modifications made later by Albright.

[12] Graphic analyses of the archaeological materials from Warka, Jemdet Nasr, Obeid, Ur, Kish, and Susa are presented in useful form by H. W. Eliot, Jr., *Excavations in Mesopotamia and Western Iran, Sites of 4000-500 B.C.*, Cambridge, Mass., 1950.

[13] See H. Frankfort, *OIC*, 19, Chicago, 1935, pp. 79-87; *OIC*, 20, Chicago, 1936, pp. 35-59, and chronological table at end, with comment.

Early Dynastic I and II (early third millennium)
Early Dynastic III (middle third millennium)
Royal tombs of Ur (about twenty-fifth century)
Akkadian period (Dynasty of Akkad, Sargonid period) (about 2360-2180)
Guti rule (about 2190-2065)
Ur III period (Third Dynasty of Ur) (about 2060-1955)
Isin-Larsa Dynasties (about 1960-1700)
Old Babylonian period (First Dynasty of Babylon) (1830-1530)

The dates given in the catalogue for Egyptian kings and dynasties are essentially those employed by John A. Wilson in the introductions to his translations in *Ancient Near Eastern Texts*, with slight modifications for the approximate dates for kings and periods before the Eighteenth Dynasty.[14] That Egyptian chronology, especially for the earlier periods, is in a fluid state may be seen from the listings of dates by W. S. Smith, *Ancient Egypt as Represented in the Museum of Fine Arts*, Boston, 1952, pp. 169-177, and in É. Drioton and J. Vandier, *L'Égypte, Les peuples de l'orient méditerranéen*, vol. 2, 1952, pp. 627-632, where as many as three different systems of dates are sometimes given. In each of the listings of dates for kings and periods up until the second half of the first millennium, it is to be understood that the dates are only approximate, with the margin of error decreasing for the later periods.

The publication of a large collection of pictures is possible only through the cooperation of many people—excavators, photographers, museum staffs, and collectors of photographic negatives. The many acknowledgments have been registered at the appropriate places within the catalogue. It is to be hoped that each of these lines carries beyond the formal acknowledgment an appreciation for courtesy and help without which the production of this volume would have been impossible. In addition to the collections of photographs belonging to the museums visited while preparing this book, other collections have been useful. Thanks are due to the following institutions and individuals for the opportunity of going through their photographic files: Bildarchiv Foto Marburg, Marburg; photographs of Bernard V. Bothmer, Museum of Fine Arts, Boston; Archives Photographiques, Paris; Giraudon, Photographe-Éditeur, Paris; collection of photographs from the Ägyptische Museum, Berlin, belonging to Rudolf Anthes, University Museum, Philadelphia.

The following have contributed in various ways toward the making of this volume: Ekrem Akurgal, professor, University of Ankara, in supplying photographs and information; Rudolf Anthes, curator, University Museum, in reading descriptions of Egyptian objects; Naji al-Aṣil, Director General of Antiquities, Iraq, in supplying photographs; I. Ben-Dor, Department of Antiquities, Israel, in providing photographs; Solomon A. Birnbaum, School of Oriental and African Studies, University of London, in drawing the table of alphabets (No. 286); Henri de Boisgelin, in granting access to the Collection de Clercq; Elie Borowski, in supplying photographs from his and other private collections; John D.

[14] For these modifications and more detailed listing of Egyptian dates see John A. Wilson, *The Burden of Egypt*, Chicago, 1951, pp. vii-viii.

Cooney, curator, Brooklyn Museum, in suggestions for illustrations of Egyptian deities; the trustees of the Crozer Theological Seminary, in providing the writer with a sabbatical year for study abroad; M. Dunand, Beirut, in sending photographs; Henry G. Fischer, University Museum, in reading some Egyptian descriptions in the catalogue; G. Lankester Harding, Department of Antiquities, Jordan, in supplying photographs; Mustafa Kalaç, Museum of the Ancient Orient, Istanbul, in giving photographs; Samuel N. Kramer, curator, University Museum, in help on matters Sumerian, and in many personal courtesies; G. R. Meyer, director, Vorderasiatische Abteilung, Staatliche Museen, in sending photographs and other information on objects in the Berlin Museum; Hans Wolfgang Müller, University of Munich, in supplying photographs; Edith Porada, Queens College, in the selection and description of cylinder seals; Hermann Ranke, in suggesting illustrations of Egyptian objects; Faisal Seirafi, National Museum, Aleppo, in sending photographs; Froelich G. Rainey, director, University Museum, in many courtesies, including office space where this work was done; C. F. A. Schaeffer, in the loan of prints of objects from Ras Shamra; Nora E. Scott, Metropolitan Museum of Art, in suggestions for Egyptian objects from daily life; Charles K. Wilkinson, Metropolitan Museum of Art, in help on illustrations of Mesopotamian objects; Helen Van Zandt, Princeton University Press, in attention to the many difficult artistic and mechanical problems connected with the making of this book. For these many services the author expresses his profound thanks.

Abbreviations

AAA *Annals of Archaeology and Anthropology,* Liverpool, 1908-.

AASOR *Annual of the American Schools of Oriental Research,* New Haven, 1920-.

AfO *Archiv für Orientforschung,* Berlin, vols. 3 ff., 1926-.

AJ *The Antiquaries Journal,* London, 1921-.

AJA *American Journal of Archaeology,* Concord, N.H., etc., 1885-.

AJSL *American Journal of Semitic Languages and Literatures,* Chicago, 1884-1941.

Albright, *AP* W. F. Albright, *The Archaeology of Palestine,* Harmondsworth, 1949.

ANET *Ancient Near Eastern Texts Relating to the Old Testament,* edited by James B. Pritchard, Princeton, 1950.

An. Or. *Analecta Orientalia,* Rome, 1931-.

AO *Der alte Orient,* Leipzig, 1900-.

AOB Hugo Gressmann, *Altorientalische Bilder zum alten Testament,* 2nd ed., Berlin and Leipzig, 1927.

ASAE *Annales du Service des Antiquités de l'Egypte,* Cairo, 1899-.

AZ *Zeitschrift für Ägyptische Sprache und Alterthumskunde,* London (later Leipzig), 1886-.

BA *The Biblical Archaeologist,* New Haven, 1938-.

BASOR *Bulletin of the American Schools of Oriental Research,* New Haven, 1919-.

BEUP *Babylonian Expedition of the University of Pennsylvania, Series A: Cuneiform Texts,* edited by H. V. Hilprecht, Philadelphia, 1893-1914.

BM The British Museum, London.

BMFA *Bulletin of the Museum of Fine Arts,* Boston, 1903-.

BMMA *Bulletin of the Metropolitan Museum of Art,* New York, 1905-.

Bossert, *Altanatolien* Helmuth Th. Bossert, *Altanatolien,* Berlin, 1942.

————, *Altsyrien* Helmuth Th. Bossert, *Altsyrien,* Tübingen, 1951.

Breasted, *AR* J. H. Breasted, *Ancient Records of Egypt,* vols. 1-5, Chicago, 1906-1907.

Br. M The Brooklyn Museum, Brooklyn, N.Y.

CIS *Corpus Inscriptionum Semiticarum,* Paris, 1881-.

Contenau, *Man.* G. Contenau, *Manuel d'archéologie orientale,* vols. 1-4, Paris, 1927-1947.

Corpus E. Porada (in collaboration with B. Buchanan), *The Collection of the Pierpont Morgan Library, Corpus of Ancient Near Eastern Seals in North American Collections,* vol. 1 (Text and Plates), Washington, 1948.

Erman-Ranke A. Erman and H. Ranke, *Ägypten und ägyptisches Leben im Altertum,* Tübingen, 1923.

Fondation Piot Fondation Eugène Piot, *Monuments et Mémoires, l'Académie des Inscriptions et Belles-Lettres,* Paris, 1894-.

Frankfort, *CS* H. Frankfort, *Cylinder Seals: a Documentary Essay on the Art and Religion of the Ancient Near East,* London, 1939.

Fremdvölker Photographic negatives listed in E. Meyer, "Bericht über eine Expedition nach Ägypten zur Erforschung der Darstellungen der Fremdvölker," *Sitz. preuss. Akad. der Wiss., phil.-hist. Klasse,* Berlin, 1913, pp. 769-801. Prints from these negatives, the property of the Staatliche Museen, Berlin, were supplied through the courtesy of Hessische Treuhandverwaltung des früheren preussischen Kunstgutes, Wiesbaden, Neues Museum.

Galling, *BR* K. Galling, *Biblisches Reallexikon,* Tübingen, 1937.

Iraq *Iraq,* London, 1934-.

JAOS *Journal of the American Oriental Society,* New Haven, 1843-.

JBP Photographs taken by James B. Pritchard.

JEA *Journal of Egyptian Archaeology,* London, 1914-.

JPOS *Journal of the Palestine Oriental Society,* Jerusalem, 1920-.

LD C. R. Lepsius, *Denkmäler aus Ägypten und Äthiopien,* Berlin, 1849-1859.

Luckenbill, *AR* D. D. Luckenbill, *Ancient Records of Assyria and Babylonia,* Chicago, 1926-1927.

MFA Museum of Fine Arts, Boston.

MJ *The Museum Journal,* University of Pennsylvania, Philadelphia, 1910-.

MMA The Metropolitan Museum of Art, New York.

No. Indicates references to illustrations in this volume.

OI The Oriental Institute of the University of Chicago.

OIC *Oriental Institute Communications,* Chicago, 1922-.

OIP *Oriental Institute Publications,* Chicago, 1924-.

PAM Palestine Archaeological Museum, Jerusalem.

PBS *Publications of the Babylonian Section,* University Museum, University of Pennsylvania, Philadelphia, 1911-.

PEFQS *Palestine Exploration Fund, Quarterly Statement* (later *Palestine Exploration Quarterly*), London, 1869-.

PML The Pierpont Morgan Library, New York.

Porter and Moss, *Bibliography* B. Porter and R. L. B. Moss, *Topographical Bibliography of Ancient Egyptian Hieroglyphic Texts, Reliefs, and Paintings,* vols. 1-7, Oxford, 1927-1951.

QDAP *Quarterly of the Department of Antiquities in Palestine,* Jerusalem, 1931-.

RA *Revue d'Assyriologie et d'archéologie orientale,* Paris, 1884-.

RB *Revue biblique,* Paris, 1892-.

SAOC *Studies in Ancient Oriental Civilization,* Chicago, 1931-.

Schäfer-Andrae H. Schäfer and W. Andrae, *Die Kunst des alten Orients, Propyläen-Kunstgeschichte,* II, Berlin, 1925.

Sumer *Sumer,* Baghdad, 1945-.

Syria *Syria,* Paris, 1920-.

TEL Éditions "TEL," Paris.

TEL, vol. 1 *Encyclopédie photographique de l'art, Le Musée du Louvre,* vol. 1, Paris, 1935.

TEL, vol. 2 *Encyclopédie photographique de l'art, Le Musée du Louvre,* vol. 2, Paris, 1936.

TEL, Cairo *Encyclopédie photographique de l'art, Le Musée du Caire,* Paris, 1949.

TTS *The Theban Tomb Series,* London, 1915-1933.

UM The University Museum, University of Pennsylvania, Philadelphia.

Watzinger, *Denk.* C. Watzinger, *Denkmäler Palästinas,* 2 vols., Leipzig, 1933-1935.

Wresz. Walter Wreszinski, *Atlas zur altägyptischen Kulturgeschichte,* Leipzig, vols. 1-3, 1923-1936 (third volume not yet complete).

WVDOG *Wissenschaftliche Veröffentlichungen der deutschen Orient-Gesellschaft,* Berlin, Leipzig, 1900-.

ZA *Zeitschrift für Assyriologie und verwandte Gebiete,* Leipzig, 1886-.

ZAW *Zeitschrift für die alttestamentliche Wissenschaft,* Berlin, Giessen, 1881-.

ZDMG *Zeitschrift der deutschen morgenländischen Gesellschaft,* Leipzig, 1847-.

ZDPV *Zeitschrift des deutschen Palaestina-Vereins,* Leipzig, 1878-.

The Ancient Near East
in Pictures

I. Peoples and Their Dress

1. Prisoners from lands bordering Egypt—Libyan, South-Hamite, Syrian, Libyan—on relief from temple of Sahu-Re at Abusir.

2. Representatives from lands to the north of Egypt—two Syrians, Cretan, Libyan—on painted relief of tomb of Puy-em-Re.

3. Ibsha, "the ruler of a foreign country," leads a caravan of "thirty-seven" Asiatics bringing stibiu[m]

4. Kneeling Syrians and Negroes form the decoration of the platform for the enthroned Amen-hotep III, wall painting at Thebes.

5. Syrians, Libyans, and a Negro(?) implore a royal servant on a relief from the tomb of Hor-em-heb at Memphis.

Egypt, on a wall painting in the tomb of Khnum-hotep III at Beni Hasan, dating from about 1890 B.C.

6. Two Syrians and three Negroes from a row of figures on a wall painting in the tomb of Seti I at Thebes.

7. Prisoners of Ramses III from his campaign in Amor—Libyan, Syrian, Hittite, Sea Peoples, Syrian.

8. Libyans, Syrians, and Negroes represented as prisoners on the interior of state chariot of Tut-ankh-Amon.

9. Six bound prisoners labeled with names of the northern peoples, a drawing of a limestone relief at Medinet Habu.

10. Prisoners taken by the army of the Assyrian King Ashurbanipal from a captured Egyptian town, on a relief from Nineveh.

11. Babylonians and Syrians bringing tribute, a relief from a stairway of the apadana at Persepolis.

12. Egyptian hunters, armed with spears, bows, and other weapons, carved on a slate palette of the predynastic period.

13. Old Kingdom official and his wife.

14. The "*Sheikh el-beled.*"

15. Methethy, an Egyptian nobleman.

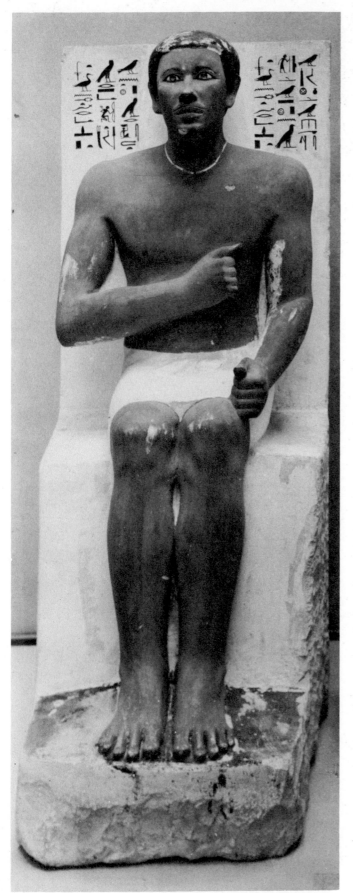

16. Painted limestone statue of Ra-hotep of the Fourth Dynasty.

17. Painted stone statue of Nefret, wife of Prince Ra-hotep.

18-19. Statues of men from Early Dynastic period at Khafajah.

20. Male figure from Tell Asmar.

21. A votive statue of Idi-Narum from Mari.

22. Woman from Khafajah.

23. Statue of male figure from Khafajah.

24. A votive statue of Ebih-il of Mari, with hands clasped before the breast and seated on a stool of basketwork.

25. Two Elamite soldiers with bows and quiver on relief from Nineveh.

26. Head of a Mede from a Persepolis stairway.

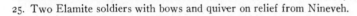

27. A Median (?) attendant, with curled beard and hair and wearing a cloak of skin, carries a whip and leads two horses.

28. Attendants with the royal footstool, grooms, and chariots (above); Medes and Persians alternate in procession (middle, below).

29. Median nobles marching up stairway at Persepolis.

30. An Elamite archer of the Persian guard with spear.

31. Heads and shoulders of seven Hittite figures approximately identical, carved in bas-relief of the thirteenth century.

32. A Hittite prisoner, from Abu Simbel.

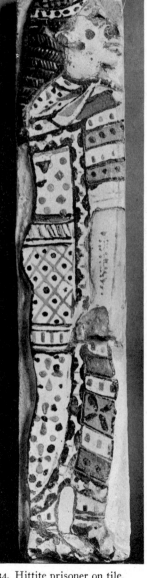

34. Hittite prisoner on tile.

35. Hittite on faïence tile.

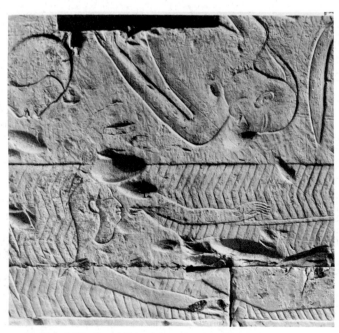

33. Bodies of Hittite soldiers slain at battle of Kadesh.

37. Two helmeted warriors from a relief at Carchemish.

36. Figure from the Late Hittite period at Zinjirli.

38. Hittite figure from Boghazköy.

39. Bowman from Arslan Tash.

40. Man with staff and sword, from Zinjirli.

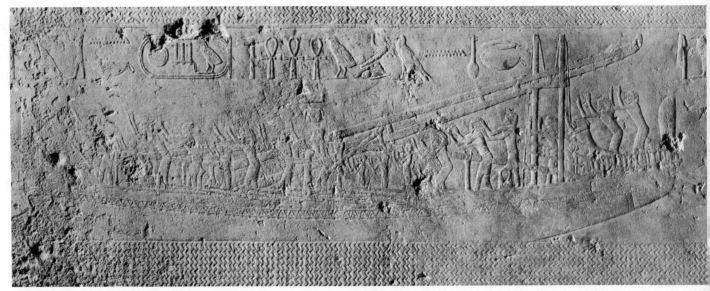

41. Ships, on which are Syrian men, women, and children, standing with upraised hands greeting the Egyptian King Sahu-Re.

42. Cast of the relief on which are ships carrying Syrian captives for the Egyptian King Sahu-Re.

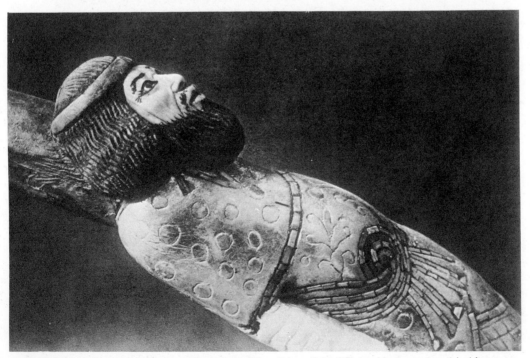

43. Bound Syrian captive on the head of a ceremonial walking stick of Tut-ankh-Amon found in his tomb.

44. Bound Syrian on gaming piece from Abydos.

45. Four figures from a line of foreigners who present gifts, on a wall painting of Men-kheper-Re-seneb.

46. Two registers from a scene of Syrians presenting gifts and children on the tomb of Amen-em-heb at Thebes.

47. Syrian tribute bearers, bringing ointment horn, quiver, vessels, rhyton, and child, on wall painting of tomb 63 at Thebes.

48. The Prince of Kadesh and other Syrians carrying tribute, on a painting of the tomb of Men-kheper-Re-seneb at Thebes.

49. Shackled Syrians on a bas-relief from tomb of Hor-em-heb.   **50.** Continuation of No. 49, showing Syrians led by Egyptians.

51. No. 50 continued; full-bearded Syrians and captors.   **52.** Syrians bringing tribute to Tut-ankh-Amon, tomb of Huy.

53. File of three Syrians wearing the long, wrapped garment with cape, on a wall painting of the tomb of Ramses III at Thebes.

55. Shackled Syrians, from temple of Ramses II at Beit el-Wali.

54. Syrian on faïence tile.

56. Syrian porter carved
on handle of wooden spoon.

57. Prisoners from among the Sea Peoples, on a relief at Medinet Habu.

58. Bearded ivory figure from Arslan Tash.

60. Warriors on sherd found at Megiddo.

59. Sherden warriors at battle of Kadesh.

61. Syrian, from Persepolis.

62. Two similarly dressed Arameans, from Zinjirli.

63. The Assyrian forces of Ashurbanipal engaged in conflict with the Arabs, who seek to escape upon their camels.

64. Statue of a man in long garment.

65. Qatabanian funerary statue.

66. Inscribed Qatabanian statue.

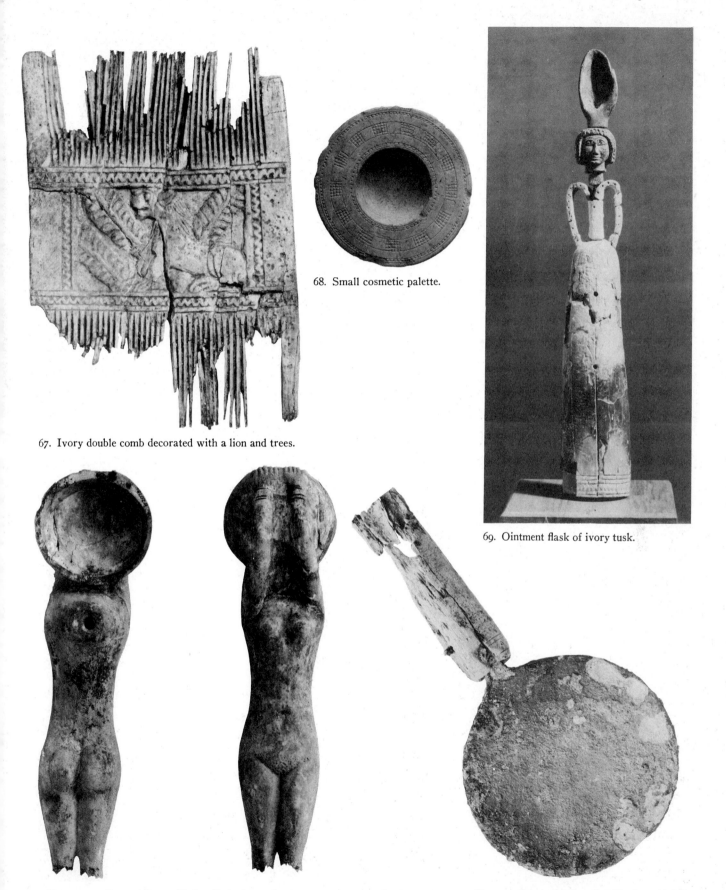

67. Ivory double comb decorated with a lion and trees.

68. Small cosmetic palette.

69. Ointment flask of ivory tusk.

70. Ivory cosmetic container with handle in form of a woman.

71. Bronze mirror with bone handle, from 'Athlit.

72. Jewelry of Queen Shubad on a model head.

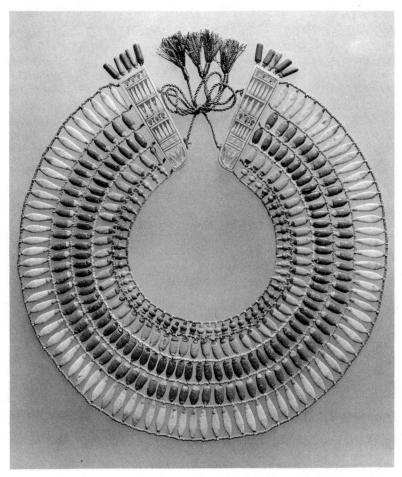

73. Broad collar, made of five rows of faïence beads, of late 18th Dynasty.

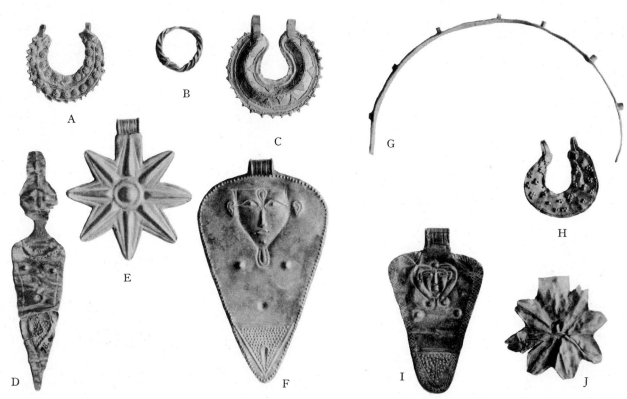

74-75. A hoard of gold and electrum jewelry found at Tell el-'Ajjul and belonging to the 14-13th centuries.

76. Hairdressing scene from the side of the sarcophagus of Princess Kawit, who is being served milk by an attendant.

77. An Egyptian hairdresser at work, on Middle Kingdom relief.

78. Woman holding mirror and applying paint to lips with a brush.

79. Figurine of woman in bath, from ez-Zib cemetery.

80. An Egyptian barber dresses the hair of one of the recruits of Amen-hotep II, on a wall painting in the tomb of User-het.

81. Limestone handle into which a flint or obsidian razor blade was set with bitumen.

82. Egyptian razor blade dating to the New Kingdom.

83. Razor blade with handle.

84. Wooden model of a man plowing with a two-handled wooden plow drawn by two yoked oxen.

85. An Egyptian plow drawn by four slaves and guided by a bearded man, on a relief from the tomb of Pa-heri at el-Kab.

87. Plow in pictograph of Uruk period.

86. Plow with seed drill on impression of Cassite period.

88. Seed plow and other symbols on stela of Esarhaddon.

89. Asses driven over a threshing floor, on a bas-relief of the Old Kingdom from Sakkarah.

90. Piles of fruit (above), granaries with rounded tops (middle), and men treading out grapes to the accompaniment of music (below).

91. Harvesting scene (above); Nakht sits in a booth watching his men cut a tree and prepare the soil (below).

92. A scene from the harvesting of flax, on a bas-relief from the tomb of Pa-heri at el-Kab.

93. Women gather lotus blossoms (right), carry them to be pressed (center); liquid from the press is presented to seated figure.

94. Lifting water into an irrigation ditch by means of a sweep (*shadūf*), on a relief from the palace of Sennacherib.

95. Egyptian gardener drawing water, painting on tomb of Ipui at Thebes.

96. Man climbing palm by a ladder, from Tell Halaf.

97. Milking scene on cylinder seal.

98. Row of five bulls, made of pieces of carved shell set in bitumen (with below).

99. Dairy scene on frieze from Tell el-Obeid: milking of cows, doorposts of the sacred precincts, preparation of milk products.

100. Cow being milked, with calf tethered to her leg, on sarcophagus of Princess Kawit, from Deir el-Bahri.

101. An emaciated desert herdsman leads three oxen in a procession of offering bearers who bring gifts to Ukh-hotep.

102. Starving people on a bas-relief from the interior wall of the temple causeway of King Unis of the Fifth Dynasty at Sakkarah.

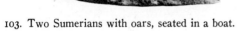
103. Two Sumerians with oars, seated in a boat.   104. Boat with high prow and stern, in a ritual scene on a seal of Uruk period.

105. Silver boat model, with paddles, thwarts, and arched band, from "King's Grave" at Ur.

106. Three-decked warship, driven by two banks of oars and equipped with a pointed ram, bears warriors on the upper deck.

107. Six boats transporting logs in tow or aboard, on Sargonid relief from Khorsabad.

108. Skin-covered boat, manned by four oarsmen, transports a heavy load of materials.

109. Models of fishing boats of papyrus which tow a large seine.

110. Wooden model of a boat equipped with rudder, mast, sail, and cabin, in which sits Meket-Re with his son and a singer.

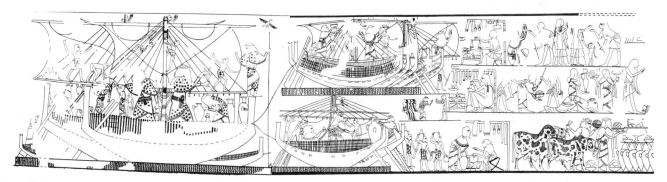

111. Ships carrying Syrians dock at an Egyptian port, where shopkeepers purchase wares brought by the sailors; tomb painting.

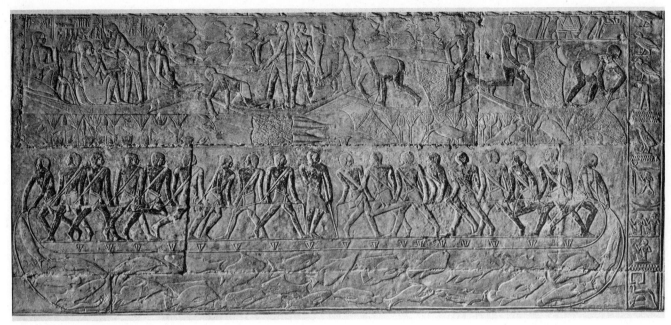

112. Egyptian fishermen: men hauling seine, a fisherman with line, men fishing with hand-nets and by means of traps.

113. Fishermen, from tomb of Ra-hotep.

114. An Assyrian fishing with a line.

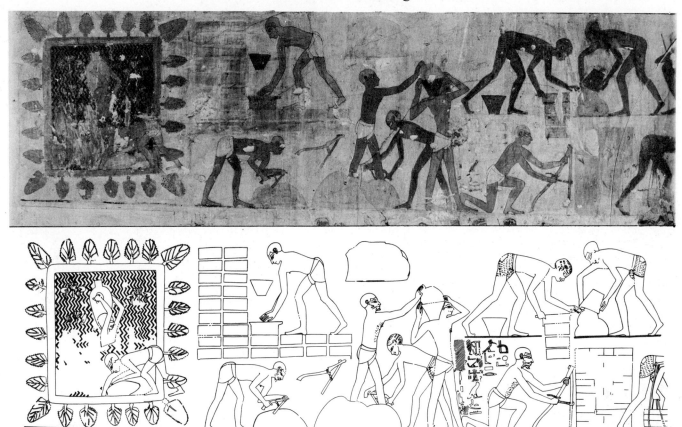

115. Brickmaking in Egypt: workmen with hoes knead clay moistened with water, as laborers carry material to two brickmakers.

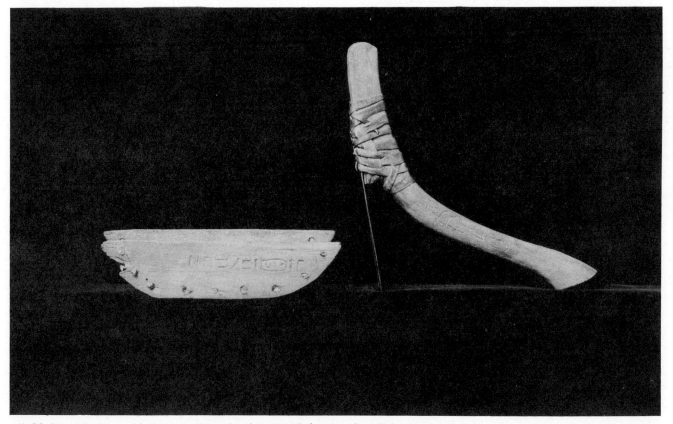

116. Model cradle for working stone and an adze, from foundation deposit at Deir el-Bahri.

118. Copy of one-mina weight of Nebuchadnezzar II.

117. Small balance held in right hand; folded balance in left.

119. Bronze lion-weight of two-thirds of mina.

121. Bronze weights inlaid in gold with figures of beetles.

120. Weight of 30 minas, carved from black basalt into the shape of a duck.

122. Scenes of arts, trades, and agricultural pursuits of the Middle Kingdom, from the tomb of Amen-em-het at Beni Hasan.

123. Three carpenters at work, tomb of Ti at Sakkarah.

124. A boatwright binds papyrus reeds as an old man looks on.

125. Woman holding staff, on Megiddo ivory.

126. Ivory carving
of nude woman,
from Megiddo.

127. Hunting scenes on Zawiyeh ivory.

128. Box from one piece of ivory with sphinxes and lions carved in high relief, from Megiddo.

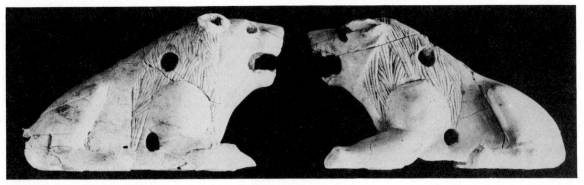

129. Two crouching lions carved in ivory, from Samaria.

130. Lion grappling with a long-horned bull, in pierced ivory relief from Samaria.

131. Woman at the window, ivory carving from Nimrud.

132. Man holding lotus and saluting.

133. Goldworking scenes from tomb of Mereru-ka: weighing and recording, melting for casting, and finishing the molded objects.

135. A pottery mold for casting implements with two axes or chisels in place.

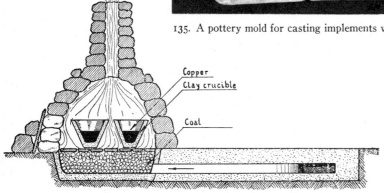

Copper
Clay crucible

Coal

134. Drawing of the reconstructed copper-smelting furnace at Tell Qasile.

136. Metalworking crucible.

137. Silver bowl and ladle with nude female figure forming the handle.

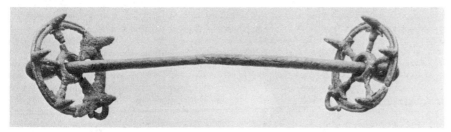

139. Bronze horse's-bit.

138. Bowl made of single piece of copper.

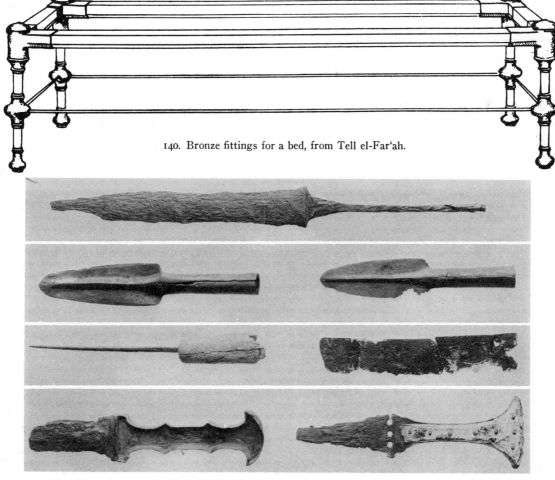

140. Bronze fittings for a bed, from Tell el-Far'ah.

141. Daggers, spearpoints, sword, knife, and awl.

142. Wooden tomb-model of a weaver's house, with women preparing flax, spinning, and weaving on a horizontal loom.

143. Reproduction of painting of spinning and weaving scene on the wall of the tomb of Khnum-hotep at Beni Hasan.

144. Lady seated on a low lion-footed stool and holding a spindle and wool, with an attendant; stone relief from Susa.

145. A dye plant consisting of two cylindrical stone vats and two rectangular basins, from eighth-century level at Tell Beit Mirsim.

146. Model of potter's shop, in which one figure turns clay on a wheel as another tends a kiln (?), from tomb at Sakkarah.

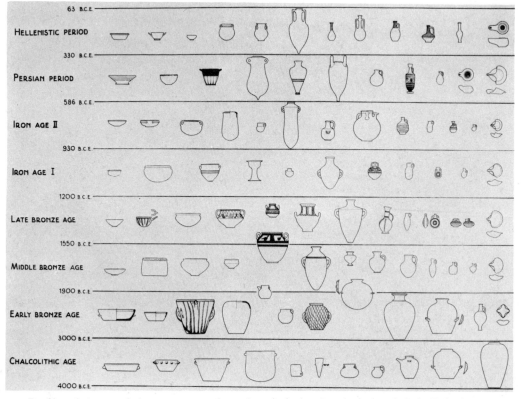

147. Profiles of characteristic pottery types from the principal archaeological periods in Palestine.

148. A selected group of pottery vessels from the periods of Early · Bronze through Iron II in Palestine.

149. A servant figure of the Old Kingdom, wearing short skirt and wig covered with a cloth, grinding grain.

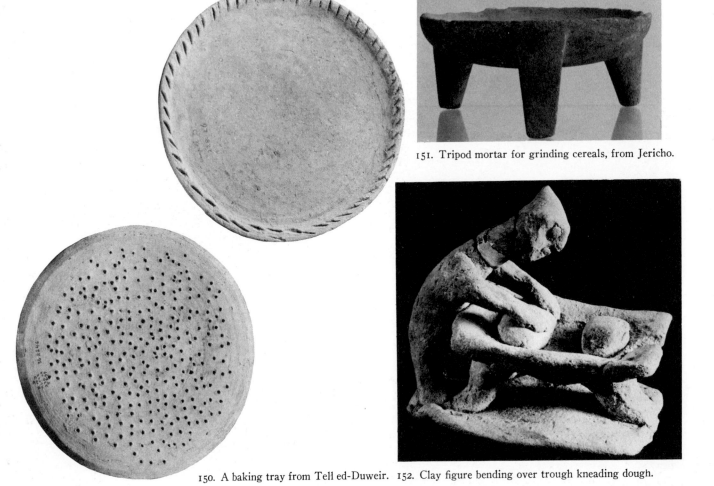

151. Tripod mortar for grinding cereals, from Jericho.

150. A baking tray from Tell ed-Duweir. 152. Clay figure bending over trough kneading dough.

153. Three registers depicting the process of making beer, on an Old Kingdom relief.

154. Model house containing a brewery (upper) and a bakery filled with men and women working, from Thebes.

155. Five men operate a wine press as two musicians (in circle) beat time to set the pace for those (not shown) who tread the grapes.

156. Gathering grapes from an arbor, treading and storage of wine in jars with stoppers, tomb of Nakht at Thebes.

158. God and worshiper drinking from tubes.

157. Syrian warrior drinking from a tube, from Tell el-Amarna.

159. Gold dagger and sheath, from Ur.

160. Gold helmet of Mes-kalam-dug (not the king), from a tomb at Ur.

161. Coat of mail made of bronze plates laced together with thongs, from Nuzi.

162. Head of helmeted warrior, Mari.

163. Two-wheeled chariot drawn by four asses, fragment of limestone plaque from Ur.

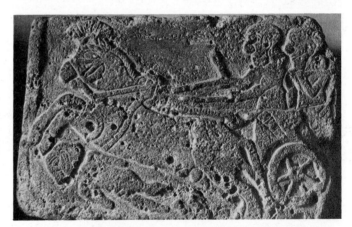

165. Warrior and charioteer in a six-spoked chariot, Tell Halaf.

164. Cavalryman with shield and sword (?), from Tell Halaf.

166. Copper quadriga from Tell 'Agrab.

167. Assyrian soldiers leading away prisoners of war and transporting women in a cart, from palace of Ashurbanipal at Nineveh.

168. Elamite prisoners partake of a meal beside a heavily loaded wagon, relief of Ashurbanipal from Nineveh.

169. Wagon model from Tepe Gawra.

170. Assyrian officer's tent, where meal and couch are prepared for him; adjoining is tent where food is being prepared.

171. Tent and part of another pitched within a defensive wall with turrets; men preparing food within.

172. Bowman and driver in chariot with six-spoked wheels and decorated by a lion's head, from Zinjirli.

173. Two soldiers from a procession on a relief from Arslan Tash.

174. Lancer wearing a spiked helmet, from Arslan Tash.

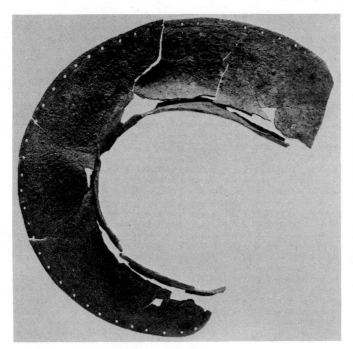

175. Crest of Assyrian helmet, Tell ed-Duweir.

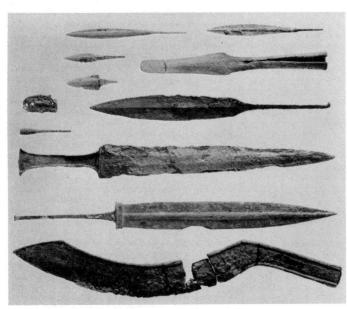

176. Weapons found in Palestine.

177. Warrior (?) with spear, found east of Dead Sea.

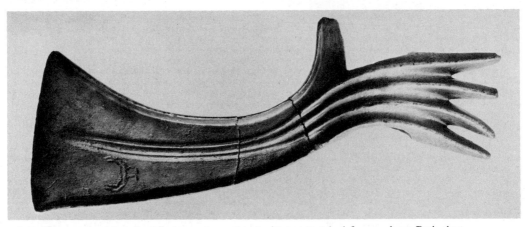

178. Bronze ceremonial axehead in form of open hand with outstretched fingers, from Beth-shan.

179. Model of Nubian bowmen marching four abreast, and each carrying bow and arrows.

180. Egyptian soldiers arranged in four columns of ten each, armed with lance and shield; model from Siut.

181. Iron dagger from tomb of Tut-ankh-Amon, fitted with gold haft and knob of rock crystal; decorated sheath.

182. Hunting of lions represented on stela from Warka.

183. Hunter in chariot charges bulls and gazelles, on gold plate from Ras Shamra.

184. Ashurnasirpal hunting lions: the king and his driver stand in a chariot drawn by two horses as two footmen assist in the hunt.

185. Assyrian hunters in a wood shooting birds and other game, on a relief from the palace of Sargon II at Khorsabad.

186. A hunt for wild asses: two attendants hold with ropes an ass as two others flee; relief of Ashurbanipal from Nineveh.

187. Captive camels led by woman carrying a pointed vase, relief of Tiglath-pileser III from Nimrud.

188. Camel ridden by a man seated on a boxlike saddle and carrying a stick in his hand, relief from Tell Halaf.

189. Fowling by means of a cagelike net spread in the marches, a relief from the tomb of Ka-gemni at Sakkarah.

190. Tut-ankh-Amon, standing in his chariot with drawn bow, charges a herd of gazelles and ostriches.

191. Eleven-stringed lyre on a relief from Tello.

192. Plaque of shell inlay from the end of the sound-box of Ur lyre.

193. Reconstructed lyre with sound-box ending in a gold bull's head, from Ur.

195. Terra-cotta figurine of woman playing double pipe.

196. Musicians playing before deities.

194. Bone playing-pipes found in the Obeid stratum at Gawra.

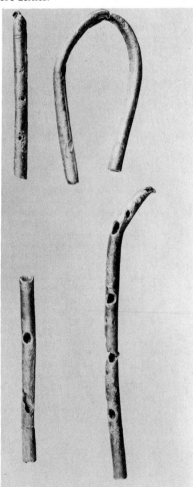

197. Two harpists from a procession of musicians on a stone vase from Bismaya.

198. Silver pipes from Ur.

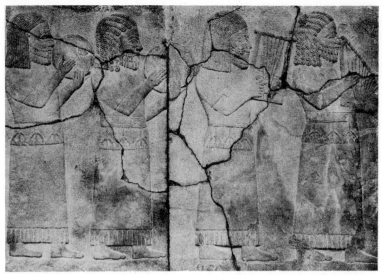

199. Four musicians, playing upon lyres and hand drums, from Zinjirli.

200. Man dancing to music of clappers, pipe, and lute; from Carchemish.

201. Horn and drum played by musicians on basalt relief from Carchemish.

202. Four musicians from a military band.

203. Musicians on an ivory from Nimrud.

204. Elamite musicians at celebration of Ashurbanipal's capture of the town of Madaktu.

205. Three captive lyrists conducted by an Assyrian soldier over a wooded mountain.

206. Egyptian lyre from Thebes.

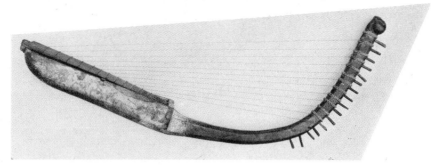

207. Twelve-stringed Egyptian harp with stem carved in form of a head.

208. Egyptian musicians: harpist, lutist, dancer, player of double pipe, lyrist; Theban tomb painting.

209. Two nude girls dance to music; musicians have unguent cones on their heads; wine jars are arranged in two tiers.

210. Male dancers perform with clasped hands; female dancers hold hands over heads; from tomb of Mereru-ka at Sakkarah.

211. Women dance as they beat upon hand drums; two nude girls keep rhythm with clappers; men march with upraised arms.

212. Inlaid game board and playing pieces from a grave at Ur.

213. Game board of ivory and ebony veneer, ivory pins, and knucklebones, for playing "hounds and jackals."

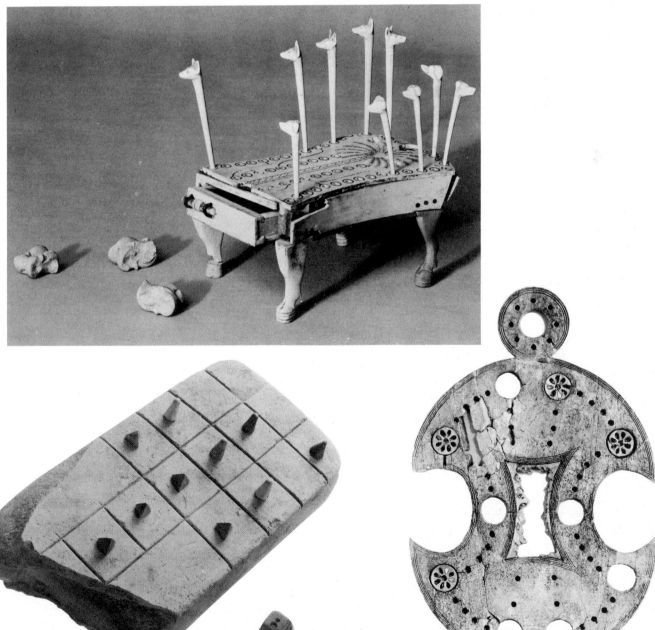

214. Game from Tell Beit Mirsim.

215. An ivory game board with fifty-eight holes, from Megiddo.

216. Girls, with hair braided in a pigtail, dancing or playing games, on a relief from the tomb of Mereru-ka at Sakkarah.

217. Boys engage in a tug of war and other games, on a relief of the Sixth Dynasty tomb of Mereru-ka at Sakkarah.

218. Contestants—perhaps wrestlers and boxers—on a limestone plaque from Khafajah.

219. Ceremonial wrestlers, in bronze, from Khafajah.

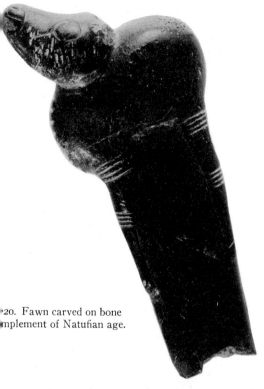

220. Fawn carved on bone implement of Natufian age.

222. Nude female figure on cylinder seal from Syria.

221. Neolithic clay head excavated at Jericho.

223. Figures with oval headgear on seal.

224. Weather-god on Syrian seal.

225. Silver stater of Ozbaal, king of Byblos.

226. Fourth-century Jewish coin.

227. Fourth-century coin, Beth-zur.

228. Two scenes of a combat between a dog and a lion (note star on shoulder), from fourteenth-century stratum at Beth-shan.

229. Statue of a Sumerian scribe inscribed "(To) the god Ningirsu, Dudu, the scribe, two (?) Imduguds has presented."

230. Fifth Dynasty statue of an Egyptian scribe, with eyes inlaid with quartz, crystal, and ebony wood, from Sakkarah.

231. Scribes recording evidence as village headmen are brought for nonpayment of taxes, tomb at Sakkarah.

232. Seated scribes, equipped with sharpened rush pens and palettes, on Fourth Dynasty mastaba of Ka-ni-nesut at Giza.

233. Eighteenth Dynasty scribe's palette inscribed with name of Ah-mose I.

234. Restored writing equipment of an Egyptian scribe: rush pen, palette, and water jar.

235. One scribe writes on clay tablet with stylus; another, on skin with brush.

236. Scribes list the booty and the slain from a town in southern Babylonia captured by Sennacherib, from Nineveh.

237. Necklace of beads and stamp seals, Tell Asmar.

238. Legal document and its envelope from Cappadocia.

239. Old Babylonian contract sealed with seven seals.

240. Cylinder seals, varying in size and shape, carved with scenes which were impressed on wet clay for purposes of identification.

241. Clay tablet inscribed with a pictographic script of the earliest period of cuneiform writing, from Uruk.

242. Archaic stone tablet.

243. Inscription of Enhegal, king of Lagash, cut on stone tablet.

244. Cuneiform script used on stela of Hammurabi.

245. Letter of Abimilki of Tyre, from Tell el-Amarna.

247. Historical record of Esarhaddon on clay prism.

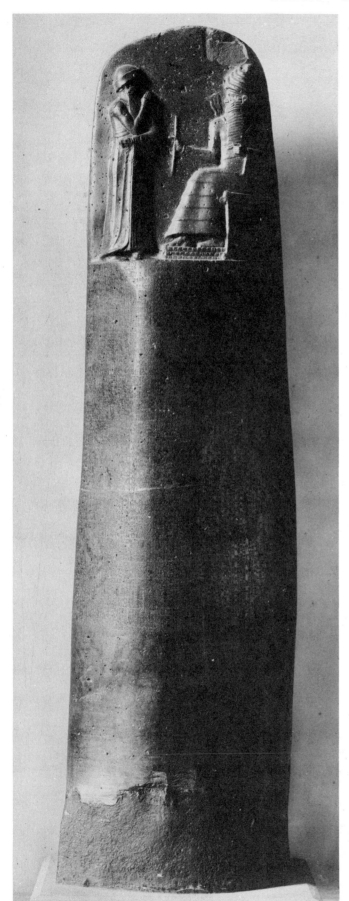

246. The stela of Hammurabi inscribed with laws.

248. Fragment of Babylonian account of the flood.

249. Relief and inscription of Darius in Old Persian, Elamite, and Akkadian, on the cliff at Behistun in Iran.

250. Script of the Old Persian text of the Darius inscription at Behistun.

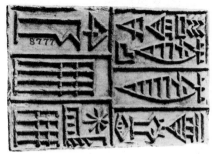

251. Stamps for inscribing building bricks, from Nippur.

252. Stamp of Naram-Sin.

253. Brick inscribed with name of Ishme-Dagon, from Nippur.

254. Cylinder inscribed with text of Nebuchadnezzar.

255. Cuneiform tablet with Aramaic endorsement.

256. Clay tag with string (restored) for attaching to basket.

257. Circular tablet which was used as a copybook, from Nippur.

Original pictograph	Pictograph in position of later cuneiform	Early Babylonian	Assyrian	Original or derived meaning
				bird
				fish
				donkey
				ox
				sun day
				grain
				orchard
				to plow to till
				boomerang to throw to throw down
				to stand to go

259. Table of the development of cuneiform script.

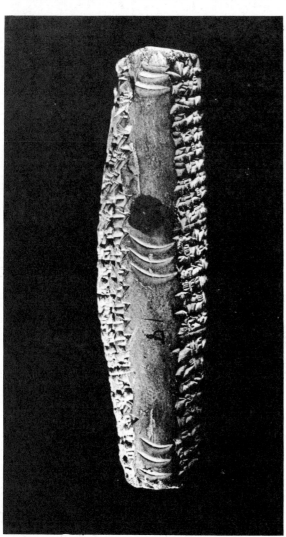

258. Thumbnail identification.

260. Fragment of clay tablet with drawing of a plan of the town Nippur.

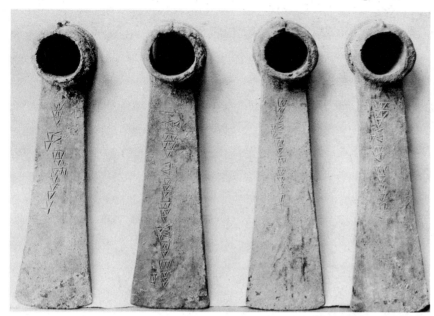

261. Ceremonial adzeheads inscribed in the cuneiform alphabet of Ugarit, from Ras Shamra.

263. Alphabet from Ras Shamra.

262. Stela from Ras Shamra recording sacrifice to Dagon.

264. Portion of the text of the legend of Aqhat on clay tablet from Ras Shamra.

265. Sheet of papyrus, rolled, tied, and sealed, containing marriage contract in Aramaic.

266. Section of the Theban recension of the "Book of the Dead," written on papyrus and illustrated with a vignette.

268. Hieroglyphs in wood, tomb of Hesi-Re, Sakkarah.

267. The Rosetta stone, inscribed in hieroglyphic, demotic, and Greek.

269. Hieroglyphs painted on end board of small Twelfth Dynasty coffin found at el-Bersheh.

270. Alphabetic inscription in Sinaitic script, on a statue from Serabit el-Khadem.

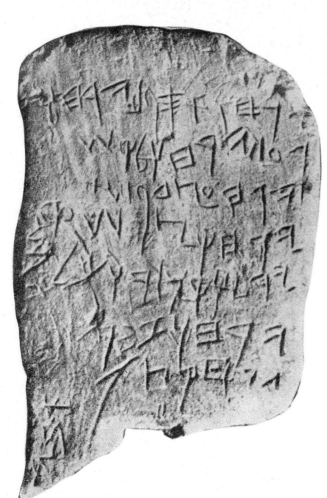

271. Dagger from Tell ed-Duweir.

272. The Gezer calendar, inscribed on soft limestone.

273. Inscribed ewer from Tell ed-Duweir.

274. Inscription of Mesha, king of Moab, discovered at Dhiban.

276. Inscribed seal: "Belonging to Shema, servant of Jeroboam."

277. Seal of Jaazaniah, found at Tell en-Nasbeh.

278. Seal impression of Eliakim, from Tell Beit Mirsim.

275. The Siloam inscription, cut in the wall of a tunnel south of temple in Jerusalem.

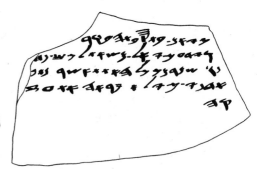

279. Reverse of ostracon IV from Tell ed-Duweir (biblical Lachish).

280. Aramaic text on Nerab stela.

281. Aramaic building inscription of Bar Rakab, from Zinjirli.

282. Portion of an Aramaic papyrus from Elephantine, describing the gift of a house by Anani bar Azariah to his daughter.

283. Inscribed sarcophagus of Eshmunazar, king of Sidon.

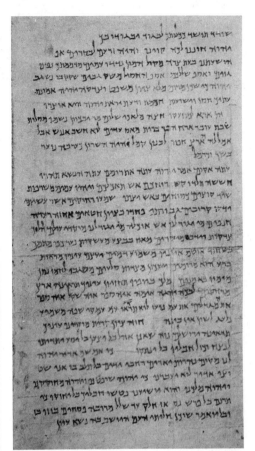

284. Column of St. Mark's Isaiah manuscript.

285. Sabaean inscription from San'a.

286. Table of Semitic alphabets. Outlined letters are carved; solid letters, written with ink.

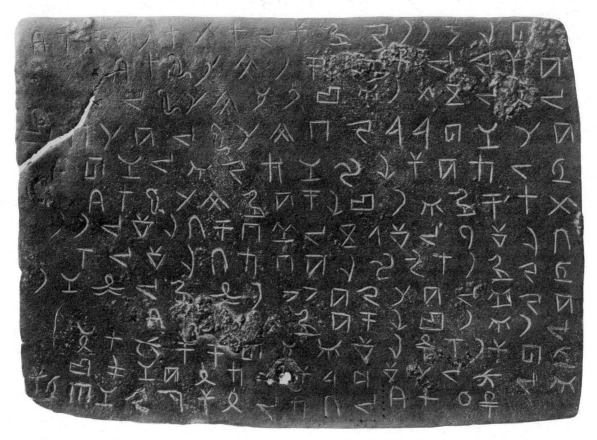

287. The obverse of a bronze tablet from Byblos, inscribed in a pseudohieroglyphic script.

288. Pictorial signs of Hittite hieroglyphic writing.

289. Cursive form of Hittite hieroglyphic writing.

IV. Scenes from History and Monuments

290. Gebel el-'Araq knife handle.

291. Fragment of a slate palette, outlined by a bull attacking a man.

292. Reverse of bull palette, with outline of two walled fortresses.

293. Usaphais smiting an easterner.

294. Stela of the king "Serpent," within a palace.

295. King Snefru smiting an Asiatic.

296. King Nar-mer, wearing the white crown of Upper Egypt, smites a kneeling prisoner, on palette from Hierakonpolis.

297. Other side of slate palette from Hierakonpolis, depicting the triumph of King Nar-mer and other scenes.

298. Enemies of Eannatum, king of Lagash, caught in a net, on two fragments of "stela of the vultures" from Tello.

299. The burial of the slain and an offering scene, on fragments of the reverse of the "vultures" stela from Tello.

300. Eannatum leading his soldiers over bodies of enemy dead (above);
troops led by Eannatum in his chariot (below).

301. Vultures carrying away the corpses of the enemy.

302. Soldiers armed with spears and axes, on edge of the "stela of the vultures" from Tello.

303. The "war panel" from a standard found at Ur, depicting the triumph of the king over his enemies.

304. Celebration of a victory with music and feasting, on the "peace panel" from the standard found at Ur.

305. Shell inlays set in bitumen and pieces of slate from a panel found in an Early Dynastic stratum at Mari. The figures inc

306. Registers of the Ur-Nammu stela, from Ur.

307. Prisoners caught in a net, from Susa.

…itaries in long robes, standard-bearer, soldiers wearing tight-fitting helmets, nude prisoners bound with ropes, chariot, and asses.

308. Stela of victory, from time of First Dynasty of Babylon.

309. Naram-Sin of Agade stands before a stylized mountain victorious over the Lullubians, on a stela from Susa.

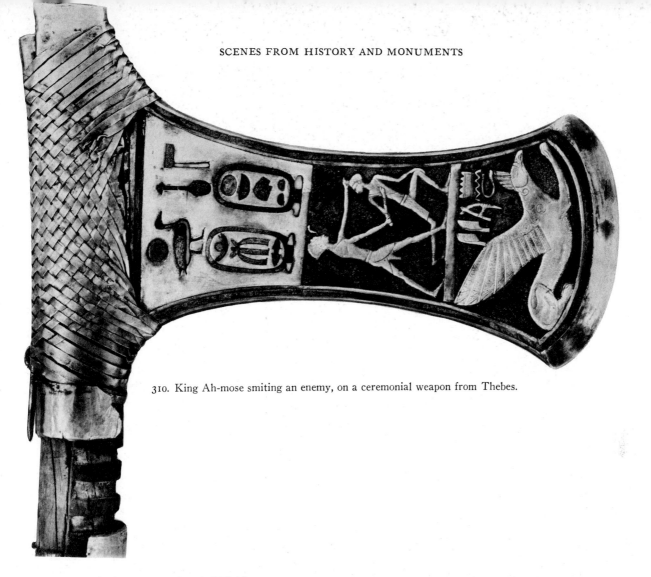

310. King Ah-mose smiting an enemy, on a ceremonial weapon from Thebes.

311. An Egyptian attack upon a fortress peopled with Asiatics, on a limestone relief of the tomb of Anta at Deshasheh.

312. Thut-mose III smites his captives, on a relief of the seventh pylon of the temple of Amon at Karnak.

313. List of the Asiatic conquests of Thut-mose III, from the sixth pylon of the temple of Amon at Karnak.

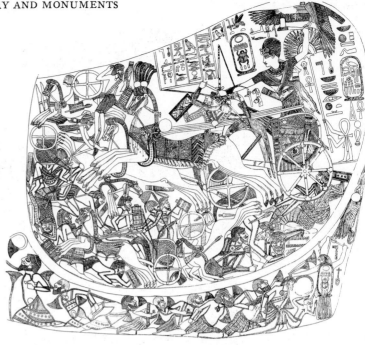

314. Thut-mose IV in his chariot (drawing of No. 316).

315. Thut-mose IV rides over wounded Asiatics on battlefield.

317. Seti I and the gods, stela found at Kadesh in Syria.

316. Exterior of chariot of Thut-mose IV.

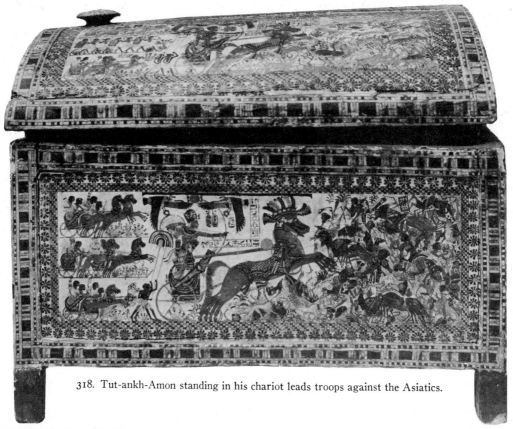

318. Tut-ankh-Amon standing in his chariot leads troops against the Asiatics.

319. Detail from No. 318. Wrecked chariots, Asiatics wounded and dead, and Egyptians cutting off the hands of corpses.

320. A stela of Seti I, found at Beth-shan.

321. Ramses II before Amon-Re, on a stela found at Beth-shan.

322. Campaigns of Seti I against Kadesh and Amor, the Libyans, and the Hittites, on the north wall of the great hall at Karnak.

323. Seti I clutching chieftains captured in Syria-Palestine and his arrival home with prisoners from the Shasu-Bedouin.

324. Attack upon Kadesh by Seti I, from No. 322.

325. Seti I holding captured chieftains from Syria-Palestine, from No. 323.

326. Prisoners from the Shasu-Bedouin taken by Seti I approaching a canal filled with crocodiles, detail from No. 323.

327. Seti I receives the submission of the chiefs of Lebanon (above) and attacks a town of the Canaan (below).

328. Seti I captures the town of Yanoam (above) and engages in battle with the Shasu-Bedouin (below).

329. Fortress of "the town of the Canaan" beside a body of water, and the Shasu, the foes of Seti I; detail from No. 327.

330. Town of Yanoam situated in a wooded region and surrounded by a moat, under attack by Seti I; detail from No. 328.

331. Chiefs of Lebanon felling cedars and assuring an Egyptian officer of Seti I of their submission; detail from No. 327.

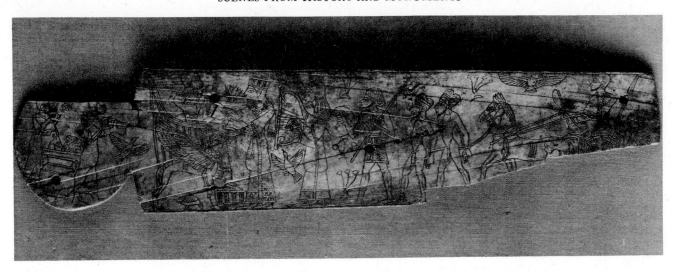

332. The celebration of victory with feasting and music and the procession of prisoners, on Megiddo ivory.

333. Troops of Ramses II attack the Hittite fortress at Deper, on Ramesseum at Thebes.

334. Ramses II's conquest of the fortress of Ashkelon, at Karnak. 335. Reliefs of Ramses II and Shalmaneser III (?) at Nahr el-Kelb.

336. The fortress of Kadesh on the Orontes, surrounded by a moat; relief on east tower of first pylon at Luxor.

337. Battle of Kadesh on second pylon of the Ramesseum: town surrounded by water, Hittite lancers, horses, and charioteers.

338. Ramses II displays his prowess before a god, on cylinder seal from Beth-shan.

339. Hittite king presents daughter to Ramses II.

340. Counting and recording hands of enemy dead.

341. Ship of Ramses III engaged in battle with the Sea People, who wear the high feathered headdress, relief at Medinet Habu.

342. A stela of Mer-ne-Ptah which mentions "Israel," from Thebes.

343. Detail of the name "Israel" from the stela of Mer-ne-Ptah, No. 342.

344. Syrian town (probably Tunip), surrounded on three sides by a moat, under attack by forces of Ramses III.

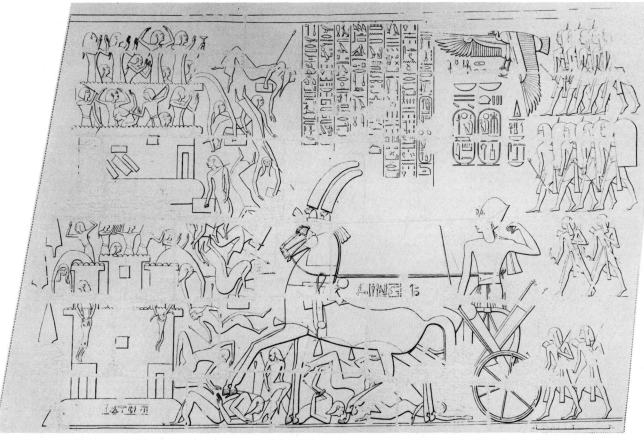

345. Ramses III mounted in his chariot charges over bodies of Hittites from two fortresses, on relief at Medinet Habu.

346. Ramses III attacks a walled fortress in Amor manned by Syrian lancers, on relief at Medinet Habu.

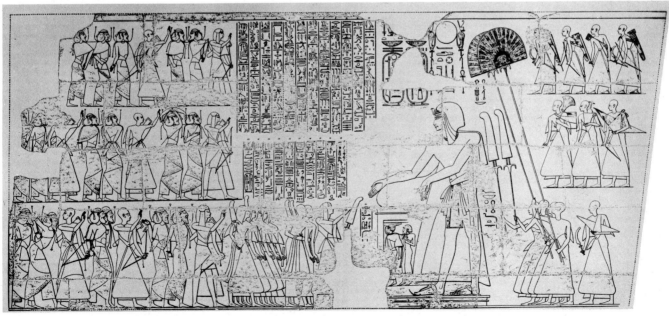

347. The Crown Prince and officials present to Ramses III three lines of bound Syrian prisoners, on relief at Medinet Habu.

348. Heap of hands severed from the enemies of Ramses III, relief at Medinet Habu.

349. List of Palestinian and Syrian towns captured by Sheshonk I, on south wall of Amon temple at Karnak.

350. Reception of tribute from conquests in foreign lands by Ashurnasirpal II, registers from a basalt obelisk from Nimrud.

I

II

III

IV

V

351. Scenes from the "Black Obelisk" of Shalmaneser III.

352. Side of obelisk, on which scenes of tribute continue.

I

II

III

IV

V

353. Camels, elephants, monkeys, and tribute bearers.

354. Continuation of scenes on fourth side of obelisk.

355. Shalmaneser III receives tribute of "Jehu, son of Omri," who is upon his hands and knees; detail from No. 351.

356. Shalmaneser III's campaign in Phoenicia: tribute from Tyre (upper) and the expedition against Hazazu (lower).

357. Tribute from Shalmaneser III's conquest of Tyre (upper), captives from Hazazu (lower); continuation of No. 356.

358. Shalmaneser III followed by his attendants and chariot (upper), and captives from Hazazu (lower); continuation of No. 357.

359. Assyrian war chariots of Shalmaneser III (upper), and storming of the town of Hazazu (lower); continuation of No. 358.

360. Chariots of Shalmaneser III (upper), slaughter of men of Hazazu (below) ; continuing No. 359.

361. Cavalry, officers, and camp (above) ; slaughter of men of Hazazu (below) ; continuing No. 360.

362. Shalmaneser III's campaign in north Syria: town of Dabigu (upper), impaled inhabitants of Syrian town (below).

363. Shalmaneser III receives Sangara, king of Carchemish, who presents his daughter, together with her dowry.

364. Shalmaneser III's expedition to source of Tigris: sacrifice (above), and the carving of the royal image (below).

365. Shalmaneser III's assault on the town of Hamath (above), and the escorting of female captives from Hamath (below).

366. Assyrian soldiers of Tiglath-pileser III lead away sheep and inhabitants from the town of Astartu (?).

367. Two Assyrian scribes record the spoil taken from a captured town as women and children are carried away in carts.

368. Attack by siege-engine supported by bowmen protected by shields.

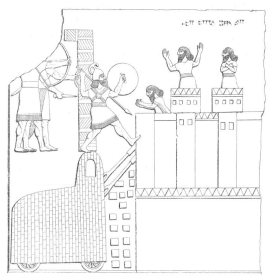

369. Siege of Gazru, on relief from Nimrud.

370. Plundering of temple of Musasir by the Assyrians, from Khorsabad.

371. Sennacherib seated on his throne receiving the booty taken from Lachish; inhabitants of the town kneel before him.

372. Attack on Lachish by siege-engines pushed up an incline and protected by archers who shoot from behind shields.

373. Defenders of Lachish fight from a tower as men and women carry their goods from the town. Three nude figures impaled.

374. Royal tent with poles and guys pitched on wooded hill before Lachish; relief of Sennacherib from Nineveh.

375. Assyrian horsemen pursuing a camel rider, on a relief from Nimrud of the time of Tiglath-pileser III.

376. King Djoser of Third Dynasty, statue from Sakkarah.

377. King Khaf-Re under the protection of the falcon-Horus.

378. Men-kau-Re (Mycerinus) between two goddesses.

379. King Pepi I in festival costume.

380. King Pepi I kneeling and holding jars.

381. Alabaster head of King Pepi II.

382. Statue of Sen-Usert II, later usurped by Ramses II.

383. Wooden figure of Sen-Usert I.

384. Sen-Usert III, an inscribed statue from Deir el-Bahri.

385. Statue of Amen-em-het III, from Hawara.

386. Twelfth Dynasty sphinx, reused by Mer-ne-Ptah.

387. Thut-mose III, upper part of Karnak statue.   388. Queen Hat-shepsut, head from Deir el-Bahri.

389. Amen-hotep II (?) under the protection of the goddess Hathor in the form of a cow, sandstone statue from Deir el-Bahri.

390. Amen-hotep II, famous for his physical prowess, stands in his chariot and shoots arrows at target.

391. Amen-hotep II kneeling and holding jars.

392. A table of offerings presented by Amen-hotep II.

393. King Thut-mose IV in the form of a sphinx treading upon his foes, from fragment of throne from his tomb at Thebes.

394. Amen-hotep III, from tomb of Kha-em-het.

395. Amen-hotep III with blue crown.

396. Amen-hotep III, head from large statue.

397. Amen-hotep III, Tiy, and three daughters.

398. Portrait head in wood of Queen Tiy, wife of Amen-hotep III.

399. Amen-hotep son of Hapu, as a scribe.

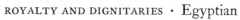

400. Amen-hotep III and Tiy seated before a table of offerings.

401. Akh-en-Aton presenting an offering tray.

402. Cast head of Akh-en-Aton from Amarna.

403. Akh-en-Aton (?), intended as inlay.

404. Portrait bust of Queen Nefert-iti, from Tell el-Amarna.

405. Akh-en-Aton, on fragment from altar-piece.

406. Akh-en-Aton and Nefert-iti, sculptor's limestone model from Tell el-Amarna.

407. Queen offering the king flowers.

408. King Akh-en-Aton and Queen Nefert-iti standing with offerings for the sun-god Aton, on balustrade at Amarna.

409. Domestic group of Akh-en-Aton, Nefert-iti, and their three daughters, on altar-piece.

410. Daughters of Akh-en-Aton, on wall painting.

411. Akh-en-Aton, Nefert-iti, and their daughters.

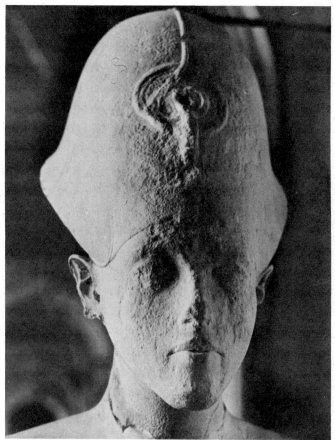

412. Akh-en-Aton wearing the blue crown, from Amarna.

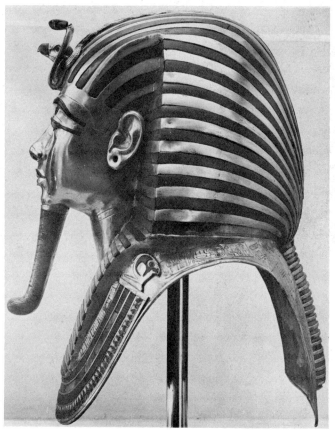

413. Mask of Tut-ankh-Amon.

414. Statue of Tut-ankh-Amon which was guarding entrance to his tomb

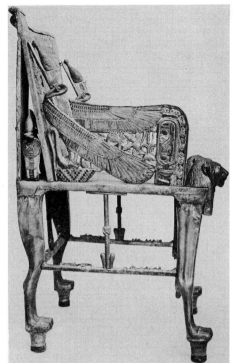

415-417. Wooden throne of Tut-ankh-Amon overlaid with sheet gold, from the tomb of the king at Thebes.

418. Hor-em-heb seated with papyrus scroll upon his lap.

419. Statue of Tut-ankh-Amon usurped by Hor-em-heb.

420. Ramses II wearing the blue crown and broad collar.

421. Seti II sitting on throne holding small shrine.

422. A goddess, wearing crowns of Upper and Lower Egypt, sits enthroned as King Seti I nurses at her breast, at Abydos.

423. King Mer-ne-Ptah wearing *nemes* headdress, from Thebes.

425. Inscribed head of Psamtik II.

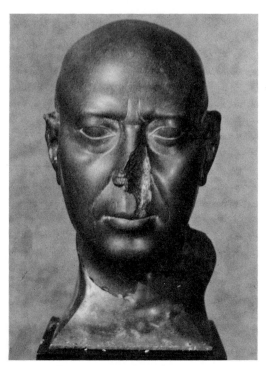

424. Head from a black granite statue of King Tirhakah.

426. Late Egyptian portrait head.

427. King Ur-Nanshe of Lagash bearing a basket on his head (above) and drinking from a cup (below), with sons.

428. Enannatum, king of Lagash, on fragment of votive plaque.

429. Lamgi-Mari, king of Mari.

430. Head from a diorite statuette of Gudea, e n s i of Lagash.

432. Bronze head from Nineveh.

431. Gudea, e n s i of Lagash, seated on his throne, from Tello.

433. Puzur-Ishtar, governor of Mari.

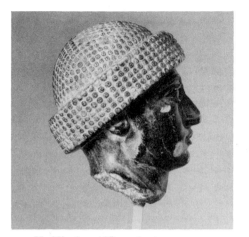

434. Ur-Ningirsu of Lagash.

435. Ur-Ningirsu, son of Gudea.

436. Ishtup-ilum, of Mari.

437. Head of "Hammurabi," from Susa.

438. Sculptured head in Old Babylonian style.

440. Assyrian king holding enemies by ropes, "Broken Obelisk" from Nineveh.

439. Ashurnasirpal II.

441. King Ashurnasirpal II of Assyria, on a relief from Nimrud.

442. Shamshi-Adad V under symbols of gods.

443. King Shalmaneser III, from Kurkh.

444. King Adad-nirari III.

445. King Tiglath-pileser III, from Nimrud.

446. Head of Sargon II of Assyria, from Khorsabad.

447. King Esarhaddon holding two royal captives, from Zinjirli.

448. Side of No. 447. 449. Side of No. 447.

450. Ashurbanipal carrying a basket for rebuilding of Esagila in Babylon.

451. King Ashurbanipal and his queen feasting in their garden, attended by servants and musicians, on relief from Nineveh.

452. King Idri-mi of Alalakh.

453. Stela of Bel-harran-bel-usur, the founder of a city, from Tell Abta.

454. Merodach-baladan making a grant to an official.

455. King Kilamuwa (?) of Sam'al with servant.

456. Sarcophagus of King Ahiram of Byblos, who is seated on a throne before a table of offerings approached by attendants.

457. Opposite side of sarcophagus of Ahiram, with eight men and women bearing offerings or making gesture of the upraised hands.

458. King Ahiram seated on a sphinx throne, with his feet on a footstool and holding a lotus (detail of No. 456).

459. Women mourning the dead King Ahiram of Byblos.

460. King Bar Rakab seated on his throne, with his scribe.

461. King Araras of Carchemish and his son Prince Kamanas, from Carchemish.

462. Darius, carved at Behistun.

463. King Darius seated on his throne with Crown Prince Xerxes behind him, with attendants and guards, from Persepolis.

VI. Gods and Their Emblems

464. A goddess, the "Queen of wild beasts," seated on her throne flanked by goats, ivory from Minet el-Beida.

465. Nude goddess from Ugarit.

466. Seated bronze figure of a Syrian goddess.

467. Molded clay figurine from Megiddo.

468. 'Astart, seal from Bethel.

469. Figurines of the nude female figure, from the Middle Bronze to the Iron II periods in the Palestine Archaeological Museum.

470. Nude goddess standing on a lion and holding lotus.

471. Goddess Qadesh on a lion and holding serpents.

472. Worshiper presenting offering to goddess on lion.

473. Qadesh on a lion, flanked by Min and Resheph.

474. Qadesh, Resheph, and Min, on a New Kingdom stela.

475. The goddess with two horns, on a stela from Beth-shan.

476. Asiatic war-god Resheph, on an inscribed stela.

477. King Yehawmilk of Byblos presents a libation to his goddess, the "Lady of Byblos."

478. Goddess with scepter, pendant from Beth-shan.

479. Nude goddess astride a horse.

480. Goddess from Ras Shamra.

481. God covered with gold
and silver, Minet el-Beida.

482. Gods found in jar at Ras Shamra.

483. Figure of god,
bronze and silver.

484. Syrian god in bronze,
covered with gold and silver.

485. Stela dedicated by Mami to Baal Ṣapuna, from Ras Shamra.

486. A god upon a lion, under winged sun-disc.

487. Mekal, god of Beth-shan, with worshipers.

488. God and a goddess on the Balu'ah stela.

489. God holding scepter, from Ras Shamra.

490. Baal of the lightning.

491. God with high headdress.

492. Goddess with winged cloak.

493. Presentation of offering to god "El," from Ras Shamra.

494. God with weapon and shield, from Megiddo.

495. Deity with silver collar, from Megiddo.

496. God of war with shield and weapon, Megiddo.

497. Bronze statuette covered with gold, Megiddo.

499. God Milqart on stela of Bar-Hadad.

498. Horned Syrian deity, from stela.

500. Storm-god standing on a bull.

501. Storm-god on bull, from Arslan Tash.

502. Alabaster vase from Warka decorated with an offering scene for the goddess, row of porters, animals, and plants.

503. Lambs emerge from the shrine of the mother-goddess, relief on the side of a troughlike stone vessel.

504. "Eye-idols" found within the temple area at Tell Brak.

505. Date-goddess on fragment of vase of Entemena of Lagash.

506. Lady from Mari.

507. Goddess Bau on geese throne, from Ur.

508. Enthroned goddess Ningal, from Ur.

509. Female figurine from Tepe Gawra.

510. Female figurines with human bodies and reptilian heads wearing crowns, from Ur.

511. Entwined serpents on
Gudea vase, from Tello.

512. The goddess Ninsun.

513. Gudea of Lagash conducted into the presence of an enthroned deity by Ningizzida and another god.

514. A worshiper before a seated god, on stela from Susa.

515. Hammurabi before the sun-god Shamash, stela from Susa.

516. Goddess with flowing vase, from Mari.

517. Shamash arising from the eastern mountain, from Mari.

518. Meli-Shipak granting lands to his daughter before the goddess, from Susa.

519. Boundary-stone of
Nebuchadnezzar I.

520. Boundary-stone of Meli-Shipak, from Susa.

521. Symbols and text from a
Nazi-Maruttash *kudurru*, Susa.

523. The god Marduk on piece of lapis, Babylon.

522. Ishtar of Arbela standing on a lion, from Til-Barsib.

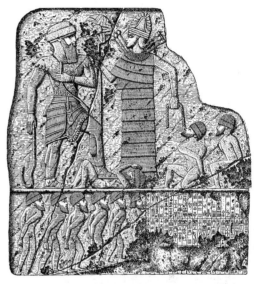

524. Goddess Ishtar on relief of Anubanini.

525. Ishtar enthroned, receiving an offering.

526. Ishtar, goddess of war, with foot on lion, and worshiper.

527. God of vegetation and his worshiper, carving on rock at Ivriz.

528. God of vegetation.

529. Shamash enthroned within his shrine, to whom Nabuaplaiddin is presented, on stone tablet from Abu Habbah.

530. Statue from Zinjirli.

531. Weather-god, from Til-Barsib.

532. Armed weather-god, Til-Barsib.

533. Shamash-resh-usur, governor of Suhi and Mari, standing before the deities Adad and Ishtar, from Babylon.

{ 179 }

534. A god standing on the back of a composite animal, from Ashur.

535. Worshiper before his god, tile from Ashur.

536. The god Ashur, with drawn bow, represented within a disc with wings and flames, is among rain clouds.

537. A procession of gods mounted on animals, between two figures of the Assyrian king, relief at Maltaya.

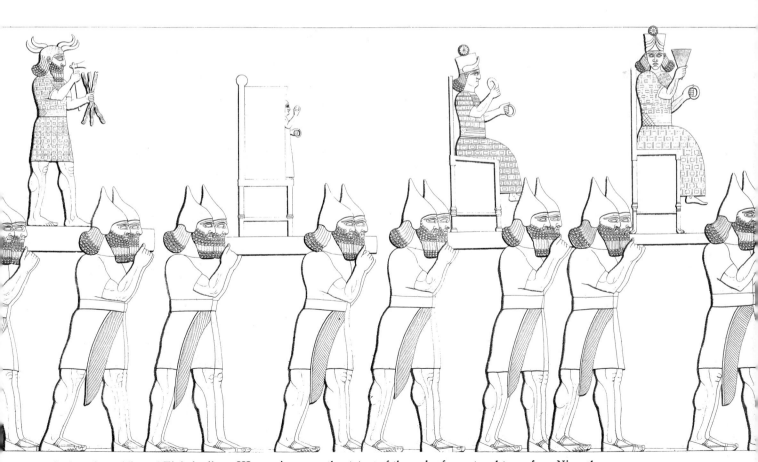

538. Assyrian soldiers of Tiglath-pileser III carrying away the statues of the gods of a captured town, from Nimrud.

539. Deities from a panel of twelve at Yazilikaya.

540. Basalt head of a Hittite deity.

541. Hittite god extends his left arm around the Hittite King Tudhaliyas, rock sculpture at Yazilikaya. (Cast at right.)

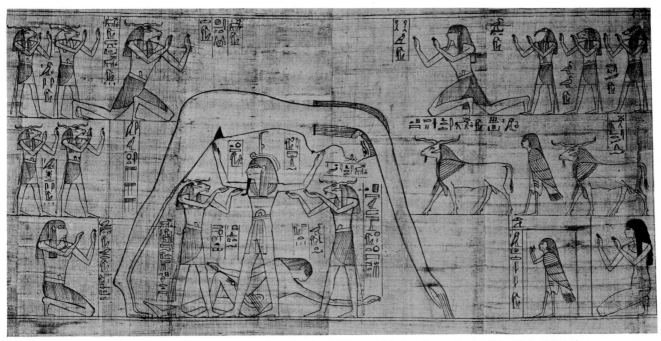

542. Sky-goddess Nut, arched as the heavens, supported by the air-god Shu; at his feet the earth-god Geb; Deir el-Bahri papyrus.

543. The sky-goddess Nut.   544. Isis protecting Osiris with her wings.

546. The air-god Shu holding the sky.

545. The goddess Isis holding King Seti I in her lap, from Abydos.

547. Head of the goddess Hathor, on capital.

548. The god Anubis as a jackal lying on a funerary chest, from the tomb of Tut-ankh-Amon at Thebes.

549. Ptah enthroned, as king kneels before him, from Abydos.

550. A king as Amon.

551. The god Amon on a Middle Kingdom relief.

552. A bronze Amon.

554. Bronze statue of Min.

553. Bronze Seth made over into god Khnum.

557. Osiris standing in his shrine, tomb painting at Thebes.

555. Seth in Asiatic dress, on "Stela of Year 400."

556. The god Osiris.

558. Sekhmet.   559. Goddess Mut. 560. Goddess Neith.   561. Goddess Maat.

562. Painted wooden figure of goddess Nephthys.   563. Granite statue of moon-god Khonsu, from Karnak.

564. The god Horus in form of a hawk wearing crown.

565. Horus with falcon head and double crown, in bronze.

566. Infant Horus on a lotus blossom, ivory from Samaria.

567. The god Horus in human form with hawk head, Abydos.

570. The bull Apis wearing a disc between his horns and a uraeus.

568. Statue of Ta-weret, Karnak.

569. Khnum fashions Prince Amen-hotep III and his *ka*.

571. The god Atum as a serpent.

572. The ibis-headed Thoth seated before Seti I, who wears the blue crown and streamer, painted limestone relief.

573. Drawings of the principal Egyptian gods and goddesses, by Étienne Drioton.

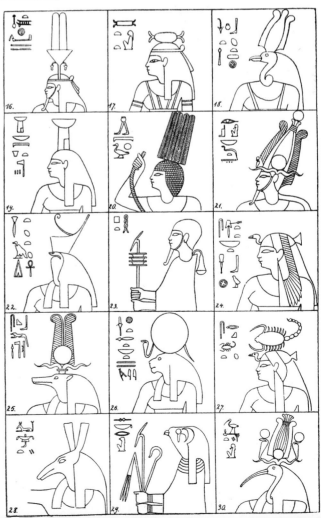

VII. The Practice of Religion

574. Frieze of gold, limestone, marble, and shale, from the altar or podium of the "Eye-Temple" at Tell Brak.

575. Horned incense altar from Megiddo.

576. Tukulti-Ninurta before Nusku.

577. Cult socket from Ashur, with king between two standards.

578. Votive shrine from a Hurrian level at Tell Billa.

579. South Arabian incense altar.

580. Round-topped altar from time of Sargon II.

581. Incense altar from South Arabia.

582. Pottery stand from Megiddo.

583. Incense stand with bowl, from Megiddo.

584. Stand with apertures and projecting tabs, from Ai.

585. Cylindrical cult object from Beth-shan.

586. Restored model shrine house, from Megiddo.

587. Stand from Megiddo.

588. Tripod from Ras Shamra.

589. Kernos ring from Megiddo.

590. Rectangular shrine model, Beth-shan.

591. Clay model house decorated with apertures, serpents, and birds, from Ashur.

592. Incense spoon in form of lion's jaw, from Tell Beit Mirsim.

593. Execration figurine, from Sakkarah.

594. Model liver made of clay and inscribed with omens and magical texts.

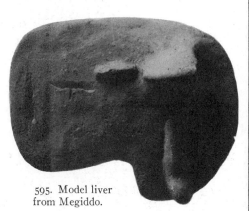

595. Model liver from Megiddo.

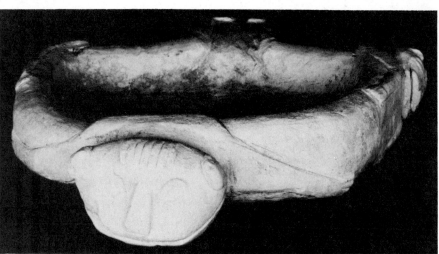

596. Offering table decorated with three lions, from Tell Beit Mirsim.

597. Nude priest pouring libation before a goddess, Tello.

598. Figure with plumed headdress, on plaque from Tello.

599. Dudu, priest of the god Ningirsu, plaque from Tello.

600. Nude priest offering libation to god, from Nippur.

601. Offering scene, limestone plaque from Nippur.

602. Part of festival scene, limestone plaque from Susa.

603. Nude priest presenting offering, plaque from Ur.

604. Festival scene, Early Dynastic plaque, Khafajah.

605. Priest with libation vase, shell plaque from Ur.

606. Enheduanna, daughter of Sargon, priestess of moon-god, on disc from Ur.

607. Attendant leading a bull, wall painting from Mari palace.

609. Sargon and officer before a god, Khorsabad painting.

608. Two men before table, stela from Ras Shamra.

610. Investiture of the king by goddess.

611. Bearded figure, perhaps a king, pours libation to four divinities, who stand in line before him, relief from Malatya.

612. Man holding animal to his breast, statue from Mari.

613. Offering bearer with sacrificial animal, from Mari.

614. Winged human figure carrying goat and barley, from Nimrud.

615. Hero holding a lion, large relief from Khorsabad.

616. Hittite royal pair making an offering before an altar and a bull, Alaça Hüyük.

617. A protective genius, holding a bucket and a cone, touches the Assyrian King Ashurnasirpal II, relief from Nimrud.

618. Sacrificial animals carried by offering bearers forming a procession, basalt relief from Carchemish.

619. Bronze model of the enactment of the ritual *ṣît šamši*, with representations of cultic objects, from Susa.

620. Statue of divine servant.

622. Statuette dedicated to Amurru.

621. Divine servant with box.

623. Courtiers with offering table, from Khorsabad.

624. Offering register of obelisk of Ashurnasirpal I (?) from Nineveh: temple with god and priest-king, altar, and king.

625. Shalmaneser III sacrificing to his gods, before his own royal image cut in the rock at Lake Van; "Tell Balawat."

626. Ashurbanipal pouring a libation over dead lions before an offering table and incense stand, to accompaniment of music.

627. Making an offering, Ashur seal.

628. Painting in color on a vessel of an Assyrian offering scene, from Ashur.

629. "Mortuary priests" perform operations on boys in a scene labeled "Circumcision," relief of Sixth Dynasty from Sakkarah.

631. Stela from Marash, with hieroglyphic Hittite.

630. Funerary stela, depicting offering for deceased, from Zinjirli.

632. Man served by two women, grave stela from Marash.

633. Man and woman partake of ceremonial meal, Zinjirli.

634. Lamentation scene on a Nineteenth Dynasty relief from Memphis: widow

635. Funerary stela of priest Agbar, from Nerab.

636. Grave stela from South Arabia.

f the deceased (upper right); behind her, servants prepare booths for funeral; two sons (lower right), viziers, and mourners.

637. Banquet scene on a relief from Carchemish: bearded figure sits before table, with attendants.

638. Group of women and girls stand with raised hands mourning for deceased, painting from Theban tomb.

639. The god Anubis leads the deceased toward the balance, where his heart is weighed against Maat; papyrus of Hu-nefer.

640. Ceremony of "opening the mouth," for giving deceased a new body in the hereafter.

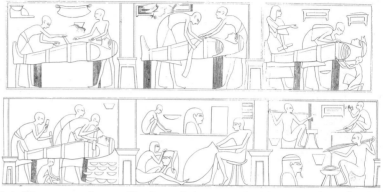

642. The process of mummification, painting on tomb of Amen-em-Opet.

641. Pottery anthropoid sarcophagus, from Beth-shan.

643. Basalt sarcophagus and lid belonging to Shamshi-Adad V, from Ashur.

644. Composite winged creature, from Carchemish.

645. Pair of monsters with upraised arms, from Carchemish.

646. Colossal winged lion from doorway of Ashurnasirpal palace.

647. Winged bull which guarded doorway to palace at Nimrud.

650. Sphinxes face each other, one at each side of the Egyptian goddess Hathor.

648. Two sphinxes which form a base for a column of the palace of Bar Rakab at Zinjirli.

649. Sphinx in lotus thicket carved in ivory, from Samaria.

651. A winged deity, armed with swords and holding lightning forks, drives out a monster, on relief from Nimrud. Reconstruction inset.

652. Two leaping genii, from Aleppo citadel.

653. Bull-men holding winged disc.

654. Stylized tree flanked by winged human creatures, on relief from Tell Halaf.

655. Winged figure, Tell Halaf.

656. A winged deity with chaplet in hand stands at each side of a stylized tree, relief of Ashurnasirpal II from Nimrud.

657. Lion-headed demon, with dog and pig at her breast.

658. Bronze Pazuzu plaque with exorcising scene.

659. Inscribed bronze statue of the demon Pazuzu.

660. Fragment of a Lamashtu amulet for exorcising demons from the sick.

661. Head of demon Pazuzu.

662. Inscribed amulet from Arslan Tash.

663. Egyptian Bes, Megiddo ivory.

664. Bes, in green faïence.

665. Bronze bell decorated with demons, human figure, priest carrying pail, etc.

666. Hittite sphinx which stood beside inner doorway of Yerkapu at Boghazköy.

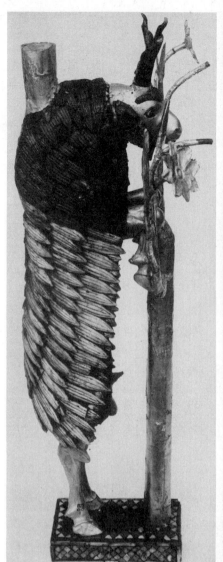

667-668. Two statues of a goat standing upright beside a tree, found in the "Great Death Pit" at Ur, Early Dynastic period.

669. The cat kills the serpent Apophis, Theban painting.

670. Contest with the great serpent-dragon, relief from Malatya.

671. Contest of a god with a seven-headed monster, on shell plaque.

VIII. Myth, Legend, and Ritual on Cylinder Seals

672. Feeding of the temple herd, on a marble cylinder seal of the Uruk period.

673. Boat with cult objects and men.

674. The presentation of temple offerings.

675. Deity seated before his shrine, drinking from tube.

676. God seated in a boat, holding an oar.

677. Sun-god in a boat (upper); carrying material for building temple tower (lower).

678. Contest frieze of fighting animals and bull-man.

679. Drinking (above), and musicians (below).

680. Ritual marriage of god and goddess.

681. Contest, on seal of Adda, major-domo of Enheduanna.

682. Seal dedicated to King Sharkalisharri of Akkad.

683. The sun-god ascending between two mountains.

684. The sun-god before the enthroned Ea, god of wisdom.

685. Liberation of the sun-god from between two mountains.

686. The sun-god, holding a plow, travels in his boat.

687. Water-god Ea, two-faced god, and minor deities.

688. Seated god of vegetation before other gods.

689. Offering presented to weather-god in his chariot.

690. Fighting gods and the building of temple tower.

691. Seven-headed fiery dragon attacked by two gods.

692. Serpent-god before his shrine faces worshipers.

693. Water-god seated within the frame of his shrine.

694. Etana scene: man astride an eagle in the sky, sheep dogs, and shepherds.

695. Man carried skyward by lion-headed eagle.

696. Contest of bearded hero with water-buffalo.

697. God of fertility seated on throne and holding plow.

698. Goddess with mace, before worshiper with kid.

699. Nergal standing with one foot on prostrate body.

700. Worshiper led by a goddess to an enthroned god.

701. A goddess leading worshiper to an enthroned king, on an inscribed cylinder seal of Ur III period.

702. The god Amurru.

703. Nude female above a bull.

704. Suppliant deities before the war-goddess.

705. Animal and human figures under a winged sun-disc on the sealing of Saushshattar, from Nuzi.

706. Assyrian worshiper stands before sacred tree flanked by two fish-men, as a hero grasps an ostrich.

IX. Views and Plans of Excavations

707. General view of three caves at Wadi el-Mugharah, at which prehistoric remains were excavated.

708. Air view of Tell el-Mutesellim, the ancient Megiddo, during its excavation by the Oriental Institute.

709. Air view of the mound (under excavation) and modern village of Jebeil, the ancient Byblos or Gebal.

710. Air view of the mound of ancient Susa (biblical Shushan) and the surrounding country.

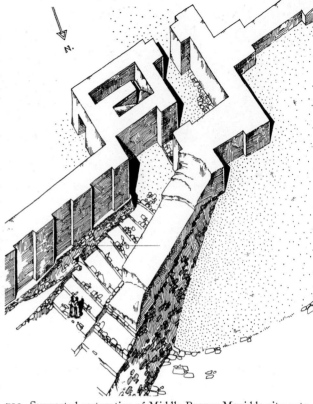

712. Suggested restoration of Middle Bronze Megiddo city gate.

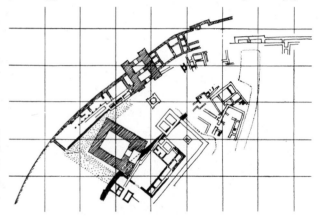

711. An Early Bronze age city wall at Megiddo.

713. City wall and gate at Middle Bronze Shechem.

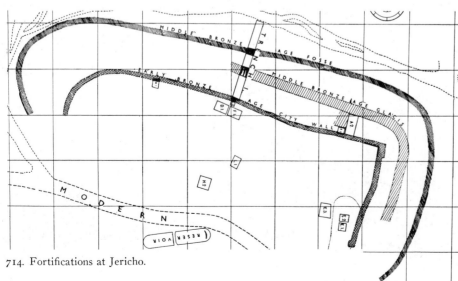

714. Fortifications at Jericho.

715. Battered wall at Jericho.

716. City wall and gate at Tell en-Nasbeh, dating to the ninth century.

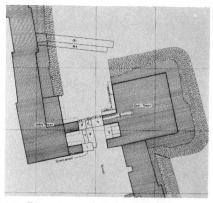

717. Plan of gate at Tell en-Nasbeh.

718. Foundation of city wall near one of main gates of ninth-century Samaria.

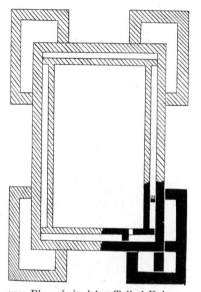

719. Plan of citadel at Tell el-Ful.

720. Hellenistic tower at Samaria, with nineteen courses of masonry preserved.

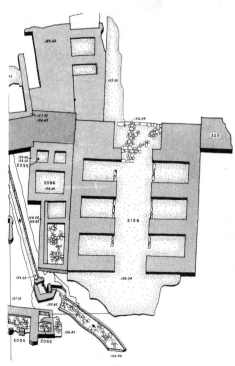

721. Tenth-century gate at Megiddo.

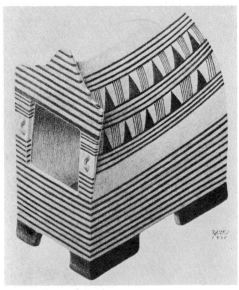

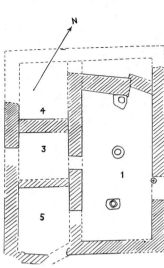

724. Plan of Middle Bronze house.

723. Patrician house at Tell Beit Mirsim.

722. House-shaped burial urn.

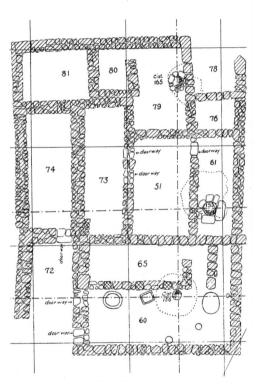

726. Aerial view of a tenth-century palace of ashlar masonry found at Megiddo.

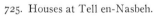
725. Houses at Tell en-Nasbeh.

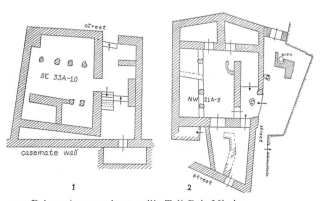

727. Private houses of pre-exilic Tell Beit Mirsim.

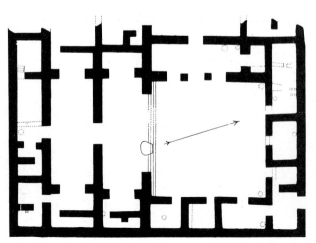

728. Plan of a palace of the Persian period at Tell ed-Duweir.

729. Broad-room type of shrine with a large altar, from the Early Bronze I period at Megiddo.

730. Corner of a small shrine with an altar made of stone and plastered, from the Early Bronze period at Ai.

731. Temple with mud-brick platform, altar, and benches for offerings, from the Late Bronze period at Lachish.

732. General view of the temple of Mekal, dating to the fourteenth century, found at Beth-shan.

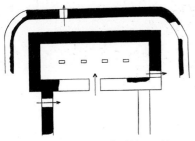

733. Early Bronze temple (?) at Ai.

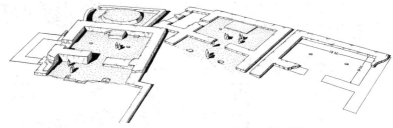

734. Three Middle Bronze temples and a great altar at Megiddo.

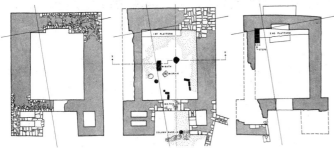

735. Three phases of a Late Bronze temple at Megiddo VIII-VIIA.

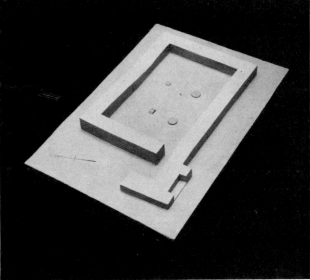

736. The northern temple at Beth-shan V.

737. Canaanite temple from Beth-shan VII.

738. Model of temple at Beth-shan VI.

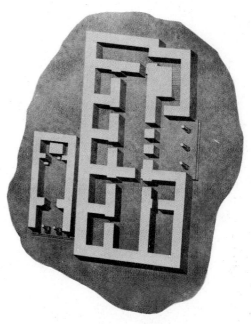

739. Palace and chapel at Tell Tainat.

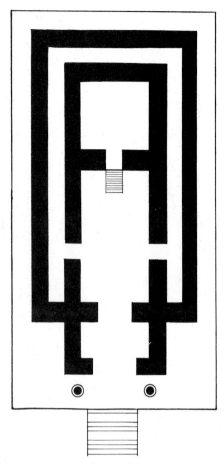

740. Suggested floor plan, Solomonic temple.

741. Partially restored model of the Solomonic stables found at Megiddo.

742. Stables with hitching-posts and mangers, of Solomonic level at Megiddo.

743. Pit for storing grain found at Megiddo, stratum III.

744. The Siloam tunnel, cut through the rock at Jerusalem.

745. Three temples of the Obeid period at Tepe Gawra.

746. Section of wall of ziggurat of Ur-Nammu at Ur. 747. Aerial view of the temple tower, or ziggurat, at Ur.

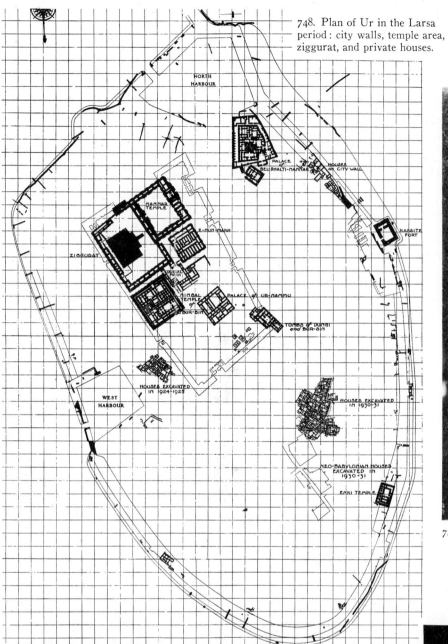

748. Plan of Ur in the Larsa period: city walls, temple area, ziggurat, and private houses.

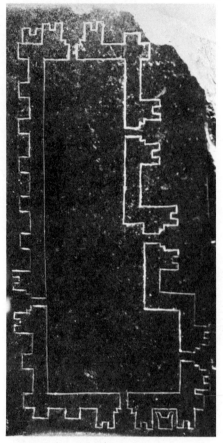

749. Building plan in lap of Gudea.

750. Bound enemy carved on a door socket from Hierakonpolis.

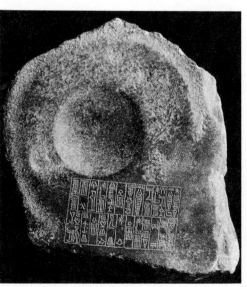

751. Door socket of Sharkalisharri.

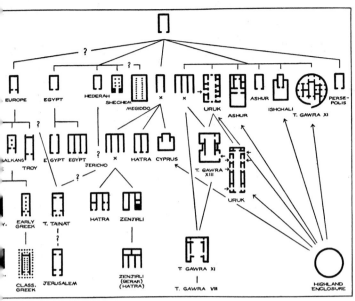

752. Types of Mesopotamian houses with connections.

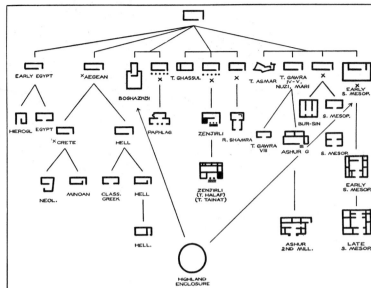

753. Mesopotamian houses related to other types.

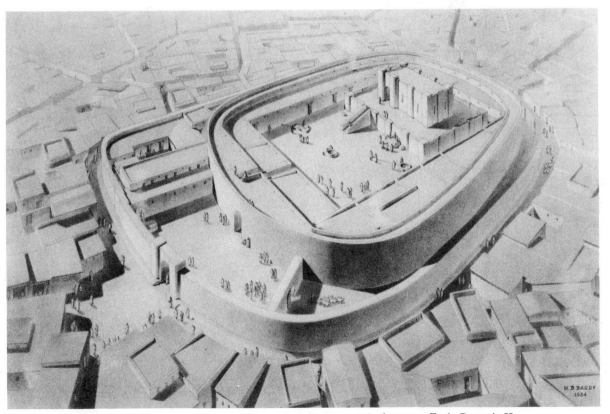

754. Temple Oval at Khafajah, covering an area of more than three-quarters of an acre, Early Dynastic II.

755. Anu-Adad temple of Tiglath-pileser I at Ashur.

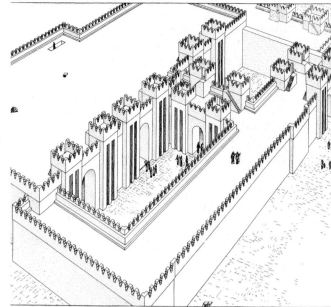

756. Nebo-Ishtar temple of Sinsharishkun at Ashur.

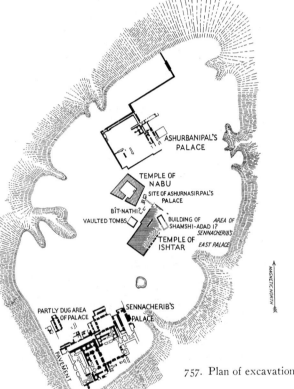

757. Plan of excavations at Kuyunjik.

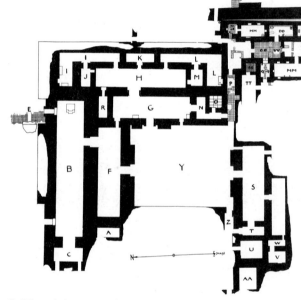

758. Plan of the palace of Ashurnasirpal II at Nimrud.

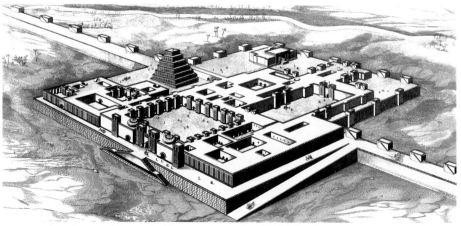

759. Reconstructed drawing of the palace of Sargon II at Khorsabad, from Place's excavations.

760. The Ishtar gate of Nebuchadnezzar II at Babylon, as reconstructed in the Staatliche Museen, Berlin.

761. Serpent-dragon from the Ishtar gate.

762. Lion from the procession street at Babylon.

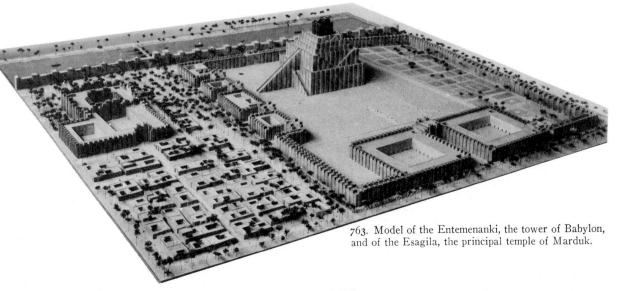

763. Model of the Entemenanki, the tower of Babylon, and of the Esagila, the principal temple of Marduk.

764. A tomb for King Djoser of the Third Dynasty, in the form of a step pyramid, at Sakkarah.

765. A sphinx with the head of King Khaf-Re guards the necropolis of Giza with its three great pyramids (two shown).

766. Apadana, or audience hall, of Darius and Xerxes at Persepolis as excavated by the Oriental Institute.

767. Susian and Persian guards along the eastern stairway of the apadana at Persepolis.

768. Tomb of Cyrus built of limestone blocks tied together with iron cramps, at Pasargadae in Iran.

769. Tombs of Darius I, Artaxerxes I, and Darius II, cut in the rock at Naqsh-i-Rustam in Iran.

X. Maps

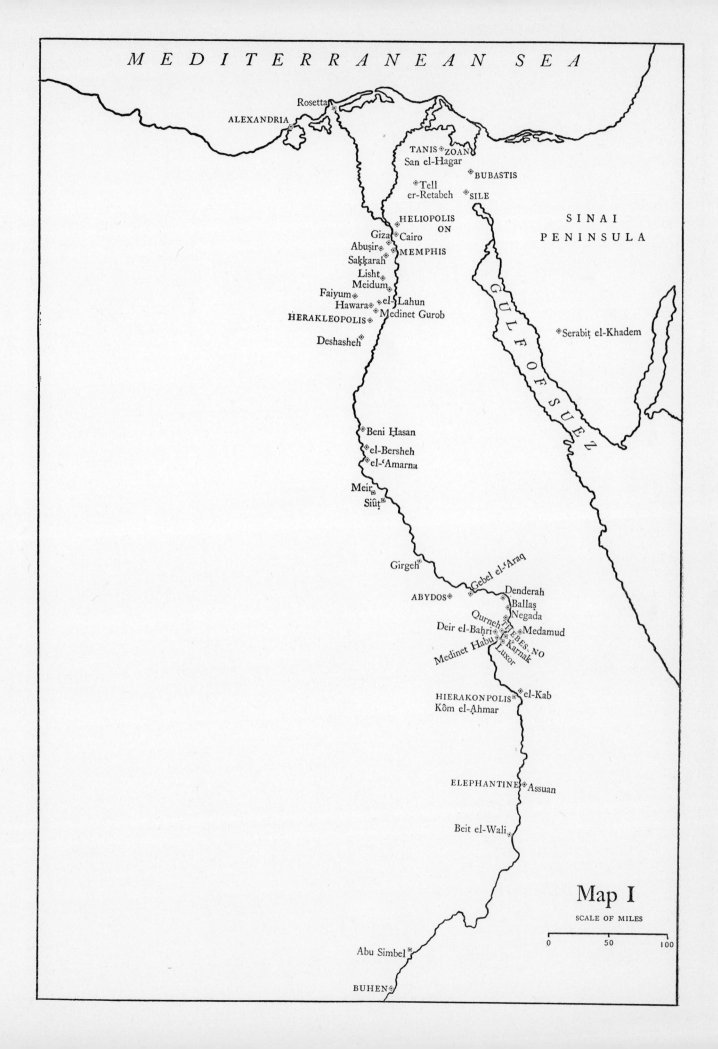

MEDITERRANEAN SEA

Rosetta

ALEXANDRIA

TANIS ZOAN
San el-Hagar

BUBASTIS

Tell
er-Retabeh

SILE

SINAI
PENINSULA

HELIOPOLIS
ON

Giza Cairo

Abuṣir

MEMPHIS

Saḳḳarah

Lisht

Meidum

Faiyum

Hawara el-Lahun

HERAKLEOPOLIS Medinet Gurob

Deshasheh

Serabiṭ el-Khadem

GULF OF SUEZ

Beni Ḥasan

el-Bersheh

el-ʿAmarna

Meir

Siûṭ

Girgeh

Gebel el-ʿAraq

Denderah

ABYDOS

Ballaṣ

Negada

Qurneh THEBES, NO Medamud

Deir el-Baḥri

Medinet Habu Karnak

Luxor

HIERAKONPOLIS el-Kab

Kôm el-Aḥmar

ELEPHANTINE Assuan

Beit el-Wali

Map I

SCALE OF MILES

0   50   100

Abu Simbel

BUHEN

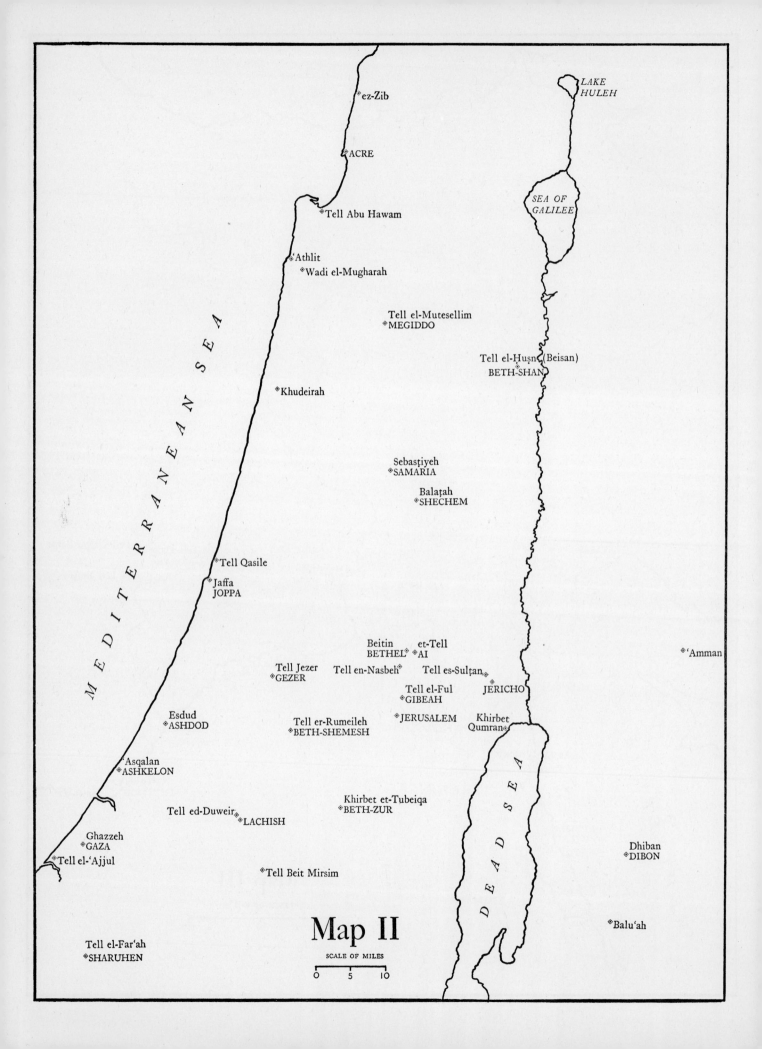

ez-Zib

LAKE
HULEH

ACRE

SEA OF
GALILEE

Tell Abu Hawam

'Athlit
Wadi el-Mugharah

M E D I T E R R A N E A N   S E A

Tell el-Mutesellim
MEGIDDO

Tell el-Huṣn (Beisan)
BETH-SHAN

Khudeirah

Sebasṭiyeh
SAMARIA

Balaṭah
SHECHEM

Tell Qasile

Jaffa
JOPPA

Beitin   et-Tell
BETHEL   AI   'Amman

Tell Jezer   Tell en-Nasbeh   Tell es-Sulṭan
GEZER   JERICHO

Tell el-Ful
GIBEAH

Esdud   JERUSALEM   Khirbet
ASHDOD   Tell er-Rumeileh   Qumran
              BETH-SHEMESH

'Asqalan
ASHKELON

D E A D   S E A

Khirbet et-Tubeiqa
BETH-ZUR

Tell ed-Duweir
LACHISH

Ghazzeh
GAZA   Dhiban
Tell el-'Ajjul   DIBON

Tell Beit Mirsim

Map II

Balu'ah

Tell el-Far'ah
SHARUHEN

SCALE OF MILES

0   5   10

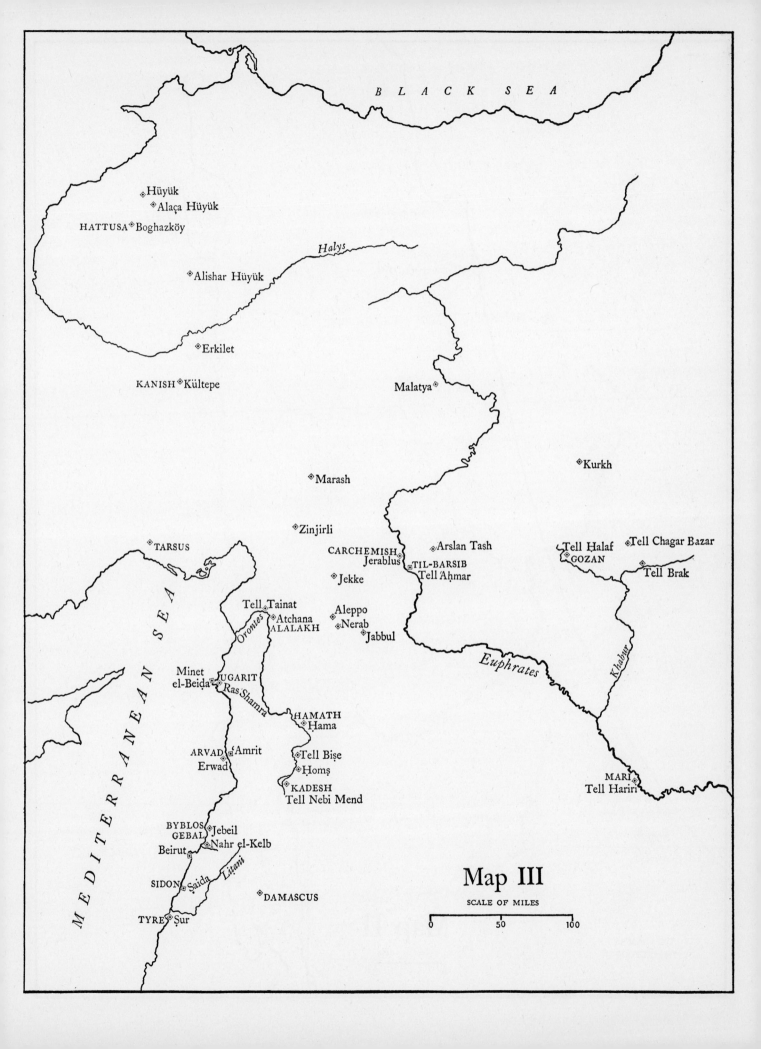

B L A C K   S E A

◇ Hüyük
◇ Alaça Hüyük
HATTUSA ◇ Boghazköy

Halys

◇ Alishar Hüyük

◇ Erkilet

KANISH ◇ Kültepe

Malatya ◇

◇ Kurkh

◇ Marash

◇ Zinjirli

◇ TARSUS

◇ Arslan Tash

CARCHEMISH ◇
Jerablus

TIL-BARSIB ◇
Tell Aḥmar

Tell Ḥalaf ◇
GOZAN

◇ Tell Chagar Bazar

◇ Tell Brak

◇ Jekke

Tell ◇ Tainat
◇ Atchana
ALALAKH

Aleppo ◇
◇ Nerab
◇ Jabbul

M E D I T E R R A N E A N   S E A

Orontes

Minet
el-Beida ◇ UGARIT
Ras Shamra

Euphrates

Khabur

HAMATH ◇
Hama

ARVAD ◇ Amrit
Erwad

◇ Tell Biṣe
◇ Homṣ

◇ KADESH
Tell Nebi Mend

MARI ◇
Tell Hariri

BYBLOS ◇ Jebeil
GEBAL
Beirut ◇ Nahr el-Kelb

SIDON ◇ Ṣaida *Litani*

◇ DAMASCUS

TYRE ◇ Ṣur

Map III

SCALE OF MILES

0   50   100

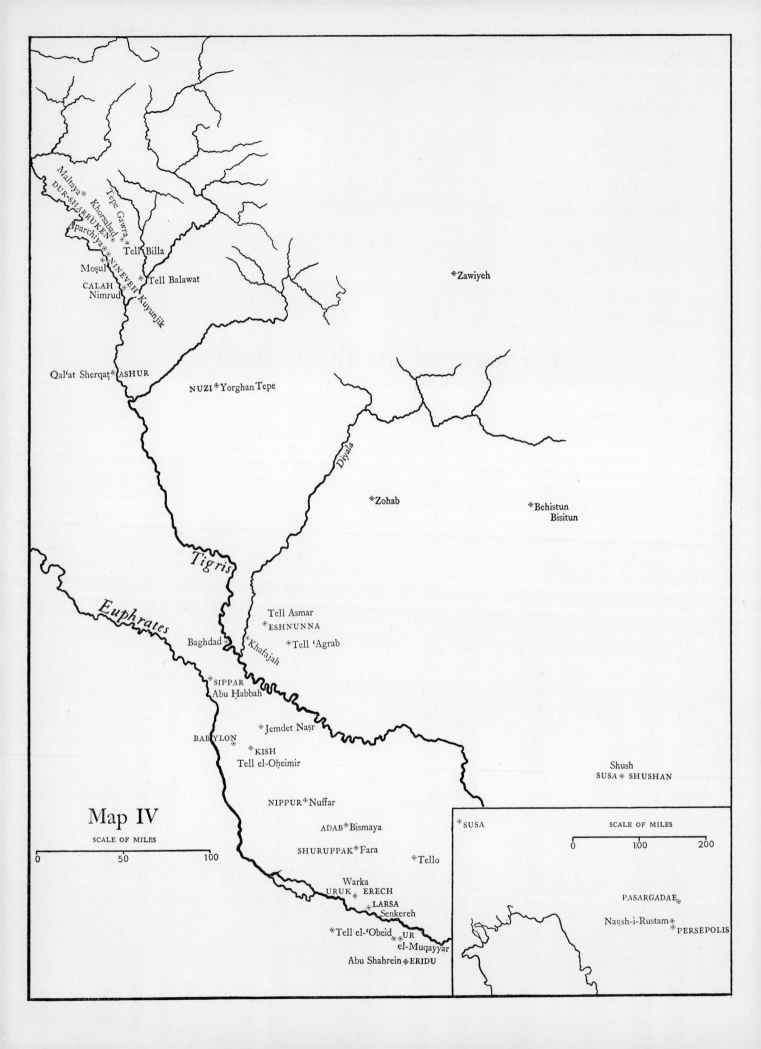

Map IV

SCALE OF MILES

0   50   100

Maltaya
Khorsabad
DUR-SHARRUKEN
Aparchiya
Moşul
CALAH
Nimrud
Tepe Gawra
Tell Billa
NINEVEH
Kuyunjik
Tell Balawat

Qal'at Sherqaṭ ASHUR

NUZI Yorghan Tepe

Tigris

Euphrates

Baghdad
Khafajah
SIPPAR
Abu Ḥabbah

BABYLON
KISH
Tell el-Oḥeimir

Jemdet Naṣr

NIPPUR Nuffar

ADAB Bismaya

SHURUPPAK Fara

Warka
URUK ERECH
LARSA
Senkereh

Tell el-'Obeid UR
el-Muqayyar

Abu Shahrein ERIDU

Tell Asmar
ESHNUNNA
Tell 'Agrab

Diyala

Zohab

Zawiyeh

Behistun
Bisitun

Tello

Shush
SUSA SHUSHAN

SUSA

SCALE OF MILES

0   100   200

PASARGADAE

Naqsh-i-Rustam PERSEPOLIS

Catalogue of the Illustrations

XI. Catalogue

I. Peoples and Their Dress

VARIOUS PEOPLES

1. Three neighboring peoples are represented on an Egyptian relief from the mortuary temple of Sahu-Re at Abusir. First: a Libyan, with pointed beard, a prominent forelock or ornament, and a mass of hair falling below the shoulders; nude except for bands crossed on the chest. A phallus sheath is held by a narrow belt to which is attached at the side a semicircular decoration or pocket and at the back a cord which holds an animal's tail hanging down behind; about the neck hangs a long tassel. Second: a South-Hamite (Egyptian except for the belt) with small pointed beard, curled hair (or wig) held in place by a fillet, with strands extending below the shoulders; clothed in a short kilt held by a sash tied in front, and a broad collar about the neck. Third: a Syrian, with prominent nose, chin beard, long straight hair extending to the shoulders, clothed in a plain kilt. Fourth: duplicate of the first figure. All are bound with ropes around the elbows, and each pair is held, with ropes attached to the waist, by a deity (represented in the register above but not shown here) who presents the prisoners to the king.

Berlin, Äg. 21782. Abusir, mortuary temple of Sahu-Re. Limestone. Height of first figure: 0.32 m. Sahu-Re (about 2500). L. Borchardt, *Das Grabdenkmal des Königs Śa'ḥu-Reʿ*, vol. 2, Leipzig, 1913, pl. 6. Schäfer-Andrae, 251. Photograph courtesy of Staatliche Museen.

2. A group of four foreign representatives from the north forms part of a larger scene depicting the presentation of gold as tribute to Egypt. First: a Syrian, with bald or shaved head, wearing a long, sleeved white garment with colored edging. Second: a bearded Syrian, with a mass of hair held in place by a white fillet, and wearing a short kilt. Third: a Cretan, beardless, with long hair falling in strands over the shoulder, clothed in a kilt. Fourth: a Libyan, bearded, with massive hair, which seems to be caught up at the back and held in place by a fillet tied behind; clothed in a kilt decorated on the side by a semicircular design or pocket, and a blue and white sash which crosses on the chest; from the neck hangs a red tassel.

Thebes, tomb of Puy-em-Re (39), west wall, north of central doorway. Painted relief. Height: about 0.45 m. Fifteenth century. Norman de G. Davies, *The Tomb of Puyemrê at Thebes*, vol. 1, New York, 1922, pl. 33A (see also pls. 1 and 36), pp. 90-92. Fremdvölker, 799. Wresz., vol. 1, pl. 149. Photograph courtesy of Metropolitan Museum of Art, New York.

3. This register from a wall painting in the tomb of Khnum-hotep III at Beni Hasan is labeled: "The arriving, bringing eye-paint, which thirty-seven Asiatics brought to him" (cf. *ANET*, 229). To the far right is the royal scribe Nefer-hotep, who holds a docket giving the date as the sixth year of Sen-Usert II (about 1890). Behind him is the Overseer of Hunters Khety, who is followed by "the Ruler of a Foreign Country Ibsha" (perhaps, Abî-shar, according to W. F. Albright, *The*

Vocalization of the Egyptian Syllabic Orthography, New Haven, 1934, p. 8). Ibsha is bearded, and is clothed in a colored garment. He is followed by a man wearing a kilt. Next comes a group of four warriors, armed with spears, throw sticks, and a bow. One carries a waterskin over his shoulder. Two wear the usual highly colored garment which leaves one shoulder free; the other two are clothed in white garments of similar design. The warriors, as well as the two men at the left end, wear sandals seemingly made of leather thongs. The register continues with a donkey covered with a blanket and carrying two children and a bellows (see Albright, *AP*, p. 107). Four women, each wearing a long garment of colored material and low boots, are preceded by a boy carrying a spear. The third woman's dress has a round neck, the others have the right shoulder bare. Another donkey follows, on which are tied a throw stick, a spear, and a bellows. At the end of the line are two men: the first carries a waterskin slung over his shoulder and uses a plectrum to play his lyre; the other carries a bow, a throw stick, and a quiver on his back. All the men are bearded and have heavy black hair; the women's hair is bound by a fillet and hanging down the back. Albright has suggested (*AP*, p. 208) that the representation is of traveling metalworkers and illustrates details in Gen. 4:19-22.

Beni Hasan, tomb of Khnum-hotep III, north wall, row 3. Wall painting. Height of figures: about 0.50 m. Sixth year of Sen-Usert II, about 1890. Porter and Moss, *Bibliography*, vol. 4, p. 146. P. E. Newberry, *Beni Hasan*, vol. 1, London, 1893, pls. 28, 30-31. N. M. Davies and A. H. Gardiner, *Ancient Egyptian Paintings*, vol. 1, Chicago, 1936, pls. 10-11 (details). *AOB*, 51. Fremdvölker, 46-49. Champollion, *Monuments de l'Égypte et de la Nubie*, vol. 4, Paris, 1845, pls. 361, 362, 393 bis. Text translated in *ANET*, 229. Photograph reproduced from *LD*, vol. 2, pl. 133.

4. These five kneeling figures form a part of the decoration of a platform upon which sits the enthroned Amen-hotep III. The enemies actually constitute his footstool (Psalm 110:1). The three Negroes are dressed alike, with ostrich feathers in their hair, necklaces, bracelets, and earrings, a short skirt, a red sash across the shoulder and around the waist, and cat's (?) tails hanging from the waist and elbows. Two types of Syrians are shown: to the left is a bearded figure with bald or shaved head, with a shawl thrown over his long white garment; to the right, the bearded figure wears a white fillet around his black hair and is clothed in a long, sleeved garment down to the ankles. The five figures kneel with upstretched hands in a gesture of worshipful submission.

Thebes, wall of tomb 226. Wall painting. Height of frieze: 0.25 m. Amen-hotep III (1413-1377). Nina de G. Davies and Norman de G. Davies, *The Tombs of Menkheperrasonb*, etc., London, 1933, pls. 41, 43. N. M. Davies and A. H. Gardiner, *Ancient Egyptian Paintings*, vol. 2, Chicago, 1936, pl. 58. Fremdvölker, 734-737. Discussion of types of dress on Syrians: James B. Pritchard, "Syrians as Pictured in the Paintings of the Theban Tombs," *BASOR*, no. 122, 1951, pp. 36-41. Photograph Fremdvölker, 734.

5. Foreigners implore a royal servant, on a relief from the tomb of Hor-em-heb at Memphis. The prostrate figures below recall the words of Amarna Letter No. 147, "on my belly, on my back I hear the word of the king" (*ANET*, 484). Five full-bearded Syrians are shown; two are bald, the others' hair is held in place by a broad fillet. The dress is a long-sleeved garment with a cape over the shoulders. A sixth Syrian wears only a kilt with long tassels and his wavy hair is tied up so that it resembles a cap. The two Libyans are distinguishable by a feather protruding from the top of the hair, long straight hair, a plait or strand falling down the side of the face before the ear, and a sharp pointed beard. The head of a beardless figure is possibly intended for a Negro.

Leiden. Tomb of Hor-em-heb at Memphis. Limestone. Height: about 0.53 m. Hor-em-heb reigned about 1349-1319. P. A. A. Boeser, *Die Denkmäler des neuen Reiches*, vol. 1, Haag, 1911, pl. 24. *AOB*, 87. Schäfer-Andrae, 385, 1. Translations from texts of the tomb of Hor-em-heb: *ANET*, 250-251. Photograph courtesy of Rijksmuseum van Oudheden.

6. To the left are two Syrians, bearded and with a mass of hair held in place by a fillet. They wear only the short kilt of woven design, decorated by tassels at the bottom and a semicircular loop in front above the belt. The three Negroes are beardless, with hair cut in the shape of an inverted bowl. They wear earrings, necklace, bracelets, and a long skirt of thin material held by a sash and a diagonal chest-band.

Thebes, tomb of Seti I. Wall painting. Seti I (1318-1301). *LD*, vol. 3, pl. 136a. G. Lefébure, *Le tombeau de Séti Ier, Mém., Miss. arch. fr.*, vol. 2, Paris, 1886, pt. 2, pls. 4, 5. Drawings: *AOB*, 1. Erman-Ranke, p. 35, fig. 7. Porter and Moss, *Bibliography*, vol. 1, p. 23. Photograph Fremdvölker, 807.

7. Detail from a large scene showing Ramses III returning home from a campaign in Amor. The figures of prisoners, from left to right: first, a Libyan, with pointed beard and side-lock of hair ending in a curl at the neck (see No. 5), wears a long robe over a belt with phallus sheath attached (see No. 1); second, a Syrian, clothed in a kilt with tassels, and wearing a pointed beard; third, a Hittite, beardless, and clothed in a long garment which seems to be wrapped around the body; fourth, one of the Sea Peoples, perhaps a Philistine, beardless, and wearing a close-fitting helmet with feathered crown; fifth, a Syrian, with full beard and heavy hair bound by a fillet, and wearing a long garment like that of the Hittite. All the prisoners are bound, and tied together by a rope which encircles the neck of each.

Medinet Habu, great temple of Ramses III, first court, north wall. Stone relief. Height: about 1.15 m. First half of twelfth century. The Epigraphic Survey, *Later Historical Records of Ramses III, Medinet Habu*, vol. 2, *OIP*, 9, Chicago, 1932, pl. 125A. Porter and Moss, *Bibliography*, vol. 2, p. 181 (21). Wresz., vol. 2, pl. 150a (upper, right of center). Photograph (reinforced by Bollacher) courtesy of Oriental Institute.

8. Figures on the interior of the first state chariot from the tomb of Tut-ankh-Amon. From left to right: first

(only partly shown), a Negro, with feather in curled hair, wearing earrings, necklace, bracelets, skirt, and chest-band; second, a Libyan, with tattooing on his arm, wearing a beard, side-lock ending in a curl, feathers in hair, a double chest-band, and phallus sheath attached to belt; third, a Negro, similar to the first, but without feather in hair; fourth, a Syrian, bearded, with shaved head, wearing a long-sleeved garment over which is a cape, and a tasseled sash wrapped around the waist, looped and tucked in on the side; fifth, a Negro, like third figure; sixth, a Syrian, wearing full beard and hair, dressed like fourth figure; seventh, a Negro, like first figure; eighth, a Libyan, like second figure.

Cairo Museum. Thebes, tomb of Tut-ankh-Amon, no. 120. Chariot of bentwood, overlaid with burnished thin sheet-gold upon gesso. Tut-ankh-Amon (1361-1352). H. Carter, *The Tomb of Tut-ankh-Amen*, vol. 2, London, 1927, pl. 18. P. Fox, *Tutankhamun's Treasure*, London, 1951, pl. 6. Bossert, *Altsyrien*, 927. Photograph courtesy of Metropolitan Museum of Art, New York.

9. A row of six bound prisoners of the northern people in kneeling posture. From left to right: first, the prince of Hatti (*ẖt*), beardless, hair held by a fillet and extending in a single curl down below the shoulders; second, the prince of Amor (*'imr*), bearded and with massive hair, around which is a fillet tied behind; third, the chieftain of the *t̲kry*, bearded with hair or helmet projecting from a band; fourth, a *šrdn* of the Sea, bearded, wearing a helmet with side points and horns between which is a ball-tipped projection; fifth, the chieftain of the *š[krš]*, bearded, and with long hair held by a band and extending backwards; sixth, a *trš* of the Sea, who seems to wear a tightly fitting cap. The figure of the chieftain of the *p[rśt]* (Philistines) is missing.

Medinet Habu, pavilion. Limestone relief. First half of twelfth century. Wresz., vol. 2, pl. 160b (upper). *LD*, vol. 3, pl. 209b. Porter and Moss, *Bibliography*, vol. 2, p. 173 (6). Text: J. Simons, *Handbook for the Study of Egyptian Topographical Lists Relating to Western Asia*, Leiden, 1937, p. 176; discussion, pp. 6, 85-86. Photograph from Wresz., vol. 2, pl. 160b (upper), courtesy J. C. Hinrich Verlag, Leipzig.

10. In the upper register, the army of Ashurbanipal is attacking a walled town of the Egyptians. Below to the left, prisoners with hands tied, and some with shackled feet, are being led away. They have shaved faces, wear their curled hair short, and are dressed in kilts. Some of the prisoners, perhaps the chiefs, wear head-feathers. All appear to exhibit negroid features.

British Museum, Assyrian Basement, 88. Kuyunjik. Limestone. Width of relief: 1.83 m. Ashurbanipal (668-633). H. R. Hall, *Babylonian and Assyrian Sculpture in the British Museum*, Paris and Brussels, 1928, pl. 40. Photograph from publication.

11. Two panels from the large scene of twenty-three groups of subject nations who send tribute to Xerxes. Upper register: procession of six Babylonians led by a Median usher. They are dressed in long flowing robes and caps with tassels, and bring gifts of bowls, woven stuff, and an ox. All wear beards, which are carefully

curled. Lower register: four bearded Syrians, wearing high turban-like caps, carry gifts of metalwork and vases; following are two men, dressed like the others, except for a more rounded cap, bringing a team and chariot. This procession is led by a Persian usher.

Persepolis, eastern stairway of the apadana. Height of figures: about 0.80 m. Xerxes (485-465). E. F. Schmidt, *Persepolis I, OIP,* 68, Chicago, 1953, pls. 31B, 32B. Details from these scenes: E. E. Herzfeld, *Iran in the Ancient East,* London, 1941, pls. 78 (upper), 82 (left). Lower register: Bossert, *Altsyrien,* 980. Photograph courtesy of the Oriental Institute.

EGYPTIAN

Egyptians and their dress are illustrated more fully in other sections, particularly in "Daily Life," "Scenes from History and Monuments," and "Royalty and Dignitaries." Here are a few examples of outstanding works of carving and sculpture. For a general discussion of Egyptian dress see: "The Dress of the Ancient Egyptians," *BMMA,* August 1916, pp. 166-171; October 1916, pp. 211-214; and the standard reference works.

12. This slate palette represents the Egyptians of the predynastic period as short, with pointed head, curly hair, pointed beard, long nose, and almond-shaped eyes. They wear head-feathers and a short kilt, from the back of which hangs a bushy tail (of a jackal?). The hunters carry spears, long recurved bows, throw sticks, maces, double-axes, and some carry standards which resemble the later hieroglyphs for "east" and "west." On the lower right-hand piece a hunter makes use of a lasso. The upper right-hand fragment is in the Louvre; the other two pieces are in the British Museum. The circular space in the center is for mixing paint.

British Museum, 20790, 20792; Louvre. Green schist. Length: 0.665 m. Predynastic period (late Gerzean, according to H. J. Kantor, *JNES,* vol. 3, 1944, p. 134). J. Capart, *Les débuts de l'art en Égypte,* Brussels, 1904, pl. 1, opp. p. 223. Discussion: British Museum, *A General Introductory Guide to the Egyptian Collections,* London, 1930, pp. 24-25. British Museum fragments published by E. A. W. Budge, *The Classical Review,* vol. 4, 1890, p. 323; Louvre fragment, *Revue archéologique,* vol. 15, 1890, pls. 4-5. J. Vandier, *Manuel d'archéologie égyptienne,* vol. 1, Paris, 1952, fig. 380, pp. 574-579. Photograph courtesy of the British Museum.

13. Statue in wood. Man clothed in simple kilt; woman, in a skin-tight dress.

Louvre. Probably from Memphis. Wood. Height of entire statue: 0.69 m. Fourth Dynasty (2650-2500). TEL, vol. 1, p. 16. J. Vandier, *Guide sommaire, Le département des antiquités égyptiennes, Musée du Louvre,* Paris, 1948, p. 38 (for description). Photograph JBP.

14. The "*Sheikh el-beled,*" so named by the workmen who discovered the statue because of its likeness to the *sheikh* of the village, was originally covered with painted stucco. Eyes are inlaid with quartz, crystal, ebony, and are surrounded by copper mounting. The man is clothed in a skirt reaching below the knees and holds a staff (replaced) in his left hand.

Cairo Museum, 34. Sakkarah, mastaba C 8. Wood, probably sycamore. Height: 1.10 m. Fourth or Fifth Dynasty (2650-

2350). L. Borchardt, *Statuen und Statuetten von Königen und Privatleuten,* pt. 1, *Cat. gén.,* Berlin, 1911, no. 34. TEL, Cairo, p. 16. Schäfer-Andrae, 239. Photograph Foto Marburg.

15. Methethy, a nobleman of the entourage of the king, the administrator of the royal estates, has close-cut black hair, a reddish-brown skin, and wears a full white skirt and a necklace of pale green and dark blue. The eyes are inlaid with alabaster and obsidian and edged with copper. Head, body, and legs are made of one piece of wood.

Kansas City, Missouri. Region of Sakkarah. Hard wood, perhaps cedar, and gesso. Height: 0.80 m. Fifth-Sixth Dynasty (2350). *Illustrated London News,* August 4, 1951, p. 196. The William Rockhill Nelson Gallery of Art, *Gallery News,* vol. 18, no. 9, October 1951. Photograph courtesy of the William Rockhill Nelson Gallery of Art.

16. Ra-hotep, the son of a king, probably Snefru, is shown with close-cut black hair, a steel-gray mustache, and clothed in a white kilt. He holds his right fist against his chest. The skin is painted orange-brown.

Cairo Museum, 3. Meidum, December 1871. White limestone, painted. Height: 1.20 m. Fourth Dynasty (2650-2500). L. Borchardt, *Statuen und Statuetten von Königen und Privatleuten,* pt. 1, *Cat. gén.,* Berlin, 1911, no. 3. TEL, Cairo, p. 12. Schäfer-Andrae, 232. Photograph Foto Marburg.

17. Nefret, a relative of the king, is clothed in a low-cut dress and a white robe, which she holds tightly around her body. She wears a full wig, over which is a diadem studded with stones, and a collar necklace painted red and blue and bordered with tear-shaped beads. The skin tint is pale yellow.

Cairo Museum, 4. Meidum, December 1871. White limestone. Height: 1.18 m. Fourth Dynasty (2650-2500). L. Borchardt, *Statuen und Statuetten von Königen und Privatleuten,* pt. 1, *Cat. gén.,* Berlin, 1911, no. 4. TEL, Cairo, p. 12. Schäfer-Andrae, pl. 3. Photograph Foto Marburg.

MESOPOTAMIAN

In addition to examples given below of representations of the inhabitants of Mesopotamia and the region to the east, notice should be taken of the figures on the Assyrian reliefs and on the bronze bands from the Balawat gates. For these and other examples of Mesopotamian dress see the Index. For a discussion of the dress of Nos. 18, 19, 20, 22, 23 see H. Frankfort, *Sculptures of the Third Millennium B.C. from Tell Asmar and Khafājah, OIP,* 44, Chicago, 1939, pp. 49-55. General works: L. and J. Heuzey, *Histoire du costume dans l'antiquité classique,* 1935; W. Reimpell, *Geschichte der babylonischen und assyrischen Kleidung,* Berlin, 1916. For beards see: H. Mötefindt, *Zur Geschichte der Barttracht im alten Orient,* Leipzig, 1923; Igor Diakonov, "On an Early Oriental Sculpture," State Hermitage, Division of Eastern Culture and Art History (*Otdel istorii kultury i iskusstva vostoka, Trudy otdela vostoka*), vol. 4, Leningrad, 1947, pp. 107-118.

18. Upper part of gypsum sculpture of a bearded man with hands clasped, wearing a simple skirt made of a fringelike or tasseled material extending downward from a heavy belt. Locks of hair and the beard hang down his chest, the beard textured by incisions in a herringbone design. The hair is parted in the middle. Holes

to which the legs were once attached appear in the base. While the statue is without inscription one may suppose from inscribed examples of this type that it represented a worshiper intent on the god's favor.

University Museum, 37-15-34. Khafajah, Nintu Temple V. Gypsum. Height: 0.26 m. Early Dynastic II (early third millennium). H. Frankfort, *More Sculpture from the Diyala Region, OIP*, 60, Chicago, 1943, pl. 4A, no. 211. For discussion of dress see: H. Frankfort, *Sculpture of the Third Millennium B.C. from Tell Asmar and Khafājah, OIP*, 44, Chicago, 1939, pp. 49-55. Photograph courtesy UM.

19. Figure representing a devotee of the god in whose temple it had been placed, with long hair extending down below the shoulders in two massive locks. The figure is clothed in a long skirt, the lower half of which consists of strips of material arranged like a broad fringe—perhaps to facilitate movement. The statue originally had a long beard but this has been chiseled away in antiquity. The eyes are inlaid.

University Museum, 37-15-29. Khafajah, Nintu Temple V. Gray limestone. Height: 0.232 m. Early Dynastic II (early third millennium). H. Frankfort, *More Sculpture from the Diyala Region, OIP*, 60, Chicago, 1943, pl. 4C, no. 210. Photograph courtesy UM.

20. Statue of a man with shaved head and face, wearing a kilt; the lower part extends down to the calves of the legs and seems to be made of strips of material. The figure is supported by a stand and base. Since it was found in context with bearded figures, the difference of beard may have served to represent a distinction of professional function (cf. No. 19). It has been suggested that this statue may represent a priest.

Oriental Institute, A 12332. Tell Asmar, Square Temple, shrine II. Veined gypsum; eyeballs of shell set in bitumen; pupils of black limestone. Height: 0.40 m. Early Dynastic II (early third millennium). H. Frankfort, *Sculpture of the Third Millennium B.C. from Tell Asmar and Khafājah, OIP*, 44, Chicago, 1939, pls. 21-23, 24B, 25AB. Photograph courtesy of the Oriental Institute.

21. Upper part of a votive statue of some important person at Mari. Head bald; short curled beard, with upper lip and part of lower shaved. Just above the break there is evidence of a belt which held skirt of robe. Hands are clasped on chest. Inscribed on back with the name of Idi-Nârum and a dedication to Ishtar (cf. No. 429).

Aleppo, National Museum. Mari, temple of Ishtar, first campaign, 1933-1934. Stone. Height: 0.21 m. Middle third millennium. *Syria*, vol. 16, 1935, pl. 9, p. 27. Inscription published by F. Thureau-Dangin, *RA*, vol. 31, 1934, p. 142. A. Parrot, *Mari*, Paris, 1948, fig. 13, pp. 107-109. Photograph JBP.

22. Female figure draped in long tufted shawl, which leaves the left shoulder bare but hides the feet. Hands are clasped in front. Hair has been parted in the middle of the head, braided into a number of small plaits, which in turn have been braided into a large plait, wound around the head counterclockwise, and the end tucked in at the back.

Iraq Museum. Khafajah, Sin Temple IX. Limestone. Height: 0.149 m. Early Dynastic II (early third millennium). H. Frank-

fort, *Sculpture of the Third Millennium B.C. from Tell Asmar and Khafājah, OIP*, 44, Chicago, 1939, pl. 76C; discussion of hairdress, pp. 50-51. Photograph courtesy of the Oriental Institute.

23. Heavy-set figure of a beardless and bald man, clothed in a skirt covered with tufts or tassels. Hands are clasped before the breast in a gesture of supplication to the god, before whom it had been placed as a representative of the devotee.

University Museum, 37-15-31. Khafajah, Nintu Temple V. Alabaster, eyeballs of shell, iris of lapis lazuli. Height: 0.30 m. Early Dynastic II (early third millennium). H. Frankfort, *More Sculpture from the Diyala Region, OIP*, 60, Chicago, 1943, pl. 9, no. 217, and pl. 10 for other views. L. Legrain, *The Babylonian Collections of the University Museum, University Museum Bulletin*, 10, June 1944, fig. 30. Photograph courtesy UM.

24. Ebih-il, with hands clasped before his breast, seated on a stool of basketwork; head bald and upper lip and part of lower shaved; short, curled beard; eyes of slate, shell, and lapis lazuli. Clothed in a long fleecelike skirt, which is tied with a knot behind. Cf. No. 429. Inscription: "Statue of Ebih-il, the steward, to Ishtar . . . he devoted it."

Louvre. Mari, temple of Ishtar, first campaign, 1933-1934. White alabaster. Height: 0.52 m. Middle third millennium. H. Frankfort, *RA*, vol. 31, 1934, p. 179, places the temple at Mari two centuries before Sargon (=ED III). *Syria*, vol. 16, 1935, pl. 8, fig. 8, pp. 25-27. TEL, vol. 1, pp. 200-202. A. Parrot, *Mari*, Paris, 1948, fig. 10, pp. 104-107. Inscription published by F. Thureau-Dangin, *RA*, vol. 31, 1934, p. 143. Photograph TEL.

ELAMITE, MEDIAN, AND PERSIAN

25. Two Elamite soldiers marching to the left; second watching the rear. Both wear short full beard and hair, which is shown in straight locks, held in place by a broad fillet, and are clothed in a short-sleeved garment which reaches to the knees. Each holds a bow in his left hand and extends his right upward in a gesture of supplication. The second carries over his back a quiver with Elamite cover. This is the costume worn in the time of the Assyrian Empire by the inhabitants of what is today eastern Iran.

Rome, Museo Barracco. Kuyunjik. Limestone. Height: 0.20 m.; width: 0.19 m. Probably Ashurbanipal (668-633). E. F. Weidner, *Die Reliefs der assyrischen Könige*, pt. 1, Berlin, 1939, fig. 40. Photograph courtesy Musei Comunali, Rome.

26. Head of a Mede, wearing high rounded cap with neck flap. Short, pointed beard, mustache, hair bunched at neck—all elaborately curled. Earring pierces ear, and protrudes from mass of hair. To be distinguished from a Persian, who wears a high fluted hat and an ankle-length flowing robe. (See Mede in No. 463.)

Persepolis. Darius (521-486)—Xerxes (485-465). A. T. Olmstead, *History of the Persian Empire*, Chicago, 1948, pl. 5 (upper). E. E. Herzfeld, *Iran in the Ancient East*, London, 1941, pl. 73 right. Photograph courtesy of the Oriental Institute.

27. A Mede(?), with curled beard, and hair curled in

ringlets and held by a fillet, wearing a fleece cloak, leading two horses, of which only the heads remain. In his right hand the man holds a whip. D. Opitz (*AfO*, vol. 6, 1930, p. 126) has identified this fragment as belonging to room x of the palace at Khorsabad (P. E. Botta, *Monument de Ninive*, vol. 2, Paris, 1849, pl. 133).

New York, Metropolitan Museum of Art, 33.16.1. Khorsabad. "Alabaster." Height: 0.49 m.; width: 0.79 m. Sargon II (721-705). *BMMA*, February 1933, fig. 5. See also C. J. Gadd, *The Stones of Assyria*, London, 1936, p. 239. See TEL, vol. 1, 319, for similar figure and horse, with inscription describing an expedition to Media. Photograph courtesy MMA.

28. In the two lower registers Medes and Persians alternate, striding forward informally in the procession of the New Year's festival. The Medes wear the high rounded hat over curled hair, knee-length tunics, trousers, a torque around the neck, and occasionally a long cape with sleeves which hang empty at the sides. The Persians wear the high fluted hat over massive curled hair, and draped robes which extend in graceful folds to the ankles. Some carry short swords thrust in the girdle, while others have bow cases suspended from the belt. All the figures wear their beards elaborately curled. The upper register depicts attendants carrying the royal footstool; grooms are leading horses; and chariots are empty except for the drivers.

Persepolis, apadana, north wing of eastern stairway. Height of figures: about 0.80 m. Xerxes (485-465). E. F. Schmidt, *Persepolis I, OIP*, 68, Chicago, 1953, pls. 51, 52. A. T. Olmstead, *History of the Persian Empire*, Chicago, 1948, pl. 38, pp. 275-277. Photograph courtesy of the Oriental Institute.

29. Medes marching up the stairway of the tripylon at Persepolis, carrying flowers or other symbols (see No. 463). All wear elaborately curled beards, mustaches, and bunched hair extending from under a high rounded hat with streamer at the back. They are clothed in a tight-fitting tunic extending to the knees and held by a narrow belt fastened around the waist, moderately tight trousers, and pointed shoes. One figure carries a bow case, which he steadies with his left hand. Another places a hand on his knee as if to support himself in the climb up the stairs; while yet another noble is shown turning to speak to his companion. The informality of pose shown here is characteristic of the long line of nobles who make their way up the stairs.

Persepolis, council hall, east wing of main stairway. Height of larger figures: about 0.60 m. Darius (521-486). E. F. Schmidt, *Persepolis I, OIP*, 68, Chicago, 1953, pl. 72A. A. T. Olmstead, *History of the Persian Empire*, Chicago, 1948, pl. 27 upper. Photograph courtesy of the Oriental Institute.

30. This Elamite soldier of the Persian "Ten Thousand Immortals" is shown in full military array: spear with pomegranate knob placed firmly on the toe, unsheathed bow, and quiver over back. The curled hair is held by a broad twisted fillet; where the curled beard meets the hair there seems to be an earring. The body is almost entirely covered by a long, wing-sleeved, rosetted robe. Low, laced shoes are worn.

Louvre. Susa. Glazed brick in blue, olive, yellow, and white. Height: 1.85 m. Fifth century. G. Contenau, *Les antiquités orientales, monuments hittites, assyriens, phéniciens, perses*, etc., Paris, n.d., pl. 21. Description: A. T. Olmstead, *History of the Persian Empire*, Chicago, 1948, pp. 238-239. Similar figure in TEL, vol. 2, p. 50. Photograph Archives Photographiques.

HITTITES AND SUCCESSORS

For discussion of four types of Hittites represented on contemporary monuments see A. Götze, *Kleinasien, Kulturgeschichte des alten Orients*, vol. 2, pt. 1, Munich, 1933, pp. 17-20. See also G. Röder, *Ägypter und Hethiter, AO*, vol. 20, Leipzig, 1919. For other representations of Hittites see section on "Scenes from History and Monuments."

31. Heads and shoulders of seven Hittite figures, nearly identical: shaved face and forehead; hair falling on the shoulders; a flat, sloping forehead continues in the same line into a prominent and slightly aquiline nose; a receding chin. See No. 33 for same profile. A. Götze lists it as Type *a* in his discussion of types (*Kleinasien*, Munich, 1933, pp. 17-20). Relief is probably from a scene depicting the battle of Kadesh.

Berlin, Äg. 14124. Length: 0.75 m. Probably from time of Ramses II (1301-1234). Wresz., vol. 2, pl. 46 (Beibild 2). Bossert, *Altanatolien*, 759. Photograph Fremdvölker, 827.

32. A beardless Hittite prisoner with a thick mass of hair falling below the shoulders and ending in a curl at the back just above the elbow. A fillet is decorated with discs. The nose is long and prominent, but the forehead is not so sloping as that represented in No. 31; the chin is stronger. The prisoner is bound with a rope about his neck. See A. Götze's Type *b* (*Kleinasien*, Munich, 1933, pp. 17-20).

Abu Simbel, great temple, right wall of entrance. Ramses II (1301-1234). Wresz., vol. 2, pl. 46 (Beibild 6). Bossert, *Altanatolien*, 731. Photograph Foto Marburg.

33. Below is the corpse of a Hittite floating in the river: prominent nose, receding chin, and hair reaching down the back (see No. 31). Above, to the left, is head of soldier. Above, in center, is corpse of a figure with face and head shaved, except for a long pigtail at the back. A. Götze (*Kleinasien*, Munich, 1933, p. 19) takes profile (Type *d*) as a representation of one of the allies of the Hittites.

Abydos, exterior of south wall, scene of battle of Kadesh. Limestone relief. Ramses II (1301-1234). Wresz., vol. 2, pl. 21a (extreme right). Porter and Moss, *Bibliography*, vol. 6, p. 39. Photograph Foto Marburg.

34. Hittite prisoner represented on a faïence tile: beardless face has low, sloping forehead, prominent nose and receding chin; hair is held by a fillet and extends down the back in a strand or plait. The robe has a woven pattern and extends to the ankles.

Berlin, Äg. 17277. Faïence tile. Height: 0.29 m. Probably Ramses III (1195-1164). Wresz., vol. 2, pl. 46 (Beibild 5). Photograph Fremdvölker, 825A.

35. Faïence tile of a Hittite prisoner, with shaved face and long hair hanging down the back. Tattooing appears on the belly. The costume is a short kilt, over which has been thrown a gaily colored (Libyan?) mantle, which leaves the left shoulder free (see No. 7), a cap with decorated border, and a beaded collar.

Cairo Museum, J 36457f. Faïence tile. Height: 0.255 m. Ramses III (1195-1164). *ASAE*, vol. 11, 1911, pl. 3, 12. *AOB*, 8. U. Hölscher, *The Mortuary Temple of Ramses III*, pt. 2, *OIP*, vol. 55, Chicago, 1951, pl. 31a. Wresz., vol. 2, pl. 46 (Beibild 4). For tattooing see L. Keimer, *Remarques sur le tatouage dans l'Égypte ancienne*, Cairo, 1948. Photograph Fremdvölker, 2B.

36. Figure carved on a slab of the Late Hittite period, probably representing the god of war, holding a lance in his right hand and a shield in the left; through his belt is thrust a long sword. The face is shown with an exaggerated nose and eye, and a long beard of four rows of curls. The hair hangs in a plait which ends in a curl at the shoulder. On the head is a horned cap ending in a ball-like top. The costume consists of a short-sleeved shirt, a kilt held by a diagonal shoulder strap, and short boots with upturned and pointed toes.

Berlin, VA 2647. Zinjirli. Dolerite. Height: 1.35 m. Ninth century. F. von Luschan, *Ausgrabungen in Sendschirli*, vol. 3, Berlin, 1902, pl. 40. *AOB*, 9. Bossert, *Altanatolien*, 927. Photograph Foto Marburg.

37. These two soldiers, dressed in kilts and carrying round shields on their backs and spears in their right hands, are of interest for their distinctive helmets. The helmet is of the same shape as that worn by the Hittite (No. 38) from the period of the Hittite Empire, but it is surmounted by a plume, divided into two parts. To the front a part stands upright, but four strands come down the back of the helmet and take the place of the much longer streamer of the earlier period. From the front of the helmet a horn protrudes. The faces of the soldiers seem to have a shaved upper lip and a short beard; the nose is prominent and aquiline; the braided hair hangs down the back.

Ankara, Hittite Museum, 9664. Carchemish. Basalt. 1.30 m. by 1.15 m. Ninth-eighth century (?). D. G. Hogarth, *Carchemish, Part I*, London, 1914, pl. B 3 b. E. Akurgal, *Späthethitische Bildkunst*, Ankara, 1949, figs. 16, 17, pp. 14-15. Photograph courtesy of the British Museum.

38. This life-sized Hittite figure, carved in the half round on a slab which was a part of the inner King's Gate at Boghazköy, has been variously interpreted as king, a god of war, Teshub, god of the gate, and as a warrior figure (*WVDOG*, 60, p. 5). The figure is clothed in a kilt, decorated by bands of spiral and diagonal designs, held by a girdle, through which is thrust a short sword with a curved point (see also sword on figure on stela from Ras Shamra, No. 490). In the right hand is a battle-axe with four prongs (see No. 178 for example found at Beth-shan). The face is shaven and on the head is a high helmet, pointed and ending in a streamer which hangs down the back to the elbow (see streamer worn by god Seth on No. 555). On the

front of the helmet are horns (not visible in this picture), and cheek flaps extend down over the side of the face. Bittel places the relief as contemporary with those of Yazilikaya, which he dates to the period extending from the fourteenth to the first part of the thirteenth centuries (*WVDOG*, 60, p. 6).

Ankara, Hittite Museum, 48. Boghazköy. Crystalline limestone. Height of relief: 2.25 m. Fourteenth-thirteenth centuries. O. Puchstein, *Boghasköi, die Bauwerke*, *WVDOG*, 19, Leipzig, 1912, pls. 17-19, pp. 67-72. K. Bittel, *Boğazköy, die Kleinfunde*, *WVDOG*, 60, Leipzig, 1937, frontispiece, pls. 2-3, pp. 5-7. Bossert, *Altanatolien*, 476. Photograph courtesy of K. Bittel.

39. This soldier, clothed in a short-sleeved shirt, fringed kilt, sword-belt, and sandals, holds a bow in his left hand and a spear in his right, the butt resting on his foot. The hair and short beard are carefully curled into ringlets; the upper lip is shaved in characteristic Hittite fashion.

Istanbul, Museum of the Ancient Orient, 1981. Probably from Arslan Tash. Basalt. Height: 1.45 m. Ninth century (Bossert). E. Akurgal, *Späthethitische Bildkunst*, pl. 19b. Bossert, *Altsyrien*, 493. E. Unger, *Die Reliefs Tiglatpilesers III. aus Arslan Tasch*, Constantinople, 1925, pl. 8, no. 28. Photograph JBP.

40. The man is dressed, unlike others shown on this plate, in a short-sleeved robe reaching to the ankles. Around the waist is a wide belt, supporting a long sword. A strap passes diagonally over the chest and ends in four cords. Sandals of the Assyrian type are worn. The profile, with a low, sloping forehead, large nose, and receding chin covered by a beard arranged in five rows of curls, is strikingly similar to that of Hittites represented on Egyptian reliefs (No. 31). The upper lip seems to be shaved.

Istanbul, Museum of the Ancient Orient, 7717. Zinjirli. Ninth century (Bossert). F. von Luschan, *Ausgrabungen in Sendschirli*, vol. 3, Berlin, 1902, pl. 37, fig. 107, p. 215. Bossert, *Altanatolien*, 913. E. Akurgal, *Späthethitische Bildkunst*, Ankara, 1951, pl. 26 and p. 142, where Akurgal places in Middle Late Hittite period on basis of Assyrian ringlets and sandals. Photograph JBP.

SYRIAN

For references to Theban tombs which contain paintings of Syrians see James B. Pritchard, "Syrians as Pictured in the Paintings of the Theban Tombs," *BASOR*, no. 122, April 1951, pp. 36-41. For the reliability of the paintings see Norman de G. Davies, *BMMA*, December 1930, ii, pp. 29 ff. See also H. F. Lutz, *Textiles and Costume among the Peoples of the Ancient Near East*, Leipzig, 1923, pp. 142-192, for costumes of the Asiatic peoples.

41-42 (cast). Ships, on which are Syrian men, women, and children, standing with upraised hands greeting Sahu-Re. The men are bearded, have long hair held by a fillet tied in back, and are clothed in the Syrian kilt. In addition to this type are other beardless figures, sometimes nude, but wearing a headdress which may be a wig. The prow of the ship to the right is decorated with the Horus-eye; the stern of the one to the left, with the *ankh* sign. The masts are lashed down and the rudder, consisting of three oars, is retracted.

Berlin, Äg. 21833,4. Abusir, mortuary temple of Sahu-Re, west passage, surrounding the hall of columns. White limestone. Height: 0.99 m.; width: 1.32 m. Fifth Dynasty (2500-2350). L. Borchardt, *Das Grabdenkmal des Königs Śa'ḥu-Re'*, vol. 1, Leipzig, 1910, fig. 14, p. 19; vol. 2, Leipzig, 1913, pls. 12, 13 for drawings. *AOB*, 40. Photograph of relief courtesy of Staatliche Museen, Berlin; of cast, courtesy of the Oriental Institute.

43. The captive on the head of a ceremonial walking stick of Tut-ankh-Amon has long hair held in place by a fillet, a rounded full beard, and a very slight mustache. He wears a long-sleeved undergarment, over which a robe of woven design is wound around the body and then over the shoulders to form a cape. The edge is decorated with an embroidered hem. The overgarment seems to be held in place by a broad belt which ends in six tassels hanging in front. This type of dress appears in representations of Syrians by Egyptians at about the last quarter of the fifteenth century and continues in popularity well after the Eighteenth Dynasty (*BASOR*, no. 122, April 1951, p. 41).

Cairo Museum. Thebes, Tomb of Tut-ankh-Amon, no. 50uu. Ivory for face, hands and feet. Length of entire stick: 1.04 m. Tut-ankh-Amon (1361-1352). H. Carter and A. C. Mace, *The Tomb of Tut-ankh-Amen*, vol. 1, London, 1923, pl. 70A, B. *AOB*, 18. Photograph courtesy of the Cairo Museum.

44. A gaming piece made of ivory, on which are carved the attenuated figure of a bound captive and an inscription, which is read by Griffith (W. M. F. Petrie, *The Royal Tombs of the First Dynasty*, pt. 1, London, 1900, p. 43) as *sty* "the Asiatic" (?), followed by an oval sign for land. The captive has a long and pointed nose, wears a full beard, but no mustache, and hair which falls in long strands or plaits below his shoulders. The clothing is a simple kilt held by a broad belt at the waist. The back of the gaming piece is carved with knots and bracts of a reed.

Cairo Museum. Abydos, tomb of Qa. Ivory. Height: 0.203 m. First Dynasty (about 3000). W. M. F. Petrie, *The Royal Tombs of the First Dynasty*, pt. 1, pl. 12 (12-13), and pl. 17 (30) for drawing, pp. 23-24. *AOB*, 15 (where the object is mistakenly listed as being in the Ashmolean Museum, Oxford). E. Meyer, *Sumerier und Semiten in Babylonien*, Berlin, 1906, p. 20. Photograph JBP.

45. Four figures from a long line of foreigners who present gifts, on the wall of the tomb of Men-kheper-Re-seneb, high priest of Amon under Thut-mose III. First, kissing the ground, is a bearded figure with shaved or bald head, wearing a banded kilt with a loop or pocket below the belt; although labeled "the Prince of Keftiu" (Crete), he is represented as a Syrian. Second, kneeling with upraised hands is a similarly dressed figure, but with long black hair bound by a fillet, and mislabeled as "the Prince of Hatti." Third, "the Prince of Tunip," who holds out an infant son, who may be intended as a hostage, has a closely cropped head and beard, and is clothed in a tight-fitting, sleeved robe reaching well below the knees. Its borders are edged in color and each

vertical band ends in two tassels. Fourth, represented with darker skin, is a beardless Cretan carrying a bull's head rhyton upon a basket and a folded (Syrian) cloth over his arm.

Thebes, tomb 86. Paint on fine plaster. 0.78 m. by 0.47 m. Fifteenth century. Wresz., vol. 1, pls. 273-277. Fremdvölker, 596-600, 720-721. Nina de G. Davies and Norman de G. Davies, *The Tombs of Menkheperrasonb*, etc., *TTS*, 5, London, 1933, pl. 4. See *ANET*, 248-249 for translations. Porter and Moss, *Bibliography*, vol. 1, p. 117 (3). Photograph from N. M. Davies and A. H. Gardiner, *Ancient Egyptian Paintings*, vol. 1, Chicago, 1936, pl. 21.

46. Upper register: the first three figures wear the long-sleeved Syrian gown with a skirt of diagonal bands of cloth; the first kisses the ground, the other two kneel with upraised hands; the fourth figure wears a closely fitting gown with decorated seams and carries a vase and a piece of cloth; the fifth is similarly dressed, carries one child, and is preceded by another. Second register: the first three figures duplicate those above; the fourth leads a child and carries a bowl or flat basket with bull's head rhyton; another child is led by a fifth figure, of which only the arm remains. The hairdress of the figures is of two kinds: first, a closely cropped head; second, full hair ending in strands which are curled at the ends and with fillet tied at the back in a knot with the ends hanging down as streamers.

Thebes, tomb of Amen-em-heb (85). Wall painting. Fifteenth century. Wresz., vol. 1, pl. 4. Fremdvölker, 494-495. *AOB*, 55. *JEA*, 20, 1934, pl. 25. Porter and Moss, *Bibliography*, vol. 1, p. 115 (5). For biography of Amen-em-heb see *ANET*, 240-241. Photograph courtesy of Metropolitan Museum of Art, New York.

47. The tribute bearers have bearded faces, which are surmounted in all but three cases—where the head is shaved or bald—by bushy hair bound with a white fillet. Generally the hair ends at the shoulders; however, in the second figure of the upper register, it extends below in strands which end in curls (see No. 46). Tight sleeves are worn except in one case. On every figure a white shawl edged with red or blue is wound around the body from the waist downward. The fourth figure of the upper register leads a nude little girl. Note the ointment horn carried by the last figure of the upper register (see No. 69). Other tribute includes a quiver, vessels, and a rhyton in the shape of a conventionalized bird.

British Museum, 37991. Thebes, tomb 63. Painted on a thin layer of white plaster over mud and straw. 1.32 m. by 1.12 m. Thut-mose IV (1421-1413). N. M. Davies and A. H. Gardiner, *Ancient Egyptian Paintings*, vol. 1, Chicago, 1936, pl. 42. Wresz., vol. 1, pl. 56a (1). Porter and Moss, *Bibliography*, vol. 1, p. 93 (3). Photograph courtesy BM.

48. Behind a partly destroyed kneeling figure stands the Prince of Kadesh, bearded and bald, clothed in a short-sleeved and tightly fitting garment, and presenting a jar and a sheath from which protrudes the handle of a dagger. Four tribute bearers follow: the first and third wear

long hair held in place by a fillet and are clothed in a kilt ending in a point between the legs; the second and fourth figures have shaved heads (or caps) and wear the long-sleeved Syrian robe decorated with colored borders. Tribute includes: ivory, vessels, strips of woven materials, a scimitar, and other objects.

Thebes, tomb 86 (the register immediately above is shown in No. 45). Paint on fine plaster. Height of register: about 0.47 m. Fifteenth century. Nina de G. Davies and Norman de G. Davies, *The Tombs of Menkheperrasonb*, etc., *TTS*, 5, London, 1933, pl. 20 (lower register). Porter and Moss, *Bibliography*, vol. 1, p. 117 (3). See *ANET*, 248-249 for translation. Photograph courtesy of the Metropolitan Museum of Art, New York.

49-51. (49 continues at the right into 50, and 50 at the right into 51.) The principal register of this fragment from a tomb relief portrays a line of Syrian captives being led into the presence of Hor-em-heb. To the right (No. 51) an Egyptian attendant leads by a rope a Syrian, who cowers before his captor. The captive is dressed in a long, sleeved robe extending in diagonal folds to his ankles and encircled at his protruding belly by a heavy girdle; he wears a full beard and has a bald or shaven head. His hands are held by a wooden shackle suspended by a cord around his neck. Following are groups of two prisoners led by two Egyptians. At the end (No. 49) a woman, wearing a dress flounced in three tiers and carrying two children, one upon her shoulder and the other in a sack slung over her back, is led by an Egyptian, who holds her firmly by the wrist. The Syrian men are dressed like the leading figure, but heads with long hair and fillet alternate with bald or shaven heads. The lower and partly destroyed register is of interest for the types of prisoners pictured to the extreme left of No. 51. One wears a mass of hair well down over the forehead and partly covering a disc, which may be an ear ornament. This is a representation of a Hittite (see A. Götze, *Kleinasien*, Munich, 1933, p. 19, where he places it under Type *c*). The other figure, to the right, has his head shaved except for two plaits, one to the side and one behind; this, too, recalls a Hittite feature (see No. 33).

Leiden. Memphis, tomb of Hor-em-heb. Limestone. Height of full figures: about 0.47 m. Latter half of fourteenth century. P. A. A. Boeser, *Die Denkmäler des Neuen Reiches*, vol. 1, Haag, 1911, pl. 21. *AOB*, 86. For translation of texts from the tomb of General Hor-em-heb see *ANET*, 250-251. Photographs courtesy of Rijksmuseum van Oudheden.

52. Four registers of Syrian tribute bearers display two types of dress. Predominant is the long robe of material with elaborate design, consisting of a band of edged cloth wrapped around the body and over the shoulders (see No. 43 for description of this type of dress). Some of the wearers of this dress have black hair encircled by a fillet and some are bald or shaven, but the latter also have the fillet, even though there is no hair to contain. Two of the figures wear hair ending in curls, after the Hittite fashion. The other type of dress, which is confined to the porters, is a simple kilt with tassels at the waist and at the bottom corners. Those who wear the kilt have shaved or closely cropped heads. Tribute includes: jars, display vessels, a lion, a horse, a panther (?), ingots of copper or blocks of wood, etc.

Thebes, tomb 40. Height: about 1.90 m. Tut-ankh-Amon (1361-1352). Nina de G. Davies and A. H. Gardiner, *The Tomb of Ḥuy, TTS*, vol. 4, London, 1926, pl. 19. *AOB*, 81. Porter and Moss, *Bibliography*, vol. 1, p. 76 (8). Translation of text in *ANET*, 249. Photograph from *LD*, vol. 3, pl. 116a.

53. Three Syrians wear the long, wrapped garment with cape, but without the sleeved undergarment (see No. 43 for description). The head is covered by a skullcap, matching the dress and encircled by a fillet tied in the back with a loop and long streamer.

Thebes, tomb of Ramses III. Wall painting. Ramses III (1195-1164). Champollion, *Monuments de l'Égypte et de la Nubie*, vol. 3, Paris, 1845, pl. 257, 2. Porter and Moss, *Bibliography*, vol. 1, p. 16 (26). Photograph Fremdvölker, 810.

54. Bound prisoner, dressed in long robe (see No. 43 for description) of highly decorated woven stuff, with hair held by a fillet tied in back and extending to the shoulder in a streamer.

Cairo. Faïence tile. Height: 0.255 m. Ramses III (1195-1164). *ASAE*, vol. 11, 1911, pl. 3, no. 5. U. Hölscher, *The Mortuary Temple of Ramses III*, pt. 2, *OIP*, 55, Chicago, 1951, pl. 30b. Fremdvölker, 4A. Photograph courtesy of the Cairo Museum.

55. Three heavily bearded Syrian prisoners, one of whom is shown with hands through a shackle, are led by a bowman (for shackles see Nos. 49-51). Two leading prisoners are bald; the third has long hair held by a fillet with ends in two streamers.

Beit el-Wali, rock temple of Ramses II. Ramses II (1301-1234). Champollion, *Monuments de l'Égypte et de la Nubie*, vol. 1, Paris, 1835, pl. 62 (upper right corner). Fremdvölker, 130. Porter and Moss, *Bibliography*, vol. 7, p. 23-24. Photograph Foto Marburg.

56. Syrian dressed in long robe (see No. 43 for description of dress) standing on the top of a lotus blossom and supporting with his hands and shoulder a large, double-handled jar. The object is a handle for an ointment spoon.

Louvre. Wood. New Kingdom (1550-1090). Wresz., vol. 1, pl. 4a (2). H. Fechheimer, *Kleinplastik der Ägypter*, Berlin, 1922, pl. 136. Bossert, *Altsyrien*, 938. Photograph Foto Marburg.

SYRIAN AND SEA PEOPLES

57. An Egyptian is leading two prisoners to Ramses III, who celebrates his victory over the Sea Peoples. The prisoners are beardless and wear high feathered helmets held firmly in place by a strap under the chin. The feathers are joined to the headgear by a band, decorated in one instance by triangles and in another by small discs. The shackle through which the hands of the prisoner are inserted is suspended by a cord about the neck (see No. 51). To the left are two more prisoners with arms bound at the back.

Medinet Habu, exterior of north wall. Height: about 1.20 m. Ramses III (1195-1164). The Epigraphic Survey, *The Earlier*

Historical Records of Ramses III, Medinet Habu, vol. 1, *OIP*, 8, Chicago, 1930, pl. 52C (detail from scene on pl. 42). Wresz., vol. 2, pls. 118-119 (right). Porter and Moss, *Bibliography*, vol. 2, p. 190 (112). Photograph courtesy of the Oriental Institute.

58. A bearded figure, with full hair parted in the middle and extending to the shoulders, is shown full face except for the feet, which are turned to the left. The costume is a long, fringed garment, over which a shawl is worn. See No. 62.

Louvre. Arslan Tash. Ivory. Height: 0.178 m. Second half of ninth century. F. Thureau-Dangin, *et al., Arslan-Tash*, Paris, 1931, pl. 33, no. 43, pp. 111-112. TEL, vol. 2, pl. 111H. Contenau, *Man.*, vol. 4, fig. 1258, pp. 2224-2229. Photograph JBP.

59. Sherden soldiers, who served as Egyptian mercenaries, from a scene of the battle of Kadesh. They are beardless, wear a helmet decorated with two horns and a spike surmounted by a small knob (see No. 9). They carry a short sword, a spear, and a round shield, and are clothed in a kilt like that worn by Egyptian soldiers.

Abydos, southwest wall of Ramesseum. Ramses III (1195-1164). Wresz, vol. 2, pl. 19. Porter and Moss, *Bibliography*, vol. 6, p. 39. Photograph Fremdvölker, 86.

60. Two warriors painted in red and black on a sherd. The better-preserved figure holds a battle-axe in his right hand and a shield in the left. Black hair and beard; costume is not clearly defined.

Istanbul, Museum of the Ancient Orient. Megiddo, south city-gate of fourth trench. Pottery. 0.15 m. by 0.09 m. Eighth-seventh century (Gressmann, *AOB*, 24). *AOB*, 24. Photograph from G. Schumacher and C. Steuernagel, *Tell el-Mutesellim*, vol. 1, Plates, Leipzig, 1908, pl. 24.

61. Syrian with a high turban, wound in broad bands and leaning slightly backward. Full beard, carefully curled except at the point, and a mustache. Hair is tightly curled and emerges from the turban in a mass of curls at the back and a row of curls across the forehead. Behind the ear a lock of hair (or a ribbon) falls down to the shoulder. Detail from No. 11.

Persepolis, eastern stairway of the apadana. Xerxes (485-465). E. F. Schmidt, *Persepolis I, OIP*, 68, Chicago, 1953, pl. 32B. A. T. Olmstead, *History of the Persian Empire*, Chicago, 1948, pl. 34 (top), p. 243 for description. Photograph courtesy of the Oriental Institute.

62. Two beardless Aramean figures dressed similarly: hair reaches to the shoulders in three rows of curls; side-lock is more pronounced in the figure to the right; high cap ending in point; costume is a long robe with band of fringe near the bottom and a capelike part which covers the right shoulder and is held by the left hand of each figure. The dress is similar to, but not so elaborate as, that of Bar Rakab (No. 281).

Istanbul, Museum of the Ancient Orient, 7737. Zinjirli. Dolerite. Height: 0.78 m. Probably to be dated to period of Bar Rakab, second half of eighth century. Cf. F. von Luschan, *Ausgrabungen in Sendschirli*, vol. 4, Berlin, 1911, pl. 58, pp. 342-345. Photograph JBP.

63. Ashurbanipal's battle against the Arabs, who seek to escape upon their camels. The Arabs are bearded and wearing their long hair shoulder-length, straight back in thick strands; they wear short kilts. There is no headdress. For other camel riders see No. 375.

British Museum, 124926. Kuyunjik, north palace, discovered by Rassam in 1854. Entire relief (as shown in Hall's publication) 1.17 m. by 2.27 m. Alabastrine limestone. Ashurbanipal (668-633). H. R. Hall, *Babylonian and Assyrian Sculpture in the British Museum*, Paris and Brussels, 1928, pl. 46. *AOB*, 23. Described in C. J. Gadd, *The Stones of Assyria*, London, 1936, p. 195. See D. Opitz, *AfO*, vol. 7, 1931, pl. 2, pp. 7-13. Photograph courtesy BM.

64. Standing figure of a man holding in his left hand a lotus stalk. His hair is encircled by a fillet and falls down to his shoulders in curls at the back and in two side-locks before each ear. The upper lip and part of the lower are shaved. The costume consists of a long garment, which appears to be pleated, reaching to the ground, with short sleeves, over it a shawl with fringed edge, which is wound about the body at the waist and passes over the left shoulder and across the back and ends in a tassel below the right shoulder. See No. 62. The figure stands on a base which is inscribed with a badly worn inscription.

'Amman, Jordan Archaeological Museum. 'Amman, north end of the citadel. Soft limestone. Height: 0.45 m. Eighth-ninth century, on basis of forms of the letters of the inscription (Barnett, p. 35). *Illustrated London News*, February 18, 1950, pp. 266-267. R. T. O'Callaghan, "A Statue Recently Found in 'Ammân," *Orientalia*, vol. 21, 1952, pp. 184-193, pl. 26. R. D. Barnett, "Four Sculptures from Amman," *Annual of the Department of Antiquities of Jordan*, vol. 1, 1951, pl. 11, pp. 34-36. Photograph courtesy of G. Lankester Harding.

65. A Qatabanian funerary statue of 'Amrum 'Abyad Karr, standing on a base inscribed with his name. The body is stylized and out of proportion to the head. He seems to wear a triple necklace and a garment which reaches to his knees. The beard and mustache are indicated by stippling; the eyes and the eyebrows are incised. The top of the head is cut flat.

University Museum, 30-47-2. Alabaster. Height: 0.32 m. First century B.C. (W. F. Albright). L. Legrain, "In the Land of the Queen of Sheba," *AJA*, vol. 38, 1934, p. 331, fig. 1A. G. Ryckmans, "Inscriptions Sud-arabes," *Le Muséon*, vol. 48, 1935, pl. 2, 119. Photograph courtesy UM.

66. A funerary statue of 'Ammyada' of Šukaymim, a Qatabanian. Base on which the figure stands is inscribed with his name. The face is decorated with small incisions to indicate a beard and a mustache. The costume appears similar to No. 65.

University Museum, 30-47-1. Alabaster. Height of statue: 0.432 m. First century B.C. (W. F. Albright). L. Legrain, "In the Land of the Queen of Sheba," *AJA*, vol. 38, 1934, p. 331, fig. 1B. G. Ryckmans, "Inscriptions Sud-arabes," *Le Muséon*, vol. 48, 1935, pl. 2, 118. Photograph courtesy UM.

II. Daily Life

Since pictures for the section on "Daily Life" have been chosen to illustrate daily activities and occupations of the peoples of ancient Palestine, first consideration has generally been given to those artifacts which have come from Palestine and Syria. When these sources have failed resort has been to illustrations from the adjacent areas of Egypt, Mesopotamia, and Asia Minor—areas in which the record of daily life has often been preserved in much richer detail. This procedure involves an assumption of a basic unity of certain cultural elements in the ancient Near East, an assumption which is borne out by the observation of a corresponding unity of daily life in the various parts of the modern Near Eastern world.

In addition to the references given in the individual entries for this section, reference may be made to the following more general works dealing with daily life within the area of the ancient Near Eastern world: A. Erman and H. Ranke, *Ägypten und ägyptisches Leben im Altertum*, Tübingen, 1923. A. Wiedemann, *Das alte Ägypten*, Heidelberg, 1920. L. Klebs, *Die Reliefs des alten Reiches*, Heidelberg, 1915; *Die Reliefs und Malereien des mittleren Reiches*, Heidelberg, 1922; *Die Reliefs und Malereien des neuen Reiches*, Heidelberg, 1934. H. Kees, *Ägypten*, Munich, 1933. B. Meissner, *Babylonien und Assyrien*, 2 vols., Heidelberg, 1920, 1925. G. Contenau, *La vie quotidienne à Babylone et en Assyrie*, Paris, 1950. A. Götze, *Kleinasien*, Munich, 1933. H. Th. Bossert, *Altanatolien*, Berlin, 1942 (volume of pictures); *Altsyrien*, Tübingen, 1951 (volume of pictures). C. Watzinger, *Denkmäler Palästinas*, 2 vols., Leipzig, 1933, 1935. K. Galling, *Biblisches Reallexikon*, Tübingen, 1937. G. Dalman, *Arbeit und Sitte in Palästina*, 7 vols., Gütersloh, 1928-1942. G. Contenau, *Manuel d'archéologie orientale*, 4 vols., Paris, 1927-1947. H. Gressmann, *Altorientalische Bilder zum alten Testament*, Berlin and Leipzig, 1927.

PERSONAL ADORNMENT

67. One of the several examples of ivory combs found at Megiddo (*OIP*, 52, pls. 16-18 for others). Two rows of teeth separated by a panel showing a lion crouching among trees. Same scene, although reversed, on other side. Other examples of combs found in Palestine listed by Galling, *BR*, cols. 255-256. For Egyptian combs see: G. Bénédite, *Objets de toilette, Cat. gén.*, Cairo, 1911, pls. 3-7.

Oriental Institute, A 22295. Megiddo, treasury. Ivory. 0.074 m. by 0.102 m. Dated to 1350-1150 in *OIP*, 52, p. 10. G. Loud, *The Megiddo Ivories, OIP*, 52, Chicago, 1939, pl. 17, no. 110b. Photograph courtesy of the Oriental Institute.

68. One from the many examples of small stone palettes found at Megiddo, extending over strata I-III (*OIP*, 42, pls. 108-111). The suggestion that they were cosmetic bowls is plausible. See example from Beth-zur (O. R. Sellers, *The Citadel of Beth-zur*, Philadelphia, 1933, fig. 53, no. 5).

Palestine Archaeological Museum, I.3562. Megiddo, 1926. White stone. 0.102 m. by 0.033 m. Iron II (ninth-early sixth centuries). R. S. Lamon and G. M. Shipton, *Megiddo I, OIP*, 42, Chicago, 1939, pl. 109, no. 14. Photograph courtesy PAM.

69. Tusk, hollowed out to make flask, forms the torso of a human figure, to which has been added a neck and head surmounted by a hand in the form of a spoon. A hole has been pierced through the head and into the hand, perhaps for the purpose of allowing a liquid (perfumed ointment?) to pass from the body when the flask is turned upside down. See object carried by Syrian in wall painting shown in No. 47. Similar object found in Egypt (W. M. F. Petrie, *Qurneh*, London, 1909, pl. 25) and at Megiddo (*OIP*, 52, pl. 43, no. 186).

Palestine Archaeological Museum, 347699. Tell ed-Duweir, shrine room, 181, campaign of 1933-1934. Ivory. Height: 0.245 m. Dated to 1400-1200 in publication, p. 59. O. Tufnell, C. H. Inge, L. Harding, *Lachish II*, London, 1940, pl. 15 above, pp. 59-60. Photograph courtesy PAM.

70. Cosmetic container or ointment spoon, with handle in shape of a nude female figurine. Arms, with bracelets, support bowl of container. Breasts protrude and genital region is marked with incised dots. Hole in back between shoulders for insertion of the doweled head of the figure (see alabaster container in Metropolitan Museum of Art, *A Brief Guide to the Egyptian Collection*, New York, 1947, p. 17).

Palestine Archaeological Museum, 38807. Megiddo. Ivory. Length: 0.183 m. Dated to 1350-1150 in *OIP*, 52, p. 10. G. Loud, *The Megiddo Ivories, OIP*, 52, Chicago, 1939, pl. 41, no. 178. Photograph courtesy of the Oriental Institute.

71. A Palestinian example of a mirror, an object frequently illustrated in Egypt and other parts of the ancient Near East. Short tang for insertion into handle which is decorated with incised rings and riveted with bronze pins. See also Nos. 76, 78, 632. For Egyptian examples see G. Bénédite, *Miroirs, Cat. gén.*, Cairo, 1907. List of other Palestinian mirrors in Galling, *BR*, cols. 493-494.

Palestine Archaeological Museum, 32551. 'Athlit, 1930-1931. Bronze and bone. Diameter: 0.118 m. Fifth century. *QDAP*, vol. 2, 1932, pl. 23, no. 551, fig. 7 on p. 53, and p. 75. Photograph courtesy PAM.

72. Elaborate headdress and other jewelry found with the crushed skull of Queen Shubad at Ur are here displayed on a model head. Among the pieces (not all shown) were the following: gold hair ribbon, 12 m. in length; wreath of lapis cylinder beads and carnelian rings with gold ring pendants; wreath of similar beads, but with gold "beech-leaf" pendants; a wreath of same "beech-leaf" pendants, but with each leaf tipped by a carnelian bead; wreath with gold willow-leaf pendants tipped with carnelian beads arranged in sets of three, and between the leaves gold flower-rosettes whose petals are inlaid with lapis and white paste; seven-pointed gold comb, each point ending in a rosette of gold with lapis centers; gold earrings of lunate type, 0.11 m. in diameter; four hair rings of spirally twisted gold wire; necklace of small gold and lapis beads with a pendant in form of a wheel-rosette of open work in gold set with carnelian.

University Museum. Ur, tomb PG/800. Early Dynastic III, about twenty-fifth century. *MJ*, vol. 20, 1929, pl. opp. p. 211 (Legrain's reconstruction). C. L. Woolley, *The Royal Cemetery*, London, 1934, pp. 84-87, pl. 128 (reconstruction by Woolley). Photograph courtesy UM.

73. A broad, beaded collar consisting of five rows of elements: the innermost is made up of conventionalized cornflowers; the three middle rows, beads resembling dates; the outermost row, pendants of form derived from water lilies.

New York, Metropolitan Museum of Art, 40.2.5. Purchased. Faïence: yellow, green, red, blue, and white. Approximate diameter: 0.315 m. Late 18th Dynasty (1550-1350). Metropolitan Museum of Art, *Egyptian Jewelry*, New York, 1940, fig. 14. *BMMA*, vol. 35, 1940, pp. 65-68, fig. 2. Photograph courtesy MMA.

74-75. A hoard of metal ornaments: (a) Gold earring decorated with grains grouped into a circular patch (publication, pl. 14, no. 30). (b) Gold torque earring (pl. 14, no. 40). (c) Gold earring made of two plates sweated together (pl. 14, no. 29). (d) Large plaque of thin electrum, representing stylized female with high headdress, necklace, breasts, and genital region—0.105 m. high (pl. 14, no. 6). (e) Gold star pendant (pl. 14, no. 15). (f) Gold plaque with face, breasts, and genital region—0.097 m. high (pl. 14, no. 8). (g) Headband or diadem of electrum, with seven short tubes or sockets to hold metal rosettes (pl. 14, no. 7). (h) Gold earring, coarsely made (pl. 14, no. 26). (i) Gold pendant on which are incised a face surmounted by a Hathor headdress, breasts, and genital incisions—0.072 m. high (pl. 14, no. 9). (j) Gold plate planned for working into a star or flower (pl. 14, no. 13).

Palestine Archaeological Museum. Tell el-'Ajjul, hoard 1299. Fourteenth-thirteenth centuries. F. Petrie, *Ancient Gaza*, vol. 4, London, 1934, pl. 13 (photographs), 14 (drawings). Photograph courtesy PAM.

Hairdressing

Scenes of hairdressing on Egyptian monuments have been collected in Gauthier-Laurent, "Les scènes de coiffure féminine dans l'ancienne Égypte," *Mélanges Maspero*, vol. 1, pt. 2, *Mém., L'inst. fran. d'arch. orient. du Caire*, vol. 66, Cairo, 1935-1938, pp. 673-696.

76. A panel from the side of the sarcophagus of Princess Kawit: left, a server pours milk from a flask into a bowl and presents it to the Princess (for milking scene to the left, see No. 100). The Princess sits holding a bowl in her right hand and a mirror in her left. Behind her stands a female servant who is dressing her mistress' hair.

Cairo Museum, 623. Deir el-Bahri. Limestone. Eleventh Dynasty (2135-2000). E. Naville, *Deir el-Bahari*, pt. 1, London, 1907, pl. 20, p. 55. G. Bénédite, *Objets de toilette, Cat. gén.*, Cairo, 1911, pl. 1. Schäfer-Andrae, 296, 2. Photograph courtesy of the Metropolitan Museum of Art, New York.

77. On a fragment of a limestone relief there is shown a woman, the hairdresser Inu, holding a triple strand of curls, originally colored blue, which repeats in form the hieroglyph *shny* "hair" in the inscription above. Inscription: "The hairdresser Inu."

Brooklyn Museum, 51.231. Purchased. Limestone, deep-sunk relief. Height: 0.132 m.; width: 0.245 m. Probably Eleventh Dynasty (2135-2000). E. Riefstahl, "An Ancient Egyptian Hair-

dresser," *Bulletin of the Brooklyn Museum*, vol. 13, Summer 1952, pp. 7-16. Photograph courtesy Br. M.

78. Detail from Turin Papyrus no. 145 (so-called "obscene papyrus"). Woman wears two strings of beads about neck and bracelets. Right hand holds brush, with which she applies paint to her lips; left holds mirror and a cosmetic box (?).

Turin, papyrus no. 145. New Kingdom (1550-1090). Erman-Ranke, fig. 101. Photograph courtesy of the Turin Museum.

79. Woman seated in shallow bowl cleaning her left leg; left hand rubbing toes, and right holding leg. Hair falls over her shoulders.

Palestine Archaeological Museum, 44.57. ez-Zib, er-Ras cemetery, excavation of 1943. Pottery, red ware. 0.083 m. by 0.108 m. Iron II (ninth-early sixth centuries). For Cypriote example see C. Daremberg and E. Saglio, *Dictionnaire des antiquités*, fig. 5896, where bath for dead is shown. Photograph JBP.

80. To the left of the lower register a barber dresses the hair of one of the recruits of Amen-hotep II, while others await their turn. The barber has tied the soldier's hair into a knot on the crown and is separating it into strands and fixing them with fat from a bowl.

Thebes, hall of tomb of User-het (56). Copy of wall painting. Amen-hotep II (1447-1421). *BMMA*, December 1926, pt. ii, fig. 11. Wresz., vol. 1, pl. 44. Photograph courtesy of the Metropolitan Museum of Art, New York.

81. Handle of gray limestone, in which there is a slit on the lower edge. Into this a flint or obsidian razor blade with set and held in place by bitumen, traces of which remain. The notch in the grip accommodated the fourth finger, while the second and third fingers rested on top of the handle.

Baghdad, Iraq Museum. Tepe Gawra. Gray limestone. Length: 0.127 m.; width: 0.03 m.; thickness: 0.012 m. Stratum XIA ("Uruk" period), end of fourth millennium. A. J. Tobler, *Excavations at Tepe Gawra*, vol. 2, Philadelphia, 1950, pl. 176, fig. 18, discussion on p. 202. Photograph courtesy of the University Museum.

82. Razor blade, similar to the broken one attached to a handle in No. 83, has holes for attaching to handle.

University Museum, E 1046. Ballas or Negada. Bronze. Length: 0.162 m. Eighteenth Dynasty (1550-1350). Photograph courtesy of UM.

83. Egyptian razor with handle. Blade is partly broken.

University Museum, E 10313. Buhen, Nubia. Bronze. Length of partly broken blade: 0.115 m. New Kingdom (1550-1090). D. Randall-MacIver and C. L. Woolley, *Buhen*, Philadelphia, 1911, Plates, pl. 64, no. 10313, Text, p. 224. Photograph courtesy of UM.

AGRICULTURE

Plows

For Palestinian plows see G. Dalman, *Arbeit und Sitte in Palästina*, 2, Gütersloh, 1932, pp. 64-93 and Galling, *BR*, cols. 427-429, where references are given to examples of plowpoints found in excavations.

84. A plowman guides a two-handled wooden plow drawn by two oxen. Attached by cord to the plow is a

bar or tongue by which the oxen draw it. The yoke consists of a bar placed on the necks of the oxen just behind the long horns.

British Museum, 51090. Wood. Height: about 0.23 m. Sixth-Eleventh Dynasty (2350-2000). British Museum, *A General Introductory Guide to the Egyptian Collections in the British Museum*, London, 1930, fig. 59. J. H. Breasted, Jr., *Egyptian Servant Statues*, Washington, 1948, pl. 3b, p. 7. Photograph courtesy of BM.

85. An Egyptian plow, drawn by four men and guided by a bearded man with long hair reaching down to the shoulders. To the right is another man with a seed bag. See *ANET*, 469 for translations of songs from reliefs of Pa-heri.

el-Kab, tomb of Pa-heri. Eighteenth Dynasty (1550-1350). J. J. Tylor, *The Tomb of Paheri*, London, 1895, pl. 5. *AOB*, 171. Photograph Fremdvölker, 116.

86. A plow with seed drill is drawn by two humped oxen. A man to the left drives the team; the figure in the middle has a bag over his shoulder and puts seed into the funnel of the drill; the third man grasps the handles of the plow. For example of drill plow from Khorsabad (eighth century) see *AOB*, 162.

University Museum, CBS 3657. Nippur. Seal impression on clay tablet. Length of seal: about 0.054 m. Nazi-Maruttash (1320-1295). A. T. Clay, *Documents from the Temple Archives of Nippur*, PBS, 11, 2, Philadelphia, 1912, p. 66. *MJ*, 1, 1910, no. 1, fig. 1. *AOB*, 161. Photograph courtesy UM.

87. The earliest representation of a plow is that on clay tablets found in Uruk IV. The pictograph continued in use, but with slight changes in form, for several centuries.

On tablets published by A. Falkenstein, *Archaische Texte aus Uruk*, Berlin, 1936, no. 214. Photograph from publication.

88. In the lower register is a seed plow; to the left, an object which may represent a hill (or perhaps a stylized ear of grain); and to the right are a palm tree with two bunches of dates and a square with four objects at the corners. In the upper register, from left to right, are: shrine or cult stand surmounted by a horned crown, bearded figure (Esarhaddon?) in gesture of adoration, sacred tree, and a bull. For discussion of meaning of symbols see D. D. Luckenbill, *AJSL*, vol. 41, 1925, pp. 165-173.

British Museum, 91027. Black basalt. Height of stela: 0.216 m. Esarhaddon (680-669). British Museum, *A Guide to the Babylonian and Assyrian Antiquities*, London, 1922, p. 228. *AOB*, 163. See also for discussion of inscription: H. Gressmann, *ZAW*, vol. 43, 1925, p. 287. Photograph courtesy BM.

89. Asses driven over a threshing floor; one reaches down for a nibble of the grain.

Leiden. Sakkarah. Limestone. Width: about 0.43 m. Old Kingdom (2700-2200). Rijksmuseum van Oudheden, *Die Denkmäler des alten Reiches*, vol. 1, Plates, Haag, 1908, pl. 22. *AOB*, 170. Photograph courtesy Rijksmuseum van Oudheden.

90. In the upper register are piles of fruit, from which porters fill their containers. In the middle register are shown granaries with rounded tops and window-like doors for emptying at the bottom. Below, to the left, men carry grapes to the enclosure where others tread them out. To the extreme right are shown two seated figures beating out a rhythm for the wine treaders.

Sakkarah, mastaba of Mereru-ka, chamber A 12. Height of three registers: about 0.97 m. Sixth Dynasty (2350-2200). The Sakkarah Expedition, *The Mastaba of Mereruka*, pt. 2, OIP, 39, Chicago, 1938, pl. 116. Photograph courtesy of the Oriental Institute.

91. Upper register: men with sickles cut tops of grain, which are forced into a carrier by means of a bar. Between, a girl gathers the heads of grain into her basket. Two women at the left may pull flax. Lower register: the owner of the tomb sits in a booth watching his laborers. Before him are piled food, containers of seed, and water jars. Beyond, a man bends over the two handles of his plow, which is drawn by yoked cows. Above, a man breaking up the soil and another cutting down a tree with an axe.

Thebes, tomb of Nakht (52). Height of two registers: about 0.76 m. Thut-mose IV (?) (1421-1413). Norman de G. Davies, *The Tomb of Nakht at Thebes*, New York, 1917, pl. 19B, pp. 60-66. Photograph courtesy of the Metropolitan Museum of Art, New York.

92. One man ties up a bundle of harvested flax, while another carries a bundle upon his shoulder. To the left, another seems to be removing the heads of flax from the stalks by means of a fixed comb. Two of the men wear long hair and beards. An inscription reads: "Hurry, don't talk too much." See *ANET*, 469 for songs from the reliefs of Pa-heri.

el-Kab, tomb of Pa-heri. Eighteenth Dynasty (1550-1350). J. J. Tylor, *The Tomb of Paheri*, London, 1895, pl. 3. *AOB*, 172. Photograph Fremdvölker, 115.

93. To the right, women gather lotus flowers in baskets and carry them to the press in the center. There, the liquid is pressed out into a large jar. Beyond, other women carry it in jars and present it to a seated figure, presumably the deceased, seated and holding a lotus flower in the left hand. It is not certain whether the liquid was used for perfume or for medicine.

Louvre. Limestone. Neo-Memphite period, perhaps 450-350. G. Bénédite, "La cueillette du lis et le 'Lirinon,'" Fondation Piot, vol. 25, 1921-1922, fig. 1, pls. 4-5, pp. 1-28. C. Boreux, *Guide-catalogue sommaire, Département des Antiquités Égyptiennes*, Paris, 1932, pl. 24, pp. 195-196. Photograph Archives Photographiques.

94. The sweep or *shadūf* consists of a long beam mounted on a stepped pillar, which acts as a fulcrum. To one end is attached a counterpoise of stone or mud, to the other a pole or rope which holds the bucket. The operator, apparently standing on a brick platform, fills the bucket from the lower stream and lifts it to the higher channel. To the extreme left, two men operate sweeps to lift the water to yet a higher level. This is a part of a relief which depicts the dragging of a sculpture of an

unfinished bull up a hill. Above are the legs of the men drawing the colossal bull.

British Museum, 124820. Kuyunjik, Sennacherib's palace. Length of beam of sweep: about 0.23 m. Sennacherib (704-681). A. H. Layard, *Monuments of Nineveh*, London, 1853, pl. 15 for drawing. Photograph courtesy BM.

95. A gardener draws water for his garden by means of the counterpoised sweep or *shadūf*. The fulcrum consists of a post, presumably of lime-washed brick. The counterpoise is a piece of irregular limestone or a ball of mud. The bucket, held by a rope and a long pole which attaches to the sweep above, is identical in shape with those in No. 94. See excursus, "The Shadūf in Egypt," in Norman de G. Davies, *The Tomb of Nefer-Hotep at Thebes*, vol. 1, New York, 1933, pp. 70-73, where a Mesopotamian origin for the *shadūf* is suggested.

Thebes, tomb of Ipui, no. 217. Drawing of wall painting. Height of register: about 0.30 m. Ramses II (1301-1234). Norman de G. Davies, *Two Ramesside Tombs at Thebes*, New York, 1927, pl. 29, pp. 52-53. Porter and Moss, *Bibliography*, vol. 1, p. 157. Photograph courtesy of the Metropolitan Museum of Art, New York.

96. Man climbing a date palm by a ladder, apparently for the purpose of fertilizing the female tree by applying the male inflorescence to the flowers with a cone. See discussion of this operation in C. J. Gadd, *The Assyrian Sculptures*, London, 1934, pp. 51-52.

British Museum, 117110. Tell Halaf. Limestone. Height: 0.635 m. The reliefs from Tell Halaf, biblical Gozan, although originally dated to a much earlier period, have more recently been placed in the ninth century (E. Akurgal, *Späthethitische Bildkunst*, Ankara, 1949, p. 143; H. Frankfort, *JNES*, vol. 11, 1952, p. 225) or in the tenth (W. F. Albright, *BASOR*, no. 119, 1950, p. 26). Cf. also A. Götze, *Hethiter, Churriter und Assyrer*, Oslo, 1936, pp. 87 ff. Photograph courtesy BM.

CATTLE KEEPING

97. Inside a stable, indicated by a gate guarded by a dog, is a man seated on a stool and milking a goat from behind. Vessels, the containers for the various products obtained from milk, appear above the man and goat.

New York, private collection. Chalcedony. Height: 0.032 m. Early Dynastic III (middle of third millennium). Cf. Frankfort, *CS*, pl. 15d. Photograph JBP.

98. A row of five bulls, each composed of pieces of carved shell, set in bitumen to form a frieze held by a copper border. The heads are shown in profile with only one horn and one ear showing. The tails brush against the hind legs and extend all the way to the ground.

University Museum, B 15880. el-Obeid. Shell and black shale. Height with border: 0.22 m.; length: 0.85 m. Temple of Ninhursag (middle third millennium). H. R. Hall and C. L. Woolley, *Al-'Ubaid*, Oxford, 1927, pl. 32, 3, p. 94. Photograph courtesy UM.

99. Inlay frieze with limestone figures set against a black shale background held within copper borders. To the right are two cows and their muzzled calves. Each cow

is being milked from behind by a man who holds a slender milking vessel between his knees. In the center of the panel is a gateway to a cattle byre made of reeds fastened together by bands and from which emerge two heifers, of which only the foreparts are shown. The scene to the left is occupied by four men with shaved heads and faces and wearing the skirt with a fringe. The figure to the left holds a large jar into which he thrusts his left hand. The next man pours milk from a milking jar into a funnel or strainer, from which it flows into a jar on the ground. The third seems to sit upon a stool and holds the strainer into which the milk is being poured. The fourth figure sits upon a stool and holds a huge pottery jar between his knees. C. L. Woolley interprets the scene as the preparation and storing of clarified butter (*Al-'Ubaid*, Oxford, 1927, p. 92).

Baghdad, Iraq Museum. el-Obeid. Limestone set against shale background. Height: 0.22 m.; length: 1.15 m. Temple of Ninhursag (middle of third millennium). H. R. Hall and C. L. Woolley, *Al-'Ubaid*, Oxford, 1927, pl. 31, 3, pp. 91-94. L. Legrain, *MJ*, vol. 15, 1924, pp. 156-170, for parallels. Photograph (of cast) courtesy of the University Museum.

100. A scene from the side of the sarcophagus of Princess Kawit depicting life in the hereafter. The cow is being milked from the side; the milk is caught by a small jar, which is balanced on the man's knee, and is to be given to the Princess, who is having her hair curled (No. 76). To the left front leg of the cow her calf is tethered. A tear drops from the cow's eye. The cow is hornless.

Cairo Museum, 623. Deir el-Bahri. Limestone. Eleventh Dynasty (2135-2000). E. Naville, *Deir el-Bahari*, pt. 1, London, 1907, pl. 20, p. 55. Photograph Foto Marburg.

101. An emaciated desert herdsman, clad only in a kilt, leads three oxen in a procession of offering bearers who bring gifts to Ukh-hotep. The herdsman's staff is a branch of a tree; his head is covered with a mass of disheveled hair; he has a pointed chin-beard.

Meir, south wall, part of register 2. Height of herdsman: about 0.42 m. Sen-Usert I (Porter and Moss, *Bibliography*, vol. 4, p. 250) (about 1971-1928). A. M. Blackman, *The Rock Tombs of Meir*, pt. 2, London, 1915, pl. 30, 1, pp. 17-18. Photograph courtesy of the Metropolitan Museum of Art, New York.

102. Two registers of starving people, from the interior wall of the temple causeway of King Unis. This unique representation of people apparently dying from starvation may have been intended to illustrate the humanitarian interest of the king or to memorialize his charity in a time of famine (see remarks of H. A. Groenewegen-Frankfort, *Arrest and Movement*, Chicago, 1951, pp. 50, 56). For a tradition of seven lean years in Egypt see *ANET*, 31-32.

Sakkarah, interior wall of temple causeway of King Unis. Limestone. Fifth Dynasty (2500-2350). *Illustrated London News*, February 26, 1944, p. 249 (top). *Bulletin de l'Institut d'Égypte*, vol. 25, 1943, pp. 45-54. See J. Vandier, *La famine dans l'Égypte ancienne*, Cairo, 1936. Photograph courtesy Service des Antiquités, Cairo.

BOATING, SHIPPING, AND FISHING
Boats

For a study of shipping by boat in Babylonia, as known from Sumerian and Akkadian sources, see A. Salonen, *Die Wasserfahrzeuge in Babylonien, Studia Orientalia*, vol. 8, 4, Helsinki, 1939, where there is a full bibliography. See also: A. Köster, *Schiffahrt und Handelsverkehr des östlichen Mittelmeeres im 3. u. 2. Jahrtausend v. Chr.*, Leipzig, 1924, Beih. z. *AO*, 1. A. Köster, *Das antike Seewesen*, Berlin, 1923. Other representations of boats: Nos. 41, 124, 225, 290, 341, 356, 673, 676, 686.

103. On this fragment of a relief from Fara are shown two Sumerian figures seated in a boat, which they propel with oars or paddles (^{gis} ǵi - m u š = *gimuššu*, according to A. Salonen, *Die Wasserfahrzeuge in Babylonien*, Helsinki, 1939, p. 104). Cf. the silver model from Ur (No. 105).

Berlin, VA 5194. Fara. Alabaster. Height: 0.10 m. Early Dynastic I (early third millennium). E. Heinrich, *Fara*, Berlin, 1931, pl. 21a, p. 52. A. Salonen, *Die Wasserfahrzeuge in Babylonien*, pl. 6, 2. Photograph Foto Marburg.

104. A small boat is shown in profile as a part of a ritual scene from a cylinder seal of the Uruk period found at Tell Billa. The boat has high prow and stern, each is surmounted by a standard, the top of which is in the shape of an inverted triangle. The nude figure at the prow holds a punting-pole (^{gis} ǵi - m u š: ^{gis}ǵi - m u š - k u d - d u = *parīsu*, according to A. Salonen, *Die Wasserfahrzeuge in Babylonien*, Helsinki, 1939, p. 102). To the rear, a seated figure paddles the craft. Also included in the scene are a rectangular shrine flanked by posts with pairs of rings (see E. D. van Buren, *Symbols of the Gods in Mesopotamian Art*, Rome, 1945, pp. 48-49), and three figures carrying offerings.

Baghdad, 11953. Tell Billa. Black diorite. Height: 0.042 m.; diameter: 0.036 m. Uruk period (end of fourth millennium). *BASOR*, no. 46, 1932, p. 5. Frankfort, *CS*, pl. 3d. Photograph courtesy of the Iraq Museum.

105. This silver model of a boat with high prow and stern was found in the vaulted tomb of the "King's Grave" at Ur. Inside were five thwarts for the rowers. The leaf-blade paddles were still in place. Amidships is an arched band of silver, probably intended as support for an awning.

Baghdad, Iraq Museum, 8259. Ur, grave PG/789. Silver. Length: 0.64 m.; height of peak: 0.20 m.; width: 0.08 m. Early Dynastic III, twenty-fifth century. C. L. Woolley, *The Royal Cemetery*, London, 1934, pl. 169a, p. 71. Photograph courtesy University Museum.

106. A three-decked warship is driven forward by oars arranged in two banks. The prow of the vessel is sharply pointed (or a pointed ram is lashed to the hull, if the incisions represent rope). Shields are hung around the upper deck, on which sit armed warriors.

British Museum, 124772. Kuyunjik, in 1850. Alabastrine limestone. Height: 0.686 m.; width: 0.94 m. Sennacherib (704-681). A. Paterson, *Palace of Sinacherib*, The Hague, pl. 11. H. R.

Hall, *Babylonian and Assyrian Sculpture in the British Museum*, Paris and Brussels, 1928, pl. 33, 1. British Museum, *Assyrian Sculptures in the British Museum from Shalmaneser III to Sennacherib*, London, 1938, pl. 40. Photograph courtesy BM.

107. Six boats, with high horse-headed prows and high sterns, are transporting logs, some of which are towed behind, and others carried aboard the crafts. To the left, at about the center, is a mitered figure with the body of a fish. The water is filled with fish and other marine animals.

Louvre. Khorsabad. Alabaster. Height: 2.83 m. Sargon II (721-705). P. E. Botta, *Monument de Ninive*, vol. 1, Paris, 1849, pl. 34. E. Pottier, *Catalogue des antiquités assyriennes*, Paris, 1924, pp. 88-89. Photograph Foto Marburg.

108. This skin-covered boat, similar to the modern *guffa*, is manned by four oarsmen who transport a heavy load of material. A fisherman, supported by an inflated skin, pulls in a line with a fish on the end.

British Museum, 124823 (part only). Kuyunjik. Sennacherib (704-681). A. H. Layard, *A Second Series of the Monuments of Nineveh*, London, 1853, pl. 12. See Contenau, *Man.*, vol. 1, fig. 29 for similar representation. Photograph courtesy BM.

109. Two solid canoe-like boats made of papyrus towing a large seine between them. Each of the boats is propelled by two oarsmen, one at the bow and the other at the stern. Three sailors on each boat hold the seine. A squatting figure in the boat to the left handles the fish taken from the seine.

Cairo Museum, 46715. Thebes. Eleventh Dynasty (2135-2000). H. E. Winlock, *BMMA*, December 1920, ii, fig. 24, p. 29, text, p. 30. J. H. Breasted, Jr., *Egyptian Servant Statues*, Washington, 1948, pl. 68a, p. 78. Cf. A. Servin, "Constructions navales égyptiennes," *ASAE*, vol. 48, 1948, pp. 55-88. Photograph courtesy of the Metropolitan Museum of Art, New York.

110. A wooden model of a boat equipped with rudder, cabin, mast, and sail. Within the cabin sits Meket-Re with his son beside him and with a singer in attendance. The boat contains at least fourteen servant figures. At the stern stands a steersman; the pilot with fender in hand is at the bow of the boat. Grouped around the mast are sailors who hoist the sail. At either side of the cabin two sailors squat to make fast the backstays attached to the mast. An overseer stands at the forward end of the cabin on the starboard side. Other sailors stand toward the bow.

Cairo Museum, 46720. Deir el-Bahri. Wood. Length: 1.22 m.; height: about 1.00 m. Eleventh Dynasty (2135-2000). H. E. Winlock, *BMMA*, December 1920, ii, fig. 20, p. 27, text, pp. 28, 30. J. H. Breasted, Jr., *Egyptian Servant Statues*, Washington, 1948, pl. 75a, p. 82. Photograph courtesy of the Metropolitan Museum of Art, New York.

111. Two ships carrying Syrians are shown approaching an Egyptian port, where seven smaller, but similar craft are already docked. The ship in the foreground to the left has a single mast with a crow's-nest on the top. Amidship stand two large figures dressed in typical Syrian garb; the first seems to be making an offering and the second, to be giving orders. On the post at the bow stands a figure, perhaps the pilot, with a long sounding pole. At the wharf are docked similar ships, from which gangplanks extend to the shore, where there are shown three booths in which Egyptian shopkeepers purchase wares brought by the sailors (for convention in representing gangplanks see *ÄZ*, vol. 73, 1937, pp. 99-100). Below, a Syrian disposes of a large jar, perhaps containing oil. Above this scene, before a woman's shop a ship's officer has some sailors whom he may be bringing before a port official. Above, a shopkeeper makes use of a small hand-balance in a commercial transaction.

Thebes, tomb no. 162. Wall painting now almost completely destroyed. Probably from time of Amen-hotep III (1413-1377). G. Daressy, "Une flottille phénicienne d'après une peinture égyptienne," *Revue Archéologique*, vol. 27, 1895, pl. 15, pp. 286-291. Norman de G. Davies and R. O. Faulkner, "A Syrian Trading Venture to Egypt," *JEA*, vol. 33, 1947, pl. 8, pp. 40-46. Photograph from *JEA*, vol. 33, 1947, pl. 8, courtesy of the Egypt Exploration Society.

112. On these two registers from the tomb of Mereru-ka are represented four means of catching fish. Below, men haul in a large seine by means of ropes to which have been spliced shoulder straps to aid in pulling. Above, to the left, is a reed boat containing Mereru-ka's eldest brother Ihi, who is lunching on a fowl and drinking from a bowl held by a server, and a seated fisherman holding a line with a hook. To the right are three other reed boats, the first of which contains men who fish by means of traps; the other two carry fishermen with small hand-nets.

Sakkarah, tomb of Mereru-ka, chamber A 4, east wall. Limestone relief, painted. Height of lower register: about 0.54 m. Reign of Teti, Sixth Dynasty (2350-2200). The Sakkarah Expedition, *The Mastaba of Mereruka*, pt. 1, *OIP*, 31, Chicago, 1938, pls. 42 (photograph), 43 (drawing). Photograph from Wresz., vol. 3, pl. 96.

113. Three fishermen pull the lines of a net which holds some fish. Relief from tomb of Ra-hotep.

Berlin. Äg. 15756. Meidum. Limestone. Width: 0.92 m. Fourth Dynasty (2650-2500). Schäfer-Andrae, 249, 1. Porter and Moss, *Bibliography*, vol. 4, p. 91. Photograph courtesy of Staatliche Museen.

114. An Assyrian, with a basket of fish on his back, stands in a pond, located in a mountainous and wooded region, and fishes with a line.

British Museum, 102072. Kuyunjik. Gypsum. Height: 0.495 m. Sennacherib (704-681). C. J. Gadd, *The Stones of Assyria*, London, 1936, p. 177. Photograph from A. H. Layard, *The Monuments of Nineveh*, London, 1849, pl. 67B.

BUILDING

115. Below, two workmen with short-handled hoes knead the clay which has been moistened by water drawn from the pool to the left. Other laborers carry the material in baskets to the two brickmakers, who form the bricks by means of a mold. To the right, a workman tightens his hoe. Among the laborers are represented

fair-skinned and bearded Syrians, and Nubians, who are darker. The scene is accompanied by an inscription: "making bricks to build anew the workshops (of Amūn) in Karnak. . . ." (Davies, *Tomb*, p. 55).

Thebes, tomb of Rekh-mi-Re (100). Height of register: about 0.48 m. Vizier of Egypt, latter part of reign of Thut-mose III and opening of reign of Amen-hotep II (Davies: about 1470-1445; *ANET*, p. 248: 1490-1436). Norman de G. Davies, *The Tomb of Rekh-mi-Rēʿ at Thebes*, New York, 1943, pl. 58 (drawing), pp. 54-55. Norman de G. Davies, *Paintings from the Tomb of Rekh-mi-Rēʿ at Thebes*, New York, 1935, pls. 16, 17. See also: C. F. Nims, "Bricks without Straw," *BA*, vol. 13, 1950, pp. 22-28. Photograph courtesy of Metropolitan Museum of Art. Drawing from Norman de G. Davies, *The Tomb of Rekh-mi-Rēʿ at Thebes*, New York, 1943, pl. 58.

116. A wooden cradle or rocker was used to mount large blocks of stone for working. This is one of fifty models of this kind found in a foundation deposit at Deir el-Bahri. To the right is an adze from the same deposit.

Boston, Museum of Fine Arts, 95.1410 (for cradle). Deir el-Bahri. New Kingdom (1550-1090). E. Naville, *The Temple of Deir el Bahari*, pt. 6, London, 1908, pl. 168, p. 9. Photograph courtesy MFA.

WEIGHTS

For other scenes depicting weighing see Nos. 111, 133, 350, 639 (Egyptian). The studies of F. H. Weissbach on weights in Mesopotamia contain convenient listings of the materials: "Über die babylonischen, assyrischen und altpersischen Gewichte," *ZDMG*, vol. 61, 1907, pp. 379-402, 948-950; "Neue Beiträge zur keilinschriftlichen Gewichtskunde," *ZDMG*, vol. 70, 1916, pp. 49-91, 354-402. For the Palestinian material on weights see Galling, *BR*, cols. 186-188, where bibliography is given.

117. Beardless man holds on his right hand a small balance ready for use, and in his left another balance, which is folded. The pans of the balances are represented as circular, as if seen from above.

Louvre, AO 19221. Purchased. Sandstone. Height: 0.550 m.; width: 0.310 m. Ninth-eighth century (Contenau, *Revue*, p. 38). G. Contenau, "Monuments mésopotamiens," *Revue des arts asiatiques*, vol. 12, 1938, pl. 24a, pp. 37-38. Contenau, *Man.*, vol. 4, fig. 1243, p. 2213. Photograph JBP.

118. A weight of one mina (or maneh, i.e. 60 shekels) with an inscription stating that it is an exact copy of a weight made by Nebuchadnezzar II (605-562) after the standard fixed by Shulgi (king of the Third Dynasty of Ur, about 2000). The weight belonged to Marduk-shar-ilâni.

British Museum, 91005. Provenience unknown. Hard green stone. Height: about 0.095 m. Weight: 978.3 gr. British Museum, *A Guide to the Babylonian and Assyrian Antiquities*, London, 1922, pp. 137-138. See *ZDMG*, vol. 61, 1907, p. 397; vol. 70, 1916, pp. 53-54. Photograph courtesy BM.

119. Bronze lion-weight of two-thirds of a mina, with cuneiform inscription: "Palace of Shalmaneser (V), king of Ashur, two-thirds mina of the king" (*ZDMG*, vol. 61, 1907, p. 401, no. 68). Aramaic inscription:

"Two-thirds [mina] of the land" (*CIS*, pt. 2, vol. 1, no. 7).

British Museum, 91230. Nimrud. Bronze. Weight: 665.795 gr. Shalmaneser V (726-722). British Museum, *A Guide to the Babylonian and Assyrian Antiquities*, London, 1922, pp. 170-171. Photograph courtesy BM.

120. Large weight carved from black basalt in the shape of a duck with its head and beak turned back over its body. Inscribed as 30 "true" minas, from the palace of Eriba-Marduk (possibly Eriba-Marduk II, 688-680, *ZDMG*, vol. 61, 1907, p. 948).

British Museum, 91433. Black basalt. Weight: 33 lbs. 4 1/2 ozs. 4 drs. Length: about 0.32 m. Described in British Museum, *A Guide to the Babylonian and Assyrian Antiquities*, London, 1922, p. 213. Inscription published by E. Norris, "On the Assyrian and Babylonian Weights," *Journal of the Royal Asiatic Society*, vol. 16, 1856, pl. opp. p. 222, no. 1. Photograph courtesy of BM.

121. Bronze weights inlaid in gold with figures of beetles; although found at Nimrud, are probably of Egyptian origin.

British Museum, 119434, 119433. Nimrud. Bronze inlaid with gold. Weight of smaller: 5 oz. 296 gr.; weight of larger: 8 oz. 263 gr. British Museum, *A Guide to the Babylonian and Assyrian Antiquities*, London, 1922, p. 237. Photograph courtesy BM.

WOODWORK

122. On a wall of the tomb of Amen-em-het, "Great Chief of the Oryx nome," at Beni Hasan are scenes of arts, trades, and agricultural pursuits of the Middle Kingdom. The rows from top to bottom represent: (1) manufacture of flint knives, sandal makers, (2) bowyers, coopers, arrow making, chairmaking, boxmaking, (3) goldsmiths, (4) potters, (5) flax cultivation and linen manufacturers, (6) harvesting, (7) plowing and sowing.

Beni Hasan, tomb no. 2. Twelfth Dynasty, Sen-Usert I (1971-1928). P. E. Newberry, *Beni Hasan*, pt. 1, London, 1893, pl. 11, p. 31. Photograph from publication courtesy of the Egypt Exploration Society.

123. Three carpenters at work. Between two men sawing boards sits a man with chisel and clublike mallet working on a large block.

Sakkarah, tomb of Ti. Beginning of Fifth Dynasty (2500-2350). Wresz., vol. 3, pl. 35 (center); description, p. 63. P. Montet, *Les scènes de la vie privée dans les tombeaux égyptiens de l'ancien empire*, Strasbourg, 1925, pl. 22. Photograph Foto Marburg.

124. To the right, a nude boatwright binds with a rope as tightly as possible the bundle of papyrus reeds which form the hull of a boat, while an old man, bearded and potbellied, and perhaps garrulous, looks on.

Meir, tomb chapel of Ukh-hotep. Height of register: about 0.50 m. Sen-Usert I (Porter and Moss, *Bibliography*, vol. 4, p. 250) (1971-1928). A. M. Blackman, *The Rock Tombs of Meir*, pt. 2, London, 1915, pl. 4 (drawing), pl. 26, 2, p. 14. Photograph Foto Marburg.

IVORY CARVING

Other examples of ivory carving are Nos. 43, 44, 58, 67, 69, 70, 203, 213, 215, 290, 293, 332, 464, 566, 649, 663. For a general discussion of ivories, see: R. D. Barnett, "The Nimrud Ivories and the Art of the Phoenicians," *Iraq*, vol. 2, 1935, pp. 179-210. For remarks on the dates of the ivories see: Albright, *AP*, pp. 136-137.

125. Fragment of openwork plaque, probably used as inset in furniture, carved on both sides into a figure of a woman dressed in a long robe and with hair hanging in a mass below the shoulders. Pupils of eyes inlaid with glass.

Oriental Institute, A 22258. Megiddo. Ivory. Height of fragment: about 0.203 m.; thickness: 0.015 m. Dated to 1350-1150 in *OIP*, 52, p. 10. G. Loud, *The Megiddo Ivories*, OIP, 52, Chicago, 1939, pl. 38, no. 173a. Photograph courtesy of the Oriental Institute.

126. This fragment of a nude female figurine shows only the back of the figure; the front is missing. A crown is worn over hair, which is braided into a plait hanging half way down the back.

Oriental Institute, A 22257. Megiddo. Ivory. Height: about 0.23 m. Dated to 1350-1150 in *OIP*, 52, p. 10. G. Loud, *The Megiddo Ivories*, OIP, 52, Chicago, 1939, pl. 39, no. 175. Photograph courtesy of the Oriental Institute.

127. A fragment of a scene on which there were originally at least three panels: the lower two, of hunting scenes; and the upper, of a procession.

Metropolitan Museum of Art, 51.131.6. Zawiyeh (southeast of Lake Urmiye, east of Sakkiz). Ivory. Height: 0.155 m. Eighth century. *BMMA*, April 1952, p. 236 (left). For similar pieces see: A. Godard, *Le trésor de Ziwiyè*, Haarlem, 1950. Photograph courtesy MMA.

128. Box with all four sides carved with sphinxes and lions in relief, from one piece of ivory. Heads of the sphinxes are missing.

Palestine Archaeological Museum, 38.816. Megiddo. Ivory. Base: 0.135 by 0.12 m.; height: 0.075 m. Dated to 1350-1150 in *OIP*, 52, p. 10. G. Loud, *The Megiddo Ivories*, OIP, 52, Chicago, 1939, pl. 2, no. 1a. Photograph courtesy of the Oriental Institute.

129. Two crouching lions with mouths open, as if roaring, are the finest pieces of ivory carving in the round discovered at Samaria. Slots in the back of each figure indicate that they may have decorated the arms or steps of a throne (see I Kings 10:19, 20). Each figure has a hole in the rump for the attachment of a tail.

Palestine Archaeological Museum, 33.2557-8. Samaria, 1932. Ivory. Height: 0.04 m. First half of ninth century, according to excavator. J. W. Crowfoot and Grace M. Crowfoot, *Early Ivories from Samaria*, London, 1938, pl. 9, 1; discussion, p. 24. Photograph courtesy PAM.

130. A lion grappling with a long-horned bull is pictured in a pierced relief with frame and long tenon on the side. The subject appears on a mold from the palace at Mari (*Syria*, vol. 18, 1937, pl. 12, 4) and on an ivory comb from Megiddo (G. Loud, *The Megiddo Ivories*, *OIP*, 52, Chicago, 1939, pl. 16, no. 107a).

Palestine Archaeological Museum, 33.2552. Samaria, 1932. Ivory. Height: 0.042 m.; length: 0.114 m. First half of the ninth century, according to excavator. J. W. Crowfoot and Grace M. Crowfoot, *Early Ivories from Samaria*, London, 1938, pl. 10, 1; discussion, p. 25. Photograph courtesy PAM.

131. A woman's head shown in the frame of a recessed window, under which are four column-like supports, provides an inset for woodwork. It has been suggested that the representation is of the goddess Ashtart (or Astarte), who like her sacred harlots, lures passers-by from her window (R. D. Barnett, *Iraq*, vol. 2, 1935, p. 182). See: Judges 5:28; Jer. 22:14; II Kings 9:30 ff.

British Museum, 118147. Nimrud. Ivory. Height: 0.107 m. Possibly first half of eighth century (R. D. Barnett, *Iraq*, vol. 2, 1935, p. 185). British Museum, *A Guide to the Babylonian and Assyrian Antiquities*, London, 1922, pl. 41, no. 13. Photograph courtesy BM.

132. Man, wearing a conical cap surmounted by an uraeus in front and a long garment which trails over his right leg, holds to a lotus tree with one hand and raises the other in a kind of salute. The piece has tenons for attaching to the woodwork of which it was a part.

British Museum, 118148. Nimrud. Ivory. Height: 0.108 m. Eighth century, possibly first half (R. D. Barnett, *Iraq*, vol. 2, 1935, p. 185). British Museum, *A Guide to the Babylonian and Assyrian Antiquities*, London, 1922, pl. 41, no. 10. Photograph courtesy BM.

METALWORK

133. To the left of the upper register gold is being weighed in a balance and recorded by a scribe; to the right, six men blow through tubes into a furnace to heat the metal for casting. Below, metalworkers fashion the molded objects upon tables. Between the two principal registers is shown a shelf on which are finished products.

Sakkarah, tomb of Mereru-ka. Limestone relief. Height of the two registers and shelf: about 0.52 m. Reign of Teti, Sixth Dynasty (2350-2200). The Sakkarah Expedition, *The Mastaba of Mereruka*, pt. 1, *OIP*, 31, Chicago, 1938, pls. 32, 30 (drawing). Wresz., vol. 3, pl. 33. Photograph courtesy of the Oriental Institute.

134. Evidence for two furnaces of a smelting plant was found in room Q8 of level XI (eleventh century) at Tell Qasile; nearby were two clay crucibles containing remains of smelted copper.

Tell Qasile. Mud brick and stone tiles. Diameter of smelting chamber: about 0.75 m. B. Maisler, *The Excavations at Tell Qasile, Preliminary Report*, Jerusalem, 1951, fig. 3 (top). Photograph courtesy of B. Maisler.

135. A pottery mold for implements, with two axes or chisels in place. For similar examples see W. F. Albright, *The Excavation of Tell Beit Mirsin, Vol. 2, The Bronze Age*, *AASOR*, 17, New Haven, 1938, pl. 43.

Palestine Archaeological Museum, I.685. Balatah (Shechem), 1927. Pottery. 0.37 m. by 0.115 m. by 0.115 m. Middle Bronze (2000-1500). E. Sellin, *ZDVP*, vol. 50, 1927, pl. 21, p. 210. Photograph courtesy PAM.

136. This flat-based, cylindrical crucible with two horn-handles was found in room 19 at Tell el-Kheleifeh. The jar was handmade of red ware, now burnt black.

Palestine Archaeological Museum, 40.602. Tell el-Kheleifeh (head of Gulf of Aqabah), 1938. Pottery. Height: 0.138 m.; diameter: 0.185 m. Iron II (ninth-early sixth centuries). Photograph courtesy PAM.

137. An elaborately decorated ladle in the form of a nude female figure, from whose hands extends the bowl, and whose feet are continued into a handle ending in a ring. Two bulls' heads are represented just before the ring handle, and there is an incised lotus at the junction of the handle and the bowl. The large silver bowl, with 24 flutings around a raised center, is similar to examples from Achaemenid tombs at Susa.

Palestine Archaeological Museum, M 1141. Tell el-Far'ah, Tomb 650, 1928. Silver. Length of ladle: 0.220 m.; weight: 159.2 gr. Persian period (550-330). Flinders Petrie, *Beth-Pelet I*, London, 1930, pl. 45 (pl. 44, bowl), p. 14. J. H. Iliffe, *QDAP*, vol. 4, 1934, pl. 91, pp. 183-186. Photograph courtesy PAM.

138. The bowl has an offset disc base; the whole was hammered from a single piece of copper.

University Museum, 31-52-262. Gawra, stratum VI. Copper. Length: 0.225 m.; maximum bowl diameter: 0.112 m. Middle third millennium. E. A. Speiser, *Excavations at Tepe Gawra*, vol. 1, Philadelphia, 1935, pl. 51b, p. 109. Photograph courtesy UM.

139. Bronze bit with circular cheek-pieces to which are fastened sharp spikes. See Egyptian example of the Eighteenth Dynasty from Amarna now in the Berlin Museum (W. Wolf, *Die Bewaffnung des altägyptischen Heeres*, Leipzig, 1926, pl. 19, 1).

Palestine Archaeological Museum, 37.271. Tell el-'Ajjul, 1933-1934. Bronze. Length: 0.265 m. Excavator dates to "Early Hyksos Age." Flinders Petrie, *Ancient Gaza*, vol. 4, London, 1934, pl. 35, 558, p. 11. Photograph courtesy PAM.

140. The bed or couch shown here, after a reconstruction by Watzinger, was made with bronze fittings for the legs and iron tie-rods which held the legs together. From same grave as No. 137.

Palestine Archaeological Museum. Tell el-Far'ah, tomb 650. Bronze. Length: about 2 m. Persian period (550-330). F. Petrie, *Beth-Pelet I*, London, 1930, pls. 45-46, p. 14. Photograph from C. Watzinger, *Denkmäler Palästinas*, vol. 1, Leipzig, 1933, fig. 44.

141. Examples of daggers, spear points, sword, knife, and awl from excavations in Palestine.

Palestine Archaeological Museum. For drawings of various types of weapons and implements see: Galling, *BR*, cols. 133-134 (daggers), 282 (tools), 354 (spears), 473-474 (swords). Photograph courtesy PAM.

TEXTILES

142. A wooden tomb-model of a weaver's house shows the processes of turning flax into cloth. The woman in the corner opposite the door prepares flax fibers for spinning by twisting them. The resulting rove is wound

into balls and put into pots from which the spinner may draw it. In front of this seated figure stands a spinner, unclothed, who rotates the spindle with its whorl on her thigh, giving the thread its twist. Along the long side of the model opposite the door is a four-posted warping frame set in the floor, at which works a woman winding the thread about the posts, so that the threads cross each other. At the end of the house is a longer warping frame consisting of pegs set in the wall. The loom is a horizontal one, common in the Middle Kingdom (the loom and some of the other details, including the threads, have been restored).

New York, Metropolitan Museum of Art, 30.7.3. Purchased. Sycamore-fig wood, coated with a thin layer of gesso. Length: 0.59 m.; width: 0.355 m.; height: 0.22 m. Twelfth Dynasty (1990-1780). C. R. Clark, "Egyptian Weaving in 2000 B.C.," *BMMA*, Summer 1944, pp. 26-27. J. H. Breasted, Jr., *Egyptian Servant Statues*, Washington, 1948, pl. 48a, pp. 54-55. See also H. F. Lutz, *Textiles and Costume among the Peoples of the Ancient Near East*, Leipzig, 1923, pp. 40-72. Photograph courtesy MMA.

143. A scene of spinners and weavers and their overseer on the wall of the tomb of Khnum-hotep at Beni Hasan. To the right are two scantily dressed women spinning thread. To the left is a loom, probably a horizontal loom, to judge from the pegs shown at the top, but represented as seen from above; operated by two women. An overseer stands in the center of the scene.

Beni Hasan, tomb 3, main chamber, west wall. Height of two figures at loom: 0.24 m. Middle Kingdom (2050-1800). P. E. Newberry, *Beni Hasan*, pt. 1, London, 1893, pl. 29 (drawing of entire wall), fourth register. C. R. Clark, "Egyptian Weaving in 2000 B.C.," *BMMA*, Summer 1944, p. 28. *BMMA*, April 1933, ii, p. 25, fig. 3. Erman-Ranke, fig. 222. See also H. Ling Roth, *Ancient Egyptian and Greek Looms*, Halifax, 1913, p. 6, fig. 6. Photograph of Nina de G. Davies' painting, courtesy of the Metropolitan Museum of Art, New York.

144. Seated on a low lion-footed stool is a lady holding a spindle in her left hand and material, perhaps wool, in the right. Behind her stands a servant with a large fan; a lion-footed table is before her, on which is represented a fish and disclike objects.

Louvre. Susa. Bituminous stone. Height: 0.10 m. Date uncertain (see Contenau, *Man.*, vol. 3, pp. 1231-1232). TEL, vol. 2, p. 45C. *AOB*, 187. Schäfer-Andrae, 503, 1. J. de Morgan, *Mémoires, Délégation en Perse*, vol. 1, Paris, 1900, pl. 11. Photograph Archives Photographiques.

145. Among several dye plants found at Tell Beit Mirsim, stratum A, is this structure consisting of two roughly cylindrical basins and two adjoining rectangular basins. A relatively small opening in the center of the top led into the basin of the vats. Around the rim of each was chiseled a circular groove, obviously to catch the dye, which was then conducted back into the basin by a small hole near the rim. This hole could be stopped by a stone when the dye was being stirred. To judge from the relatively small opening at the top of the vat, thread rather than woven cloth was dyed.

Tell Beit Mirsim, stratum A, SE 32A-2, 1928. Vats between 0.70 m. and 0.90 m. in height. Eighth century (excavator,

AASOR, vol. 21-22, p. 59). W. F. Albright, *The Excavation of Tell Beit Mirsim, Vol. 3, The Iron Age, AASOR*, vol. 21-22, New Haven, 1943, pl. 53a, discussion, pp. 55-62, where copious references are given. Photograph courtesy of W. F. Albright.

POTTERY MAKING

146. In this model of a potter's shop are three figures. The one in the center molds a clay vessel with his right hand as he turns the wheel with the left. To his right sits another worker beside a cylindrical object, intended perhaps to represent a kiln. The third figure squats at the right of the shop, apparently sawing a piece of wood.

Cairo Museum, 3124. Sakkarah, tomb of Karenen. Tenth Dynasty (twenty-first century). Base: 0.38 m. by 0.26 m. J. E. Quibell, *Excavations at Saqqara (1906-07)*, Cairo, 1908, pl. 17, nos. 1, 3, p. 75. J. H. Breasted, Jr., *Egyptian Servant Statues*, Washington, 1948, pp. 51-52. Photograph courtesy of the Metropolitan Museum of Art, New York.

147. Of the many hundreds of types of pottery vessels found in the course of excavation in Palestine only a few of the more characteristic forms for the principal archaeological periods are shown in this chart. While the designations for the general archaeological periods are standard, the specific dates assigned to them are subject to debate. Those given here are suggested by the Department of Antiquities of the State of Israel.

Photograph courtesy of the Department of Antiquities, State of Israel.

148. A selected group of pottery vessels from Palestine, from the Early Bronze through the Iron II periods, now in the Lemon Bible Lands Museum, Louisville Presbyterian Theological Seminary, Louisville, Kentucky. Some forms published by W. F. Albright in *The International Standard Bible Encyclopaedia*, vol. 4, Chicago, 1930, plate and page between pp. 2422 and 2423.

Photographs JBP, courtesy of Lemon Museum.

BREADMAKING

149. This servant figure of the Old Kingdom is shown clothed only in a short skirt and wearing a wig protected from the dust by a small cloth on top. At the ends of the grinding stone are represented piles of meal or grain. Traces of paint remain.

Boston, Museum of Fine Arts, 21.2601. Giza. Limestone. Height: 0.282 m.; length: 0.45 m. Old Kingdom (2700-2200). J. H. Breasted, Jr., *Egyptian Servant Statues*, Washington, 1948, pl. 16b, p. 18. Photograph courtesy MFA.

150. A disc-shaped platter, with holes on the underside, but not bored through, and incisions around the rim of the upper side, may have been used for forming cakes of bread, or for baking them, in the shrine in which it was found. Cf. Lev. 2:5.

Palestine Archaeological Museum, 36.2246. Tell ed-Duweir, shrine, structure I. Pottery with coarse, gray grits. Diameter: about 0.30 m. Structure I dated to about 1475-1400 by excavators (p. 24). O. Tufnell, C. H. Inge, L. Harding, *Lachish II*, London, 1940, pl. 54A, 338, p. 39 for discussion. Photograph courtesy PAM.

151. This small mortar, found with pestle, was used for grinding cereals.

Palestine Archaeological Museum, 32.1377. Jericho, excavation of 1932, tomb 9, layer C, no. 869. Basalt. Diameter: about 0.26 m. Middle Bronze II (1800-1500). *AAA*, vol. 19, 1932, pl. 30, 16. Photograph courtesy PAM.

152. A crudely modeled human figure bends over a trough kneading dough.

Palestine Archaeological Museum, 44.51. ez-Zib excavation of 1941, Buqbaq cemetery, tomb III, no. 4. Pottery, buff ware. Height: 0.075 m. Iron II (ninth-early sixth centuries). Photograph courtesy PAM.

BREWING

A recent treatment of brewing in Mesopotamia is that of Louis F. Hartman and A. L. Oppenheim, *On Beer and Brewing Techniques in Ancient Mesopotamia, Supplement, Journal of the American Oriental Society*, December 1950. For methods used in Egypt see: A. Lucas, *Ancient Egyptian Materials and Industries*, 3rd ed., London, 1948, pp. 16-23. See also H. F. Lutz, *Viticulture and Brewing in the Ancient Orient*, Leipzig, 1922, especially pp. 72-96 for discussion of beer. P. Montet, *Les scènes de la vie privée dans les tombeaux égyptiens de l'ancien empire*, Strasbourg, 1925, pp. 230-254.

153. In the center of the upper register a worker removes the grain from the stalk; to the right two men pound the grain with pestles; and on the left two workers grind the grain into flour. In the second register a man mixes dough in a vessel (to the left), two men knead the dough into loaves, and another man tends the oven on which the loaves are being baked. In the lower register, a brewer pours water into a brewing vat which contains the fermented bread; two workers pour the beer into jars fitted with stoppers.

Leiden. Sakkarah. Old Kingdom (2700-2200). Rijksmuseum van Oudheden, *Die Denkmäler des alten Reiches*, Plates, The Hague, 1908, pl. 10. Wresz., vol. 1, pl. 109. Photograph courtesy of the Rijksmuseum van Oudheden.

154. The bakery and the brewery are in one building separated into two rooms by a partition wall. The room nearest to the entrance door (uppermost in the photograph) is the brewery, which has a staff of seven people, among whom are: a doorkeeper with a baton, men who tread and knead dough, a man bruising grain with a pestle, and two women grinding grain into flour. Adjoining this room is a bakery with a staff of thirteen figures (some not visible). They include: a man bruising grain with a pestle, two women grinding grain, two men tending ovens, two men mixing dough, two women forming dough into cakes, and others. The heads of the men are shaven; they usually wear white skirts and are nude to the waist.

New York, Metropolitan Museum of Art, 20.3.12. Thebes, tomb of Meket-Re, expedition of 1920. Wood. Length: 0.732 m. Eleventh Dynasty (2135-2000). *BMMA*, December 1920, ii, p. 21, fig. 12. J. H. Breasted, Jr., *Egyptian Servant Statues*, pl. 36b, p. 38. Photograph courtesy MMA.

WINE MAKING AND DRINKING

155. To the right, five men operate a wine press. In the circle to the left are shown two musicians beating time to set the pace for those who tread the grapes (not shown).

Sakkarah, tomb of Mereru-ka. Height of register: about 0.33 m. Reign of Teti, Sixth Dynasty (2350-2200). The Sakkarah Expedition, *The Mastaba of Mereruka*, pt. 2, *OIP*, 39, Chicago, 1938, pl. 114. Photograph courtesy of the Oriental Institute.

156. To the right of the register, two men gather grapes from branches trained to form an arbor. To the left, five men tread out the grapes in a covered vat, as they hold on to straps attached to the roof. The wine flows out into a container to the right of the vat, and an attendant stores it into the jars with stoppers shown above him.

Thebes, tomb of Nakht. Height of register: about 0.30 m. End of reign of Amen-hotep II or to the early years of Thut-mose IV (1421-1413) (p. 50 of publication). Norman de G. Davies, *The Tomb of Nakht at Thebes*, New York, 1917, pl. 23b, 26 (in color), pp. 69-70. *AOB*, 183. Photograph courtesy of the Metropolitan Museum of Art, New York.

157. Seated on a stool is a Syrian warrior, clad in a skirt of variegated material and a necklace-collar. He is fully bearded and has his hair held in place by a white fillet. Before him is seated his wife and a boy, who gives the seated warrior a long reed through which he draws the beer or other drink from a large two-handled jar.

Berlin, Äg. 14,122. Tell el-Amarna. Painted limestone. Height: 0.30 m. Akh-en-Aton (1380-1362). W. Spiegelberg and A. Erman, "Grabstein eines syrischen Söldners aus Tell Amarna," *ÄZ*, vol. 36, 1898, pl. 17, pp. 126-128. *AOB*, 79 (in color). H. Schäfer, *Amarna in Religion und Kunst*, Berlin, 1931, pl. 53. Photograph Fremdvölker, 828.

158. An enthroned deity drinks through a long reed from a vessel on a stand. Before him stands a server who fills the larger vessel from a smaller one. Beyond, a worshiper drinks from the same large jar through a long reed, thus partaking with the god in a kind of communion with him. The space is filled in with symbols: sun-disc and moon, bee, sheep, star, fish, and braid-border.

Berlin, VA, 522. Height: 0.21 m.; diameter: 0.009. Second millennium. A. Moortgat, *Vorderasiatische Rollsiegel*, Berlin, 1940, no. 526. Photograph from publication.

WARFARE

In addition to the representations of the various aspects of military activity found in the following section are numerous illustrations of soldiers and warfare in the section "Scenes from History and Monuments." For Elamite soldiers see Nos. 25 and 30. Other Assyrian soldiers are represented in Nos. 63, 205, 538. Sherden warriors are shown in No. 59.

Babylonia and Assyria

159. Attached to a belt in grave PG/580 at Ur was this gold dagger and sheath. The hilt is made of a single piece of lapis studded with gold and is pierced by a hole edged

with gold. The gold blade is inscribed with a mark, which may be a property mark (see E. Burrows, in *The Royal Cemetery*, London, 1934, p. 317). The sheath is also of gold and is decorated in front with openwork done in a design derived from sheaths of woven grass.

Baghdad, Iraq Museum. Ur, U.9361. Gold and lapis. Length of dagger: 0.37 m. Early Dynastic III, twenty-fifth century. C. L. Woolley, *The Royal Cemetery*, London, 1934, pl. 151, p. 51. Photograph courtesy of the University Museum.

160. Gold helmet, hammered out of one piece of metal, with features in relief and detail engraved, was found in a tomb belonging to Mes-kalam-dug (not King Mes-kalam-dug). Since fragments of cloth and wool stuffing were found, it is likely that the inside of the helmet was fitted with a quilted cap to make the wearer more comfortable. The cloth of the inner cap was brought up on to the outside of the rim of the helmet and held in place by laces which passed through the small holes around the rim.

Baghdad, Iraq Museum. Ur, U.10000, tomb PG/755. Gold, 15-carat. Length from front to back: 0.26 m.; height: 0.23 m. Early Dynastic III, twenty-fifth century. C. L. Woolley, *The Royal Cemetery*, London, 1934, frontispiece of Plates volume, pp. 156, 552. Photograph courtesy of the University Museum.

161. Fragment of a coat of mail, consisting of bronze plates laced together with cord or thongs. This piece was probably from an unfinished armor, since the rounded ends of one row were toward those of the other. A tablet from Nuzi (S.M. no. 2087) lists four suits of armor, varying in the number of plates from 680 to 1,035 (p. 479 of publication).

Baghdad. Nuzi, house of Shilwi-teshub, 18. Bronze. Size of plates in corselet: 0.118 m. by 0.063 m. by 0.002 m. Shortly after middle of second millennium. R. F. S. Starr, *Nuzi*, Cambridge, Mass., 1937, vol. 2, pl. 126B; discussion, vol. 1, pp. 475-480. E. A. Speiser, *JAOS*, vol. 70, 1950, pp. 47-49. Photograph courtesy of the Iraq Museum.

162. Head of a warrior covered with a helmet held tightly in place by bands which encircle the chin and neck.

Aleppo, National Museum, 1648. Mari, fourth campaign, 1936-1937. Alabaster. Height: 0.20 m. Dated to about time of First Dynasty of Babylon (1830-1530) by excavator (*Syria*, vol. 19, 1938, pp. 19-20). *Syria*, vol. 19, 1938, pl. 8, pp. 18-21. Photograph courtesy of National Museum, Aleppo.

163. Fragment of a limestone plaque, which seems to be identical with No. 604, shows a two-wheeled chariot drawn by four asses. The pole springs from the top of the body in a high curve and then descends to the yoke of the asses. The back of the chariot is high, possibly constructed of wickerwork, and is covered by a spotted skin thrown over it. In the forward part of the body of the chariot is a quiver filled with axes and spears. Behind the chariot walks a driver, followed by a second figure.

University Museum, 17086. Ur, U.8557. Limestone. Width: 0.27 m. Discovered in rubbish mound, so that date can only be guessed on basis of similarity with No. 604 (Early Dynastic

III, middle third millennium). C. L. Woolley, *The Royal Cemetery*, London, 1934, pl. 181b, pp. 376-377, 535. A. Salonen, *Die Landfahrzeuge des alten Mesopotamien*, Helsinki, 1951, pl. 14. A. Salonen, "Notes on Wagons and Chariots in Ancient Mesopotamia," *Studia Orientalia*, vol. 14, no. 2, Helsinki, 1950. Photograph courtesy UM.

164. A cavalryman astride a prancing horse is armed with a shield, having a boss and a bound rim, and a club or sword. The man has hair hanging in locks to his shoulders, and is beardless.

Berlin, VA 8851. Tell Halaf. Basalt. Height: about 0.70 m. Ninth century (see No. 96). M. von Oppenheim, *Der Tell Halaf*, Leipzig, 1931, pl. 18b. Photograph Foto Marburg.

165. A warrior and a charioteer—both bearded—stand in a chariot with six-spoked wheels, usually drawn by two horses (although in this profile only one is represented). Beneath the horse is the prostrate nude body of an enemy. Inscription over the horse.

Aleppo, National Museum. Tell Halaf. Basalt. Height: 0.58 m.; length: 0.90 m. Ninth century (see No. 96). Bossert, *Altsyrien*, 475. W. Wreszinski, *Löwenjagd im alten Ägypten*, Leipzig, 1932, fig. 48. Photograph JBP.

166. Two-wheeled chariot with driver, drawn by four asses. The driver stands astride a kind of centerboard which forms almost the whole body of the chariot. This type of vehicle may have served as a conveyance in peacetime.

Baghdad, Iraq Museum. Tell 'Agrab, Shara temple. Copper. Height: 0.072 m. Early Dynastic (first half of third millennium). H. Frankfort, *More Sculpture from the Diyala Region*, OIP, 60, Chicago, 1943, pl. 58A, no. 310. Contenau, *Man.*, vol. 4, fig. 977 (drawing). Photograph courtesy of the Oriental Institute.

167. An Assyrian cart with spoked-wheels and tires is drawn by a team of oxen. Seated on the cart are four women captives who are being transported by their conquerors.

Louvre, AO 19907. Nineveh, palace of Ashurbanipal. Alabaster. Height of register: about 0.36 m. Ashurbanipal (668-633). TEL, vol. 2, p. 23. V. Place, *Ninive et l'Assyrie*, vol. 3, Paris, 1867, pl. 60, 3. Photograph Foto Marburg.

168. A two-wheeled wagon heavily loaded stands with upturned tongue, under which sit two men (Elamite prisoners?) at a meal. Beyond, to the right, is another man with a waterskin, and the tongue of a second wagon.

Louvre. Kuyunjik, north palace, chamber T, 1854. Gypseous alabaster. Height of register: about 0.20 m. Ashurbanipal (668-633). V. Place, *Ninive et l'Assyrie*, vol. 3, Paris, 1867, pl. 60, 2. C. J. Gadd, *The Stones of Assyria*, London, 1936, pl. 44, pp. 204-205. TEL, vol. 2, p. 20 (lower right). Photograph Foto Marburg.

169. This terra-cotta model represents an original which was open in front and back except for low ledges at the ends. The covering for the wagon consisted of two curved poles joined together by three wooden supports and the entire frame covered with wickerwork or woven material. Two holes in the front probably served to take the tongue or pole. The excavator suggests a foreign origin

for this type and traces it to Transcaucasia or Transcaspia (p. 163).

Philadelphia, Dropsie College. Gawra, stratum VI, room 620. Pottery, greenish gray ware. Height: 0.062 m.; length: 0.068 m. Middle third millennium. E. A. Speiser, *Excavations at Tepe Gawra*, vol. I, Philadelphia, 1935, pl. 35a, p. 75. Photograph courtesy of the University Museum.

170. A cross section of a tent, to which an Assyrian officer returns, and where a meal and couch are being prepared for him. In the adjoining tent a butcher prepares a carcass; above, a man reaches into a deep cylindrical vessel; outside the tents are animals, including two camels. Although some (*AfO*, vol. 7, 1931, p. 12) have suggested Arabia as the locale, because of the camels, it seems more likely that the representation belongs to the Elamite campaigns of Ashurbanipal (C. J. Gadd, *Iraq*, vol. 10, 1948, p. 20). At the top is a defensive wall with bastions.

Berlin, VA 965. Kuyunjik, 1854. Alabaster. Height: 0.39 m. Ashurbanipal (668-633). C. J. Gadd, *The Stones of Assyria*, London, 1936, pl. 29A, p. 218. A. Paterson, *Palace of Sinacherib*, The Hague, pl. 101. Schäfer-Andrae, 570. Contenau, *Man.*, vol. 3, fig. 813. Photograph Foto Marburg.

171. Cross section of one tent and part of another, pitched within a defensive wall with turrets. In the tent to the left, two men prepare food; to the right of this tent another man bends over a low-domed object (bread oven?) and seems to be pouring or rubbing something down a board. Below the tent to the left may be fat-tailed sheep.

Baghdad, IM 31065. Directorate General of Antiquities, *A Guide to the 'Iraq Museum Collections*, Baghdad, 1942, fig. 105. C. J. Gadd, *Iraq*, vol. 10, 1948, pl. 5, pp. 19-21. Photograph courtesy of the Iraq Museum.

North Syria and Anatolia

For representations of other soldiers from this area see Nos. 37-39.

172. In a chariot stand a bowman with drawn bow and spear behind, and a driver, who holds a whip in one hand and reins in the other. Both men are bearded and wear shortsleeved garments. Under the plumed horse lies a nude enemy pierced by two arrows. The chariot has two six-spoked wheels and is decorated with a lion's head at the back.

Istanbul, Museum of the Ancient Orient, 7725. Zinjirli. Basalt. Width: 1.86 m. Perhaps eighth century (E. Akurgal, *Späthethitische Bildkunst*, Ankara, 1949, p. 143). F. von Luschan, *Ausgrabungen in Sendschirli*, vol. 3, Berlin, 1902, pl. 39, pp. 211-213. Bossert, *Altsyrien*, 488. Photograph JBP.

173. Two swordsmen with batons from a row of five, marching in procession. Unlike the representation in No. 174, these soldiers wear no helmet and do not carry the lance, but wear earrings and bracelets.

Istanbul, Museum of the Ancient Orient, 11-12. Arslan Tash. Height: 0.87 m. Tiglath-pileser III (744-727). F. Thureau-Dangin, *et al.*, *Arslan-Tash*, Paris, 1931, pl. 8, p. 80. E. Unger, *Die Reliefs Tiglatpilesers III. aus Arslan Tasch*, Constantinople, 1925, pl. 5, nos. 19, 20. Photograph JBP.

174. This figure stands in a row of three soldiers, each of whom is armed with a lance and a sword, and carries a baton in his right hand. A spiked helmet fits tightly over the head. He is clothed in a knee-length, short-sleeved, plain garment held at the waist by a belt; and sandals.

Istanbul, Museum of the Ancient Orient, 7. Arslan Tash. Height: 0.905 m. Tiglath-pileser III (744-727). F. Thureau-Dangin, *et al.*, *Arslan-Tash*, Paris, 1931, pl. 9, no. 1, pp. 80-81. E. Unger, *Die Reliefs Tiglatpilesers III. aus Arslan Tasch*, Constantinople, 1925, pl. 6, no. 23. Photograph JBP.

Palestine

For illustrations from the Syro-Palestinian area of soldiers or gods dressed in the form of warriors see Nos. 60, 491, 494, 495, 496.

175. This curved piece of bronze with holes along the outer edge is thought to be a part of the crested helmet worn by the Assyrians (see H. R. Hall, *Babylonian and Assyrian Sculpture in the British Museum*, Paris and Brussels, 1928, pl. 36, p. 42).

Palestine Archaeological Museum, 34.133. Tell ed-Duweir, tomb 119, no. 1504, excavation of 1933. Bronze. Diameter at widest points: 0.226 m. Iron II (ninth-early sixth centuries). J. L. Starkey, *PEFQS*, October 1933, pl. 8, p. 198. O. Tufnell, *Lachish III*, London, 1953, pl. 39, no. 1, pp. 98, 387. Photograph courtesy of PAM.

176. At the bottom is a curved sword (see Galling, *BR*, col. 474 for other examples); above it are two daggers (see Galling, *BR*, cols. 133-134 for examples); above to right, are two spearheads (Galling, *BR*, col. 354); in addition are shown arrowheads (Galling, *BR*, col. 418) and a small piece of an armor (Galling, *BR*, col. 417).

Palestine Archaeological Museum. See references cited above; H. Bonnet, *Die Waffen der Völker des alten Orients*, Leipzig, 1926; W. Wolf, *Die Bewaffnung des altägyptischen Heeres*, Leipzig, 1926. Photograph courtesy PAM.

177. This relief, found in 1851 to the east of the Dead Sea, has been variously interpreted as a god, a warrior, or a king. It shows a figure clothed only in a short kilt held by a belt at the waist and holding a spear with the point downward.

Louvre, AO 5055. Rujm el-'Abd (between Dhiban and Shihan). Basalt. Height: 1.03 m.; width: 0.58 m. Contenau, *Man.*, vol. 1, fig. 123. AOB, 617. R. Dussaud, *Les monuments palestiniens et judaïques*, Paris, 1912, no. 1, p. 3. Photograph Archives Photographiques.

178. A bronze ceremonial axehead in the form of an open hand with outstretched thumb and fingers. Four ridges run from the finger tips to the curved blade. See axe held by figure from the gate at Boghazköy, No. 38.

Palestine Archaeological Museum, 36.1662. Beth-shan, upper altar room (1068). Bronze. Length: 0.205 m. "Amenophis III" = VII city-level (thirteenth century). A. Rowe, *The Topography and History of Beth-shan*, Philadelphia, 1930, pl. 35, no. 2. A.

Rowe, *The Four Canaanite Temples of Beth-shan*, Philadelphia, 1940, pls. 32, no. 2; 49A, no. 5. Photograph courtesy PAM.

Egypt

179. Nubian bowmen, arranged in four columns of ten each (only partly shown here), are represented as marching. Each figure carries a bow in the left hand and a bunch of arrows in his right; each is clothed in a short skirt, from the front of which hangs a piece of material with diamond design. The skin is painted dark brown and the hair black.

Cairo Museum, 257. Siut. Wood. Length: 1.93 m. Middle Kingdom (2050-1800). L. Borchardt, *Statuen und Statuetten von Königen und Privatleuten im Museum von Kairo*, pt. 1, *Cat. gén.*, Berlin, 1911, no. 257, pp. 164-165. See also W. Wolf, *Die Bewaffnung des altägyptischen Heeres*, Leipzig, 1926, pp. 23-25. Photograph Archives Photographiques.

180. Forty soldiers, arranged in four rows of ten each. Each figure holds in his right hand a lance, which is about the height of the figure. The left arm holds a shield, which is painted to represent a leather covering. The soldiers wear short skirts and are represented with reddish-brown skin.

Cairo, 258. Siut. Wood. Length: 1.93 m. Middle Kingdom (2050-1800). L. Borchardt, *Statuen und Statuetten von Königen und Privatleuten im Museum von Kairo*, pt. 1, *Cat. gén.*, Berlin, 1911, no. 258, p. 165. Photograph courtesy of the Cairo Museum.

181. An iron dagger of Tut-ankh-Amon, quite bright and clean except for a few rust spots, is fitted with a gold haft and a knob of rock crystal. The front of the sheath is decorated with a feather-design terminating in the head of a jackal.

Cairo. Thebes, tomb of Tut-ankh-Amon. Tut-ankh-Amon (1361-1352). H. Carter, *The Tomb of Tut-ankh-Amen*, vol. 2, London, 1927, pl. 137B, pp. 135-136. *JEA*, vol. 28, 1942, pl. 1. Photograph courtesy of the Cairo Museum.

HUNTING AND ANIMALS

182. Above, a bearded man with long hair held by a fillet and wearing a skirt with broad belt spears a lion, which appears to be attacking him. Below, a similar figure stands with drawn bow opposite two lions, which have already been transfixed by several arrows. Behind the bowman is the head of another lion pierced with three arrows. It has been suggested that the two human figures probably represent the same person (H. A. Groenewegen-Frankfort, *Arrest and Movement*, Chicago, 1951, p. 152).

Baghdad, Iraq Museum, IM 23477. Warka, level III, but not *in situ*, expedition of 1932-33. Black basalt. Height: 0.80 m.; width: 0.57 m.; thickness: 0.37 m. Attributed to Jemdet Nasr period (around 3000) by excavators; for arguments for dating to the Uruk period see F. Basmachi, "The Lion-hunt Stela from Warka," *Sumer*, vol. 5, 1949, pp. 87-90. A. Nöldeke, Fünfter vorläufiger Bericht, *Abh. der preuss. Ak. der Wiss., Phil.-hist. Kl.*, 1933, no. 5, Berlin, 1934, pls. 12, 13, pp. 11, 12. Contenau, *Man.*, vol. 4, fig. 1075, pp. 1984-1986. Photograph courtesy of Staatliche Museen, Berlin.

183. In the inner circle of a gold plate from Ras Shamra are wild goats (cf. No. 464). The principal scene, in the outer circle, deals with hunting savage bulls and gazelles. The hunter stands in a two-wheeled chariot, with drawn bow, and with a supply of arrows in the quiver over his back. He has a long beard, clipped head, and seems to wear a long garment, over which there are two diagonally crossed bands at the chest. Three wild bulls are shown, all with prominent genitals; also in the field are two dogs and a gazelle.

Louvre. Ras Shamra, 1933. Gold. Diameter: 0.19 m. From "Ugarit Récent 2" (1450-1365, according to excavator). C. F. A. Schaeffer, *Ugaritica II*, Paris, 1949, pls. 1, 7 (drawing), pp. 3-23. *Syria*, vol. 15, 1934, pp. 124-131. Photograph Archives Photographiques.

184. King Ashurnasirpal and his driver stand in a chariot drawn by two horses (the head of a third horse is shown). Beneath the horses lies a lion (or possibly two) pierced by two arrows. Another lion, into which four arrows have already been shot, charges the chariot from behind after having been prodded on by two "beaters" armed with bows, shields, and dirks. The chariot has six-spoked wheels and crossed quivers attached to the side.

British Museum, Nimrud Gallery, 4A. Nimrud. Alabaster, Height: 0.864 m. Ashurnasirpal (883-859). E. A. W. Budge, *Assyrian Sculptures in the British Museum*, London, 1914, pl. 12, 2. A. H. Layard, *The Monuments of Nineveh*, London, 1849, pl. 10. Schäfer-Andrae, 537. Photograph J. E. Bulloz, Paris.

185. To the left, a beardless hunter draws a bow, obviously aimed at a bird, since some are represented about the tops of the trees. In the center is a small, bearded figure with bow and arrows; to the right, another hunter carries his game.

British Museum, 118829. Khorsabad. Black stone. Length: 1.78 m. Sargon II (721-705). C. J. Gadd, *The Assyrian Sculptures*, London, 1934, pl. 5, pp. 20, 65. A. H. Layard, *A Second Series of the Monuments of Nineveh*, London, 1853, pl. 32. British Museum, *Assyrian Sculptures in the British Museum from Shalmaneser III to Sennacherib*, London, 1938, pl. 31. Photograph courtesy BM.

186. Two beardless men hold with ropes a wild ass which has been captured; below, two wild asses in flight. Cf. Job 39:5 ff.

British Museum, 124882. Nineveh. Alabaster. Width: 0.863 m. Ashurbanipal (668-633). *AOB*, 180. B. Meissner, *Babylonien und Assyrien*, vol. 1, Heidelberg, 1920, pl.-fig. 51. Photograph courtesy BM.

Camels

On the subject of camels in the ancient Near East see: R. Walz, "Zum Problem des Zeitpunkts der Domestikation der altweltlichen Cameliden," *ZDMG*, vol. 101, 1951, pp. 29-51; E. D. van Buren, *The Fauna of Ancient Mesopotamia as Represented in Art*, Analecta Orientalia, vol. 18, Rome, 1939, pp. 36-37; *Orientalia*, vol. 19, 1950, pp. 251-253; *AfO*, vol. 7, 1931, pp. 7-13; C. J. Gadd, *The Stones of Assyria*, London, 1936, pp. 195-196.

187. A woman wearing a cloak, which also covers her head, and carrying a pointed vase, leads four camels.

British Museum, 118901. Nimrud, central palace, 1847. Height: 1.01 m. Tiglath-pileser III (744-727). A. H. Layard, *The Monuments of Nineveh*, London, 1849, pl. 61. H. R. Hall, *Babylonian and Assyrian Sculpture in the British Museum*, Paris and Brussels, 1928, pl. 25, 2. *AOB*, 131. C. J. Gadd, *The Stones of Assyria*, London, 1936, pl. 9, p. 155. British Museum, *Assyrian Sculptures in the British Museum from Shalmaneser III to Sennacherib*, London, 1938, pl. 21. Photograph courtesy BM.

188. Seated on a boxlike saddle tied to the one-humped camel with crosswise girths, is a driver with stick in hand. He wears his hair in a bun, which extends to the shoulders and is encompassed at the top by a fillet. Cf. Gen. 31:34.

Baltimore. Tell Halaf. Limestone, tinted red with ochre. Height: about 0.70 m. Ninth century (see No. 96). D. K. Hill, *The Fertile Crescent*, Baltimore, 1944, fig. 20, p. 22. M. von Oppenheim, *Der Tell Halaf*, Leipzig, 1931, pl. 21a. Photograph courtesy of the Walters Art Gallery.

189. To the left, is shown a cagelike net spread in the marshes and filled with birds. Hidden from sight of the birds by a blind stands the fowler, who holds with one hand the rope and with the other gives the signal to his three companions to close the trap by pulling the rope.

Sakkarah, tomb of Ka-gemni. Beginning of the Sixth Dynasty (2350-2200). Wresz., vol. 3, pl. 73A (bottom register). Photograph courtesy of Service des Antiquités, Cairo.

190. Tut-ankh-Amon, standing in his chariot with drawn bow, charges into a herd of gazelles and ostriches which are fleeing before the king's hounds. In the field is desert flora. See No. 318 for box on which this scene appears.

Cairo Museum. Thebes, tomb of Tut-ankh-Amon, box no. 21. Painting upon the right-hand side of the lid of the box. Tut-ankh-Amon (about 1361-1352). H. Carter and A. C. Mace, *The Tomb of Tut-ankh-Amen*, vol. 1, London, 1923, pl. 50, pp. 110-111. Photograph courtesy of the Metropolitan Museum of Art, New York.

MUSIC AND GAMES

For a general discussion of musical instruments, in which many of the illustrations given below are discussed, see Curt Sachs, *The History of Musical Instruments*, New York, 1940, especially pp. 67-127. Also important are the following: F. W. Galpin, *The Music of the Sumerians and their Immediate Successors, the Babylonians and Assyrians*, Cambridge, 1937; Curt Sachs, *Die Musikinstrumente des alten Ägyptens*, Berlin, 1921; M. Wegner, *Die Musikinstrumente des alten Orients*, Münster, 1950; S. B. Finesinger, "Musical Instruments in OT," *Hebrew Union College Annual*, vol. 3, Cincinnati, 1925, pp. 21-76; O. R. Sellers, "Musical Instruments of Israel," *BA*, vol. 4, 1941, pp. 33-47. H. Hickmann, "Miscellanea Musicologica," *ASAE*, vol. 49, 1949, pp. 417-449; ———, "Cymbales et crotales dans l'Égypte ancienne," *ASAE*, vol. 49, 1949, pp. 451-545; ———, "Miscellanea Musicologica," *ASAE*, vol. 48, 1948, pp. 639-663.

191. Fragment in two registers: upper, procession of four figures dressed in long robes; lower, a standing figure, behind whom is a lyre played by a seated figure.

The lyre consists of a soundboard ending in a bull's head, to which are attached two arms that extend upward and support a crossbar, which projects over the support to the right. The figure of a bull stands on the front of the soundboard and constitutes a part of the front support. The eleven strings of the lyre are plucked with both hands as the player sits behind the instrument.

Louvre. Tello. Limestone. Height: 1.25 m.; width: 0.63 m.; thickness: 0.21 m. Period of Gudea (beginning of twenty-first century). E. de Sarzec, *Découvertes en Chaldée*, Paris, 1884-1912, pl. 23. A. Parrot, *Tello*, Paris, 1948, pl. 20a, pp. 174, 176. *AOB*, 532. TEL, vol. 1, p. 246. Photograph JBP.

192. The plaque of shell inlay set in bitumen originally belonged to the end of the sound-box of a lyre. The top panel shows a bull-man wrestling with two bulls. The scene below is that of a dog, with dagger thrust in his belt, carrying a light table on which are animal heads and a joint of meat; behind him a lion walks in an upright position with a cup in his right hand and a tall, wicker-covered vase in his left. In the third register a donkey, seated on the ground, plays a lyre with eight strings and a sound-box in the form of a bull; in front of him a bear dances and a small jackal shakes a sistrum and beats a hand drum. In the lowest register stands a scorpion-man with some unidentifiable object in his left hand; following is a gazelle holding two tall tumblers, which have probably been filled from the large jar standing at the back. For discussion of the possible meanings of these scenes see C. L. Woolley, *The Royal Cemetery*, London, 1934, pp. 280-282.

University Museum, 17694. Ur, grave PG/789. Shell and bitumen. Height: about 0.22 m. Early Dynastic III, twenty-fifth century. C. L. Woolley, *The Royal Cemetery*, London, 1934, pl. 105, pp. 280-282. Photograph courtesy UM.

193. This reconstructed lyre consists of a sound-box, ending in a gold head of a bearded bull, to which are attached two uprights sheathed with bands of mosaic in shell, lapis, and red limestone, separated by bands of sheet gold. Attached to the uprights is a crossbar, half of which consists of a silver tube. The strings were probably fixed at the bottom of the sound-box, where there is a break in the design of the mosaic border, and then attached to the crossbar at the top. It is also likely that there was a bridge over which the strings passed at the middle of the side of the sound-box.

Baghdad, Iraq Museum, 8694. Ur, PG/1237. Shell, lapis, red limestone, gold, and wood (destroyed). Height: 1.20 m. Early Dynastic III, twenty-fifth century. C. L. Woolley, *The Royal Cemetery*, London, 1934, pl. 114, pp. 252-253. Photograph courtesy of the University Museum.

194. These four bone pipes were found in levels XII-XV at Gawra. The example to the right is complete and has four holes or stops bored into it. All the specimens bear incised chevrons on the flat lower surface, possibly to afford a grip for the thumbs.

University Museum (three to left) and Baghdad, Iraq Museum (example to the right). Gawra, levels XII-XV. Bone.

Length of example to right: 0.165 m. Obeid period (fourth millennium). A. J. Tobler, *Excavations at Tepe Gawra*, vol. 2, Philadelphia, 1950, pl. 99d, p. 215. Photograph courtesy UM.

195. A crudely modeled figurine of a nude woman playing a double pipe. The pipes could have been blown through a reed (Curt Sachs, *The History of Musical Instruments*, New York, 1940, p. 72); if they were so used, the instrument was an oboe or clarinet.

University Museum. Nippur. Clay. Height: 0.103 m. L. Legrain, *Terra-Cottas from Nippur, PBS*, XVI, Philadelphia, 1930, no. 88. Photograph courtesy UM.

196. A god, characterized by a bow and quiver with long tassel, holds a bough over his shoulder. At the left are two deities with clasped hands, the one to the left holding a weapon with curved blade surmounted by the head of a feline or a snake. To the right are two musicians, one with a harp, the other with percussion instruments.

New York, private collection. Gray marble. Height: 0.034 m. Akkadian period (about 2360-2180). Photograph JBP.

197. Two harpists form part of a procession leading up to a figure holding a staff in the form of a tree-branch. The first figure plays a horizontal arched harp of seven strings; the second figure plays a similar harp with five strings.

Oriental Institute. Bismaya. Steatite, with marble inlay on skirt of man to left. From vase with vertical walls, approximately 0.22 m. in diameter. Early Dynastic I (early third millennium). For date see H. Frankfort, *OIC*, 20, Chicago, 1936, pp. 68-71. E. J. Banks, *Bismya*, New York, 1912, p. 268. José Pijoán, *Summa Artis*, vol. 2, Madrid, 1931, fig. 39. *Mitteilungen der vorderasiatisch-ägyptischen Gesellschaft*, vol. 22, 1917, p. 392, figs. 26-27 (drawing). Photograph courtesy of the Oriental Institute.

198. Fragments of silver pipes found at Ur. On a fragment at the bottom can be seen four equidistant finger holes. For the probable use of these pipes see No. 195.

University Museum, CBS 17554. Ur, grave PG/333. Silver. Total length of tubing found: 0.408 m.; finger holes placed at intervals of 0.025 m. Early Dynastic III, twenty-fifth century. L. Legrain, *The Babylonian Collections of the University Museum*, Philadelphia, 1944, fig. 14. C. L. Woolley, *The Royal Cemetery*, London, 1934, pp. 258-259, fig. 68. Photograph courtesy UM.

199. Four musicians are dressed similarly, each in a long, fringed robe reaching to the bare feet and confined at the waist by a broad belt, from which hang three-pronged tassels; the first and third wear their hair long and curled in spiral locks, the second and fourth are represented with straight hair hanging to the shoulders; all are full-bearded with a mustache. The first plays with his right hand a twelve-stringed lyre; the second holds a plectrum in his right hand and a six-stringed lyre in his left; the third and fourth figures play upon the hand drum.

Istanbul, Museum of the Ancient Orient, 7723. Zinjirli. Dolerite. Height: 1.13 m. About eighth century (Bossert). F. von Luschan, *Ausgrabungen in Sendschirli*, vol. 4, Berlin, 1911, pl.

62, pp. 355-356. Bossert, *Altanatolien*, 949. Schäfer-Andrae, 596, 2. Photograph JBP.

200. To the right, a bearded man, dressed in a short skirt, dances to the music of three musicians. A small figure beats two clappers; the figure in the center plays upon a double pipe; the third musician plays upon a lute attached to his left wrist by a strap, from which hang two long tassels.

Ankara, 119. Carchemish. Limestone. Height: 1.12 m.; width: 1.50 m. Ninth-eighth century (?). C. L. Woolley, *Carchemish, Part II*, London, 1921, pl. B 17b. Photograph courtesy of the British Museum.

201. To the left, a man blows upon a curved horn; to the right, a drum is carried by one man as two musicians beat upon it with their open hands. The man to the right seems to have about his neck a strap which helps to support the drum.

Ankara, 141; British Museum, 117810. Carchemish. Basalt. Height: 0.90 m.; width: 1.30 m. Ninth-eighth century (?). C. L. Woolley, *Carchemish, Part II*, London, 1921, pl. B 18b. Photograph courtesy of the British Museum.

202. Four musicians occupy part of the second register of a four-register scene, which in other registers deals with military activity. This association suggests a military band. The musicians are dressed in long, fringed garments which extend to their bare feet; they are full-bearded with a mustache, and their hair is done in ringlet curls. One plays upon a hand drum; another beats cymbals; the man to the right plays with both hands upon an eight-stringed lyre with curved upright supports; the remaining musician plays a rectangular lyre of five strings.

Louvre. Kuyunjik. Gypseous alabaster. Height of register of musicians: about 0.37 m. Ashurbanipal (668-633). E. Pottier, *Catalogue des antiquités assyriennes*, Paris, 1924, no. 66. TEL, vol. 2, p. 16. Photograph Archives Photographiques.

203. Three musicians form a part of a procession of women advancing to worship an enthroned goddess. The first plays double pipes (see No. 195); the second, the hand drum or tambourine; the third, of which only a part remains, plays a kind of zither, having ten strings on a rectangular frame. Curt Sachs (*The History of Musical Instruments*, New York, 1940, p. 118) suggests identification with the biblical *'asor* "ten-stringed instrument."

British Museum, 118179. Nimrud. Ivory. Height: 0.064 m. R. D. Barnett, "The Nimrud Ivories and the Art of the Phoenicians," *Iraq*, vol. 2, 1935, pl. 26, 1, p. 189. Photograph courtesy BM.

204. Procession of Elamite musicians (middle register) is a part of a larger scene describing Ashurbanipal's defeat of Teumman, king of Elam (*ANET*, 451). The musicians play in celebration of the subsequent enthronement of the Elamite refugee prince Ummanigash. In procession, from left to right, are: six figures—four with harps, one with a double pipe, and another with a hand drum—followed by six women and nine children, who are clapping their hands and probably singing. Upper register: the town of Madaktu, with its palm trees and well-planned streets, surrounded by water. Lower register: a river filled with dead soldiers, horses, parts of chariots, bows, quivers, and fish.

British Museum, Kuyunjik Gallery 50. Kuyunjik, southwest palace. Limestone. Ashurbanipal (668-633). A. H. Layard, *A Second Series of the Monuments of Nineveh*, London, 1853, pl. 49 (pls. 45-48 belong to same scene). A. Paterson, *Palace of Sinacherib*, The Hague, pl. 66. C. J. Gadd, *The Assyrian Sculptures*, London, 1934, pl. 17, p. 71. *AOB*, 152. Photograph courtesy BM.

205. Three captive lyrists conducted through a mountainous area by an Assyrian soldier armed with a club and a bow slung over his shoulder. The barefoot captives have short beards and are dressed in simple long garments. Two of the men wear caps; one is bareheaded. Note the similarity between these figures and those depicted in the siege of Lachish (No. 371).

British Museum, 124947. Kuyunjik, palace of Sennacherib, 1853. Alabaster. Sennacherib (704-681). C. J. Gadd, *The Stones of Assyria*, London, 1936, pl. 20, p. 176. *AOB*, 151. Photograph courtesy BM.

206. Egyptian oblique lyre consists of a sound-box (restored), two arms of unequal length, and a crossbar, to which the six strings (restored) are attached.

New York, Metropolitan Museum of Art, 16.10.504. Thebes, Asasif, excavation of 1915-1916. Wood, bronze staple. Length of crossbar: 0.313 m. Eighteenth Dynasty (1550-1350). H. E. Winlock, *The Rise and Fall of the Middle Kingdom in Thebes*, New York, 1947, pl. 32 (left). N. E. Scott, *The Home Life of the Ancient Egyptians*, New York, 1947, fig. 35. Photograph courtesy MMA.

207. A twelve-stringed harp, consisting of a stem ending in a human head and a sound-box (restored). Some missing pegs, the tailpiece, and strings are new.

New York, Metropolitan Museum of Art, 43.2.1. Purchased. Wood. Total length, taken diagonally: 0.82 m. Eighteenth-Nineteenth Dynasty (1550-1200). N. E. Scott, *The Home Life of the Ancient Egyptians*, New York, 1947, fig. 35. Photograph courtesy MMA.

208. The leader of the band plays upon a harp, the lower part of which is covered with a leopard skin. The lutist who follows is nude, except for ornaments. Behind her is a small girl, who dances with clenched fists. The player of the double pipes is clothed in a transparent linen garment. The last figure plays with a plectrum upon a seven-stringed lyre. The first and last figures are clothed in long white garments and wear unguent cones on their heads.

Thebes, tomb 38, back wall of hall, right-hand portion. Painting by N. M. Davies of tomb painting. Height: 0.39 m. Thutmose IV (1421-1413). N. M. Davies and A. H. Gardiner, *Ancient Egyptian Paintings*, Chicago, 1936, pl. 37. Wresz., vol. 1, pl. 144. Porter and Moss, *Bibliography*, vol. 1, p. 72 (5). Photograph courtesy of the Metropolitan Museum of Art, New York.

209. Two nude girls dance to the music made by seated women. The first plays upon double pipes; the second

and fourth clap their hands to mark the rhythm; the third woman may be a singer, although her mouth is closed. The musicians wear unguent cones on their heads. To the right of the dancers are wine jars arranged in two tiers, festooned with vines and bunches of leaves.

British Museum, 37984. Tomb at Thebes. Wall painting. Height of register: about 0.30 m. Thut-mose IV (1421-1413) or Amen-hotep III (1413-1377). N. M. Davies and A. H. Gardiner, *Ancient Egyptian Paintings*, Chicago, 1936, pl. 70 (lower register only). Curt Sachs, *Die Musikinstrumente des alten Ägyptens*, Berlin, 1921, fig. 10 (lower register only). British Museum, *Wall Decorations of Egyptian Tombs*, London, 1914, pl. 4. Photograph courtesy BM.

210. In the lower register are male dancers arranged in pairs. A man of each couple clasps hands with the other. In the middle register are represented female dancers, who hold their hands over their heads. Each has a long pigtail hanging down the back and ending in a ball.

Sakkarah, tomb of Mereru-ka, chamber A 10, east wall, scene 2. Limestone. Height of the three registers: about 1.12 m. Reign of Teti, Sixth Dynasty (2350-2200). The Sakkarah Expedition, *The Mastaba of Mereruka*, pt. 1, *OIP*, 31, Chicago, 1938, pl. 86 (right half). Photograph courtesy of the Oriental Institute.

211. To the left, women clad in transparent garments dance and beat hand drums; in the center, two nude girls keep time with clappers as they dance; to the right, three rows of men march with upraised arms.

Cairo Museum. Sakkarah, tomb of Khai. Limestone. Height: about 0.40 m. Eighteenth or Nineteenth Dynasty (1550-1200). *ASAE*, vol. 49, 1949, p. 531, fig. 51 where H. Hickmann dates to Twenty-second Dynasty. Wresz., vol. 1, 419. Schäfer-Andrae, 397, 2. Curt Sachs, *Die Musikinstrumente des alten Ägyptens*, Berlin, 1921, fig. 5. Photograph Foto Marburg.

212. The game board was originally hollowed to contain the playing pieces. It consists of two rectangular parts of unequal size, joined by a bridge. Also shown are 14 roundels: 7 of black shale inlaid with 5 white shell spots; 7 of shell inlaid with 5 lapis spots.

British Museum, 120834. Ur, grave PG/513. Shell, bone, red limestone, strips of lapis, set in bitumen. Length of board: 0.27 m.; diameter of roundels: 0.022 m. Early Dynastic III, twenty-fifth century. C. L. Woolley, *The Royal Cemetery*, London, 1934, pl. 95b, p. 276. See also: E. D. van Buren, "A Gaming-Board from Tall Halaf," *Iraq*, vol. 4, 1937, pp. 11-15. Photograph courtesy BM.

213. An elaborate game board made of ivory and ebony veneer, found with ten carved ivory pins, with heads of dogs and jackals; the pins were moved up and down the board according to the cast of knucklebones.

New York, Metropolitan Museum of Art, 26.7.1287. Thebes, tomb of Ren-seneb, 1910. Ivory and ebony veneer; ivory playing pieces. Length: 0.152 m.; height: 0.063 m. Twelfth Dynasty (1990-1780). Earl of Carnarvon and H. Carter, *Five Years' Explorations at Thebes*, London, 1912, pl. 50, 1-2, pp. 56-59, fig. 14. See also: C. J. Gadd, "An Egyptian Game in Assyria," *Iraq*, vol. 1, 1934, pp. 45-50. Photograph courtesy MMA.

214. A game board, an ivory teetotum pierced on four sides with varying number of holes, ranging from one

to four; and ten playing pieces, five in the form of a cone, and five tetrahedra, all of blue faïence. For a discussion of the use of these objects, see W. F. Albright, *Mizraim*, vol. 1, 1933, pp. 130-134.

Palestine Archaeological Museum, 33.1856 for the board; and Tell Beit Mirsim, D palace for the pieces. Height of teetotum: 0.017 m.; length of board: 0.23 m. Teetotum and playing pieces, MB II (1800-1500). W. F. Albright, *The Excavation of Tell Beit Mirsim, Vol. II, The Bronze Age, AASOR*, vol. 17, New Haven, 1938, pl. 20b, pp. 48-49 (where appear many references to analogous material). Photograph courtesy PAM.

215. An ivory game board for the "game of fifty-eight holes," with center inlaid with gold and blue paste. Every fifth hole is inlaid with a medallion of gold filled with leaves of blue paste. Back of the board is plain.

Oriental Institute, A 22254. Megiddo. Ivory. Length: about 0.27 m. Dated to 1350-1150 by excavators. G. Loud, *The Megiddo Ivories, OIP*, 52, Chicago, 1939, pl. 48. Photograph courtesy of the Oriental Institute.

216. In this register of a tomb relief are shown girls, nude (all but one) with hair braided into a pigtail which ends in a ball, dancing or playing games. Four of the figures hold mirrors and two also hold objects which end in a hand.

Sakkarah, tomb of Mereru-ka. Limestone. Height of the register: about 0.37 m. Reign of Teti, Sixth Dynasty (2350-2200). The Sakkarah Expedition, *The Mastaba of Mereruka*, pt. 2, *OIP*, 39, Chicago, 1938, pl. 165 (top). Photograph courtesy of the Oriental Institute.

217. In the upper register nude boys with hair braided into pigtails engage in a kind of tug of war; to the right, three boys run toward two others who are seated on the ground with arms and feet extended before them (*BMFA*, vol. 35, August 1937, pp. 54-55). Below, boys are playing a game with two types of objects which are carried in the right hand: a stick which ends in a hand and another which ends as a feather.

Sakkarah, tomb of Mereru-ka. Limestone. Height of the two registers: about 0.74 m. Reign of Teti, Sixth Dynasty (2350-2200). The Sakkarah Expedition, *The Mastaba of Mereruka*, pt. 2, *OIP*, 39, Chicago, 1938, pl. 163. Photograph courtesy of the Oriental Institute.

218. Three groups of two contestants each may represent successive phases of a single combat or two groups of wrestlers (to the left) and a boxing bout (to the right). To the extreme left, one contestant, who stands firmly on the ground, grasps his opponent by the ankle and lifts his foot from the ground.

Baghdad, Iraq Museum (cast in University Museum, 37-15-101). Khafajah. Limestone. Height: 0.135 m.; length: 0.245 m. Early Dynastic II-IIIa (first half of third millennium). H. Frankfort, *More Sculpture from the Diyala Region, OIP*, 60, Chicago, 1934, pl. 62, no. 313. Photograph courtesy of the University Museum.

219. Two figures wrestle, nude except for a belt, with what appear to be large jars upon their heads.

Baghdad, Iraq Museum (cast in University Museum, 37-15-100). Khafajah, Nintu Temple VI. Bronze. Height: about 0.11

m. Early Dynastic (first part of third millennium). P. Delougaz and S. Lloyd, *Pre-Sargonid Temples in the Diyala Region, OIP*, 58, Chicago, 1942, fig. 77, C. H. Gordon, "Belt-Wrestling in the Bible World," *Hebrew Union College Annual*, vol. 23, pt. 1, Cincinnati, 1950-1951, pp. 131-136. Photograph courtesy of E. A. Speiser.

MISCELLANEOUS

220. Carving of a young deer on a piece of long bone, which was probably used as a sickle haft. The object has the high glaze or polish observed on bone points which have been in contact with fire. Although this object was found in a disturbed area, it is dated by the excavators to the Lower Natufian period.

Palestine Archaeological Museum, I.1727. Mugharet el-Wad, layer B 2, found in sounding made by Lambert in 1928. Bone. Height: about 0.107 m. Lower Natufian. D. A. E. Garrod and D. M. A. Bate, *The Stone Age of Mount Carmel: Excavations at the Wady el-Mughara*, vol. 1, Oxford, 1937, pl. 13, 3, pp. 38-39. Photograph courtesy PAM.

221. This clay head was originally a part of a group of three human figures—a man, a woman, and a child. The hair and beard are represented by reddish-brown lines; the eyes are fashioned of shells.

Palestine Archaeological Museum, 35.3289/1. Jericho, area 195, elev. 6.59-6.36, excavation of 1934-1935. Clay, unbaked. Height: 0.203 m. Neolithic period. J. Garstang, "Jericho: City and Necropolis, Fifth Report," *AAA*, vol. 22, 1935, pl. 53, pp. 166-167. Photograph courtesy PAM.

222. A recurring subject of seal engraving from Syria is the nude female figure lifting the ends of her veil and displaying her nudity (for discussion of the role of the figure see E. Porada in *Corpus*, pp. 124-125). In the center is a worshiper holding a hare by the hind leg before a seated figure with a stirrup-handle cup. Also shown in the scene are three vultures along the upper border, a fish, a sitting antelope above two small female figures, star, and sun-disc in crescent.

New York, Pierpont Morgan Library. Hematite. Height: 0.021 m.; diameter: 0.010 m. About 1600-1350 (Porada's date). *Corpus*, no. 937. Photograph courtesy PML.

223. The figure with an oval headgear is frequently represented on cylinder seals and in statuary (see No. 452). For suggestion that the portrayal is of a royal person see E. Porada, *Corpus*, p. 126. The pair of central figures wear mantles with fringed borders and striped undergarments. Between the two is an altar topped by a jug, over which is a star-disc in a crescent. To the right stands a female figure holding a falcon (?) above a triple-ringed cup and Egyptian *ankh* sign. Also shown, under a guilloche, is a goddess with Egyptian sacred ram's horns facing a seated figure with cup; between is a scorpion.

New York, Pierpont Morgan Library. Hematite. Height: 0.020 m.; diameter: 0.011 m. Middle of second millennium. *Corpus*, no. 950. Photograph courtesy PML.

224. A figure with the oval headgear stands before a partly veiled nude female, who holds a jug before a god with spiked helmet. The latter holds an axe and a curved weapon, and brandishes a mace as he vaults three mountains. For suggestion that this figure represents the weather-god see E. Porada, *Corpus*, p. 129. To the left of the nude female figure are a bull's head, hand, and triple-ringed vase; at the right, a bird, a vase, and a monkey. Beside the curved weapon of the god is a hand; below his pigtail is a ringed vase. Also shown are two seated figures filling cups out of streams flowing from a vase on a stand between them, a guilloche, and three walking figures. The seal is Syrian.

New York, Pierpont Morgan Library. Hematite. Height: 0.020 m.; diameter: 0.015 m. Perhaps middle of second millennium. *Corpus*, no. 968. Photograph courtesy PML.

225. One hundred and twenty silver staters of Ozbaal, king of Byblos, were found in the course of the excavations of M. Dunand. On the obverse is a Phoenician galley with lion-headed prow; within are three soldiers, wearing helmets with streamers, and armed with round shields. Below, is a sea horse, a conch, and the letters *ʿz* in the Phoenician script. On the reverse there is a lion seizing a bull and the inscription *ʿzbʿl mlk gbl* "Ozbaal, king of Byblos."

From Byblos. Silver. Fourth century. M. Dunand, *Fouilles de Byblos, 1926-1932*, Paris, 1939, p. 407, pl. 92, nos. 2, 4. See G. F. Hill, *Catalogue of the Greek Coins of Phoenicia*, London, 1910, pp. 94-96. Photograph from M. Dunand, *Fouilles de Byblos, 1926-1932*, Paris, 1939, pl. 92, nos. 2, 4.

226. Reverse of coin on which is a bearded male figure seated on a winged wheel. His right hand is wrapped in his garment; his left holds a hawk. Above the figure is what was once read as *yhw* "Yahu," but taken by Sukenik (*JPOS*, vol. 14, 1934, pp. 178-184) as *yhd* "Judaea."

British Museum. Silver. Diameter: 0.015 m.; weight: 3.29 gr. About fourth century. G. F. Hill, *Catalogue of the Greek Coins of Palestine*, London, 1914, pl. 19, no. 29, pp. lxxxvi-lxxxviii, 181. E. L. Sukenik, *JPOS*, vol. 14, 1934, pp. 178-184, pl. 1. Photograph from *JPOS*, vol. 14, 1934, pl. 1.

227. Before a well executed owl are the archaic Hebrew letters *yḥzqyh* "Hezekiah." Behind the owl is another group of letters, which Albright reads as *yhwḥn* [*n*].

Palestine Archaeological Museum. Beth-zur. Silver. Diameter: 0.007 m.; weight: 0.21 grm. Obverse blank. Late fourth century. O. R. Sellers, *The Citadel of Beth-zur*, Philadelphia, 1933, fig. 72, pp. 73-74. Photographs from E. L. Sukenik, *JPOS*, vol. 14, 1934, pl. 1, fig. 2; p. 180, fig. 2.

228. In upper register, a dog and a lion, each standing on his two hind legs, oppose each other; below, a dog bites the rump of a standing lion. In each representation the lion has a star on its shoulder.

Palestine Archaeological Museum, I.3861. Beisan excavation, 1928. Basalt. Height: 0.92 m.; width: 0.72 m.; thickness: 0.23 m. City-level IX (fourteenth century). A. Rowe, *The Topography and History of Beth-shan*, Philadelphia, 1930, frontispiece and p. 16. For rosettes on lions see H. Kantor, *JNES*, vol. 6, 1947, pp. 250 ff. See W. F. Albright, *JPOS*, vol. 16, 1936, p. 54, for opinion that slab belongs to sixteenth-fourteenth centuries. Photograph courtesy PAM.

III. Writing

Written documents comprise the most important single class of monuments which have survived from the ancient Near East. From the hundreds of thousands of documents which are now known a few have been chosen to illustrate such features as materials on which writing was done, types and sizes of objects, the various scripts which were employed, and other details which should help to visualize the documents that lie behind the translations available in modern languages. Other documents have been included because of the prominent part they have had either in the decipherment of a script or in the recovery of the history of the ancient Near East. A few illustrations have been given of scribes and of the equipment which they used. The bibliography found in I. J. Gelb, *A Study of Writing*, Chicago, 1952, pp. 254-264, lists some of the more recent literature on the subject of writing. Mention should be made also of G. R. Driver, *Semitic Writing*, London, 1948, which is concerned with the origins and developments of cuneiform and alphabetic writing; J. G. Février, *Histoire de l'écriture*, Paris, 1948; and H. Jensen, *Die Schrift in Vergangenheit und Gegenwart*, Glückstadt and Hamburg, 1935. For a popular account of the beginnings of writing in Mesopotamia, see E. Chiera, *They Wrote on Clay*, Chicago, 1938, pp. 50-66. A. Falkenstein, *Archaische Texte aus Uruk*, Leipzig, 1936, pp. 5-36, contains a detailed discussion of the early stages of writing in Mesopotamia. A recent standard work on the alphabet is D. Diringer, *L'alfabeto nella storia della civiltà*, Florence, 1937; English edition under title *The Alphabet, a Key to the History of Mankind*, London and New York, 1948. Further references to details peculiar to the individual illustrations are to be found in the Catalogue.

SCRIBES AND EQUIPMENT

229. A Sumerian, with shaved head and face and clothed only in a heavy skirt covered with tufts or tassels, is seated with folded hands upon a chair with curved seat. Upon his bare back is incised an inscription: "(To) the god Ningirsu, Dudu, the scribe, two (?) Imduguds has presented."

Baghdad. Thought to have come from Lagash. Black volcanic stone. Height: about 0.39 m. Early Dynastic period, perhaps from time of Ur-Nanshe (twenty-fifth century) (see mention of "Dudu, the Banar," on Ur-Nanshe plaque (No. 427). Naji al-Asil, "Dudu, the Sumerian Scribe," and Fuad Safar, "The Identification of Dudu," *Sumer*, vol. 5, 1949, pp. 131-135. Photograph courtesy of the Iraq Museum.

230. An Egyptian scribe, clothed in a short skirt, sits holding a partly opened roll of papyrus. He is shaved and wears his black hair closely cropped. The skin is painted reddish-brown; the skirt and the papyrus are white. The eyes are inlaid with white opaque quartz, crystal, and ebony wood.

Louvre. Sakkarah. Painted limestone. Height: 0.53 m. Fifth Dynasty (2500-2350). TEL, vol. 1, p. 29. Schäfer-Andrae, 237. G. Maspero, Fondation Piot, vol. 1, 1894, pl. 1, pp. 1-6. J. Capart, *JEA*, vol. 7, 1921, pp. 186-190. Photograph TEL.

231. In a columned hall, scribes sit and record evidence, as village headmen are brought before local tax officials for nonpayment of taxes.

Sakkarah, tomb of Mereru-ka, chamber A 4, west wall, scene 1. Limestone. Height of register: about 0.32 m. Reign of Teti,

Sixth Dynasty (2350-2200). The Sakkarah Expedition, *The Mastaba of Mereruka*, pt. 1, *OIP*, 31, Chicago, 1938, pl. 36. Photograph courtesy of the Oriental Institute.

232. Four seated scribes, each writing with a sharpened rush which served as a pen. Two additional pens are stuck behind the ear of each scribe. Three of the palettes are in the shape of a mussel shell; the fourth is rectangular in shape.

Giza, mastaba of Ka-ni-nesut, son of Snefru. Fourth Dynasty (2650-2500). H. Junker, *Giza*, vol. 2, Vienna and Leipzig, 1934, pl. 7b, fig. 19 (drawing). Photograph from publication, courtesy of Österreichische Akademie der Wissenschaften, Vienna.

233. Palette, equipped with sharpened rushes which served as pens, is inscribed with the name of Ah-mose I, (1570-1545). At the end is a circular hollow to hold ink or paint.

British Museum, 12784. Wood. Length: 0.285 m. Eighteenth Dynasty (1550-1350). British Museum, *A General Introductory Guide to the Egyptian Collections in the British Museum*, London, 1930, fig. 21. Photograph courtesy BM.

234. A palette with two circular hollows attached to a writing reed and a water jar by means of a thong (palette only is original; remainder reconstructed). This combination of writing equipment is a hieroglyph for *sash* "scribe, writing." See it repeated four times on No. 232. A wooden relief in the Cairo Museum shows a scribe with this equipment over his shoulder (L. Klebs, *Die Reliefs des alten Reiches*, Heidelberg, 1915, p. 7, fig. 4.).

Oriental Institute, 11069. Palette: slate. Length of palette: 0.071 m. J. A. Wilson, *The Burden of Egypt*, Chicago, 1951, fig. 4c. See also: A. Lucas, *Ancient Egyptian Materials and Industries*, 3rd ed., London, 1948, pp. 413-419 (for ink, pigments, palettes, etc.). Photograph courtesy of the Oriental Institute.

235. To the right, a bearded Assyrian scribe holds a tablet in his left hand and impresses it with a stylus held awkwardly—as it would seem to us—between the first finger and the thumb and with the four fingers closed over it. (See G. R. Driver, *Semitic Writing*, London, 1948, pp. 22-23 for discussion of the way in which the stylus was held and the suspicion that the awkwardness in representation is due to the artist's lack of skill.) The figure to the left is writing with a brush on a piece of skin or papyrus and is probably intended to represent a scribe writing in Aramaic. See also No. 367.

Tell 'Ahmar, ancient Til-Barsib. Wall painting, now destroyed. Height of register: about 1.40 m. Perhaps early eighth century, or even to reign of Adad-nirari III (810-783). F. Thureau-Dangin and M. Dunand, *Til-Barsib*, Paris, 1936, pl. 50, pp. 54-56. See also: L. Messerschmidt, "Zur Technik Tontafel-Schreibens," *Orientalistische Literaturzeitung*, vol. 9, 1906, cols. 185-196, 304-312, 372-380, esp. col. 187 for other examples then known of the two scribes; D. Opitz, "Die älteste Darstellung des Schreibens in Babylonien," *AfO*, vol. 6, 1930, pp. 63-64; E. Unger, *Babylonisches Schrifttum*, Leipzig, 1921, pp. 8-9 for list of Assyrian monuments depicting scribes. Photograph from publication by F. Thureau-Dangin and M. Dunand, courtesy of Librairie Orientaliste Paul Geuthner, Paris.

236. Toward the right of this part of a register, which shows the booty taken from a captured town in southern Babylonia, stand two scribes, evidently listing the booty and the slain, represented by a pile of heads before them. The nearer one, like the scribe to the left in No. 235, is beardless, and holds a piece of writing material of papyrus or skin in one hand and a brush or pen in the other. The second scribe, the one only partly visible, wears a full beard and holds what may be a clay tablet.

British Museum, 124955. Kuyunjik. Gypsum. Height of register: about 0.75 m. Sennacherib (704-681). A. Paterson, *Palace of Sinacherib*, The Hague, pls. 53-56. Photograph from A. H. Layard, *A Second Series of the Monuments of Nineveh*, London, 1853, pl. 35.

CUNEIFORM

237. The stamp seals, shown here interspersed with beads, have an engraved sealing surface, which when pressed on pliable material left an impression that was the distinctive mark of its owner or that had some magical property. Stamp seals were employed from the beginning of civilization in the Near East, but were supplanted at about the end of the fourth millennium by the cylinder seal. In other parts of the Near East, however, the stamp seal continued as the common seal form, regaining its popularity in Mesopotamia in the seventh century.

Oriental Institute and Baghdad, Iraq Museum. Tell Asmar, shrine I of Square Temple, level 1. Smaller diameter of necklace: about 0.20 m. P. Delougaz and S. Lloyd, *Pre-Sargonid Temples in the Diyala Region*, *OIP*, 58, Chicago, 1942, fig. 142, p. 184. Photograph courtesy of the Oriental Institute.

238. Legal texts and letters were sometimes inclosed in an outer envelope, which served to protect from damage or forgery and to identify the enclosure and usually contained only an excerpt from the document. (See G. R. Driver, *Semitic Writing*, London, 1948, pp. 11-12, for references to Akkadian terminology for case tablets.) This is an affidavit before the council of Kanish.

Yale Babylonian Collection, NBC 1906. Kültepe. A. T. Clay, *Letters and Transactions from Cappadocia*, New Haven, 1927, no. 114. See E. Chiera, *They Wrote on Clay*, Chicago, 1938, pp. 69-73, for discussion of the use of the envelope. Photograph courtesy of Yale University News Bureau.

239. A record of the division of an inheritance between several heirs bears twenty-five impressions made by seven different seals belonging to the contracting parties and witnesses. On the side of the tablet shown here there are seven impressions made by three different seals. The impression in the center of the upper part of the tablet contains the hand symbol surmounted by the crescent and star in a disc and flanked by two goddesses. Traces of the same seal appear in two more impressions immediately below the clearer impression. Frankfort, *CS*, pl. 30a, reproduces two of the impressions of this tablet and the entire face in pl. 2m.

Cambridge, Mass., Harvard Semitic Museum, 109. Purchased. Clay. Height: 0.064 m. Reign of Samsu-iluna (about 1685-1647). D. G. Lyon, "The Seal Impressions on an Early Babylonian Contract," *JAOS*, vol. 27, 1906, pp. 135-141. Photograph courtesy of the Harvard Semitic Museum.

240. A group of cylinder seals from the Pierpont Morgan Library in New York illustrates the appearance of seals, which are more generally known from their impressions. See note before No. 672 for bibliography. For the view that writing grew out of the use of the cylinder seal see E. A. Speiser, "The Beginnings of Civilization in Mesopotamia," *Supplement, JAOS*, December 1939, pp. 20-21, 26. An opposing view is expressed by I. J. Gelb, *A Study of Writing*, Chicago, 1952, p. 65.

Photograph courtesy of Edith Porada.

241. This tablet, written in an essentially pictographic script, from an early period at Uruk, when the characteristic cuneiform script had not yet evolved, lists on the obverse (to the left) personal names by means of one or more signs and with each name gives a number expressed by semicircles. Each name with its number is enclosed by lines drawn on the tablet. On the reverse (to the right) is what is being recorded, in this case 54 g u d á b, "54 oxen (and) cows."

From Uruk, level IV. End of fourth millennium. A. Falkenstein, *Archaische Texte aus Uruk*, Leipzig, 1936, pl. 31, no. 339. See I. J. Gelb, *A Study of Writing*, Chicago, 1952, fig. 29 (drawing), p. 64. See M. Rutten, "Notes de paléographie cunéiforme," *Revue des études sémitique et Babyloniaca*, Paris, 1940, pp. 1-53. Photograph from publication by A. Falkenstein, courtesy of Otto Harrassowitz, Leipzig.

242. The obverse of a small tablet of black stone on which are inscribed pictographic signs; the circles indicate numbers.

University Museum, CBS 16105. Purchased. Soft, black stone. Height: 0.068 m. End of fourth millennium. G. A. Barton, *Sumerian Business and Administrative Documents from the Earliest Times to the Dynasty of Agade, PBS*, IX, 1, Philadelphia, 1915, pls. 65, 1 (drawing), pp. 9-11. See G. A. Barton, *Orientalistische Literaturzeitung*, vol. 16, 1913, cols. 6-12, for proposed translation. Photograph courtesy UM.

243. A tablet of stone, on which are listed various accounts in a script which has passed out of an essentially pictographic stage. Here the originally pictographic signs are more conventionalized in form. The inscription is that of Enhegal, king of Lagash.

University Museum, CBS 10000. Purchased. Cream-colored stone. Height: 0.124 m. Several centuries later than No. 242. G. A. Barton, *Sumerian Business and Administrative Documents from the Earliest Times to the Dynasty of Agade, PBS*, IX, 1, Philadelphia, 1915, pls. 66, 2 (drawing), pp. 11-16. Photograph courtesy UM.

244. Paragraph 196 from the reverse of the stela of Hammurabi (No. 246): "If a seignior has destroyed the eye of a member of the aristocracy, they shall destroy his eye" (*ANET*, 175). Cf. Exod. 21: 23-25; Lev. 24: 19-20; Deut. 19:21.

For description of monument see No. 246. Photograph *JBP* from cast of stela.

245. This letter from Abimilki, of Tyre, to Akh-en-Aton, king of Egypt, is one of a collection of cuneiform tablets found in 1887 at Tell el-Amarna, the capital of Akh-en-Aton in the early fourteenth century. See *ANET*, 483-490 for translations of selected Amarna tablets.

New York, Metropolitan Museum of Art, 24.2.12. Purchased in 1924. Clay. Height: 0.077 m. Akh-en-Aton (1380-1362). *BMMA*, July 1926, p. 170, fig. 2. J. A. Knudtzon, *Die El-Amarna-Tafeln*, Leipzig, 1915, no. 153. Photograph courtesy MMA.

246. The stela of Hammurabi, discovered at Susa in the winter of 1901-1902, is inscribed with prologue, 282 laws, and an epilogue (translated in *ANET*, 163-180). For a description of the relief at the top see No. 515.

Louvre. Susa. Diorite. Height: 2.25 m. Hammurabi (1728-1686). V. Scheil, *Mémoires, Délégation en Perse*, vol. 4, Paris, 1902, pl. 3 (for top), pp. 11-162. A. Deimel, *Codex Hammurabi: transscriptio et translatio Latina*, Rome, 1930. Photograph Giraudon, Paris.

247. A common form for historical records during the Assyrian empire was the prism with six, eight, or ten sides. This text, written on an octagonal prism, deals with the reconstruction of the Esharra temple of the god Ashur, which was in the capital city of Ashur.

University Museum, 32-22-5. Purchased. Clay. Height: 0.216 m. Second year of reign of Esarhaddon (680-669). F. R. Steele, "The University Museum Esarhaddon Prism," *JAOS*, vol. 71, 1951, pp. 1-12 and plate. Photograph courtesy UM.

248. A fragment of a clay tablet inscribed with the Assyrian version of Tablet XI of the Gilgamesh epic. The fragment contains lines 55-106, 108-269 (Thompson edition, "B").

British Museum, K.3375. Kuyunjik. Clay. Height: 0.146 m.; width: 0.133 m. British Museum, *A Guide to the Babylonian and Assyrian Antiquities*, London, 1922, pl. 46. Photograph courtesy BM.

249. The trilingual inscription in Old Persian, Elamite, and Akkadian, with accompanying sculptures, is cut in the living rock of a cliff about 225 feet above the road and purposely made inaccessible by those who carved the monument. To the left of the relief stands the figure of Darius, followed by two attendants, with his foot planted on the prostrate figure of Gaumata. Before the king stand nine rebels roped together, with hands tied behind their backs. Above is the figure of the god Ahuramazda. For detail of the head of Darius see No. 462.

Behistun (modern Bisitun), on main caravan route from Baghdad to Teheran. Darius (521-486). For description and bibliography of the inscription see: R. G. Kent, *Old Persian: Grammar, Texts, Lexicon*, New Haven, 1950, pp. 107-108, pl. 1 (photograph). A. T. Olmstead, "Darius and his Behistun Inscription," *AJSL*, vol. 55, 1938, pp. 392-416. Photograph courtesy of G. G. Cameron.

250. The script of the Old Persian inscriptions, a syllabary which goes back to the Akkadian cuneiform syllabary, provided the key to decipher other forms of cuneiform writing. The inscription shown here is from lines 27-35 of column II of the Darius inscription at Behistun.

Behistun (modern Bisitun). Darius (521-486). For transliteration: R. G. Kent, *Old Persian: Grammar, Texts, Lexicon*, New Haven, 1950, p. 121. Photograph courtesy of G. G. Cameron.

251. This clay stamp (with stamping surface shown to the right), is of the type used for stamping bricks used in building. Inscription (here shown in reverse): "Sharkalisharri, king of Agade, builder of the temple of Enlil." To the left is the handle side of another stamp.

University Museum, CBS 8777. Nippur. Baked clay. Height: 0.135 m. Sharkalisharri (latter part of twenty-third century). H. V. Hilprecht, "Old Babylonian Inscriptions Chiefly from Nippur," *Transactions of the American Philosophical Society*, vol. 18, NS, pt. 1, Philadelphia, 1893, pl. 3, no. 3 (for drawing of obverse). Photograph courtesy UM.

252. The stamping surface of a brick stamp inscribed (in reverse): "Naram-Sin, builder of the temple of Enlil."

University Museum, CBS 8764. Nippur. Baked clay. Height: 0.118 m. Naram-Sin (first half of twenty-third century). H. V. Hilprecht, "Old Babylonian Inscriptions Chiefly from Nippur," *Transactions of the American Philosophical Society*, vol. 18, NS, pt. 1, Philadelphia, 1893, pl. 3, no. 4. Photograph courtesy UM.

253. A building brick of clay inscribed with the name of Ishme-Dagan.

University Museum, CBS 8641, 8649, 8650. Nippur. Clay. 0.28 m. by 0.31 m. Ishme-Dagan (early nineteenth century). L. Legrain, *Royal Inscriptions and Fragments from Nippur and Babylon*, PBS, XV, Philadelphia, 1926, pl. 17, no. 46 (copy of text). Photograph courtesy UM.

254. This cylinder, inscribed with three columns of text, each containing 96 lines, was inscribed shortly after 586 by order of Nebuchadnezzar and buried in the foundation of a temple.

University Museum, CBS 9. Purchased. Clay. Height: about 0.26 m. Nebuchadnezzar (605-562). L. Legrain, *Royal Inscriptions and Fragments from Nippur and Babylon*, PBS, XV, Philadelphia, 1926, pl. 9, pp. 36-45. L. Legrain, "The Golden Boats of Marduk and Nabu in Babylon," *MJ*, vol. 14, 1923, pp. 266-281. Photograph courtesy UM.

255. Fragment of a cuneiform tablet bearing an endorsement in Aramaic: "In the first year, the document concerning the house." Cuneiform inscription is here pictured upside down.

University Museum, CBS R 5160. Nippur. Clay. 0.047 m. by 0.058 m. by 0.022 m. First year of Darius II (423-404). A. T. Clay, *Business Documents of Murashû Sons of Nippur*, BEUP, Series A, vol. 10, Philadelphia, 1904, pl. 32, no. 56, photograph reproduction, pl. 8, no. 17, p. 7, note 2. Photograph courtesy UM.

256. A clay tag with string (restored), probably made for attaching to a basket of official records or legal documents.

University Museum, CBS 7095. Clay. Early Sargonid period (about 2360-2180). L. Legrain, *Historical Fragments, PBS*, XIII, Philadelphia, 1922, no. 12, p. 47. Photograph courtesy UM.

257. A circular tablet used by an ancient schoolboy for practice in writing. The last two lines are probably clumsy copies of the first two lines, which served as a model.

University Museum, B 14215. Nippur. Clay. Diameter: about 0.07 m. Old Babylonian period (1830-1530). Photograph courtesy UM.

258. The impressions of the thumbnail on a tablet were used as marks of identification alongside, or instead of, seal impressions. Here the custom of thumbnail marking has become conventionalized in regular impressions made probably by some instrument rather than by the nail.

University Museum, JS 18. Baked clay. 0.095 m. by 0.052 m. by 0.028 m. Fifth year of reign of Kandalanu, about 642. A. T. Clay, *Legal and Commercial Transactions, BEUP*, Series A, vol. 8, pt. 1, Philadelphia, 1908, pl. 5, no. 12 top (photograph), pl. 3, p. 3. See also G. R. Driver, *Semitic Writing*, London, 1948, pp. 62-63. Photograph courtesy UM.

259. Table showing the development of the cuneiform script from original pictographs to the normal Assyrian forms of the signs.

Photograph from J. H. Breasted, *Ancient Times*, 2nd ed., Boston, 1935, fig. 86 (compiled and drawn by Arno Poebel). Also reproduced in I. J. Gelb, *A Study of Writing*, Chicago, 1952, fig. 31. Photograph courtesy of the Oriental Institute and Ginn and Co.

260. Map of Nippur with legends, showing locations of temple, walls, gates, and canals.

Present location unknown. Nippur. Clay. 0.15 m. by 0.20 m. (restored). C. S. Fisher, *The Excavations at Nippur*, vol. 1, New York, 1905, pl. 1 (left), discussion p. 12 f. Reproduced earlier in H. V. Hilprecht, *The Excavations in Assyria and Babylonia*, Philadelphia, 1904, p. 518. Photograph courtesy of the University Museum.

UGARITIC

The alphabetic script used at ancient Ugarit is illustrated by inscriptions on bronze, stone, and clay. While the bibliography of the original publication of the texts as well as of the discussions of their many problems is voluminous, mention should be made of the useful handbook of C. H. Gordon, *Ugaritic Handbook: Revised Grammar, Paradigms, Texts in Transliteration, Comprehensive Glossary*, Rome, 1947, where the material is made available in convenient form. Translations of some of the myths, epics, and legends, made by H. L. Ginsberg, are given in *ANET*, pp. 129-155. C. H. Gordon has published translations in *Ugaritic Literature*, Rome, 1949. A recent detailed bibliography of the literature on the texts from Ras Shamra is to be found in R. de Langhe, *Les textes de Ras Shamra-Ugarit et leurs rapports avec le milieu biblique de l'Ancien Testament*, vol. 1, Gemblous and Paris, 1945, pp. xv-lvii.

261. These inscribed ceremonial adzeheads belonged to a cache of 74 weapons found at Ras Shamra. Inscription on first, third, and fourth: *rb khnm* "(Belonging to) the highpriest." Inscription on the second: *ḫrṣn rb khnm* "Adze of the highpriest." See C. H. Gordon, *Ugaritic Literature*, Rome, 1949, p. 108.

Louvre. Ras Shamra. Bronze. Height: about 0.23 m. Fourteenth century. *Syria*, vol. 10, 1929, pl. 60, nos. 2, 3, 4. C. F. A. Schaeffer, *Ugaritica I*, Paris, 1939, pl. 24 (for two adzes). Photograph Archives Photographiques.

262. Broken stela inscribed in the alphabetic script of

Ugarit with a dedication to the god Dagan (cf. Judg. 16:23).

Aleppo, National Museum. Ras Shamra, 1934. Limestone. Fourteenth century. *Syria*, vol. 16, 1935, pl. 31, 2. For inscription see R. Dussaud, *Syria*, vol. 16, 1935, pp. 177-180; C. H. Gordon, *Ugaritic Literature*, Rome, 1949, p. 108. Photograph JBP.

263. The alphabet used at ancient Ugarit in the fourteenth century consisted of 30 characters which appear in the following order, an order into which the letter sequence of the 22 letters of Hebrew, as it is known from acrostic passages in the Old Testament, fits: 'a b g ḫ d h w z ḥ ṭ y k š l m ẕ n z ṣ ʿ p ṣ q r t̲ ġ t 'i 'u ś. (making use of scheme of transliteration suggested by E. A. Speiser in *BASOR*, no. 121, 1951, pp. 17-21).

Damascus Museum. Ras Shamra. Clay. Fourteenth century. C. H. Gordon, *Orientalia*, vol. 19, 1950, pp. 374-376. W. F. Albright, *BASOR*, no. 118, 1950, pp. 12-14; no. 119, 1950, pp. 23-24. Photograph of tablet courtesy of C. F. A. Schaeffer; drawing from *Orientalia*, vol. 19, 1950, p. 374.

264. The reverse of a two-column tablet containing part of the legend of Aqhat (I, cols. iii and iv = lines 107-224, *ANET*, 154-155).

Louvre, AO 17323. Ras Shamra. Fourteenth century. C. Virolleaud, *La légende phénicienne de Danel*, Paris, 1936, pl. 13. Photograph Archives Photographiques.

EGYPTIAN

In addition to the examples of Egyptian writing shown here are the many inscriptions shown on reliefs which are included in other sections of the book. For a discussion of Egyptian writing see A. H. Gardiner, *Egyptian Grammar*, 2nd ed., London, 1950, pp. 6-15, 25-28.

265. A single sheet of papyrus, on which is written a marriage contract in Aramaic. The papyrus is tied with a braided string, seemingly of linen, and sealed with a mud seal on which is a seal impression. Recto of opened papyrus has fifteen lines of text; verso, single line.

Brooklyn Museum, 47.218.89. Papyrus. Length as folded: 0.104 m.; size of sheet when opened: 0.265 m. by 0.32 m. E. G. Kraeling, ed., *The Brooklyn Museum Aramaic Papyri*, New Haven, 1953, no. 2, pl. 21 top. Photograph courtesy Br. M.

266. A section of the Theban recension of the "Book of the Dead," from a papyrus scroll 5.29 m. in length. The text of the inscription is written in cursive hieroglyphic signs (sometimes including hieratic signs) with black ink; red is used for the headings of spells and other outstanding parts. In the vignette at the top of this section is seen the owner of the papyrus roll in a boat with the sun-god and a baboon.

University Museum, E 2775. Thebes. Papyrus. Height of scroll: 0.36 m. New Kingdom (1550-1090). H. Ranke, *The Egyptian Collections of the University Museum*, Philadelphia, 1950, fig. 50. Photograph courtesy UM.

267. This fragment of a stela, found in 1799 near Rashid, or "Rosetta," contains an inscription written in two languages, Egyptian and Greek. The Greek text (at the bottom) consists of 54 lines, the last 26 being imperfect at the ends. The Egyptian text is written in demotic (middle), an abbreviated and modified form of the hieratic, and occupies 32 lines, of which the first 14 are imperfect at the beginning; and in hieroglyphs (at the top), of which 14 lines are preserved and correspond to the last 28 lines of the Greek text. The inscription, a copy of the decree of Egyptian priests assembled at Memphis in 196 B.C. to celebrate the first commemoration of the coronation of Ptolemy V, Epiphanes, king of all Egypt, is of interest for the prominent place which it has had in the decipherment of Egyptian hieroglyphs.

British Museum, 24. Rosetta. Black basalt. Length: 1.14 m. Second century. E. A. W. Budge, *The Rosetta Stone*, London, 1913, frontispiece; and in many other publications. E. A. W. Budge, *The Rosetta Stone in the British Museum*, London, 1929, for publication of texts, translations, and a short history of the decipherment of Egyptian hieroglyphs. Photograph courtesy BM.

268. Hieroglyphs carved in raised relief on a wooden panel from the tomb of Hesi-Re at Sakkarah.

Cairo Museum, 1426. Sakkarah, mastaba A3. Wood. Height of entire panel: 1.15 m. (of which about one-fourth is shown here). Fourth Dynasty (2650-2500). L. Borchardt, *Denkmäler des alten Reiches, Cat. gén.*, Berlin, 1937, pl. 25, no. 1426, p. 108. Photograph Foto Marburg.

269. Carefully painted hieroglyphs from the end board of a Twelfth Dynasty coffin found at el-Bersheh.

Boston, Museum of Fine Arts, 21.969. el-Bersheh. Wood. Height: 0.248 m. Twelfth Dynasty (1990-1780). Popular note on the discovery in *BMFA*, vol. 19, August 1921, pp. 43-46. Photograph courtesy of Museum of Fine Arts.

ALPHABETIC

270. Front of the statue of a squatting figure, on which is an inscription in the Sinaitic script containing the phrase *lbʿlt*, "for Baʿalat."

Cairo Museum. Serabit el-Khadem. Sandstone. Height of statue: 0.20 m.; width of this inscribed area: about 0.12 m. Fifteenth century (W. F. Albright, *BASOR*, no. 110, 1948, pp. 6-22). W. M. F. Petrie, *Researches in Sinai*, London, 1906, figs. 138-139. A. H. Gardiner and T. E. Peet, *The Inscriptions of Sinai*, London, 1917, pl. 82, 346. Photograph from H. Grimme, *Althebräische Inschriften vom Sinai*, Darmstadt, 1923, pl. 9 below.

271. The inscription on the blade of a dagger has been variously interpreted (see G. R. Driver, *Semitic Writing*, London, 1948, p. 198, for summary of interpretations). The four clearly incised signs exhibit some similarity to the script of the Sinai inscriptions (see No. 270).

Palestine Archaeological Museum, 34.2791. Tell ed-Duweir. Bronze. About 1500. *PEFQS*, October 1937, pl. 8, 1, pp. 239-240. A. H. Gardiner, *Antiquity*, vol. 11, 1937, pl. 12, pp. 359-360 (Hyksos date). For discussion of reading see J. Obermann, *Supplement, JAOS*, September 1938, pp. 25-33. Photograph courtesy PAM.

272. An inscription, probably a school exercise tablet, on limestone, written in verse.

Istanbul. Gezer. Limestone. Length: 0.11 m. Variously dated; W. F. Albright, *ANET*, 320: about 925. R. A. S. Macalister, *The Excavation of Gezer*, London, 1912, vol. 2, pp. 24-28; vol. 3, pl. 127. Extensive bibliography in D. Diringer, *Le iscrizioni antico-ebraiche palestinesi*, Florence, 1934, pp. 18-20. See also: S. Moscati, *L'epigrafia ebraica antica, 1935-1950*, Rome, 1951, pp. 8-26; F. M. Cross, Jr. and D. N. Freedman, *Early Hebrew Orthography*, New Haven, 1952, pp. 45-47. Translation: *ANET*, 320. Photograph from D. Diringer, *Le iscrizioni antico-ebraiche palestinesi*, Florence, 1934, pl. 1, courtesy of Felice le Monnier, Florence.

273. A ewer, reconstructed from 42 fragments, has its shoulder decorated with goats and trees, a stag, a lion, and a bird. Above is a line of signs, which are similar to the Sinai script (see No. 270), and which have been variously interpreted (see G. R. Driver, *Semitic Writing*, London, 1948, p. 199, for a summary of the interpretations). The inscription runs from left to right, and is probably a dedicatory inscription.

Palestine Archaeological Museum, 34.7738/1. Tell ed-Duweir. Pottery. Height, when reconstructed: about 0.60 m. Thirteenth century, according to excavator. O. Tufnell, C. H. Inge, L. Harding, *Lachish II*, London, 1940, frontispiece, pls. 51, no. 287; 60, fig. 3; pp. 47-54. Photograph courtesy PAM.

274. The Moabite stela was discovered in 1868 at Dhiban, in Transjordan, and later broken into pieces by Arabs; in 1873 it was taken to the Louvre. By the contents of the inscription the stela seems to date from between 840 and 820 (*ANET*, 320).

Louvre, AO 5066. Dhiban. Black basalt. Height: about 1.00 m.; width: 0.60 m. Perhaps between 840 and 820. R. Dussaud, *Les monuments palestiniens et judaïques*, Paris, 1912, pp. 4-21. F. M. Cross, Jr. and D. N. Freedman, *Early Hebrew Orthography*, New Haven, 1952, pp. 35-44, where recent bibliography is listed. *ANET*, 320-321. Photograph Archives Photographiques.

275. This inscription of six lines was discovered in 1880 in the rock wall of the lower entrance to the Siloam tunnel south of the temple area in Jerusalem. Contents and script point to a date during the reign of Hezekiah (about 715-687).

Istanbul. Jerusalem. Stone. Height: about 0.38 m.; length: about 0.72 m. Reign of Hezekiah (about 715-687). D. Diringer, *Le iscrizioni antico-ebraiche palestinesi*, Florence, 1934, pl. 11, pp. 81-102, where extensive bibliography up until 1932 is listed. For more recent references see: S. Moscati, *L'epigrafia ebraica antica, 1935-1950*, Rome, 1951, pp. 40-43; F. M. Cross, Jr. and D. N. Freedman, *Early Hebrew Orthography*, New Haven, 1952, pp. 49-51. Translation: *ANET*, 321. Photograph courtesy of S. H. Horn.

Stamp Seals

A wealth of epigraphic material is to be found on stamp seals and stamp-seal impressions which have come from Palestine. From the hundreds of seals which have been published three are reproduced here as illustrative of this type of object and of the script which was employed. The important seals and seal impressions from Palestine are published in D. Diringer, *Le iscrizioni antico-ebraiche palestinesi*, Florence, 1934, pls. 14-22, pp. 111-261, which is supplemented to 1950 by S. Moscati, *L'epigrafia ebraica antica, 1935-1950*, Rome, 1951, pls. 11-23, pp. 47-98. For a popular discussion of Hebrew seals see A. Reifenberg, *Ancient Hebrew Seals*, London, 1950. See also: D. Diringer, "The Royal Jar-Handle Stamps," *BA*, vol. 12, 1949, pp. 70-86; K. Galling, "Beschriftete Bildsiegel des ersten Jahrtausends v. Chr. vornehmlich aus Syrien und Palästina," *ZDPV*, vol. 64, 1941, pp. 121-202.

276. Seal carved with figure of roaring lion and inscription, *lšmʻ ʻbd yrbʻm* "Belonging to Shema, the servant of Jeroboam."

From Megiddo. Jasper. Diameters: 0.037 m. and 0.026 m. Eighth century, Jeroboam II (about 786-746). G. Schumacher and C. Steurnagel, *Tell el-Mutesellim*, vol. 1, Leipzig, 1908, fig. 147, pp. 99 ff. D. Diringer, *Le iscrizioni antico-ebraiche palestinesi*, Florence, 1934, pl. 21, no. 5, pp. 224-228. Photograph courtesy of A. Reifenberg.

277. Seal engraved with the figure of a fighting cock and the inscription *lyʼznyhw ʻbd hmlk* "Belonging to Jaazaniah, servant of the king." Note the mention of Jaazaniah in II Kings 25:23.

Palestine Archaeological Museum. Tell en-Nasbeh. Onyx. Diameters: 0.019 m. and 0.018 m. About 600. C. C. McCown, *Tell en-Naṣbeh*, vol. 1, Berkeley, 1947, pl. 57, 4 and 5, p. 163. D. Diringer, *Le iscrizioni antico-ebraiche palestinesi*, Florence, 1934, pl. 21, 6, pp. 229-231. More recent bibliography given in S. Moscati, *L'epigrafia ebraica antica, 1935-1950*, Rome, 1951, p. 70. Photograph from C. C. McCown, *Tell en-Naṣbeh*, vol. 1, pl. 57, 4, courtesy of the Palestine Institute of the Pacific School of Religion.

278. Impression made on a jar handle by a seal inscribed *lʼlyqm nʻr ywkn*, "Belonging to Eliakim steward of Joiachin."

Palestine Archaeological Museum. Tell Beit Mirsim. Largest diameter: about 0.016 m. Sixth century (by excavator). W. F. Albright, *The Excavation of Tell Beit Mirsim*, vol. 1, *AASOR*, 12, New Haven, 1932, par. 101 (p. 78), fig. 13. D. Diringer, *Le iscrizioni antico-ebraiche palestinesi*, Florence, 1934, pp. 126-127. Addition bibliography in S. Moscati, *L'epigrafia ebraica antica, 1935-1950*, Rome, 1951, p. 82. Photograph from publication by Albright.

279. One of twenty-one ostraca discovered at Tell ed-Duweir, consisting of letters and lists of names, from the time of the beginning of the siege of Lachish by the Babylonians, perhaps in 589 or 588. This particular inscription mentions the town of Lachish and thus makes possible the identification of Tell ed-Duweir with ancient Lachish.

Palestine Archaeological Museum. Tell ed-Duweir. Clay. 0.13 m. by 0.08 m. Dated 589 or 588. H. Torczyner, *Lachish I*, London, 1938, p. 76 (photograph), p. 77 (drawing). Translation: *ANET*, 322, where additional bibliography is given. Photograph courtesy PAM.

280. Funerary stela of Sen-zer-ibni found at Nerab, near Aleppo, in 1891. The figure is beardless and barefoot and is clothed in a long, fringed garment. On his head he wears a heavy cap which completely covers his hair. His right hand is raised in a gesture of prayer; his left holds a piece of folded material fringed at the ends. The inscription, written in the old Aramaic script, mentions the Babylonian gods: Sin, Shamash, Nergal, and Nusku. For translation see G. A. Cooke, *A Text-Book of North-Semitic Inscriptions*, Oxford, 1903, pp. 186-189 ("probably seventh century"). See also No. 635.

Louvre. Nerab. Basalt. Height: 0.93 m. First half sixth century. Contenau, *Man.*, vol. 1, fig. 68; vol. 3, pp. 1365-1367. G. Contenau, *Les antiquités orientales, monuments hittites, assyriens, phéniciens, perses, judaïques, chypriotes, araméens*, Paris, n.d., pl. 26, p. 17. Photograph Archives Photographiques.

281. A twenty-line inscription in Aramaic (see M. Lidzbarski, *Handbuch der nordsemitischen Epigraphik*, vol. 1, Weimar, 1898, pp. 443-444; and G. A. Cooke, *A Text-Book of North-Semitic Inscriptions*, Oxford, 1903, pp. 180-185). King Bar Rakab wears a full beard and a side curl which falls down before his ear. His head is covered by a tight-fitting cap with a knoblike projection at the top, from which a tassel hangs down at the back. He wears sandals and is clothed in a long, fringed robe draped over his shoulders. In his left hand he holds a blossom, perhaps a lotus. Represented at the top of the relief are five symbols: a horned cap, a kind of loop surmounted by a knot, a five-pointed star in a circle, a winged sun-disc, and a crescent. Behind the king are the arms of an attendant holding a fly-whisk and a roll of fringed material.

Istanbul, 7697. Zinjirli. Dolerite. Second half of eighth century. F. von Luschan, *Ausgrabungen in Sendschirli*, vol. 4, Berlin, 1911, pl. 67, pp. 377-380, figs. 275, 276. Photograph courtesy of the Museum of the Ancient Orient.

282. A portion of an Aramaic papyrus, dated November 26, 404 B.C. In it Anani bar Azariah, the servitor of the god Yahu in Yeb (Elephantine), makes a gift of a house to his daughter Yehoyishma.

Brooklyn Museum 47.218.92. Acquired in 1893 from natives at Elephantine. Papyrus. Size of entire papyrus: 0.693 m. by 0.309 m. 404. E. G. Kraeling, ed., *The Brooklyn Museum Aramaic Papyri*, New Haven, 1953, no. 9, pl. 9. Photograph courtesy Br. M. and Emil G. Kraeling.

283. This sarcophagus, made in the Egyptian fashion for Eshmunazar, king of Sidon, is inscribed with a Phoenician inscription which has been well preserved. For script see No. 286.

Louvre. Sidon. Black basalt. Length: 2.51 m. Fifth century. G. Contenau, *Les antiquités orientales, monuments hittites, assyriens, phéniciens*, etc., Paris, n.d., pl. 31. Contenau, *Man.*, vol. 3, fig. 902. Text and translation: G. A. Cooke, *A Text-Book of North-Semitic Inscriptions*, Oxford, 1903, pp. 30-40. Photograph Archives Photographiques.

284. Column 27 of the St. Mark's Isaiah manuscript, containing the text of Isaiah 33:1-24, discovered in Palestine in 1947 (for accounts of discovery and subsequent transaction see *BA*, vol. 11, 1948, pp. 46-57; vol. 12, 1949, pp. 26-31). The entire scroll consists of seventeen sheets of coarse parchment sewn together with linen thread. The writing is in square Hebrew characters and suspended from carefully ruled lines which were made upon the skins by a semi-sharp instrument.

Photographed in 1948 at the American School of Oriental Research in Jerusalem with the permission of the Syrian Orthodox Metropolitan at St. Mark's Monastery. Said to have come from cave near Khirbet Qumran. Coarse parchment. Height of manuscript: 0.262 m.; width of widest line of this column: 0.111 m. M. Burrows, *The Dead Sea Scrolls of St. Mark's Monastery*, vol. 1, New Haven, 1950, pl. 27. Photograph courtesy of the American Schools of Oriental Research.

285. An inscription, written in the symmetrically carved Sabaean alphabet of 29 letters, dedicated to the god Ta'lab of Riyâm, deals with wars in the time of 'Alhān Nahfān.

Louvre. Ṣan'â (southern Arabia). Height: 0.44 m.; width: 0.25 m.; thickness: 0.103 m. About second century A.D. (W. F. Albright). *CIS*, pt. 4, vol. 1, pl. 3. See K. Conti Rossini, *Chrestomathia Arabica meridionalis epigraphica*, Rome, 1931, p. 63. Photograph from *CIS*.

286. The table of alphabets, drawn by S. A. Birnbaum mostly from photographs of the original documents, gives the forms of letters used on engraved inscriptions (letters in outline) and in writings (solid black letters) in Phoenician, Hebrew, and Aramaic. Below are references to the publication of photographs of the documents, cross references to illustrations in this volume, and the approximate date to which the documents are ascribed.

1. Ahiram Inscription. P. Montet, *Byblos et l'Égypte*, Atlas, Paris, 1929, pls. 139-141. No. 456. Tenth century.

2. Yehimilk Inscription. M. Dunand, *Fouilles de Byblos*, vol. 1, Paris, 1937, pl. 31, no. 2. Tenth century.

3. Samaria Ivories. J. W. Crowfoot, G. M. Crowfoot, E. L. Sukenik, *Early Ivories from Samaria*, London, 1938, pl. 25, pp. 47-48. Ninth century.

4. Gezer Calendar. R. A. S. Macalister, *The Excavation of Gezer*, London, 1912, vol. 3, pl. 127. No. 272. Tenth century (or early ninth, according to Birnbaum).

5. Moabite Stone. R. Dussaud, *Les monuments palestiniens et judaïques*, Paris, 1912, pp. 4-21. No. 274. Ninth century.

6. Kilamuwa Inscription. F. von Luschan, *Ausgrabungen in Sendschirli*, vol. 4, Berlin, 1911, pp. 374-377. Ninth century.

7. Samaria Ostraca. G. A. Reisner, C. S. Fisher, D. G. Lyon, *Harvard Excavations at Samaria*, Cambridge, Mass., 1924, pp. 227-246. Eighth century.

8. Shema Seal. G. Schumacher and C. Steuernagel, *Tell el-Mutesellim*, vol. 1, Leipzig, 1908, fig. 147. No. 276. Eighth century.

9. Bar Rakab Inscription. F. von Luschan, *Ausgrabungen in Sendschirli*, vol. 4, Berlin, 1911, pl. 67. Nos. 281 and 460. Second half of eighth century.

10. Siloam Inscription. D. Diringer, *Le iscrizioni antico-ebraiche palestinesi*, Florence, 1934, pl. 11. No. 275. Eighth-seventh century.

11. Nerab Stelae. G. Contenau, *Les antiquités orientales, monuments hittites, assyriens, phéniciens, perses,*

judaïques, chypriotes, araméens, Paris, n.d., pls. 26, 27. Nos. 280 and 635. First half sixth century.

12. Pharaoh Letter. A. Dupont-Summer, "Un papyrus araméen d'époque saïte découvert à Saqqarah," *Semitica,* vol. 1, 1948, pl. opp. p. 68, pp. 43-68 (Cairo Museum, 86.984). End of seventh century.

13. Lachish Ostraca. H. Torczyner, *Lachish I,* London, 1938. Nos. 279. First part of sixth century.

14. Jewish Seals. D. Diringer, *Le iscrizioni antico-ebraiche palestinesi,* Florence, 1934, pls. 14-22. S. Moscati, *L'epigrafia ebraica antica, 1935-1950,* Rome, 1951, pls. 11-23. Nos. 276-278. Sixth century.

15. Meissner Papyrus. H. Bauer and B. Meissner, "Ein aramäischer Pachtvertrag aus dem 7. Jahre Darius' I," *Sitz. der Preuss. Ak. der Wiss., Philo.-hist. Kl.,* no. 30, Berlin, 1936, pp. 414-424. 515 B.C.

16. Leviticus Fragments. R. de Vaux, *RB,* vol. 56, 1949, pl. 18. S. A. Birnbaum, *BASOR,* no. 118, 1950, p. 21. Middle of fifth century.

17. Elephantine Papyri. A. Cowley, *Aramaic Papyri of the Fifth Century B.C.,* Oxford, 1923, no. 35. Cf. No. 282. About 400 B.C.

18. Eshmunazar Sarcophagus. G. Contenau, *Les antiquités orientales, monuments hittites, assyriens, phéniciens, perses, judaïques, chypriotes, araméens,* Paris, n.d., pl. 31. No. 283. Fifth century.

MISCELLANEOUS

287. The obverse of a bronze tablet which contains 217 characters of a pseudohieroglyphic script among which are 53 different signs. The inscription has not yet been read with certainty.

Byblos. Bronze. Length: 0.155 m.; width: 0.11 m. M. Dunand, *Byblia Grammata,* Beirut, 1945, pl. 9, upper, pp. 74-76. E. Dhorme, "Déchiffrement des inscriptions pseudo-hiéroglyphiques de Byblos," *Syria,* vol. 25, 1946-48, pp. 5-12. Photograph courtesy of M. Dunand.

288. Hittite hieroglyphic writing, which was in use about 1500 to 700 in the area from central Anatolia to northern Syria, employed pictorial signs.

Suvasa C (eastern Anatolia, south of the Halys). I. J. Gelb, *A Study of Writing,* Chicago, 1952, fig. 38, pp. 82-83. Photograph from I. J. Gelb, *Hittite Hieroglyphic Monuments, OIP,* 45, Chicago, 1939, pl. 75 upper, courtesy of the University of Chicago Press.

289. A cursive form of Hittite hieroglyphic writing of the latest period. Gelb translates: "This monument 'Astawalus placed; it then nobody should damage!" (I. J. Gelb, *A Study of Writing,* Chicago, 1952, p. 114).

Erkilet II, now Kayseri, no. 5. Height: 0.81 m.; width: 0.63 m. I. J. Gelb, *Hittite Hieroglyphic Monuments, OIP,* 45, Chicago, 1939, pl. 37, fig. 21. Photograph from publication.

IV. Scenes from History and Monuments

290. The ivory handle to a carefully worked flint knife is carved with scenes from warfare and hunting in predynastic Egypt. At the top of the verso of the handle a bearded figure, but without mustache, wearing a cap (or fillet) and a kilt extending below the knees, stands between two lions to form a heraldic scene like that which appears in a Mesopotamian seal engraving (No. 672). Below and to either side of a pierced boss, probably for a suspensory thong, are two dogs, each wearing a collar. Below are various animals: a gazelle, ibexes, a lion attacking a bull (?) from behind, a wildcat (or dog on a leash), and a bull (?). To the left is a part of a hunter, wearing a codpiece and probably (to judge from the other hunter shown on the recto of the handle) armed with a lasso.

On the upper part of the recto of the handle are nine combatants, all completely nude except for a codpiece. Two groups can be distinguished: those with shaved heads, who seem to be the better armed, having sticks, a mace, and knives; and those with long flowing hair. Below are pictured two registers of boats separated by several human bodies, presumably in the water. The two boats above have high prows and sterns which are surmounted by standards and suggest forms which appear on cylinder seals in Mesopotamia (Nos. 104, 673). The boats below are shaped as an arc from a circle and have the head of a bull attached to the prow. This type has its parallels in representations of Egyptian boats.

Louvre, E 11517. Said to have come from Gebel el-'Araq. Ivory. Length of handle: about 0.10 m. Gerzean Period, generally assigned to S.D. 60 (possible range of S.D. 50-60, according to H. J. Kantor, *JNES,* vol. 3, 1944, pp. 130-131). G. Bénédite, "Le couteau de Gebel el 'Arak," Fondation Piot, vol. 22, 1916, pl. 1, pp. 1-34. J. Vandier, *Manuel d'archéologie égyptienne,* vol. 1, Paris, 1952, pp. 533-539, figs. 358-359. Schäfer-Andrae, 185, 2 and 3. H. J. Kantor, "The Final Phase of Predynastic Culture: Gerzean or Semainean (?)," *JNES,* vol. 3, 1944, pp. 119-124. H. Frankfort, *Studies in Early Pottery of the Near East, I,* London, 1924, pp. 118 ff. Photographs Foto Marburg.

291. Fragment of a large slate palette carved on both sides. The outline of the top of the palette is formed by the back of a horned bull, which is represented on each side as attacking a man wearing a codpiece. On one side, where the head and face of the man are shown, he wears a long beard in three strands, but has his upper lip shaved. His hair is curled in ringlets. Below the bull are five standards ending in hands which grasp a rope. Two are surmounted by wolves (representing the god Up-wawet), one by an ibis (Thoth), one by a falcon (Horus), and the other by a symbol of Min. At the bottom is the head of a bearded man.

292. On the other side of the Bull Palette, below the scene of the bull goring a man, are representations of two walled fortresses. The upper, which is almost completely preserved, contains a lion standing before a small vase; the lower, a bird. These were probably intended to give the names of the fortresses which contain them. The palette may have served to celebrate the victory of King Nar-mer over the people of the Delta (J. Vandier, *Manuel d'archéologie égyptienne,* Paris, 1952, p. 594) or a victory of Egypt over the nomads of the eastern desert (S. Schott, *Hieroglyphen*, Wiesbaden, 1951, p. 23, n. 3).

Louvre. Slate. Height of fragment: 0.26 m. Archaic period. *Bulletin de correspondance hellénique*, vol. 16, 1892, pl. 1, pp. 307-319. G. Bénédite, Fondation Piot, vol. 10, 1903, p. 114, figs. 6, 7. Schäfer-Andrae, 188, 1 and 3. Photographs Archives Photographiques, Paris.

293. King Usaphais (see *ANET*, 495) stands with upraised club and smites a bearded figure, who kneels before him. Behind the king's enemy is a standard bearing the symbol of Up-wawet (wolf). An inscription giving the Horus name of the king adds, "first time of smiting the East."

British Museum, 55586. Abydos. Ivory. Height: about 0.05 m. First Dynasty (about 3000). E. Amélineau, *Les nouvelles fouilles d'Abydos 1895-1896*, Paris, 1899, pl. 33. British Museum, *A General Introductory Guide to the Egyptian Collections in the British Museum*, London, 1930, fig. 154. *AOB*, 29. W. Spiegelberg, *ÄZ*, vol. 35, 1897, pp. 7-11. Photograph courtesy BM.

294. The Horus name of the king is a "serpent" represented within the frame of palace, which has three towers and two doors. On the top is a falcon, a form of Horus.

Louvre. Abydos. Limestone. Width: 0.65 m. First Dynasty (about 3000). G. Bénédite, Fondation Piot, vol. 12, 1905, pl. 1, pp. 5-17. Schäfer-Andrae, 190. *AOB*, 30. TEL, vol. 1, p. 4. Th. Dombart, "Die Grabstele des Horus 'Schlange,'" *Festschrift Max von Oppenheim*, Berlin, 1933, pp. 18-26. Photograph JBP.

295. Relief on which Snefru is shown smiting a crouching bearded figure, whom he holds by the hair.

Cairo Museum. Serabit el-Khadem, in Sinai. Sandstone. Height of crouching figure: about 0.30 m. Fourth Dynasty, Snefru (about 2650). W. M. F. Petrie, *Researches in Sinai*, London, 1906, fig. 50. A. H. Gardiner and T. E. Peet, *The Inscriptions of Sinai*, pt. 1, London, 1917, pl. 2, no. 5 (drawing). See *ANET*, 227 for translation of inscription. Photograph Fremdvölker, 30.

296. The upper register of both sides of the palette contains two heads of Hathor and the name of King Narmer on the façade of a palace. On the verso stands King Nar-mer, wearing the white crown of Upper Egypt and a decorated kilt to which an animal tail is attached, smiting with a mace a kneeling prisoner, whom he holds by the hair. The nude prisoner has a beard and massive hair; he belongs, according to the hieroglyphs to the right of his head, to the harpoon nome (VII) of the Delta. Above the prisoner is an oval, which terminates at the left in the head of a prisoner, and from which grow six papyrus stalks. Above them a falcon stands on one foot and holds with the other a rope attached to the nose of the prisoner (for summary of interpretations see J. Vandier, *Manuel d'archéologie égyptienne*, Paris, 1952, p. 596). Behind the king is the small figure "The sandal-bearer of the King of Upper Egypt." At the bottom, are two completely nude enemies, with hieroglyphs which may indicate the country of their origin.

297. The recto depicts in the upper register the triumph of the king, who is shown dressed as on the other side, except that here he wears the red crown of the north. He is followed by a sandal-bearer, above whom is represented a rectangular object with a hieroglyph (for interpretations see Vandier, *op. cit.*, p. 598). Before the king is a long-haired scribe carrying a writing palette. He is preceded by four men bearing standards, on the tops of which are two falcons (Horus), a wolf (Up-wawet), and the royal placenta (?). The right part of the register is occupied by ten bound and decapitated corpses with their heads lying between their legs. Above are a boat, a falcon, and two hieroglyphs. In the middle register are two panthers, with long necks which are entwined to form a figure-8, and held on leashes by two small figures which resemble the prisoners. Below, a bull attacks with his horns a partly demolished fortress and treads on an enemy.

Cairo. Hierakonpolis (Kom el-Ahmar). Slate. Height: 0.64 m. First Dynasty (about 3000). J. E. Quibell, *Hierakonpolis*, pt. 1, London, 1900, pl. 29. *AOB*, 26-27. Schäfer-Andrae, 189. For description and a listing of some recent literature see J. Vandier, *Manuel d'archéologie égyptienne*, Paris, 1952, pp. 595-599. See H. Frankfort, *Studies in Early Pottery of the Near East, I*, London, 1924, pp. 119 ff., for discussion of interrelations between Egypt and Mesopotamia. Photographs courtesy of the Cairo Museum.

298. Two fragments (D and E) from the obverse (or mythological) side of the stela of Eannatum, the "stela of the vultures." The large human figure, nude above the waist, wears a long chin-beard, arranged in five locks curled at the ends, and massive hair which is contained in a chignon which rests upon the shoulder. The figure has been interpreted as representing the god Ningirsu or Eannatum, the king of Lagash (see A. Parrot, *Tello*, Paris, 1948, p. 96, for a summary of the arguments for each of these interpretations and the author's preference for identification with Ningirsu). In the right hand is held a mace with which he smites the nude figures, with shaved faces and heads, contained in a net. The net is surmounted by the symbol of Ningirsu (see E. D. van Buren, *Symbols of the Gods in Mesopotamian Art*, Rome, 1945, p. 30), a lion-headed eagle which grasps with its talons the backs of two lions.

Louvre. Tello. Limestone. Height of two fragments: 0.75 m. Middle third millennium. E. de Sarzec, *Découvertes en Chaldée*, Paris, 1884-1912, pl. 4 bis. A. Parrot, *Tello*, Paris, 1948, pl. 6, pp. 95-97. Schäfer-Andrae, 487. *AOB*, 33. TEL, vol. 1, p. 190. For account of restoration and text see L. Heuzey and F. Thureau-Dangin, *Restitution matérielle de la stèle des vautours*, Paris, 1909. Photograph TEL.

299. Three fragments (C', F', G') of the reverse (historical) side of the stela of Eannatum. To the left are two piles of corpses, neatly stacked. Two men with baskets of earth on their heads make their way up the second pile, perhaps to make tumuli. To the right is depicted an offering scene. A bull is tied securely to two stakes and the bodies of six smaller animals are piled up ready for the offering. Above them stands a nude

offerer, who pours a libation, which falls into one of two vases. The vases contain growing plants and palm branches draped over the sides. To the extreme right are the feet and flounced robe of a large figure, perhaps that of the king. In the fragment of the lower register a lance is directed at the forehead of what may be the king of Kish.

Louvre. Tello. Limestone. Height: about 0.51 m. Middle third millennium. E. de Sarzec, *Découvertes en Chaldée*, Paris, 1884-1912, pl. 4 ter (for F' only). TEL, vol. 1, p. 193G. A. Parrot, *Tello*, Paris, 1948, pl. 6, p. 100. Photograph TEL.

300. The upper register of the fragments (D', E') from the reverse of the stela of Eannatum (No. 298) shows troops marching in six columns after their leader, Eannatum. The soldiers wear tight-fitting helmets and are heavily armed with shields, spears, maces, and axes. They march over a road made of the bodies of their enemies laid feet to feet and head to head. The leader wears a more elaborate helmet, with ears and a bun represented (see No. 160), and is clothed in a flounced skirt and a skin thrown over his left shoulder. In the lower register the troops are shown marching in close formation and carrying spears and axes. Again they are lead by Eannatum, who rides in a chariot. His left hand holds an outstretched spear and his right grasps a sickle-sword. At the front of the chariot are a quiver and an axe.

Louvre. Tello. Limestone. Height of fragments: 0.75 m. Middle third millennium. E. de Sarzec, *Découvertes en Chaldée*, Paris, 1884-1912, pl. 3 bis. A. Parrot, *Tello*, Paris, 1948, pl. 6, p. 99. Schäfer-Andrae, 486. *AOB*, 32. TEL, vol. 1, p. 192. Photograph Archives Photographiques.

301. On this fragment (A') vultures, or perhaps eagles, carry away from the battlefield with their beaks and claws the heads and an arm of the slain.

Louvre. Tello. Limestone. Middle third millennium. E. de Sarzec, *Découvertes en Chaldée*, Paris, 1884-1912, pl. 3A. TEL, vol. 1, p. 193H. A. Parrot, *Tello*, Paris, 1948, pl. 6, p. 99. Photograph TEL.

302. On the edge of the stela, the scene shown on the lower register of fragments D' and E' (No. 300) is continued with four soldiers clad in flounced skirts and tight-fitting helmets, carrying spears and axes. They constitute a part of the troops led by Eannatum in his chariot.

Louvre. Tello. Limestone. Height: about 0.30 m. Middle third millennium. E. de Sarzec, *Découvertes en Chaldée*, Paris, 1884-1912, pl. 4 ter. TEL, vol. 1, p. 194. Photograph TEL.

303. This and the following mosaic panel from a standard show the triumph of a king over his enemies and the celebration of the victory by a banquet. Upper register: To the left is an empty four-wheeled chariot driven by a helmeted soldier armed with an axe, and drawn by four asses or onagers. The chariot consists of a framework of low, paneled sides and a higher front-shield (shown in the same plane as the side) mounted on axles, to which are attached four solid wheels, each made of two semicircles of wood fastened together by tenons

(see A. Salonen, *Die Landfahrzeuge des alten Mesopotamien*, Helsinki, 1951, pp. 155-159, for listing of examples of four-wheeled wagons). In front of the animals are a groom and three soldiers carrying axes and spears. In the center of the register is a larger figure, probably a king. Before him are nude prisoners, escorted by soldiers, who are presented to the king. Middle register: To the left is a line of helmeted soldiers, wearing fringed skirts and capes and armed with short spears. In the right half of the register are depicted soldiers engaged with the naked enemies. Lower register: Four chariots (similar to that in the upper register), each with a driver and a fighting-man. The first three chariots charge, their asses at a gallop, over a battlefield covered with corpses, while the fourth proceeds with its asses at a walk.

British Museum, 121201. Ur, U.11164. Mosaic in shell, lapis lazuli, and red limestone. Height: 0.20 m.; width: 0.47 m. Early Dynastic III, twenty-fifth century. C. L. Woolley, *The Royal Cemetery*, London, 1934, pl. 92, pp. 269-273. Schäfer-Andrae, 476. Photograph courtesy BM.

304. The upper register of the "peace panel" shows a large figure, presumably the king, dressed in a many-flounced skirt and seated facing six other seated figures (captains of the hosts, according to excavator). Each of the seated figures holds a cup in his right hand. In the register are also three smaller figures, probably servers, a lyrist (see No. 193), and a woman with black hair, perhaps a singer. In the middle and lower registers men bring food or other spoil captured from the enemy. To the right of the middle register two men are followed by a third who leads a bull by a rope as his companion guides it by the horns. Then appear three goats and an attendant; he is followed by a man with four fish and another group of three men with a bull. Behind is a bearded man with an oryx; another man carries a gazelle (?). The lower register (from right to left) shows a man with a feathered (?) cap, followed by a servant; another man leads four asses. A man wearing a feathered headdress carries a bundle on his shoulder. Another porter supports a heavy load on his back by means of a band across his forehead. The remainder of the register is made up of similar figures.

British Museum, 121201. Ur, U.11164. Mosaic in shell, lapis lazuli, and red limestone. Height: 0.20 m.; width: 0.47 m. Early Dynastic III, twenty-fifth century. C. L. Woolley, *The Royal Cemetery*, London, 1934, pl. 91, pp. 273-274. Schäfer-Andrae, 477. Photograph courtesy BM.

305. Fragments of figures which once formed an inlaid panel of shell set in bitumen among pieces of cut slate and cased in wood. To the right is a line of four dignitaries clothed in long robes with fringes, with cushions at the back. They wear headdress with sharp points. Over the left shoulder they wear a kind of scarf and carry an axe. Three are beardless; one is bearded. Before them is a standard-bearer, who is nude above the waist, and elevates a standard topped by a bull. Facing him are soldiers (bearded and beardless) clothed like the dignitaries except for the tight-fitting helmet. They

bring nude prisoners who are bound by ropes about their waists and arms. Below are fragments of a chariot drawn by asses, prisoners, and soldiers.

Louvre. Mari, 1933-1934, court of temple of Ishtar. Shell. Height of one of the dignitaries: 0.11 m. Middle third millennium. *Syria*, vol. 16, 1935, pl. 28, pp. 132-137. TEL, vol. 1, pp. 188-189. A. Parrot, *Mari*, Paris, 1948, fig. 14, pp. 125-134, 221-222. Photographs TEL.

306. Part of the first, with the second, the third, and part of the four registers of the obverse of the restored stela of Ur-Nammu from Ur. Above, the king stood before a deity (perhaps Ningal) seated on a throne holding a child, whose feet can be seen on the edge of the break in the throne. In the second register are two antithetical scenes, each showing the king offering a libation to a deity. On the platform to the right sits a god wearing a horned miter, a long beard, and a flounced robe; holding in his right hand the rod, ring, and line, and in his left, an adze which rests on his shoulder. Before him is a libation vase from which grow palms and dates, and into which the king (all but lower part of skirt and feet restored) pours a libation. Behind him is a minor deity, an attendant. To the left of the register the scene is repeated, except that a goddess appears as the recipient of the offering. What remains of the third register shows the king carrying a basket, and surveying and building instruments; he is identified as Ur-Nammu by an inscription on the skirt. He is preceded by a god, and followed by a servant. Fragments of the scene from the fourth register include part of a ladder and bricks (at lower right) built into a wall. These suggest that the subject was the building of a ziggurat.

University Museum. Ur. Limestone. Width: 1.52 m. Ur-Nammu, first king of the Third Dynasty of Ur (about 2060-1955). L. Woolley, *MJ*, vol. 16, 1925, pp. 48-55. L. Legrain, "The Stela of the Flying Angels," *MJ*, vol. 18, 1927, pp. 74-98. L. Legrain, "Restauration de la stèle d'Ur-nammu," *RA*, vol. 30, 1933, pp. 111-115. Photograph courtesy UM.

307. On this fragment of what may have been a stela of victory is shown a large net containing prisoners. The scene is similar to that on No. 298, except that the prisoners do not have shaved heads. One head (to the extreme left, and not visible in this photograph) not only has long hair but also a beard.

Louvre. Susa. Diorite. Height: 0.54 m. Sargonid period (about 2360-2180). V. Scheil, *Mémoires, Délégation en Perse*, vol. 10, Paris, 1908, pp. 4-8. E. Nassouhi, "La stèle de Sargon l'ancien," *RA*, vol. 21, 1924, pp. 65-74, figs. 5-7. Photograph Archives Photographiques.

308. The principal figure of this fragment of a stela of victory wears a shawl-like garment over an undergarment and stands with his left foot on the body of an enemy, which he smites with a battle-axe and pierces with a spear. The foe wears a long garment which extends to his ankles. A third person is represented to the right of the scene.

Louvre, AO 2776. Grayish-green volcanic stone. Height: 0.45 m.; width: 0.55 m. First Dynasty of Babylon (about 1830-1530), to judge from the script and language of inscription on reverse. H. de Genouillac, "Ancienne stèle de victoire," *RA*, vol. 7, 1909, pls. 5 and 6, pp. 151-156. Contenau, *Man.*, vol. 2, fig. 596, pp. 836-839. L. and J. Heuzey, *Histoire du costume . . .*, 1935, pl. 37. Photograph Archives Photographiques.

309. Naram-Sin of Agade stands before a stylized mountain as the victor over the Lullu(bians). The bearded figure of the king is clothed with the same costume as worn by his soldiers below; on his head he wears a pointed helmet, from the sides of which emerge two horns, the insignia of divinity. He is armed with axe, bow, and spear. He places his left foot upon the prostrate bodies of two enemies. A third lies before him, pierced by a spear, while a fourth stands clad in a garment of skin, making supplication. Below, a fifth enemy stands with broken spear. Beneath the figure of the king are his troops, carrying standards, spears, and axes. A tree suggests that the mountainous region is wooded. At the top of the stela are two star symbols and fragments of a third.

Louvre. Susa. Sandstone. Height: 2 m. Naram-Sin (first half twenty-third century). J. de Morgan, *Mémoires, Délégation en Perse*, vol. 1, Paris, 1900, pl. 10, pp. 144-158. E. Meyer, *Sumerier und Semiten in Babylonien*, Berlin, 1906, pl. 4 (detail), pp. 10 ff. Schäfer-Andrae, 493 (detail). *AOB*, 41, 43. TEL, vol. 1, p. 214. Inscription: G. A. Barton, *The Royal Inscriptions of Sumer and Akkad*, New Haven, 1929, p. 143. Photograph TEL.

310. On this side of the blade of a ceremonial weapon of King Ah-mose are shown the name of the king (for texts dealing with the role of Ah-mose in expelling the Hyksos see *ANET*, 232-234), the king smiting an enemy, and a griffin.

Cairo Museum. Thebes. Wood, bronze, gold, etc. Length of blade: 0.135 m. Ah-mose I (1570-1545). W. von Bissing, *Ein thebanischer Grabfund*, Berlin, 1900, pl. 1. Schäfer-Andrae, 402, 5. Photograph courtesy of the Metropolitan Museum of Art, New York.

311. To the left are four registers which depict a battle among Egyptians armed with shallow battle-axes (and perhaps quivers, in the upper row) and bearded Asiatics, who are distinguishable by their long hair held by a fillet. The Asiatics are being defeated, since they are shown either bound or transfixed by arrows. To the left of the lowest register, prisoners, including women and children, are bound with ropes and are being led away from the town. To the right of the lowest register, two Egyptians mine the wall of the fortified town with pikes and another raises a ladder to the top of the wall. Inside the wall of the town are five scenes, in which women seem to be caring for the wounded (for another interpretation see W. M. F. Petrie, *Deshasheh*, London, 1898, pp. 6-7, who sees the women as struggling with the attackers). To the left of the lowest register within the fortress, an Asiatic kneels with his head to the wall, as if to detect where the attack is being made. In the accompanying text are the names Nedia and Ain- . . . , but neither the reference nor the location can be determined with certainty (*ANET*, 227, fn. 2).

Deshasheh, tomb of Anta, north half, east wall. Relief in limestone. Height: about 1.28 m. Late Fifth or early Sixth Dynasty (about 2350). W. M. F. Petrie, *Deshasheh*, London, 1898, pl. 4, pp. 4-7. *AOB*, 39. Photograph from Wresz., vol. 2, pl. 4, courtesy of J. C. Hinrichs Verlag, Leipzig.

312. Thut-mose III holds a batch of prisoners by their hair that he may smite them. The prisoners are bearded; they kneel and raise their hands in supplication. Beyond the group of prisoners stands a goddess, who leads by a rope the figures of conquered chiefs which surmount the name-rings of the three upper rows of the topographical list. In the upper right-hand corner is the partly destroyed figure of the god Amon. The scene contains one of the topographical lists (text b) of Thut-mose III.

Karnak, great temple of Amon, pylon VII, southern face of western tower. Thut-mose III (1490-1436). Wresz., vol. 2, pl. 184a, fig. 7. G. Jéquier, *L'architecture et la décoration dans l'ancienne Égypte, Les temples memphites et thébains*, Paris, n.d., pl. 55, 1 left. J. Capart, *Thebes*, New York, 1926, p. 46, fig. 26. For diagram of names and text see J. Simons, *Handbook for the Study of Egyptian Topographical Lists Relating to Western Asia*, Leiden, 1937, pp. 109-122. Photograph courtesy of A. Gaddis, Luxor.

313. Engraved on the western face of the northern tower of pylon VI at Karnak is a list of five rows of name-rings, each surmounted by the upper part of the figure of a bound Asiatic. The entire list (list a) contains 115 names (see *ANET*, 242-243 for a digest of Asiatic place names on this and subsequent lists of Egyptian conquerors). Originally the five rows of name-rings had above them a relief, of which only a fragment remains.

Karnak, great temple of Amon, pylon VI, western face of northern tower. Thut-mose III (1490-1436). G. Jéquier, *L'architecture et la décoration dans l'ancienne Égypte, Les temples memphites et thébains*, Paris, n.d., pl. 48, 3. *AOB*, 54. For diagram of names and text see J. Simons, *Handbook for the Study of Egyptian Topographical Lists Relating to Western Asia*, Leiden, 1937, pp. 109-122. Photograph courtesy of A. Gaddis, Luxor.

314-316. On the exterior of the chariot of Thut-mose IV are two panels, each showing the king riding in his chariot over a battlefield in which are represented wounded Asiatics and their chariotry. Below each of the panels is a frieze composed of prisoners bound together by a rope. The heads of the wounded and the prisoners are all shown as bearded; some have shaved heads, others have long hair contained by a fillet, while others wear a tight-fitting, tasseled cap. Nos. 314 and 316 are of the right-hand side of the exterior of the chariot; No. 315, of the left-hand side. For details of dress see Nos. 41-56. For reference to Astarte in the inscription see *ANET*, 250.

Cairo. Thebes, tomb of Thut-mose IV. Wood coated with canvas, stucco, and fine linen. Height of body of chariot: 0.86 m. Thut-mose IV (1421-1413). H. Carter and P. E. Newberry, *The Tomb of Thoutmôsis IV*, London, 1904, pls. 10 and 11, pp. 24-33. *AOB*, 62. Photographs from Wresz., vol. 2, pls. 1, 2, courtesy of J. C. Hinrichs Verlag, Leipzig; and courtesy of the Cairo Museum.

317. To the right is Seti I, who receives from Amon the sickle-sword. Behind Amon is an Asiatic god wearing the pointed cap; then Mut and Khonsu.

Aleppo, National Museum. Tell Nebi Mend = Kadesh on the Orontes. Black basalt. Height: 0.45 m. Seti I (1318-1301). *Syria*, vol. 3, 1922, pl. 22, p. 108, fig. 6. M. Pézard, "Une nouvelle stèle de Séti Ier," Fondation Piot, vol. 25, pl. 26, pp. 387-389. *AOB*, 91. Photograph JBP.

318. Box no. 21 from the tomb of Tut-ankh-Amon viewed from the side which shows the king standing in his chariot with drawn bow as he leads his troops into battle against the Asiatics. Detail to the right shown in No. 319. For detail of the hunting scene on the lid see No. 190. For translation of legend of box see *ANET*, 251, fn. 1.

Cairo Museum. Thebes, tomb of Tut-ankh-Amon, box no. 21. Wood covered with gesso. Height of side: 0.47 m. Tut-ankh-Amon (1361-1352). H. Carter and A. C. Mace, *The Tomb of Tut-ankh-Amen*, vol. 1, London, 1923, pl. 53. TEL, Cairo, no. 115 (side panel). Photograph Foto Marburg.

319. The scene (detail from No. 318) is full of wrecked chariots, enemy wounded and dead, a few desert plants, and Egyptian soldiers, who are either spearing the enemy or cutting off the hands of the corpses for the purpose of keeping count of the dead (see No. 348). At the lower left can be seen two of the royal hounds which take part in the chase. The details of the dress of the enemy are similar to those from this period depicted elsewhere (Nos. 43, 52). See *ANET*, 251, col. 1, fn. 1.

Cairo Museum. Thebes, tomb of Tut-ankh-Amon, box no. 21. Wood covered with gesso. Tut-ankh-Amon (1361-1352). P. Fox, *Tutankhamun's Treasure*, London, 1951, pl. 15. Photograph courtesy of the Metropolitan Museum of Art, New York.

320. This stela of Seti I, found at Beth-shan in Palestine, gives an account of the king's success in overthrowing a coalition of Asiatic princes (*ANET*, 253-254 for translation of text). At the top of the stela is the winged sun-disc. Below it, to the right, stands Re-Har-akhti holding the *was* scepter in his right hand and the *ankh* emblem in the left. He is hawk-headed and wears the solar-disc crown. Before him stands Seti I, who is said to be "making (offerings of) incense and libations." Between the two figures is an altar stand holding a libation pot and a lotus.

Palestine Archaeological Museum, S 884. Beisan excavation, 1923-1925, from city-level V. Basalt. Height: 2.42 m. First year of reign of Seti I (1318-1301). A. Rowe, *The Topography and History of Beth-shan*, Philadelphia, 1930, pl. 41, pp. 24-29. *AOB*, 98. Photograph courtesy UM.

321. A stela of Ramses II, found at Beth-shan in Palestine, evidences his activity in Asiatic campaigning (see *ANET*, 255 for translation of important passage). Below the winged sun-disc stand two figures. To the left is Amon-Re, who wears a crown with double plumes and holds a scimitar in the right hand and a *was* scepter in his left. Facing the god is Ramses II, carrying a bow and raising his right hand in a gesture of address. Be-

tween the two figures are vessels, probably captured booty offered to Amon. At the bottom of the stela are name-rings of the foes of the king, each surmounted by the upper part of the body of a bound captive.

University Museum, 29-107-958. Beisan, city-level V. Basalt. Height: 2.67 m. Ninth year of Ramses II (1301-1234). A. Rowe, *The Topography and History of Beth-shan*, Philadelphia, 1930, pl. 46, pp. 33-36. *AOB*, 97. Photograph courtesy UM.

322. The upper register (Breasted, scene 16) shows Seti I attacking a fortress in a wooded region in the land of Kadesh (see No. 324 for detail and discussion of the problem of identification). The right half of the middle register describes the first and second battle with the Libyans (Breasted, scenes 12-13) and contains two figures inserted later to represent sons of the king (see Breasted, *AR*, vol. 3, §129 for a recapitulation of the three stages in the working of this scene). To the left of the middle register is shown the king returning with prisoners from the Libyan war (Breasted, scene 14). The lowest register (Breasted, scenes 17, 18) shows at the right the king in his chariot attacking "the wretched land of the Hittites" (*ANET*, 254), and to the left, carrying off his prisoners from this campaign.

Karnak, exterior of north wall of great hall. Limestone. Seti I (1318-1301). Wresz., vol. 2, pl. 53 (for top register), 50, 51 (for middle register), 45, 46, 47 (for lowest register). Breasted, *AR*, vol. 3, p. 39 for plan of reliefs (included here are Breasted's scenes 12, 13, 14, 16, 17, 18). Photograph courtesy A. Gaddis, Luxor.

323. In the upper register (Breasted, scene 7) the king, walking behind his chariot, carries two bound prisoners under each arm and leads two rows of bound captives (for detail see No. 325), between which is "Great chiefs of Retenu, whom his majesty carried off as living captives" (Breasted, *AR*, vol. 3, §97). The lower register (Breasted, scene 8) shows Seti I returning to Egypt with prisoners (for detail see No. 326) of the Shasu-Bedouin. A stream (or canal) beside the fortress of Sile divides the prisoners from the Egyptian officials who have come to greet the king upon his return. For translation of the important text of this scene see *ANET*, 254 (a).

Karnak, exterior of north wall of great hall. Limestone. Seti I (1318-1301). Wresz., vol. 2, 36a (upper register), 40, 43 (lower register). A. H. Gardiner, "The Ancient Military Road between Egypt and Palestine," *JEA*, vol. 6, 1920, pls. 11 and 12, pp. 99-116. Breasted, *AR*, vol. 3, p. 39, scenes 7 and 8. Photograph courtesy A. Gaddis, Luxor.

324. This detail from the extreme upper right of No. 322 shows the walled town of Kadesh set in a mountainous and wooded country. The defenders of the town are shown as bearded, some with long hair falling down to the shoulders and held by a fillet around the top, and others with shaved heads or wearing a tight-fitting cap or helmet from which hangs a narrow queue. Below is a herdsman with his bulls. The inscription within the fortress names "the land of Kadesh and the land of *Amurru*" (*ANET*, 254e). The reference has been taken

as referring to Kadesh on the Orontes (Wilson in *ANET*, 254e), but there are some arguments for identification with another town by this name (Breasted, *AR*, vol. 3, p. 71, fn. a). The bearded figures suggest Syrians.

Karnak, exterior of north wall of great hall. Limestone. Seti I (1318-1301). Wresz., vol. 2, 53 (right half). See also R. O. Faulkner, *JEA*, vol. 33, 1947, pp. 34-39. M. Noth, "Die Stadt Kades am Orontes in der Geschichte des zweiten Jahrtausends v. Chr.," *Die Welt des Orients*, 1948, pp. 223-233. Photograph Fremdvölker, 232.

325. Detail from No. 323 showing the king holding in his right arm two captured princes from Retenu (Syria-Palestine). Following are two rows of manacled prisoners dressed in long robes with a capelike top. (For dress see Nos. 41 ff.)

Karnak, exterior of north wall of great hall. Limestone. Seti I (1318-1301). Wresz., vol. 2, pl. 36a (center). Photograph Fremdvölker, 211.

326. This detail from the scene in No. 323 shows two rows of prisoners taken by Seti I in his campaign against the Shasu-Bedouin approaching a canal filled with crocodiles. All the prisoners wear sharply pointed beards, and two types of headdress are in evidence. One is a loose-fitting cap, very much like a beret; the other is a higher conical cap (or hair held by a fillet) from which stream locks of hair or other decoration.

Karnak, exterior of north wall of great hall. Limestone. Seti I (1318-1301). Wresz., vol. 2, pl. 43. *AOB*, 89. Photograph Fremdvölker, 202.

327. In the upper register (Breasted, scene 5), the chiefs of Lebanon are cutting down cedars for the "great barque upon the river . . . as well as for the great flagpoles of Amon," (detail in No. 331), while Seti's officer assures the king, who has left his chariot, of their submission. Between the legs of the horses there is a fortress, "the town of Qeder in the land of Henem" (*ANET*, 254c). In the lower register (Breasted, scene 3), Seti I attacks, in his first year, a town of Canaan (detail in No. 329). The foe is the Shasu "from the fortress of Sile to the Canaan."

Karnak, exterior of north wall of great hall, east projection. Limestone. Seti I (1318-1301). Wresz., vol. 2, pl. 34. Upper register: Wresz., vol. 2, pl. 35A, B; texts: Breasted, *AR*, vol. 3, p. 39, §§91-94; *ANET*, 254 b. Lower register: Wresz., vol. 2, pl. 39; *AOB*, 96; texts: Breasted, *AR*, vol. 3, p. 39, §§87-88; Photograph courtesy A. Gaddis, Luxor.

328. Above (Breasted, scenes 4 and 6), Seti I captures the town of Yanoam (detail in No. 330), which is named in the inscription on the fortress. Around the fortress are trees, between which the heads of Syrians can be seen. At the extreme right, Seti binds his prisoners. Below (Breasted, scenes 1 and 2), the king is shown in his chariot drawn by his team "Anath-is-content." To the right, he is engaged in a battle with the Shasu.

Karnak, exterior of north wall of great hall. Limestone. Seti I (1318-1301). Upper register: Wresz., vol. 2, pls. 36, 37; texts: Breasted, *AR*, vol. 3, §§89-90, 96. Lower register: Wresz., vol. 2, pl. 40; A. H. Gardiner, *JEA*, vol. 6, 1920, pl. 12 (drawing); texts: Breasted, *AR*, vol. 3, §§83-86. Photograph courtesy A. Gaddis, Luxor.

329. In this detail from No. 327 (Breasted, scene 3) is a two-staged fortress situated on a hill and bearing the label "the town of the Canaan" (*ANET*, 254c). Below the fortress and to the left is represented a body of water. The bearded foes of Seti I are the Shasu (see Nos. 323 and 326), who carry spears and axes. Above, one of the Shasu breaks his spear handle.

Karnak, exterior of north wall of great hall, east projection. Limestone. Seti I (1318-1301). Wresz., vol. 2, pl. 39. *AOB*, 95. Breasted, *AR*, vol. 3, p. 39, §88. See also A. H. Gardiner, "The Ancient Military Road between Egypt and Palestine," *JEA*, vol. 6, 1920, pp. 99-116. Photograph Fremdvölker, 191.

330. Detail from No. 328 (Breasted, scene 4) shows the walled town of Yanoam situated in a wooded region and surrounded by a moat. The inhabitants of the town are pictured as bearded and wearing the long Syrian robe with capelike top. The heads are portrayed either with long hair falling in a mass to the shoulders and tied with a fillet around the top, or shaved. Some carry oblong shields; one rides a horse. Below, one of the Syrians is shown between two trees with his hands on his head in a gesture of surrender.

Karnak, exterior of north wall of great hall. Limestone. Seti I (1318-1301). Wresz., vol. 2, pl. 36. Breasted, *AR*, vol. 3, p. 39, §§89-90. *ANET*, 254c. Photograph Fremdvölker, 207A.

331. Detail from No. 327 (Breasted, scene 5) depicting the chiefs of Lebanon felling cedars. Before those actually engaged in cutting the trees are four princes who make gestures of obeisance to an Egyptian officer, who assures the king of their submission. The garments worn by the Syrian princes are similar to those worn by Syrians in No. 5 and elsewhere.

Karnak, exterior of north wall of great hall. Limestone. Seti I (1318-1301). Wresz., vol. 2, pl. 35. *AOB*, 93 (drawing). Breasted, *AR*, vol. 3, p. 39, §§91-94. *ANET*, 254c. Photograph Fremdvölker, 190.

332. On a throne, the side of which is a sphinx, an important person (a king or prince) is seated, drinking from a bowl. He wears a chin-beard, but no mustache, a long robe which reaches to his ankles; on his head is a tight-fitting cap or helmet; his feet are bare and rest upon a footstool. Before him stands a woman wearing a tiara or crown, who offers him a lotus blossom and a part of her head-shawl as a napkin. She is followed by a woman playing a lyre of nine strings. A soldier, armed with shield and spear, leads two nude prisoners with hands bound behind them and joined by a rope to the team which follows. The prisoners are bearded, wear their hair done up in two loops on top of their heads, and are circumcised. In the chariot, drawn by two horses, stands a figure similar to that seated on the throne. Following the chariot is a soldier with a sickle-sword. Behind the throne are two servers, a jar with a cover, on which are the heads of a gazelle and a lion, and birds.

Dussaud has interpreted the scene as the celebration of the triumph of the king after a victorious expedition; if this be correct, the king is shown twice, once upon the throne and again in his chariot (*Syria*, vol. 19, 1938, pp. 353-354). The plant motif may then have been intended to separate the scenes. For throne see No. 457.

Palestine Archaeological Museum, 38.780. Megiddo, level VIIA. Ivory. Length: 0.26 m. Dated by excavator to 1350-1150. G. Loud, *The Megiddo Ivories, OIP*, 52, Chicago, 1939, pl. 4, 2a and 2b. R. Dussaud, *L'art phénicien du IIe millénaire*, Paris, 1949, pp. 89-90. Contenau, *Man.*, vol. 4, pp. 2234-2235. Photograph courtesy of PAM.

333. To the left, the steeds of Ramses II charge over the battlefield, as two of his sons (named in accompanying inscriptions) fight on foot. Farther to the right are four more of the king's sons, represented and named immediately below the fortress. The turreted fortress, bearing the name of Deper, is topped with a standard in the form of an inverted bell and four arrows. The defenders are shown beardless and wearing their hair extending in a long braid down the back in the Hittite fashion (see Nos. 31, 32, 33). Deper, although once identified with Debir of Judges 1:11, is more probably to be located in north Syria. In the lower part of the scene some of the inhabitants are shown coming forth from the town, accompanied by their children and possessions.

Thebes, Ramesseum, great hall, left wall of entrance. Limestone. Eighth year of Ramses II (1301-1234). Wresz., vol. 2, pls. 107-109. *AOB*, 105. Breasted, *AR*, vol. 3, §§359-362 for translation of texts. Photograph courtesy A. Gaddis, Luxor.

334. The fortress of Ashkelon, situated on a hill, is being stormed by Egyptian soldiers armed with shields, sickle-swords, and spears. Storming ladders have been set against the wall and one soldier is hacking at a door with an axe (No. 310). The fortress is composed of two walls, an outer and an inner. The outer has two doors or gates, over which are three windows, and has a turret in the middle. The inner wall has two windows, one barred and the other open, and is surmounted by two turrets. The tops of the walls are decorated with scallops. The men of the town of Ashkelon are bearded and wear the characteristic long garment with capelike top; some have shaved heads, others wear long hair and a fillet. A man at the extreme right of the upper tower holds a flaming incense burner and others raise their hands in a gesture of surrender. Three women upon their knees are shown between the men of the upper tower. Other defenders let down a woman and a child from the upper tower.

Karnak, exterior of south wall of great hall. Limestone. Ramses II (1301-1234). Wresz., vol. 2, pl. 58. *AOB*, 102. Breasted, *AR*, vol. 3, §§353-355, for translation of text. *ANET*, 256. Photographs, Fremdvölker, 239.

335. An almost totally illegible relief probably once gave the records of Ramses II's campaign into Syria. In the upper part, the king is shown before a god (Re-Harakhti). To the left is a relief of an Assyrian king, possibly Shalmaneser III.

Nahr el-Kelb (between Beirut and Byblos). Height of Assyrian relief: 1.93 m. Ramses II (1301-1234) and Shalmaneser III (?) (858-824). F. H. Weissbach, *Die Denkmäler und Inschriften an der Mündung des Nahr el-Kelb*, Berlin and Leipzig, 1922, fig. 5, pp. 17-22. *AOB*, 146. Breasted, *AR*, vol. 3, §297. R. Dussaud, P. Deschamps, and H. Seyrig, *La Syrie antique et médiévale illustrée*, Paris, 1931, pl. 28. R. Mouterde, *Le Nahr el-Kelb*, Beirut, 1932, pl. 5. Photograph courtesy of M. Dunand.

336. The fortified town of Kadesh is represented as almost completely surrounded by a moat, access being had to it only by two bridges or embankments over which Hittite chariots enter. To the right and below the moat are shown files of Hittite lancers. These are beardless and wear long hair falling down the back and long garments. Within the moat and below the town is a line of soldiers of various types. Among them are those of the distinctive headdresses of the Shasu-Bedouin (see No. 326), Syrians (see Nos. 334 and elsewhere), and Hittites (see Nos. 31 and 32). The town of Kadesh has four high towers and one at a lower level. These and the tops of the connecting walls are manned by soldiers of the three types represented in the line below.

Luxor, first pylon, outer wall of east tower. Ramses II (1301-1234). Wresz., vol. 2, pl. 87. *AOB*, 107. Breasted, *AR*, vol. 3, §335 (for listings of drawings of the town of Kadesh). Photograph Fremdvölker, 424.

337. To the upper right is the town of Kadesh, represented as though it were in the middle of the river. Below are rows of Hittite lancers marching toward the river, in which swim horses and charioteers who have escaped the Egyptian onslaught on the other side. Some are being pulled ashore by their comrades. For a listing of the six times this scene was reproduced on monuments; see Breasted, *AR*, vol. 3, §328.

Thebes, Ramesseum, second pylon, west wall of north tower. Ramses II (1301-1234). Wresz., vol. 2, pl. 105. Photograph courtesy of A. Gaddis, Luxor.

338. On this impression of a cylinder seal Ramses II shoots arrows at a target supported by a pole (see No. 333), to which his Syrian foes are tied back to back. To the right is the figure of a god, perhaps Seth, wearing a conical crown with two streamers attached and gazelle horns (cf. No. 487); he holds a scimitar in his left hand and an *ankh* sign in his right. Behind the figure of the king are a vulture and lotus plants.

Palestine Archaeological Museum. Beisan, city-level V. Serpentine. Height: 0.052 m.; diameter: 0.022 m. Ramses II (1301-1234). A. Rowe, *The Topography and History of Beth-shan*, Philadelphia, 1930, pl. 34, no. 4, pp. 31-32. A. Rowe, *The Four Canaanite Temples of Beth-shan*, Philadelphia, 1940, pl. 38, no. 3, pp. 27-28. A. Rowe, *Catalogue of Egyptian Scarabs, etc., in the Palestine Archaeological Museum*, Cairo, 1936, pl. 28, S.61, pp. 252 and 253. B. Parker, "Cylinder Seals from Palestine," *Iraq*, vol. 11, 1949, no. 30. Photograph courtesy of the University Museum.

339. On a stela from Abu Simbel is the figure of "Maat-nefru-Re, the daughter of the Great Prince of Hatti" (*ANET*, 258), presented by the king of the Hittites to Ramses II in marriage. See *ANET*, 256-258.

Abu Simbel. 34th year of Ramses II (1301-1234). Wresz., vol. 2, pl. 46, fig. 7. *AJSL*, vol. 43, 1926, p. 80, fig. 2. Ch. Kuentz, *ASAE*, vol. 25, 1925, pp. 181-238. Breasted, *AR*, vol. 3, §415. Photograph from *LD*, vol. 3, pl. 196.

340. In order to determine the number of enemy dead the hands of the corpses were cut off and piled for recording by the scribe. Two registers of the counting of the hands of Hittites killed in battle with Ramses II. See No. 318 for scene of the actual cutting off of the hands. Cf. I Sam. 18:25 ff.

Abydos, temple of Ramses II, exterior of southern long wall. Limestone. Ramses II (1301-1234). Wresz., vol. 2, pl. 24 (center). *AOB*, 113. Photograph Foto Marburg.

341. Detail from large scene of the naval battle of Ramses III with the Sea Peoples. The ship shown here is one of four Egyptian ships which are engaged in battle with five enemy vessels (to be distinguished by a bird's head on both prow and stern). The Egyptian ship consists of a crescent-shaped keel, a single mast topped by a crow's-nest just above the yard arm with its furled sail, a row of oars, and a large paddle used as a rudder. The prow of the boat ends in the head of a lioness which holds the head of an Asiatic in her mouth. From the deck bowmen fight against the Sea Peoples, who are pictured falling into the water. The enemies are shaved and wear the high feathered headdress (see No. 57).

Medinet Habu, exterior of north wall, second court. Length of ship: about 1.88 m. Ramses III (1195-1164). The Epigraphic Survey, *Earlier Historical Records of Ramses III, Medinet Habu*, vol. 1, *OIP*, 8, Chicago, 1930, pl. 40A. H. H. Nelson, "The Naval Battle Pictured at Medinet Habu," *JNES*, vol. 2, 1943, pp. 40-55. *AOB*, 112 (upper left). See *ANET*, 263. Breasted, *AR*, vol. 4, §§74-75, for description of entire scene. Photograph courtesy of the Oriental Institute.

342. The text of this stela contains in line 27 the only mention of the name "Israel" in all ancient Egyptian writing. For translation of the hymn of victory see *ANET*, 376-378. In the center of the relief at the top of the stela stands the god Amon represented twice under the winged sun-disc. The king also is shown twice, standing before the god with sickle-sword and scepter. At the extreme right stands the god Horus, and at the left, the goddess Mut.

343. Detail of "Israel."

Cairo Museum, 34025. Thebes, Mer-ne-Ptah's mortuary temple. Granite. Height: 3.18 m. Fifth year of Mer-ne-Ptah (1234-1222). W. M. F. Petrie, *Six Temples at Thebes*, London, 1897, pls. 13, 14. P. Lacau, *Stèles du nouvel empire, Cat. gén.*, Cairo, 1909, pl. 17. *AOB*, 109. Photograph courtesy of the Cairo Museum and Archives Photographiques (for detail).

344. A Syrian town (probably Tunip) surrounded on three sides by a moat, is represented as a fortress in three stages. The attacking Egyptians have reached by ladders the lower (or outside) turret, where they engage the defenders in hand-to-hand combat. An Egyptian trumpeter signals the victory. Above, the inhabitants of the town raise their hands in a gesture of sur-

render and hold up braziers. They are all bearded and have heavy hair about which a fillet is tied behind. Egyptian soldiers with shields tied to their backs hack away at the door (below) of the fortress and at trees (upper right). Others may be setting fire to heaps of grain. Also shown are a grapevine and a pomegranate. See *ANET*, 262, fn. 21 for suggestion that this may be "pious or propagandistic forgery."

Medinet Habu, exterior of north wall. Limestone relief. Height: about 2.65 m. Ramses III (1195-1164). The Epigraphic Survey, *Later Historical Records of Ramses III, Medinet Habu*, vol. 2, *OIP*, 9, Chicago, 1932, pl. 89. Wresz., vol. 2, pl. 151 (left). Breasted, *AR*, vol. 4, §118. H. H. Nelson, *Medinet Habu Reports, OIC*, 10, Chicago, 1931, fig. 19. Photograph (drawing reinforced by Chubb) courtesy of Oriental Institute.

345. Ramses III in his chariot charges over the bodies of Hittites from the two towns represented by the fortresses at the left. The Hittites are shown beardless and with long hair hanging down below the shoulders. The scene is a degenerate rendering of a traditional representation and its accuracy as a historical record is questionable (*ANET*, 262, fn. 21). The tower fortress bears the inscription: "the town of Arzawa ['*Irt*]."

Medinet Habu, exterior of first pylon, north tower, west face. Limestone relief. Height: about 5.30 m. Ramses III (1195-1164). The Epigraphic Survey, *Later Historical Records of Ramses III, Medinet Habu*, vol. 2, *OIP*, 9, Chicago, 1932, pl. 87 (left). Wresz., vol. 2, pl. 145. Breasted, *AR*, vol. 4, §120. W. F. Edgerton and John A. Wilson, *Historical Records of Ramses III, SAOC*, 12, Chicago, 1936, pp. 94-95, for translation of text. H. H. Nelson, *Medinet Habu Reports, OIC*, 10, Chicago, 1931, fig. 17. Photograph courtesy of the Oriental Institute.

346. The towers and walls of this fortress in Amor are manned by Syrian lancers, as the chief of the town stands on one of the gate towers at the left holding out a brazier in a gesture of surrender. The fortress is surrounded by four crenelated walls; above the highest are three towers, before which is the triangular standard of the town hanging from a pole which is topped by two arrows. See *ANET*, 262, fn. 21.

Medinet Habu, first court, north wall. Limestone relief. Height: about 4.20 m. Ramses III (1195-1164). The Epigraphic Survey, *Later Historical Records of Ramses III, Medinet Habu*, vol. 2, *OIP*, 9, Chicago, 1932, pl. 95. Wresz., vol. 2, pl. 146. Breasted, *AR*, vol. 4, §117. W. F. Edgerton and John A. Wilson, *Historical Records of Ramses III, SAOC*, 12, Chicago, 1936, pp. 100-101, for translation of text. H. H. Nelson, *Medinet Habu Reports, OIC*, 10, Chicago, 1931, fig. 20. Photograph (reinforced by Bollacher) courtesy of the Oriental Institute.

347. King Ramses III is shown receiving three lines of bound Syrian prisoners, who are dressed alike in the typical Syrian garment (see No. 43), and who are presented to him by the Crown Prince and Egyptian officials.

Medinet Habu, first court, north wall. Limestone relief. Height: about 4 m. Ramses III (1195-1164). The Epigraphic Survey, *Later Historical Records of Ramses III, Medinet Habu*, vol. 2, *OIP*, 9, Chicago, 1932, pl. 96. Wresz., vol. 2, pl. 148 (photograph). Breasted, *AR*, vol. 4, §124. W. F. Edgerton and John A. Wilson, *Historical Records of Ramses III, SAOC*, 12,

Chicago, 1936, pp. 101-102, for translation of text. H. H. Nelson, *Medinet Habu Reports, OIC*, 10, Chicago, 1931, fig. 16. Photograph courtesy of the Oriental Institute.

348. Heap of hands severed by the soldiers of Ramses III in his victory over the Libyans. See also No. 340.

Medinet Habu, second court, south wall. Limestone relief. Height: about 0.55 m. Ramses III (1195-1164). The Epigraphic Survey, *Earlier Historical Records of Ramses III, Medinet Habu*, vol. 1, *OIP*, 8, Chicago, 1930, pl. 54A. Photograph courtesy of the Oriental Institute.

349. Although the figure of Sheshonk was never completed, the scene was designed after the usual scheme of showing a king's conquest (see No. 312). To the right are the massed enemies with upraised hands. In the center is a large figure of Amon with sickle-sword in his right hand and cords by which he leads the bound captives represented over the five rows of name-rings to the left of the lower part of his figure. Below, the goddess Wast holds cords by which other name-ring figures are drawn. The names (originally about 180) are important for the light which they shed on the Egyptian invasion of Palestine (I Kings 14:25-26; II Chron. 12:2-4). For convenient listing of places identifiable see *ANET*, 242-243.

Karnak, exterior of the south wall of Amon temple. Limestone relief. Sheshonk I (945-924). For discussion, full bibliography of publications, and translation see J. Simons, *Handbook for the Study of Egyptian Topographical Lists Relating to Western Asia*, Leiden, 1937, pp. 90-101, 178-186. Breasted, *AR*, vol. 4, §§709-722. Photograph courtesy of A. Gaddis, Luxor.

350. Four registers from an obelisk carved on two sides with scenes depicting the reception of tribute by King Ashurnasirpal II, who is shown in the fourth register, first side receiving his officers. The king stands upon a crenelated wall; behind him are an attendant and a fortress with towers and turrets; beyond, to the left, is a forest, in which a hunter is shooting a deer. To the right, tribute is being weighed on a balance. The bottom register, first side, is a procession of porters with tribute, which includes a table suspended from poles, vessels, and two bulls (with calf represented on the back of one). The fourth register, second side, consists of a line of men with poles on their shoulders, bearing tribute or booty of cloth, vessels, and furniture; at the end, a porter carries a heavy object, perhaps an ingot of copper. Below, is another line of tribute bearers; at the end, a calf leaps before a cow. The fragmentary inscriptions duplicate passages in the standard inscriptions of Ashurnasirpal.

British Museum, 118800. Nimrud, 1853. Black basalt. Width: 0.736 m. Ashurnasirpal II (883-859). C. J. Gadd, *The Stones of Assyria*, London, 1936, pl. 6 (for upper half), pp. 128-129. Photographs courtesy BM.

351-355. Scenes from the Black Obelisk of Shalmaneser III. The twenty panels are from the sides of a monument which resembles an obelisk; the top (not shown) is not in the form of a pyramid, but ends in three steps, all of which are inscribed with annalistic inscriptions. At the base, below the last row of panels, there are additional inscriptions. The panels were intended to be viewed in five rows (I, II, III, IV, V, from top to bottom), each running around the four sides of the obelisk as though in a continuous frieze. Over each row of panels is an inscription describing the scene below. The top row of reliefs (I) depicts Sua, the Gilzanite, bringing tribute of "silver, gold, lead, copper vessels, staves for the hand of the king, horses, camels whose backs were doubled" to Shalmaneser III. To the left (351), the Assyrian king, armed with bow and arrows and accompanied by an attendant and a soldier, receives Sua, who bows before the king under the symbols of the winged sun-disc and the eight-pointed star. Two officers, each followed by an attendant, stand behind Sua and before the captives, who bring their tribute. One leads a horse, two bring camels, and five carry other tribute. The Gilzanites are shown with beard and wearing a tasseled cap and fringed robe. On their feet are high shoes with pointed and slightly upturned toes. In the second row (II) Shalmaneser receives the tribute of "Jehu, son of Omri," who is upon his hands and knees, with his face to the ground (detail shown in No. 355). The Assyrian king is holding a bowl in his raised hand. He is followed by an attendant holding a parasol and another with a club in his hand. Four Assyrians—one bearded officer and three attendants—stand behind Jehu and precede the procession of thirteen Israelite porters. Each of these figures is bearded, wears the pointed cap and a long garment, over which is thrown a fringed mantle with tasseled ends, which are long enough to be thrown over the shoulder. Like the people shown in the first row, they too seem to wear the pointed shoe. The tribute carried is not clearly identifiable, but the objects listed in the inscription may fit the representation of the relief. Listed are: "silver, gold, a golden *saplu*-bowl, a golden vase with pointed bottom, golden tumblers, golden buckets, tin, a staff for a king (and) wooden *puruhtu*." In row III the tribute of the country Musri is shown. It consists entirely of animals led or driven by attendants dressed in simple, knee-length garments. The men are bearded and barefoot. The animals are mentioned in the inscription as "camels whose backs are doubled, a river ox (hippopotamus), a *sakea*-animal (rhinoceros), a *susu*-antelope, elephants, *bazitu*- (and) *uqupu*-monkeys." In the fourth register (IV) there is shown the tribute of Marduk-apal-uṣur of Suhi. To the left (351), one panel shows two lions and a stag in a heavily wooded mountainous region. The remainder of the frieze depicts thirteen porters with their tribute. They are all shown as bearded, with long hair held in place by a band, clothed in a long, fringed garment, and barefoot. Among the objects carried as tribute can be seen woven material, tusks of elephants, and pieces of wood. The inscription mentions: "silver, gold, pitchers of gold, ivory, javelins, *bûia*, brightly colored (and) linen garments." The fifth register (V) is labeled as the

tribute of Karparunda from Hattina. With the bearers of tribute are an Assyrian officer and his attendant. Some of the porters wear the pointed cap, while others have their hair held in place by a fillet. Some are barefoot; others wear shoes with pointed toes. In general, it seems that here the artist merely repeated details from the panels above.

British Museum, 118885. Nimrud, 1846. Entire obelisk, height: 2.02 m; width, below: about 0.60 m. Shalmaneser III (858-824). A. H. Layard, *The Monuments of Nineveh*, London, 1849, pls. 53-56. C. J. Gadd, *The Stones of Assyria*, London, 1936, pp. 147-148. *AOB*, 121-125. Text published by A. H. Layard, *Inscriptions in the Cuneiform Character*, London, 1851, pls. 87-98. (pl. 98 has the lines over the panels, which are translated in Luckenbill, *AR*, vol. 1, §§589-593; *ANET*, 281 (II, III, V, only). Photographs courtesy BM.

Bronze Bands from Balawat

The following scenes (Nos. 356-365) and No. 625 are from hammered and engraved bronze bands once attached as ornaments to the gates of a palace of Shalmaneser III (858-824) and illustrate incidents from his military campaigns. According to the natives of the district of Nimrud, who discovered them in 1876, the bands came from a mound near the village of Tell Balawat. Although considerable doubt has been expressed as to this alleged provenience (L. W. King, *Bronze Reliefs from the Gates of Shalmaneser*, London, 1915, pp. 5-6), the name of the "Gates of Balawat" has become attached to these objects. From the bands now in the British Museum, it is possible to estimate that each door of the gates to which these bands were tacked measured about 1.83 m. in width and was over 6 m. in height. The metal of which the bands were made was only about 0.0015 m. in thickness; the width was about 0.28 m. and the length about 2.44 m. In addition to the thirteen bands now in the British Museum there are smaller collections of fragments in the Collection de Clercq (now deposited in the Louvre), in the Museum of the Ancient Orient in Istanbul, and in the Walters Art Gallery in Baltimore. See in addition to the publication cited in the following bibliographies E. Unger, *Zum Bronzetor von Balawat*, Leipzig, 1912. For translations of inscriptions see Luckenbill, *AR*, vol. 1, §§612-614.

356. The fortified town of Tyre, shown to the left of the upper register, is surrounded by water. Tribute is being ferried from the island to the mainland in boats, which are drawn up to the shore by ropes. Porters wade into the water and carry on their shoulders bales of goods. The text over the scene reads: "I received the tribute (brought) on ships from the inhabitants of Tyre and Sidon" (*ANET*, 281). In the lower register chariots and footmen advance from the Assyrian camp (to the left) toward the town of Hazazu, which is under attack. Each chariot is drawn by a team of horses and contains two men. The footsoldiers are armed with swords, maces, bows, and quivers.

British Museum. "Tell Balawat." Bronze. Height: about 0.28 m. Shalmaneser III (858-824). L. W. King, *Bronze Reliefs from the Gates of Shalmaneser*, London, 1915, pl. 13, p. 23. Photograph courtesy BM.

357. (continuation of No. 356.) In the register above (from left to right) porters carry bales supported on shoulder pads; three men carry cauldrons on their heads;

two carry trays, perhaps filled with ivories; two smaller figures carry some small objects, apparently of value; then come two taller figures. Two officers, each with his attendant, present the tribute to the king (not shown). The Phoenician porters are shown wearing pointed caps; in some cases a turban is wound around, with the ends falling down over the shoulders. The long garment extending to the ankles worn by the Phoenicians is easily distinguishable from the long Assyrian garment by the absence of a fringe. In the lower register, the Assyrian king stands in the center, followed by his attendants, and receives from his officers and their attendants the prisoners from Hazazu.

British Museum. "Tell Balawat." Bronze. Height: about 0.28 m. Shalmaneser III (858-824). L. W. King, *Bronze Reliefs from the Gates of Shalmaneser*, London, 1915, pl. 14, p. 23. Photograph courtesy BM.

358. (continuation of No. 357). The king is followed by four attendants and a groom, who leads the horses attached to his chariot. Following the chariot is an extra pair of horses, on one of which is mounted a soldier. In the lower register is a procession of prisoners from Hazazu; the men are nude and some have their arms tied behind their backs, while others carry objects on their shoulders. Three women and one child form a part of the procession.

British Museum. "Tell Balawat." Bronze. Height: about 0.28 m. Shalmaneser III (858-824). L. W. King, *Bronze Reliefs from the Gates of Shalmaneser*, London, 1915, pl. 15, p. 23. Photograph courtesy BM.

359. (continuation of No. 358). Three Assyrian war chariots are shown, each with two horses, a driver, and an officer. Below, stands the town of Hazazu on a tell, with but two of its inhabitants in its towers. Flames are leaping up from the walls of the evacuated town. To the right, Assyrian soldiers with ladder, shields, and bow are storming the wall.

British Museum. "Tell Balawat." Bronze. Height: about 0.28 m. Shalmaneser III (858-824). L. W. King, *Bronze Reliefs from the Gates of Shalmaneser*, London, 1915, pl. 16, p. 23. Photograph courtesy BM.

360. (continuation of No. 359). Above, is an Assyrian war chariot followed by a spare pair of horses. Below, the Assyrian soldiers are slaying the little men of Hazazu. Several of the slain are lying on the ground.

British Museum. "Tell Balawat." Bronze. Height: about 0.28 m. Shalmaneser III (858-824). L. W. King, *Bronze Reliefs from the Gates of Shalmaneser*, London, 1915, pl. 17, p. 23. Photograph courtesy BM.

361. (continuation of No. 360). Two fully armed soldiers go forth from a fortified military camp, inside of which are a horse and his groom, and a man who is probably preparing food (see Nos. 170 and 171 for other camp scenes). Below, the slaughter of the men of Hazazu continues; two soldiers seem to have hung the heads of two of the slain to the harness about the horses' necks; below the horses lies a decapitated corpse.

British Museum. "Tell Balawat." Bronze. Height: about 0.28 m. Shalmaneser III (858-824). L. W. King, *Bronze Reliefs from the Gates of Shalmaneser*, London, 1915, pl. 18, p. 23. Photograph courtesy BM.

362. The text for the band (IV): "Smiting of Dabigu, the city of Ahuni, son of Adini" (Luckenbill, *AR*, vol. 1, §614). The town is represented as surrounded by a double wall and flanking towers, all crenelated. Mail-clad archers attack it from the left; while a sapper and a scaler lead the attack from the right. Below, an unnamed Syrian town which contains houses with beehive roofs, is under attack. Outside the walls are the bodies of six inhabitants impaled on the ramp leading to the upper entrance of the town.

British Museum. "Tell Balawat." Bronze. Height: about 0.28 m. Shalmaneser III (858-824). L. W. King, *Bronze Reliefs from the Gates of Shalmaneser*, London, 1915, pl. 21, p. 24. Photograph courtesy BM.

363. The inscription in the field of the upper register of this band (VI), "tribute of Sangara of Carchemish," would seem to refer to the scenes in both registers. In the upper register are bearers of tribute who are being led to the king. Below, a Syrian figure (third from left) may represent Sangara, and the small figure before him may be that of his daughter, who is conducted by attendants to the Assyrian king (shown at the extreme right). Two porters with tribute follow Sangara.

British Museum. "Tell Balawat." Bronze. Height: about 0.28 m. Shalmaneser III (858-824). L. W. King, *Bronze Reliefs from the Gates of Shalmaneser*, London, 1915, pl. 34, p. 26. Photograph courtesy BM.

364. Inscription in field of the lower register: "I entered the sources of the river; I offered sacrifices to the gods; my royal image I set up." (Luckenbill, *AR*, vol. 1, §614). This brief statement is amplified in the record of the seventh year on the "Black Obelisk" (lines 67-72): "I advanced to the source of the Tigris, where the waters gush forth. The weapon of Ashur I washed therein, I offered sacrifices to my gods, I spread a gladsome banquet. I fashioned a heroic image of my royal self" (Luckenbill, *AR*, vol. 1, §564). In the upper register, a ram is led forward and a bull is being slaughtered by soldiers who stand before a cave in the rock (?), in which are shown a stonemason with chisel and hammer and a scribe holding tablet and stylus (?). The four conelike objects with spheres over them may have been intended for representations of stalagmites. In the lower register, the king is shown upon a horse, preceded by soldiers and attendants who lead animals for slaughter. In the center, a stonemason is carving the royal image on the live rock at the opening of a tunnel through which the stream comes from the mountain. Men, perhaps with torches, are shown wading waist-deep through the water of the tunnel. An armed sentry stands on the hill above the tunnel.

British Museum. "Tell Balawat." Bronze. Height: about 0.28 m. Shalmaneser III (858-824). L. W. King, *Bronze Re-*

liefs from the Gates of Shalmaneser, London, 1915, pl. 59, pp. 30-31. *AOB*, 127. Photograph courtesy BM.

365. An inscription on band XIII, of which this scene is a part, reads: "Ashtamaku, the royal city of Irhulêni of the land of Hamath, together with eighty-six cities I captured" (Luckenbill, *AR*, vol. 1, §614). In the upper register archers assault a town in Hamath, situated in a wooded region. Scaling ladders have been set up at each side of the fortress. Below, soldiers are seen swimming in the water. In the lower register, chariots drive away, leading a line of female captives.

British Museum. "Tell Balawat." Bronze. Height: about 0.28 m. Shalmaneser III (858-824). L. W. King, *Bronze Reliefs from the Gates of Shalmaneser*, London, 1915, pl. 75, p. 34. Photograph courtesy BM.

366. The town of Astartu (?)—perhaps biblical Ashtaroth—sits on a hill and is surrounded by a double wall flanked with turreted towers. Both the walls and the towers are crenelated. To the right, Assyrian soldiers lead away the sheep and the inhabitants, who carry their possessions in bags over their shoulders. For the Syrian dress see Nos. 351-355.

British Museum, 118908. Nimrud. Gypsum. Height: about 1.06 m. Tiglath-pileser III (744-727). British Museum, *Assyrian Sculptures in the British Museum from Shalmaneser III to Sennacherib*, London, 1938, pl. 9. C. J. Gadd, *The Assyrian Sculptures*, London, 1934, pl. 8. *AOB*, 133. B. Meissner, *ZDPV*, vol. 39, 1916, pl. 2, pp. 261-263. Photograph courtesy BM.

367. A double-walled and turreted town, situated in a palm-growing region, has been captured; battering-rams stand beside the wall. Above, two scribes, one with stylus and tablet and the other with pen or brush and writing material of skin or papyrus, record the spoil (see Nos. 235, 236). Cattle are driven away by the captors. Below, the inhabitants, possibly women and children, are driven away in carts drawn by teams of oxen.

British Museum, 118882. Nimrud. Gypsum. Length: 2.90 m. Tiglath-pileser III (744-727). British Museum, *Assyrian Sculptures in the British Museum from Shalmaneser III to Sennacherib*, London, 1938, pl. 11. C. J. Gadd, *The Stones of Assyria*, London, 1934, pl. 11, p. 154. Photograph courtesy BM.

368. The walls of a town are attacked by a four-wheeled siege-engine supported by bowmen, who shoot from behind large shields made of reeds. From the tower of the town an inhabitant extends his hands in surrender; the bodies of three townsmen are impaled outside the wall.

British Museum, 118903. Nimrud. Gypsum. Height: 1.09 m. Tiglath-pileser III (744-727). British Museum, *Assyrian Sculptures in the British Museum from Shalmaneser III to Sennacherib*, London, 1938, pl. 14. *AOB*, 132. C. J. Gadd, *The Stones of Assyria*, London, 1936, p. 156. Photograph courtesy BM.

369. Drawing of a relief, now lost, which shows the town of Gazru (Gezer?) under attack by Assyrian battering-ram, lancer, and archer who shoots from behind a thick shield made of reeds. The inhabitants of the town stand in its turrets and on its walls making gestures of sur-

render. Bricks from the wall have begun to fall out under the assault.

From Nimrud. Tiglath-pileser III (744-727). A. H. Layard, *The Monuments of Nineveh*, London, 1849, pl. 62, 2. *AOB*, 134. B. Meissner, *ZDPV*, vol. 39, 1916, pl. 3a, pp. 261-263. Photograph from Layard's publication.

370. In the center of the scene of the plundering of Musasir stands a temple with gable roof surmounted at the ridge by a spear point. The building has a porch supported by columns, on which are hung round shields. Two, which are shown in profile, are decorated with animal heads. A spear decorates each side of the entrance into the porch. To the right, is the figure of a cow with sucking calf. Before the building stand two large vessels supported by stands. Assyrian soldiers have climbed to the roof of the building, from which they make their way to the adjoining buildings. On the building to the left an Assyrian official is seated before two scribes.

From Khorsabad. Sargon II (721-705). P. E. Botta, *Monument de Ninive*, vol. 2, Paris, 1849, pl. 141. *AOB*, 136. Photograph from Botta's publication.

371. Sennacherib sits upon a high throne, with his feet on a footstool, holding a bow and arrow, receiving the prisoners and the spoil from Lachish. An inscription before him reads: "Sennacherib, king of the world, king of Assyria, sat upon a *nîmedu*-throne and passed in review the booty (taken) from Lachish (*La-ki-su*)" (*ANET*, 288). Before the king are an officer, soldiers, and kneeling and prostrate figures of the inhabitants of the town; behind him are two attendants with fly-whisks. The inhabitants of Lachish are dressed in a short-sleeved long garment which reaches to the ankles; they wear short hair and beard, both tightly curled; and they are barefoot. In the background of the scene are pictured palm trees and vines laden with clusters of grapes.

British Museum, 124911. Kuyunjik. Sennacherib (704-681). Gypsum. Width: 1.75 m. A. H. Layard, *A Second Series of the Monuments of Nineveh*, London, 1853, pl. 23 (right). A. Paterson, *Palace of Sinacherib*, The Hague, pl. 74. C. J. Gadd, *The Assyrian Sculptures*, London, 1934, pl. 6, *AOB*, 138. Photograph courtesy BM.

372-373. This part of a series of reliefs, to which No. 371 belongs, shows the storming of the town of Lachish by Sennacherib. In the upper part of both pieces can be seen the double-walled town of Lachish. Both walls have towers at regular intervals, manned by bowmen and soldiers who hurl stones and firebrands upon the attackers. To the right (No. 373), the tower over the gateway to the town is under attack. Against it the Assyrians have built a track of three layers of logs laid end to end, over which they have moved a siege-engine equipped with a spearlike beam by which the attackers seek to destroy the superstructure of the tower. Within the siege-engine can be seen a bowman and another soldier who holds a long-handled ladle with which he pours water on the front of the engine to extinguish the firebrands which are hurled from the wall above. There follow an Assyrian bowman under the protection of a large shield with curved top, three lancers with round shields, and two bowmen. Other tracks are shown built for the siege-engines attacking other parts of the walls. The turret of the tower is manned by four soldiers: one bowman, and three soldiers who hurl stones and firebrands (?). The superstructure of the tower is made of a frame into which are set disclike objects or shields. Below three small windows is a door from which emerge men and women carrying their possessions from the doomed town. To the right are three nude figures impaled. The area around the tower is filled with the debris of battle: quivers, lances, stones, shields, and a broken ladder.

British Museum, 124905, 124906. Kuyunjik. Gypsum. Height: about 1.77 m. Sennacherib (704-681). A. H. Layard, *A Second Series of the Monuments of Nineveh*, London, 1853, pl. 21. A. Paterson, *Palace of Sinacherib*, The Hague, pls. 69-70. *AOB*, 141 (drawing). Photograph courtesy BM.

374. Immediately behind the king seated on his throne (No. 371) is the royal tent, with its poles and guys, pitched on a wooded hill. Above, is an inscription: "Tent of Sennacherib, king of Assyria" (Luckenbill, *AR*, vol. 2, §496).

British Museum, 124911, 124912. Kuyunjik. Gypsum. Height: about 1.30 m. A. H. Layard, *A Second Series of the Monuments of Nineveh*, London, 1853, pl. 23 (upper right). A. Paterson, *Palace of Sinacherib*, The Hague, pls. 74-75. Photograph courtesy BM.

375. This relief, from the time of Tiglath-pileser III, shows two Assyrian horsemen equipped with long spears pursuing an unarmed enemy (perhaps an Arab) riding a camel. Below are three bodies, one of which is headless.

British Museum, 118878. Nimrud. Gypsum. Height: 1.18 m. Tiglath-pileser III (744-727). A. H. Layard, *The Monuments of Nineveh*, London, 1849, pl. 57. C. J. Gadd, *The Stones of Assyria*, London. 1936, pl. 10, pp. 151-152. British Museum, *Assyrian Sculptures in the British Museum from Shalmaneser III to Sennacherib*, London, 1938, pl. 19. Photograph courtesy BM.

V. Royalty and Dignitaries

EGYPTIAN

376. A statue of King Djoser who is wrapped in a long cloak and seated on a throne. He wears the *nemes* headdress over a long wig, and a beard, now partly broken away, was fastened to the chin. Eyes, which were set in copper sockets, have disappeared. Djoser was responsible for mining operations at Sinai (*ANET*, 227). See No. 764 for pyramid of Djoser.

Cairo Museum. Sakkarah, 1924-1925. Gray siliceous limestone. Life-size. Third Dynasty (2700-2650). *ASAE*, vol. 25, 1925, pl. 4, pp. 149-150. Schäfer-Andrae, 228. Photograph Foto Marburg.

377. King Khaf-Re (Chephren) sits upon a throne, wearing on his head the *nemes* headdress and a ceremonial beard. On the back of the throne stands the falcon Horus with its wings extended to cover the king's neck. See No. 765 for pyramid of Khaf-Re.

Cairo, 14. Giza. Dark gray diorite. Height of entire statue: 1.68 m. Fourth Dynasty (2650-2500). L. Borchardt, *Statuen und Statuetten von Königen und Privatleuten*, pt. 1, *Cat. gén.*, Berlin, 1911, no. 14. Schäfer-Andrae, pl. 2. *AOB*, 35. Photograph courtesy of Cairo Museum.

378. Men-kau-Re (Mycerinus), builder of the third pyramid of Giza, wears the white crown of Upper Egypt, a ceremonial beard, a collar necklace, and kilt. Beside him are two goddesses: at his right, Hathor; at his left, the nome-goddess of Diospolis Parva.

Cairo Museum, 180. Giza. Slate. Fourth Dynasty (2650-2500). G. A. Reisner, *Mycerinus*, Cambridge, Mass., 1931, pl. 45d, pp. 109-110. J. Leibovitch, *Ancient Egypt*, Cairo, 1938, fig. 47. Photograph courtesy of the Museum of Fine Arts, Boston.

379. King Pepi I is seated on a throne, wearing the white crown of Upper Egypt and holding the symbols of royal power. Behind him is the protecting falcon perched on the back of the throne. The king's name is inscribed on the back of the throne, with falcon as the first word of the inscription. For Asiatic campaigns under Pepi I see *ANET*, 227-228.

Brooklyn Museum, 39.120. Purchased. Alabaster. Sixth Dynasty (2350-2200). Height: 0.265 m. Brooklyn Museum, *Egyptian Art in the Brooklyn Museum Collection*, Brooklyn, 1952, no. 21. C. Aldred, *Old Kingdom Art in Ancient Egypt*, London, 1949, nos. 62-63. Photograph courtesy Br. M.

380. King Pepi I kneels holding in each hand a wine jar. On his head he wears the *nemes* headdress. The eyes are alabaster and obsidian inlays set in copper.

Brooklyn Museum, 39.121. Purchased. Green slate. Height: 0.152 m. Sixth Dynasty (2350-2200). Brooklyn Museum, *Egyptian Art in the Brooklyn Museum Collection*, Brooklyn, 1952, no. 20. C. Aldred, *Old Kingdom Art in Ancient Egypt*, London, 1949, nos. 60, 61. Photograph courtesy Br. M.

381. Pepi II (Nefer-ka-Re) is seated on the lap of his mother (not shown) and wears the *nemes* headdress with the uraeus serpent. See *ANET*, 3 for translation of "The Creation by Atum," carved on the inside of the pyramid of Pepi II.

Brooklyn Museum, 39.119. Purchased. Alabaster. Height from pelvis to top of headdress: 0.106 m. Sixth Dynasty (2350-2200). Brooklyn Museum, *Egyptian Art in the Brooklyn Museum Collection*, Brooklyn, 1952, no. 19. Photograph courtesy Br. M.

382. Sen-Usert II, wearing the *nemes* headdress, sits on a throne, the side of which has the symbol of the uniting of the two lands. The name of Sen-Usert II appears in No. 3. Statue later usurped by Ramses II.

Cairo Museum, 432. Tanis. Black granite. Height: 2.65 m. Sen-Usert II (1897-1878). L. Borchardt, *Statuen und Statuetten von Königen und Privatleuten*, pt. 2, *Cat. gén.*, Berlin, 1925, no. 432. W. F. M. Petrie, *Tanis*, pt. 2, London, 1888, pl. 11, no. 171, for inscription. Photograph Foto Marburg.

383. Painted wooden figure of King Sen-Usert I, wearing the white crown of Upper Egypt and holding a staff in his hand. For story of Si-nuhe from time of Sen-Usert I, see *ANET*, 18-22.

Cairo. Lisht. Painted wood. Height: 0.57 m. Sen-Usert I

(1971-1928). TEL, Cairo, no. 52. Schäfer-Andrae, 284 (left). H. G. Evers, *Staat aus dem Stein*, Munich, 1929, vol. 1, pl. 46. Photograph courtesy of Cairo Museum.

384. King Sen-Usert III wears the *nemes* headdress, a necklace with pendant, and a closely pleated tunic which projects outward over his knees. From the belt, inscribed with the king's prenomen Kha-kau-Re, there hangs a long lappet ornamented with two uraei. For an Asiatic campaign of Sen-Usert III see *ANET*, 230.

British Museum, 169 (685) Deir el-Bahri. Gray granite. Sen-Usert III (1880-1840). E. Naville, *The XIth Dynasty Temple at Deir el-Bahari*, pt. 1, London, 1907, pl. 19D. See E. A. W. Budge, *Egyptian Sculptures in the British Museum*, London, 1914, pl. 11. Photograph courtesy BM.

385. Seated figure of Amen-em-het III, wearing the *nemes* headdress with uraeus serpent, and pendant. For inscription of the time of Amen-em-het III dealing with the mines of Sinai, see *ANET*, 229-230.

Cairo Museum, 385. Hawara. Limestone. Height: 1.60 m. Amen-em-het III (1840-1790). L. Borchardt, *Statuen und Statuetten von Königen und Privatleuten*, pt. 2, Cat. gén., Berlin, 1925, no. 385. Schäfer-Andrae, 282. Photograph courtesy of the Metropolitan Museum of Art, New York.

386. This sphinx of the Twelfth Dynasty belonged to Amen-em-het III; it was reused by Mer-ne-Ptah.

Cairo Museum, 394. Tanis. Granite. Length: 1.25 m. Twelfth Dynasty (1990-1780). L. Borchardt, *Statuen und Statuetten von Königen und Privatleuten*, pt. 2, Cat. gén., Berlin, 1925, no. 394. É. Drioton, *Art égyptien*, Paris, 1950, no. 40. A. Weigall, *Ancient Egyptian Works of Art*, London, 1924, p. 102. Photograph Foto Marburg.

387. The upper part of a standing statue of Thut-mose III, wearing the crown of Upper Egypt. For translation of texts dealing with the Asiatic campaigns of Thut-mose III see *ANET*, 234-241.

Cairo, 42053. Karnak, 1904-1905. Basalt. Height of entire statue: 2 m. Thut-mose III (1490-1436). G. Legrain, *Statues et statuettes*, vol. 1, Cat. gén., Cairo, 1906, pl. 30. Schäfer-Andrae, pl. 13. *AOB*, 52. Photograph courtesy of the Cairo Museum.

388. The upper part of a statue of Queen Hat-shepsut, who wears the *nemes* headdress and a broad, beaded collar. The body was discovered by Lepsius and taken to Berlin in 1845; it later went to the Metropolitan Museum in New York as an exchange. The head is from the excavations of the Metropolitan, 1927-1928.

New York, Metropolitan Museum of Art, 29.3.2. Deir el-Bahri. Indurated limestone. Height of entire statue: about 1.95 m. Hat-shepsut (1486-1469). N. E. Scott, *Egyptian Statues*, New York, 1945, front cover. H. Ranke, *The Art of Ancient Egypt*, Vienna, 1936, pl. 110. C. Aldred, *New Kingdom Art in Ancient Egypt*, London, 1951, pl. 21, p. 47. Photograph courtesy MMA.

389. The cow-goddess Hathor wears a headdress of two plumes over a sun-disc between two horns. Under her head is the figure of a king, who is identified as Amen-hotep II by a cartouche, but which may have been orig-

inally intended for the figure of Thut-mose III, the builder of the chapel in which the statue was found. On each side of the cow's neck are papyrus stalks. Another human figure (the king as a youth) drinks milk from the cow's udder.

Cairo. Deir el-Bahri, 1906. Sandstone. Length: 2.25 m. Eighteenth Dynasty (1550-1350). TEL, Cairo, no. 86. J. Leibovitch, *Ancient Egypt*, Cairo, 1938, fig. 76. Porter and Moss, *Bibliography*, vol. 2, p. 129. Photograph courtesy of the Cairo Museum.

390. Amen-hotep II, famous for his physical prowess (see *ANET*, 244-245), stands in his chariot discharging arrows into a target before him. Below is a copper (?) target already pierced by five of the king's arrows.

Karnak. Granite. Amen-hotep II (1447-1421). H. Chevrier, *ASAE*, vol. 28, 1928, p. 126. J. A. Wilson, *The Burden of Egypt*, Chicago, 1951, fig. 21a, pp. 195-199. See also *BMMA*, November 1935, ii, p. 49, figs. 4 and 7. Photograph Foto Marburg.

391. The King Amen-hotep II kneels as he offers two libation jars. He wears the double crown of Upper and Lower Egypt, a ceremonial beard, and a short kilt. For the Asiatic campaigns of Amen-hotep II see *ANET*, 245-248.

New York, Metropolitan Museum of Art, 13.182.6. Purchased. Limestone. Height: 0.30 m. Amen-hotep II (1447-1421). N. E. Scott, *Egyptian Statuettes*, New York, 1946, no. 19. *BMMA*, vol. 11, October 1916, p. 211, fig. 1. Photograph courtesy MMA.

392. King Amen-hotep II, wearing the *nemes* headdress and a short kilt, kneels as he presents a table of offerings. See *ANET*, 245-248 for accounts of the king's campaigns in Asia.

Cairo Museum, 42073. Karnak, 1904. Gray granite. Height: 1.20 m. Amen-hotep II (1447-1421). G. Legrain, *Statues et statuettes*, Cat. gén., Cairo, 1906, pl. 43. Photograph courtesy of the Metropolitan Museum of Art, New York.

393. On a fragment of a throne of Thut-mose IV, the king is shown in the form of a sphinx treading upon his Asiatic enemies.

Boston, Museum of Fine Arts, 03.1131. Thebes, tomb of Thut-mose IV. Cedar wood. Height: 0.25 m. Thut-mose IV (1421-1413). H. Carter and P. E. Newberry, *The Tomb of Thoutmôsis IV*, London, 1904, pl. 6, 1A, pp. 20-21. Photograph courtesy MFA.

394. Head of Amen-hotep III carved on a limestone slab; the lower part has been altered. The king wears a wig with a band about which uraei serpents are wound; a double necklace is about his neck.

Berlin, Äg. 14503. Thebes, tomb of Kha-em-het. Limestone. Height: about 0.30 m. Amen-hotep III (1413-1377). Schäfer-Andrae, 368 (left). *AOB*, 63. Photograph Foto Marburg.

395. King Amen-hotep III wearing the blue crown with uraeus.

Berlin, Äg. 14442. Thebes, tomb of Kha-em-het. Limestone. Height: 0.69 m. Amen-hotep III (1413-1377). J. Pijoán, *Summa Artis*, vol. 3, Madrid, 1932, p. 263, fig. 344. Photograph Foto Marburg.

396. Fragments of a head from a colossal statue of Amen-hotep III.

British Museum, 6. Thebes. Hard sandstone. Height: 1.168 m. Amen-hotep III (1413-1377). E. A. W. Budge, *Egyptian Sculpture in the British Museum*, London, 1914, pl. 21. British Museum, *A General Introductory Guide to the Egyptian Collections*, London, 1930, fig. 98. Photograph courtesy BM.

397. A colossal group consisting of the seated King Amen-hotep III, wearing the ceremonial beard and *nemes* headdress, the Queen Tiy, wearing a heavy wig surmounted by a crown, and their three daughters, who are represented by diminutive figures along the front of the throne seat.

Cairo Museum, 610. Medinet Habu. Limestone. Height: 7 m. Amen-hotep III (1413-1377). G. Jéquier, *L'architecture et la décoration dans l'ancienne Égypte, Les temples memphites et thébains*, Paris, n. d., pl. 77. Photograph Foto Marburg.

398. Portrait head of Queen Tiy, wife of Amen-hotep III and mother of Akh-en-Aton, originally painted red and covered with a silver cap with gold band about the forehead. Over this cap is a linen and stucco covering decorated with blue pearls. The top of the headdress was decorated with a pointed peg as a support for some object. Earrings are worn.

Berlin, Äg. 21834. Medinet Gurob. Yew wood. Height: 0.107 m. Time of Amen-hotep III (1413-1377). L. Borchardt, *Der Porträtkopf der Königin Teje, WVDOG*, 18, Leipzig, 1911, pl. 4. *AOB*, 64. Schäfer-Andrae, 348. Photograph Foto Marburg.

399. Amen-hotep son of Hapu, minister to Amen-hotep III, wearing a heavy wig, is seated in a squatting position.

Cairo, 42127. Karnak, 1901. Granite. Height: 1.42 m. Period of Amen-hotep III (1413-1377). G. Legrain, *Statues et statuettes*, vol. 1, *Cat. gén.*, Cairo, 1906, pl. 76. Schäfer-Andrae, 338. Photograph courtesy of the Cairo Museum.

400. Amen-hotep III and Tiy, his queen, are seated before a table piled high with offerings. In front of the king is the *ankh* sign extending from the solar disc with rays ending in hands. The king, wearing the blue crown and a long, loose fitting robe, appears in a languid pose.

British Museum, 57399. Tell el-Amarna. Limestone. Height: 0.30 m. From the time of Akh-en-Aton (1380-1362). British Museum, *A General Introductory Guide to the Egyptian Collections*, London, 1930, fig. 189. F. Ll. Griffith, *JEA*, vol. 12, 1926, pl. 1, pp. 1-2. Photograph courtesy BM.

Akh-en-Aton

For translation of the hymn to the Aton, which embodies the religious beliefs of Akh-en-Aton, see *ANET*, 369-371.

401. Akh-en-Aton stands with feet together, presenting an offering tray, on which are etched various foods: breads, trussed ducks, and bouquets of lotus. The limestone statuette is painted with yellow ochre, except for the blue crown.

Cairo. Limestone. Height: 0.40 m. Akh-en-Aton (1380-1362).

TEL, Cairo, no. 96. R. Hamann, *Ägyptische Kunst*, Berlin, 1944, fig. 265. Photograph courtesy of the Cairo Museum.

402. Cast head of Akh-en-Aton.

Berlin, Äg. 21351. Tell el-Amarna, house P.47.1-3. Gypsum. Height: 0.26 m. Akh-en-Aton (1380-1362). A. Weigall, *Ancient Egyptian Works of Art*, London, 1924, p. 194. H. Fechheimer, *Die Plastik der Ägypter*, Berlin, 1923, pl. 84. Porter and Moss, *Bibliography*, vol. 4, p. 203. Photograph Foto Marburg.

403. This profile head of Akh-en-Aton (or of Smenkh-ka-Re) was intended as an inlay.

Brooklyn Museum, 33.685. Tell el-Amarna, 1932-1933. Red quartzite. Height: 0.118 m. Akh-en-Aton (1380-1362). *JEA*, vol. 19, 1933, pl. 16, no. 1, p. 116. Photograph courtesy Br. M.

404. This painted limestone bust of Queen Nefert-iti shows the queen wearing a high conical blue headdress encircled by a band, to which a uraeus is attached, and ending in streamers. About her neck is a beaded collar.

Berlin, Äg. 21300. Tell el-Amarna, 1912. Painted limestone. Height: 0.48 m. Akh-en-Aton (1380-1362). L. Borchardt, *Porträts der Königin Nofret-ete*, Leipzig, 1923, pls. 2-6, pp. 30-38. *AOB*, 68. Schäfer-Andrae, 350. Porter and Moss, *Bibliography*, vol. 4, pp. 202-203. Photograph Foto Marburg.

405. King Akh-en-Aton is seated on a throne, wearing a wig encircled by a band to which is attached the uraeus (cf. hairdress of the king in No. 407). Above him are the radiating hands from the sun-disc; before him are the hands—perhaps of a princess (see No. 409)—holding a bowl. The fragments would seem to belong to an altarpiece like that shown in No. 409.

British Museum, 24431. Limestone. 0.27 m. by 0.14 m. Akh-en-Aton (1380-1362). British Museum, *A General Introductory Guide to the Egyptian Collections*, London, 1930, p. 355, fig. 195. L. Borchardt, *Porträts der Königin Nofret-ete*, Leipzig, 1923, fig. 13. Porter and Moss, *Bibliography*, vol. 4, p. 233. Photograph courtesy BM.

406. This piece of limestone, with a hole for suspension at the top, may have served as a model for the workmen who built the city of Akhet-Aton at Tell el-Amarna. The incomplete head of Akh-en-Aton at the left is on a larger scale than the head of Nefert-iti at the right.

Brooklyn Museum, 16.48. Tell el-Amarna. Limestone. Height: 0.157 m. Akh-en-Aton (1380-1362). Brooklyn Museum, *Egyptian Art in the Brooklyn Museum Collection*, Brooklyn, 1952, no. 37. C. Aldred, *New Kingdom Art in Ancient Egypt*, London, 1951, no. 126. Photograph courtesy Br. M.

407. The king is shown in a casual pose, leaning on his staff and with legs crossed, as the queen offers him flowers. The identification of the figures is uncertain. Akh-en-Aton and Nefert-iti, Smenkh-ka-Re and Merit-Aton, Tut-ankh-Amon and his wife have been suggested.

Berlin, Äg. 15000. Purchased. Painted limestone. Height: 0.23 m. Time of Akh-en-Aton (1380-1362). H. Schäfer, *Amarna in Religion und Kunst*, Berlin, 1931, pl. 33. *AOB*, 66. C. Aldred, *New Kingdom Art in Ancient Egypt*, London, 1951, no. 125. L. Borchardt, *Porträts der Königin Nofret-ete*, Leipzig, 1923, fig. 22, p. 28. Porter and Moss, *Bibliography*, vol. 4, p. 233. Photograph Foto Marburg.

408. King Akh-en-Aton and his wife Nefert-iti standing with offerings for the sun-god Aton, who is represented above them by the sun-disc with uraeus and *ankh* sign (hieroglyph for "life"), from which extend fourteen rays, each ending in a hand. Two of these, those directly over the faces of the king and the queen, hold *ankh* signs. Behind the queen is a third figure, presumably a princess, who holds a sistrum in her upraised right hand. Before the king are two stands, each of which supports a bunch of lotus blossoms.

Cairo Museum. Tell el-Amarna, part of balustrade from a temple ramp. Limestone. Height: 1.05 m. Akh-en-Aton (1380-1362). J. D. S. Pendlebury, *The City of Akhenaten*, pt. 3, vol. 2, London, 1951, pl. 69, no. 5. TEL, Cairo, pl. 105. J. Leibovitch, *Ancient Egypt*, Cairo, 1938, fig. 74. Photograph courtesy of the Metropolitan Museum of Art, New York.

409. This painted limestone plaque, similar to No. 411, served as a chapel altar in a house at Tell el-Amarna. The queen sits holding two of the daughters, while the king gives something to the eldest.

Cairo. Tell el-Amarna, house Q.47.16. Limestone. Height: 0.435 m. Akh-en-Aton (1380-1362). L. Borchardt, *Porträts der Königin Nofret-ete*, Leipzig, 1923, pl. 1. Schäfer-Andrae, pl. 12. Porter and Moss, *Bibliography*, vol. 4, p. 204. Photograph courtesy of the Cairo Museum.

410. Two daughters of Akh-en-Aton are seated on cushions, wearing only bracelets, earrings, and beaded collars about their necks. These two figures, with their elongated skulls, form a part of a larger scene, of which only the heel of a foot can be identified at the upper right corner.

Oxford, Ashmolean Museum. Tell el-Amarna, 1891. Paint on thin plaster. Height: about 0.30 m. Akh-en-Aton (1380-1362). W. M. F. Petrie, *Tell el Amarna*, London, 1894, pl. 1, no. 12. Porter and Moss, *Bibliography*, vol. 4, p. 199. Photograph from N. M. Davies and A. H. Gardiner, *Ancient Egyptian Paintings*, Chicago, 1936, vol. 2, pl. 74, courtesy of the Oriental Institute.

411. Seated on chairs in a hall of the palace are the King Akh-en-Aton (left) and the Queen Nefert-iti (right) holding the royal princesses. The king wears the blue crown; the queen, a high turban-like headdress similar to that in No. 404. The queen holds two daughters, one upon her lap, and the other in her arm. The king kisses the daughter whom he holds with both hands. Above this family scene is the sun-disc with radiating arms.

Berlin, Äg. 14145. Tell el-Amarna. Limestone. Height: 0.32 m. Akh-en-Aton (1380-1362). H. Schäfer, *Amarna in Religion und Kunst*, Berlin, 1931, pl. 28. L. Borchardt, *Porträts der Königin Nofret-ete*, Leipzig, 1923, fig. 10. AOB, 67. Porter and Moss, *Bibliography*, vol. 4, p. 232. Photograph Foto Marburg.

412. Limestone bust of King Akh-en-Aton wearing the blue crown.

Louvre, E 11076. Tell el-Amarna. Limestone. Height: 0.58 m. Akh-en-Aton (1380-1362). G. Bénédite, Fondation Piot, vol. 13, 1906, pls. 1 and 2. TEL, vol. 1, pl. 72A. Porter and Moss, *Bibliography*, vol. 4, p. 234. Photograph JBP.

413. King Tut-ankh-Amon is shown wearing the *nemes* headdress with the uraeus and vulture symbols, representing Upper and Lower Egypt. Around his neck is a broad, beaded collar ending in hawk heads; on his chin is the long Osirian beard. This mask for the royal mummy is of gold inlaid with lapis lazuli, calcite, obsidian, quartz, carnelian, and colored glass. Individualized features of the face would suggest that the mask was intended for a likeness of the king.

Cairo. Thebes, tomb of Tut-ankh-Amon, no. 256A. Gold etc. Height: 0.54 m. Tut-ankh-Amon (1361-1352). H. Carter, *The Tomb of Tut-ankh-Amen*, vol. 2, London, 1927, frontispiece. TEL, Cairo, no. 134. P. Fox, *Tutankhamun's Treasure*, London, 1951, pl. 32. Photograph courtesy of the Cairo Museum.

414. One of two identical statues of King Tut-ankh-Amon which were found guarding the sealed entrance to the sepulchral chamber of the king. In his left hand he holds a scepter and in his right, a mace. The flesh is painted black and the accessories are gilded.

Cairo. Thebes, tomb of Tut-ankh-Amon. Wood. Height of statue: 1.85 m. Tut-ankh-Amon (1361-1352). H. Carter and A. C. Mace, *The Tomb of Tut-ankh-Amen*, vol. 1, London, 1923, pl. 1. TEL, Cairo, no. 108. Photograph courtesy of the Metropolitan Museum of Art, New York.

415-417. This wooden throne, overlaid with sheet gold, has feline legs, surmounted by lions' heads. The arms of the throne are in the form of serpents with wings, wearing the crowns of Upper and Lower Egypt and supporting with their wing tips the cartouches of Tut-ankh-Amon. On the inside of the back (No. 415) there is a family scene in the style of the Amarna Age. The king, wearing a composite crown, a broad collar, and pleated skirt, sits in a casual pose on a cushioned throne, with his feet on a footstool. Before him stands the Queen Ankhes-en-Amon holding a bowl in her left hand and touching the king with her right. Behind her is a stand on which is a beaded collar, shown as if seen from above. The entire scene is bordered with columns at the side and a frieze at the top, which is broken only in the center by the sun-disc with radiating arms.

Cairo. Thebes, tomb of Tut-ankh-Amon, no. 91. Wood, overlaid with gold, silver, blue faïence, calcite, and glass. Height: 1.04 m. Tut-ankh-Amon (1361-1352). H. Carter and A. C. Mace, *The Tomb of Tut-ankh-Amen*, vol. 1, London, 1923, pls. 2 (back only), 62, 63, 64. AOB, 82-83. P. Fox, *Tutankhamun's Treasure*, London, 1951, pl. 9 (side view). C. Aldred, *New Kingdom Art in Ancient Egypt*, London, 1951, no. 158 (back scene only). Photographs courtesy of the Cairo Museum (No. 415) and the Metropolitan Museum of Art, New York (Nos. 416 and 417).

418. Hor-em-heb, before he became king, clothed in a shirt with pleated sleeves and a pleated skirt, sits cross-legged with papyrus scroll unrolled across his lap. On the papyrus a psalm to Thoth is inscribed; on the base are prayers to Thoth, Ptah, Sekhmet and other gods. Nose has been restored. For texts from the tomb of Hor-em-heb see *ANET*, 250-251.

New York, Metropolitan Museum of Art, 23.10.1. Probably from Memphis. Porphyritic diorite. Height: 1.17 m. Hor-em-heb (reigned 1349-1319). *JEA*, vol. 10, 1924, pls. 1-3, pp. 1-5. *BMMA*, October 1923, ii, pp. 3-16. N. E. Scott, *Egyptian Statues*, New York, 1945, no. 20. C. Aldred, *New Kingdom Art in Ancient Egypt*, London, 1951, no. 169. Photograph courtesy MMA.

419. Detail of the head of the king, who is standing beside the larger seated figure of Amon. While the inscription names King Hor-em-heb, it is possible that the statuary originally belonged to Tut-ankh-Amon and was later usurped by Hor-em-heb.

Turin Museum. Thebes. Fine white limestone. Height of entire group: 2.11 m. Hor-em-heb (reigned 1349-1319). W. von Bissing, *Denkmäler ägyptischer Sculptur*, Munich, 1911-1914, pl. 46A. Photograph J. Felbermeyer, courtesy of Hans Wolfgang Müller, Munich.

420. Detail of the head of a statue of Ramses II (seated). The king wears the blue crown and a broad collar, and holds the royal staff.

Turin Museum. Probably from Karnak. Granite. Height of statue: 1.94 m. Ramses II (1301-1234). W. von Bissing, *Denkmäler ägyptischer Sculptur*, Munich, 1911-1914, pl. 49. *AOB*, 99. Schäfer-Andrae, 357. Photograph J. Felbermeyer, courtesy of Hans Wolfgang Müller, Munich.

421. Seti II, wearing a heavy wig with uraeus over the forehead, a pleated skirt, and sandals, sits upon his throne holding a small shrine surmounted by a ram's head. On the side of the throne is the symbol of the union of Upper and Lower Egypt.

British Museum, 616. Karnak. Quartzite sandstone. Height: 1.64 m. Seti II (1222-1212). E. A. W. Budge, *Egyptian Sculptures in the British Museum*, London, 1914, pl. 41. W. von Bissing, *Denkmäler ägyptischer Sculptur*, Munich, 1911-1914, pl. 55. Photograph courtesy BM.

422. A goddess, wearing the crowns of Upper and Lower Egypt, sits upon a throne, with her arm around the standing figure of Seti I, who nurses at her breast. The king wears the blue crown, broad collar, arm bands, and pleated skirt. For the campaigns of Seti I in Asia, see Nos. 322-331. Cf. No. 545.

Abydos. Seti I (1318-1301). G. Jéquier, *L'architecture et la décoration dans l'ancienne Égypte, Les temples ramessides et saïtes*, Paris, n.d., pl. 15 left. J. Capart, *Le temple de Séti Ier*, Brussels, 1912, pl. 14. *AOB*, 88. Photograph courtesy of G. Seif, Luxor.

423. King Mer-ne-Ptah is shown wearing the *nemes* headdress. See Nos. 342, 343 for stela of Mer-ne-Ptah.

Cairo Museum. Thebes, Qurneh. Granite. Mer-ne-Ptah (1234-1222). W. M. F. Petrie, *Six Temples at Thebes*, London, 1897, pl. 6, nos. 12, 13. *AOB*, 108. Photograph courtesy of the Metropolitan Museum of Art, New York.

424. This head from a statue of Tirhakah contains a part of the cartouche of the king on the back. Tirhakah, Ethiopian king of Egypt, is mentioned in the inscriptions of Esarhaddon and Ashurbanipal, kings of Assyria (*ANET*, 290, 292-297).

Cairo, 560. Purchased in Luxor. Black granite. Height: 0.35 m. Tirhakah (689-664). L. Borchardt, *Statuen und Statuetten*

von Königen und Privatleuten, pt. 2, *Cat. gén.*, Berlin, 1925, no. 560. *AOB*, 145. Photograph courtesy of the Cairo Museum.

425. Head of a statuette of Psamtik II, a king of the Twenty-sixth Dynasty (Saïte), to which belonged the Egyptian kings mentioned in the Bible under the names of Necho (II Kings 23:29 etc.) and Hophra (Apries) (Jer. 44:30).

Paris, Musée Jacquemart-André, 438. Green stone. Height: 0.12 m. Psamtik II (594-588). *Revue archéologique*, vol. 26, 1946, pp. 141-142, figs. 3 and 4. Photograph courtesy of Hans Wolfgang Müller, Munich.

426. Portrait head in green stone from the late Egyptian period, perhaps about 400 B.C. See B. V. Bothmer, *AJA*, vol. 56, 1952, pp. 86-87, for dating to first century B.C.

Berlin, Äg. 12500. Memphis. Green stone. Height: 0.21 m. About 400. Schäfer-Andrae, 436. *AOB*, 153. Photograph Foto Marburg.

MESOPOTAMIAN

427. This limestone plaque, perforated in the center, possibly for suspension, is divided into two registers, in each of which Ur-Nanshe of Lagash is the dominating figure. Above, Ur-Nanshe stands, clad only in a flounced skirt, bearing upon his head a basket, perhaps containing the first brick for the foundation of a temple. Behind him is the small figure of the cupbearer Anita; before him are five figures. The first, Lidda, is clothed in a flounced skirt and wears long hair and a garment over the left shoulder. This figure is followed by four sons: Akurgal (who became the successor to Ur-Nanshe), Lugalezen, Anikurra, and Muninnikurta. Below, Ur-Nanshe is seated on a throne with a goblet in his hand and is served by the cupbearer Sagantug, who stands behind him. Before him are Dudu the Banar (a title), and three sons: Anunpad, Menudgid, and Addatur. The lower register may represent the celebration of the dedication of the temple.

Louvre, AO 2344. Tello, tell K. White limestone. Height: 0.40 m. Ur-Nanshe (middle third millennium). E. de Sarzec, *Découvertes en Chaldée*, Paris, 1884-1912, pl. 2 bis. A. Parrot, *Tello*, Paris, 1948, pl. 5a, pp. 90-91. *AOB*, 528. Schäfer-Andrae, 469b. Photograph Giraudon, Paris.

428. Corner of a votive plaque on which appears Enannatum, king of Lagash.

British Museum, 130828. Heavy stone. Height: about 0.186 m. Enannatum (middle third millennium). *British Museum Quarterly*, vol. 16, 1951, pl. 19a, pp. 43-44. Photograph courtesy BM.

429. King Lamgi-Mari stands in an attitude of adoration, clothed only in a flounced robe which leaves his right shoulder free, wearing a long beard and his hair tied in a knot at the back of his head. The Akkadian inscription on the back gives his name and titles, and states that his statue had been dedicated to Ishtar (F. Thureau-Dangin, *RA*, vol. 31, 1934, p. 140). See also Nos. 21, 24.

Aleppo. Mari, first campaign, 1933-1934, temple of Ishtar.

White stone. Height: 0.272 m. Middle third millennium. *Syria*, vol. 16, 1935, pls. 6 and 7, pp. 23-24. A. Parrot, *Mari*, Paris, 1948, fig. 9, pp. 102-104. Photograph JBP.

430. Head from a statuette of Gudea, e n s i (local ruler) of Lagash. He wears the turban-like headdress which is characteristic of many representations of Gudea. For texts concerning Gudea, see *ANET*, 268-269. The head belongs to the body of a statuette now in the Iraq Museum (IM 2909).

University Museum, 16664. Diorite. Height: 0.064. Beginning of twenty-first century. L. Legrain, "A Diorite Head of Gudea," *MJ*, vol. 18, 1927, pp. 241-245. A. Parrot, *Tello*, Paris, 1948, pl. 19b (mislabeled), pp. 169-170. Photograph courtesy UM.

431. This small statue of Gudea, seated on a throne, is the only complete statue of this ruler which has come from scientific excavations. On his head he wears the turban-like headdress decorated with spiral bosses. He wears a long, fringed garment which leaves his right shoulder free. The inscription, which is carved on his skirt and the back of the chair, contains a dedication to Ningizzida.

Louvre, AO 3293. Tello. Diorite. Height: 0.45 m. Beginning of twenty-first century. A. Parrot, *Tello*, Paris, 1948, pl. 15a, p. 165. TEL, vol. I, pp. 228-229. *AOB*, 44. Schäfer-Andrae, 500. Photograph Giraudon, Paris.

432. This bronze head, first cast and then modeled in finer detail with a chisel, was probably intended to represent a prominent person (for suggestion that it is Sargon of Akkad see M. E. L. Mallowan, *Iraq*, vol. 3, 1936, pp. 109-110). The hair, encircled by a fillet and a plait, is carefully plaited and tied into a bun behind the head (see No. 160). The mustache and beard consist of rows of curls. Prominent features of the face are the high-arched eyebrows, prominent nose, and fleshy lips.

Baghdad, 11331. Kuyunjik, 1931. Bronze (or copper). Height: about 0.36 m. Last half of third millennium (on stylistic grounds). *AAA*, vol. 19, 1932, pl. 50, nos. 1 and 2. M. E. L. Mallowan, "The Bronze Head of the Akkadian Period from Nineveh," *Iraq*, vol. 3, 1936, pls. 5, 6, 7, pp. 104-110. Photograph courtesy of the Iraq Museum.

433. The body of this inscribed statue of Puzur-Ishtar, governor of Mari, was found at Babylon, where it had been carried anciently as a trophy of war, and is now in Istanbul. To the body belongs a head which was acquired by the Berlin Museum. Puzur-Ishtar is shown wearing an elaborately curled beard, a horned cap (a feature which has suggested to some that a god was intended), and a fringed and tasseled mantle which leaves the right arm and shoulder free. His hands are shown crossed in an attitude of adoration.

Berlin, VA 8748 (head); Istanbul, 7813 (body). Babylon. Diorite. Height: 1.73 m. Ur III period (about 2060-1955). R. Koldewey, *Die Königsburgen von Babylon*, pt. 2, *WVDOG*, 55, Leipzig, 1932, pls. 22, 23. E. Unger, *Sumerische und Akkadische Kunst*, Breslau, 1926, fig. 52, p. 53. E. Nassouhi, "Statue d'un dieu de Mari vers 2225 av. J.-C.," *AfO*, vol. 3, 1926, pp. 109-114 (text), who holds the representation to be that of a god. Photograph courtesy of Museum of the Ancient Orient.

434. Head of a statue of Ur-Ningirsu (No. 435), successor to Gudea, e n s i of Lagash. The headdress is similar to No. 430.

New York, Metropolitan Museum of Art, 47.100.86. Tello. Brown-veined "alabaster." Height: 0.114. Twenty-first century. *BMMA*, March 1949, p. 190. Photograph courtesy MMA.

435. Ur-Ningirsu, son of Gudea, e n s i of Lagash, stands clothed in a large shawl draped over the left shoulder and arm. Below the feet are represented eight porters bringing tribute in baskets. The two leaders (shown here) are bearded and have plumes sticking from the band around the hair. The inscription carved on the back gives the name of Ur-Ningirsu, son of Gudea, and a dedication to Ningizzida. See No. 434 for head.

Louvre, AO 9504. Tello, clandestine excavation of 1924. "Alabaster." Height: 0.46 m. Twenty-first century. A. Parrot, *Tello*, Paris, 1948, pl. 23b, c, p. 208. TEL, vol. I, pp. 240-241. *Fondation Piot*, vol. 27, 1924, pl. 9. Photograph Archives Photographiques.

436. Inscribed statue of "Ishtup-ilum, *šakkanak* of Mari." He wears a headband or turban, mustache, long beard, and a fringed robe which leaves his right arm, shoulder, and three-fourths of his chest bare. He stands barefoot, with hands joined in a gesture of worship.

Aleppo, National Museum, 1658. Mari, second campaign, 1934-1935, palace of Mari, court 65. Black stone. Height: 1.52 m. Eighteenth century. *Syria*, vol. 17, 1936, pl. 7, pp. 24-25. Contenau, *Man.*, vol. 4, p. 2116, fig. 1170. A. Parrot, *Mari*, Paris, 1948, fig. 30, pp. 184-185. Photograph JBP.

437. The headdress of this damaged head from a diorite statue is similar to that worn by Hammurabi (No. 515). The beard is carefully curled in ringlets and arranged in rows; the mustache is represented. The identification with Hammurabi is only conjectural.

Louvre. Susa. Diorite. Height: 0.15 m. First half second millennium. Contenau, *Man.*, vol. 4, fig. 1174, p. 2125. TEL, vol. I, p. 257A, B. Photograph Archives Photographiques.

438. This diorite head, so remarkably similar to No. 437, also suggests the appearance of Hammurabi as he is portrayed on the stela containing his laws (No. 515).

Kansas City, Missouri. Diorite. Height: 0.343. First half second millennium. *The William Rockhill Nelson Collection*, Kansas City, 3rd ed., p. 30, and cover. Photograph courtesy of William Rockhill Nelson Gallery of Art.

439. King Ashurnasirpal II is shown wearing a long garment decorated with fringe and holding in his right hand a weapon usually carried by gods and in his left a mace. He has long beard and mustache, long hair, but wears no headdress. On the chest are carved eight lines of text, giving his name and titles, and recording his exploits.

British Museum, 118871. Nimrud. Sandstone. Height: 1.02 m. Ashurnasirpal II (883-859). E. A. W. Budge, *Assyrian Sculptures in the British Museum*, London, 1914, pl. 1. C. J. Gadd, *The Assyrian Sculptures*, London, 1934, pl. 4, pp. 15, 17, 21. Photograph courtesy BM.

440. In a panel at the top of a broken obelisk is shown the Assyrian king (identification uncertain) standing before four of his enemies, whom he holds by ropes tied to rings through their noses (see Isa. 37:29; II Kings 19:28; Ezek. 38:4). Above, two hands reach down from the sun-disc, one blessing the king and the other offering him a bow, perhaps a token of the god's help in battle. The inscription is translated in Luckenbill, *AR*, vol. 1, §§388-395. For various proposals for the authorship of the monument see *AfO*, vol. 6, 1930, 92-94.

British Museum, 118898. Kuyunjik. Gypsum. Height: about 0.40 m. Perhaps end of tenth century. E. A. W. Budge and L. W. King, *Annals of the Kings of Assyria*, vol. 1, London, 1902, p. LI. C. J. Gadd, *The Assyrian Sculptures*, London, 1934, p. 9. C. J. Gadd, *The Stones of Assyria*, London, 1936, p. 123. Photograph courtesy BM.

441. King Ashurnasirpal II is shown facing left, his right hand grasping a staff and his left resting on a sword, which is thrust through his belt. He wears a long and elaborately curled beard, a mustache, and long hair which rests upon his neck. On his head is the royal helmet, surmounted by a pointed projection and encircled by a band which is tied at the back, the two ends hanging down behind. The dress consists of a shirt with short sleeves, a skirt with fringe at the bottom, and a shawl which is tasseled at the edges and thrown over the left shoulder. The king wears sandals and jewelry consisting of earrings, necklaces, bracelets and arm bands. Two daggers are thrust into his belt.

British Museum, Nimrud Gallery 20. Nimrud, northwest palace, chamber S, no. 3. Gypsum. Height: 2.31 m. Ashurnasirpal II (883-859). E. A. W. Budge, *Assyrian Sculptures in the British Museum*, London, 1914, pl. 29. C. J. Gadd, *The Stones of Assyria*, London, 1936, p. 137. *AOB*, 117. Photograph courtesy BM.

442. Shamshi-Adad V, king of Assyria, and husband of Sammuramat (original of Semiramis), stands facing left under the symbols of gods (horned miter, winged disc, disc and crescent, fork, and eight-pointed star). In addition to the long garment, fringed at the bottom, he wears two shoulder straps which cross his chest diagonally. Suspended from his neck is a cross. He is shown in the gesture of upraised right hand with pointed forefinger; the left hand holds a mace. He also wears the royal headdress (see No. 441) and sandals.

British Museum, 118892. Nimrud. White calcareous limestone. Height: 2.18 m. Shamshi-Adad V (823-811). British Museum, *Assyrian Sculptures in the British Museum from Shalmaneser III to Sennacherib*, London, 1938, pl. 2. H. R. Hall, *Babylonian and Assyrian Sculpture in the British Museum*, Paris and Brussels, 1928, pl. 24, 1. C. J. Gadd, *The Stones of Assyria*, London, 1936, pp. 149-150. Translation of text: Luckenbill, *AR*, vol. 1, §§714-726. On Semiramis see H. Lewy, "Nitokris-Naqi'a," *JNES*, vol. 11, 1952, pp. 264-266. Photograph courtesy BM.

443. King Shalmaneser III, clad in a long garment with fringed edges, and sandals, stands with upraised hand before symbols of the gods (winged disc, star, horned miter, and disc and crescent). The king wears other symbolic emblems on his collar: the fork, a segment of a circle, an eight-pointed star in a disc, and a winged disc. In his left hand he holds a mace (?). For translation of inscription see *ANET*, 277-279. For a study of the gesture of the upraised hand see G. Furlani, "Di un supposto gesto precatorio assiro," *Accademia dei Lincei, Rend. d. Cl. d. Sc. morali*, ser. 6, vol. 3, Rome, 1927, pp. 234-272.

British Museum, 118884. Kurkh. Limestone, Height: 2.20 m. Shalmaneser III (858-824). British Museum, *Assyrian Sculptures in the British Museum from Shalmaneser III to Sennacherib*, London, 1938, pl. 1. Photograph courtesy BM.

444. Cut in rough provincial style is the figure of King Adad-nirari III standing under and before a number of divine symbols, some of which are set in sockets. The king is represented in traditional pose (see Nos. 442, 443). For translation of a part of the text, which reports on a campaign against Palestine, see *ANET*, 282.

Istanbul, 2828. Saba'a (discovered in 1905, in desert, south of the Sinjar hills). Basalt. Height: 1.92 m. Adad-nirari III (810-783). E. Unger, *Reliefstele Adadniraris III. aus Saba'a und Semiramis, Publicationen der Kaiserlich osmanischen Museen*, Istanbul, 1916, pl. 1. Photograph courtesy of the Museum of the Ancient Orient.

445. On this fragment of a slab is the upper part of a figure of Tiglath-pileser III. He wears the royal cap with pointed top. Around the headdress are bands; at the back there hang two ribbons, which seem to emerge from the inside of the headdress. In his right hand the king holds a staff.

British Museum, 118900. Nimrud, central palace. Gypsum. Height: 1.10 m. Tiglath-pileser III (744-727). British Museum, *Assyrian Sculptures in the British Museum from Shalmaneser III to Sennacherib*, London, 1938, pl. 5 upper. Photograph courtesy BM.

446. King Sargon II wears the royal Assyrian headdress, a mustache curled at the ends, a long beard which extends down over the chest in ringlets, long hair reaching to his shoulders, and a pendant earring in the form of a cross. The details of the nose, eyebrow, and eye have been carefully carved and give the impression of an attempt at portraiture.

Turin Museum. Khorsabad, palace of Sargon II. Limestone. Height: 0.89 m. Sargon II (721-705). E. F. Weidner, *Die Reliefs der assyrischen Könige*, Berlin, 1939, fig. 48, pp. 56-57. Photograph courtesy of Museo di Antichità.

447. Esarhaddon stands facing right, before the symbols of his deities, holding in his upraised right hand a cup (?), and in his left, a mace and ropes by which he secures two captives. The king wears the Assyrian royal helmet decorated with bands and discs, a full and elaborately curled beard, mustache, long hair, a long robe with fringed edges, and shoes which are laced across the tops. In the upper part of the stela are four deities riding upon their respective animals, and symbols, which include the crescent, the winged sun-disc, the star, the lance, and others. The first captive, with ring through his

lip and shackled, has negroid features and seems to wear the uraeus serpent at his forehead. He represents Tirhakah, king of Egypt and Ethiopia (see No. 424), or his son Ushanahuru, both of whom are mentioned in the text carved on the stela (*ANET*, 293, and Luckenbill, *AR*, vol. 2, §§574-581). The second captive is bearded, wears a pointed cap, and a long garment reaching to the ankles. He may be Ba'lu, king of Tyre.

Berlin, VA 2708. Zinjirli. Dolerite. Height: 3.22 m. Esarhaddon (680-669). F. von Luschan, *Ausgrabungen in Sendschirli*, vol. 1, Berlin, 1893, pl. 1, pp. 11-29. *AOB*, 143, 144. Schäfer-Andrae, 554. Photograph courtesy of Staatliche Museen.

448-449. The two figures on the sides of the Esarhaddon stela (No. 447) stand with hands clasped before them in an attitude of respect and may represent the two sons of Esarhaddon: Ashurbanipal, king of Assyria, and Shamashshumukin, king of Babylon. The figure in No. 448 wears a decorated headdress which continues in a neck flap down the back; his fringed robe, wound diagonally around the body, is in Assyrian style. No. 449 wears a cap which ends in streamers down the back and a long robe tasseled at the bottom, in the Babylonian style (as would be proper for Shamashshumukin). Both are bearded, wear earrings, bracelets, and sandals.

Berlin, VA 2708. Zinjirli. Dolerite. Height of entire stela: 3.22 m. Esarhaddon (680-669). F. von Luschan, *Ausgrabungen in Sendschirli*, vol. 1, Berlin, 1893, pl. 3. Photographs courtesy of Staatliche Museen.

450. Ashurbanipal, king of Assyria, is shown fullface with arms upraised to support a basket which he carries for the rebuilding of the temple of Esagila in Babylon. See No. 427 for another representation of this type. The king wears long hair, curled beard, a royal headdress with pointed top, and a robe decorated along the borders by fringe. For translation of the text, see Luckenbill, *AR*, vol. 2, §§979-980.

British Museum, 90864. Babylon. Stone. Height: 0.368 m. Ashurbanipal (668-633). British Museum, *A Guide to the Babylonian and Assyrian Antiquities*, London, 1922, pl. 28, p. 74. Contenau, *Man.*, vol. 3, fig. 822, p. 1299. Photograph courtesy BM.

451. King Ashurbanipal reclines upon a high couch as he drinks from a bowl and holds a blossom in his left hand. Upon a high throne at the foot of the couch sits the queen, who also drinks from a bowl, which has been supplied by her attendants. Before her is a table, similar in design to the other furniture and on which are several small objects. Another table to the right holds the bow, sword, and quiver of the king. Two braziers stand upon the ground, one at the head of the couch and the other behind the queen's attendants. Eight attendants appear in the scene: four stand with fly-whisks, two behind each of the principal figures; two servers bring food for the feast, while another assists with the fly-whisk; to the left are a musician with a harp and the hands of another musician who plays upon a cone-shaped drum. In the scene are represented also palms, bushes, evergreen trees, and vines with leaves and clusters of grapes, which form

a shelter for the royal couple. Birds are perched on the trees or fly between them. On the branches of the evergreen tree before the harpist is tied the head of a man, perhaps that of Te-umman, king of Elam.

British Museum, 124920. Kuyunjik, north palace, 1854. Alabaster. Width: 1.35 m. Ashurbanipal (668-633). H. R. Hall, *Babylonian and Assyrian Sculpture in the British Museum*, Paris and Brussels, 1928, pl. 41, 2. *AOB*, 148, 149. Schäfer-Andrae, 572-573. Photograph courtesy BM.

452. King Idri-mi of Alalakh is seated on his throne, wearing a high conical headdress around which is a narrow band. It may be assumed that the headdress and the beard were painted and that curls were indicated. The garment worn by the king is indistinct and schematized in such a way as to allow the maximum surface for the field of the inscription. The edge of the garment was rolled in such a manner that it has been said to represent a serpent coiled around the body of the king. The inscription has been published and translated in the publication mentioned below.

British Museum, 130738. Atchana, spring of 1939. Dolomite and magnesite. Height: 1.04 m. Not later than the first quarter of the fourteenth century. W. F. Albright, *BASOR*, no. 118, 1950, p. 19, dates Idri-mi to about 1480-1450. S. Smith and L. Woolley, *The Statue of Idri-mi*, London, 1949, frontispiece. Photograph courtesy BM.

453. Bel-harran-bel-usur stands facing left with his hands extended in a gesture of adoration toward the symbols of his gods. From left to right the symbols are: the *marru* of Marduk, the stylus of Nabu, the disc of Shamash, the crescent of Sin, and the star of Ishtar (deities are mentioned in text, Luckenbill, *AR*, vol. 1, §§824-827). Bel-harran-bel-usur is beardless; he wears long hair, a mantle of square design, over which is a fringed shawl. This Assyrian art is distinctively provincial in style. The stela commemorates one who served as chamberlain under Shalmaneser IV and Tiglath-pileser III and later founded a city in the desert.

Istanbul. Tell Abta, west of Mosul. Alabaster. Height: 1.83 m. Tiglath-pileser III (744-727). E. Unger, *Die Stele des Bel-Harran-Beli-Ussur, ein Denkmal der Zeit Salmanassars IV*, Istanbul, 1917, pl. 1. Contenau, *Man.*, vol. 3, p. 1219. Photograph JBP.

454. This inscribed stone (in the form of a *kudurru*-stone, see Nos. 518-521) illustrates the act of the investiture of an official with land by the Babylonian King Merodach-baladan (Marduk-apal-iddin II). To the left, stands the king holding a staff in his left hand and a small object in his right. He wears a beard; long hair, over which is a pointed cap with streamer; a long robe; and shoes. The official is shown as smaller in stature, holding a staff in his left hand, and with his right upraised in a gesture of respect. He is dressed like the king, except that for the cap he wears only a headband and is barefoot. Above the two figures are the emblems of four deities: (left to right) the two rods of Nabu, mounted on a shrine forming the body of a <u>dragon</u> with *Tiamat* straight horns; swaddling-bands (*omega*), an emblem of Ninhursag, also mounted on a shrine; a ram-headed scepter, mounted on a shrine forming the body of a goat, the symbol of Ea; and the *marru*-emblem of Marduk, mounted on a shrine and the straight-horned dragon (for discussions of these emblems see E. D. van Buren, *Symbols of the Gods in Mesopotamian Art*, Rome, 1945, nos. I4b, F2, K4, and A2). For publication of text see F. Delitzsch, Beiträge zur Assyriologie, vol. 2, Leipzig, 1894, pp. 258-273; F. E. Peiser and H. Winckler, in *Keilinschriftlich Bibliothek*, vol. 3, 1, Berlin, 1892, pp. 184-193. See II Kings 20:12; Isa. 19:1.

Berlin, VA 2663. Black marble. Height: 0.46 m. Merodach-baladan II (722-711). E. Meyer, *Sumerier und Semiten in Babylonien*, Berlin, 1906, pl. 1, pp. 8-9. Schäfer-Andrae, 517. *AOB*, 142. Photograph Foto Marburg.

OTHERS

455. An important person, probably King Kilamuwa of Sam'al (appearance is like the figure on the Kilamuwa stela, F. von Luschan, *Ausgrabungen in Sendschirli*, vol. 4, Berlin, 1911, fig. 273; see also W. F. Albright, *BASOR*, no. 105, p. 13), stands facing right, holding a blossom in his left hand and pointing with his right. His beard is curled into locks, which are arranged in three rows; the upper lip is shaved. His hair is similarly curled and hangs to the shoulders. On his head is a pointed cap, from which hang two bands. The king is clothed in a long, fringed robe, held by a belt at the waist. He wears arm bands and bracelets, and sandals. The beardless attendant is dressed similarly, except he has no cap, the hair being held in place by a narrow fillet. Four tassels hang from his belt at the front; in one hand he holds a large blossom; in the other, the handle of some small vessel or object.

Berlin, VA S.6580. Zinjirli, southern Hallenbau, P. Height: 0.57 m. Second half of the ninth century. F. von Luschan, *Ausgrabungen in Sendschirli*, vol. 4, Berlin, 1911, pl. 66, pp. 372-374. Bossert, *Altanatolien*, 951. Contenau, *Man.*, vol. 1, fig. 83. Photograph from F. von Luschan, courtesy of the Staatliche Museen.

456-459. The principal side of the sarcophagus (No. 456 and detail in No. 458) shows Ahiram, king of Byblos, seated on a throne, with his feet resting on a triple-staged footstool. The side of the throne consists of a winged sphinx, having the body and feet of a lion and the head of a woman. The bearded king is clothed in a long, sleeved robe and holds in his left hand a lotus blossom, with blossom hanging downward, and in his right hand a cup. Facing the king are seven figures, all of whom have hair extending to the shoulders, but are without beards, and are dressed in a long robe which is held tightly around the waist by a belt tied in front. The first holds a fly-whisk, which he waves over the offering placed on a table before the king. Two men follow, carrying dishes or cups; the last four figures merely salute the king with upraised and out-turned hands. Above this scene is a border of inverted lotus blossoms and buds, and a rope design; below, are the outlines of two crouching lions, whose heads extend, carved in the round, at the ends of the sarcophagus. Visible on the lid is the life-sized figure of Ahiram (which is repeated on the other half of the lid) and the dedicatory inscription in Phoenician (see No. 286 for alphabet employed). The opposite side of the sarcophagus (No. 457) exhibits a row of eight figures: at the head are two women, dressed like the mourners in No. 459, except that they do not have their breasts bared, carrying baskets on their heads; two porters carry jars on their shoulders; a goat is led by a fifth figure, who is bearded; three bearded attendants with upraised hands are at the end of the procession. At one end of the sarcophagus (No. 459) are figures of four women, standing with bared breasts. The first two hold or beat their breasts; the other two have their hands over their heads, perhaps, either beating their heads or tearing their hair in a gesture of grief.

Beirut, National Museum. Byblos. Stone. Length of sarcophagus, without lion projections: about 2.30 m. Dated by excavator to thirteenth century; W. F. Albright assigns inscription to tenth century (*JAOS*, vol. 67, 1947, pp. 155-156). P. Montet, *Byblos et l'Égypte*, Text, Paris, 1928, pp. 228-238; Atlas, Paris, 1929, pls. 128-141. N. Aimé-Giron, *ASAE*, vol. 42, 1943, pp. 283-338. K. Galling, "Die Achiram-Inschrift im Lichte der Karatepe-Texte," *Die Welt des Orients*, 1950, pp. 421-425. Photographs JBP.

460. King Bar Rakab, identified by an inscription "I am Bar Rakab, son of Panammu," is seated on a throne of the Assyrian type with arms ending in bulls' heads, his feet on a footstool. On his head he wears a pointed cap, from which curled locks emerge, one falling down before the ear. He is bearded and wears a mustache. His left hand holds a stylized flower; his right is upraised. Before him stands a beardless scribe; his right hand is upraised in a gesture of respect (?) and his left holds a writing palette (see No. 233); under his arm is writing material. Between the two figures is a symbol composed of a disc and crescent, to which is attached a handle with tassels. To the right is the inscription "My lord is Baal Harran."

Berlin, VA 2817. Zinjirli. Dolerite. Height: 1.12 m. Second half of eighth century. F. von Luschan, *Ausgrabungen in Sendschirli*, vol. 4, Berlin, 1911, pl. 60 (lower), pp. 345-349. Schäfer-Andrae, pl. 36. Contenau, *Man.*, vol. 3, fig. 759, pp. 1150-1152. Photograph Foto Marburg.

461. To the right is King Araras, beardless and with long hair, wearing a long garment and sandals, and holding a scepter. To the left is his son Kamanas, whom he holds by the arm. The prince holds a staff and has slung over his shoulder a strap to which is attached a long sword.

Ankara, Hittite Museum, 91. Carchemish. Basalt. Height: 1.10 m. Second half of eighth century (Akurgal). D. G. Hogarth, *Carchemish, Part I*, London, 1914, pl. B 7 a. E. Akurgal, *Späthethitische Bildkunst*, Ankara, 1949, pl. 47a. Bossert, *Altanatolien*, 837. Contenau, *Man.*, vol. 3, fig. 753. Photograph courtesy of the British Museum.

462. Carved in the live rock is the life-sized figure of Darius (see No. 249 for entire scene). The king's elaborately curled beard extends to his chest; his hair is arranged in ringlets at the front and hangs in a bun at the back; the mustache is curled at the tip. On his head the king wears a battlemented crown, decorated with rosettes and representations of jewels. Behind the figure of the king are the bearers of the royal bow and spear.

Behistun (modern Bisitun), on main caravan route from Baghdad to Teheran. Darius (521-486). About 3 m. For description see A. T. Olmstead, *History of the Persian Empire*, Chicago, 1948, pp. 117-118. Photograph courtesy of G. G. Cameron.

463. King Darius sits upon an elaborately carved throne, with his feet on a footstool, holding a scepter in his right hand and a symbol, consisting of a lotus blossom with two buds, in his left. He wears a mustache, a beard which reaches to his chest, hair elaborately curled, and a tall headdress. He is clothed in an undergarment and a long, pleated outer garment, and shoes with heels. Behind the enthroned king is the standing figure of the Crown Prince Xerxes, who is represented in a similar fashion, except that his right hand is merely extended, not yet having received the royal scepter. Both figures are on an elevated platform. Before the king are two incense burners and a dignitary dressed in the Median costume (see No. 26). His right hand is raised to his mouth in a gesture of respect; his left holds a staff. Behind the Median dignitary are two attendants, one with a staff and the other carrying a pail, perhaps containing material for the incense burners. Behind the figure of Xerxes are two attendants: the first is beardless and wears a muffler cap, carries a piece of folded cloth, and perhaps is to be identified as the royal cupbearer; the second is dressed as a Mede and carries the royal axe and bow, and wears at his side a finely carved sword. Two Persian guards complete the scene. The relief is without inscription, but the identification of the figures of Darius and Xerxes is suggested by the archaeological context (see E. F. Schmidt, *The Treasury of Persepolis, OIC*, 21, Chicago, 1939, p. 21).

Teheran. Persepolis, treasury, southern relief in court of reception. Dark gray limestone. Height: about 2.50 m. Darius (521-486). E. F. Schmidt, *The Treasury of Persepolis, OIC*, 21, Chicago, 1939, fig. 14, pp. 21-33. Contenau, *Man.*, vol. 4, fig. 1284. A. T. Olmstead, *History of the Persian Empire*, Chicago, 1948, pl. 30 (top), pp. 315-318. E. F. Schmidt, *Persepolis I, OIP*, 68, Chicago, 1953, pl. 121, pp. 162 ff. Photograph courtesy of the Oriental Institute.

VI. *Gods and Their Emblems*

SYRIAN

464. A seated goddess, probably the Aegean *potnia thêrôn* "queen of wild beasts," is nude to the waist, wears a full skirt, and holds stalks of grain (or branches) in her upraised hands. Flanking her are two goats, each standing on his hind legs with one foreleg on a projection from the seat of the goddess and the other pressing against her arm, as though reaching for the vegetation. The goddess wears a necklace and a diadem around her hair, which is arranged in ringlets above her forehead and falls down her neck at the back. The coiffure has a

spiral projection at the front and a streamer which extends from the top. See discussion of H. Kantor listed below, as to whether the artist was an Asiatic attempting to imitate LH III style.

Louvre. Minet el-Beida, tomb III. Ivory. Height: 0.137 m. Fourteenth century (excavator). C. F. A. Schaeffer, *Ugaritica I*, Paris, 1939, frontispiece and pl. 11, pp. 32-33. *Syria*, vol. 10, 1929, pl. 56, pp. 292-293. Contenau, *Man.*, vol. 2, fig. 739. R. Dussaud, *L'art phénicien du IIe millénaire*, Paris, 1949, pp. 84-88, where references to other literature are given. H. Kantor, "The Aegean and the Orient in the Second Millennium B.C.," *AJA*, vol. 51, 1947, pp. 86-89, pl. 22 (for comparative material). R. D. Barnett, "Phoenician and Syrian Ivory Carving," *PEFQS*, 1939, pp. 4-19. Photograph Archives Photographiques.

465. A nude goddess is shown fullface, but with feet turned to the right, holding in each hand a goat by its hind legs. The goddess wears bracelets, bands about her ankles, and perhaps a necklace, represented by the incisions about the neck. Her hair is arranged in two curled locks, which extend to the shoulders; she wears a massive headdress consisting of a high crown ending in a knob and a plumelike decoration at each side. Bordering the pendant are two lotus plants.

Louvre. Ras Shamra. Gold. R. Dussaud, *L'art phénicien du IIe millénaire*, Paris, 1949, fig. 16 (right) for drawing. Contenau, *Man.*, vol. 4, fig. 1309 (right). Photograph Archives Photographiques.

466. Goddess clothed in a long robe and wearing pendant in form of double spiral attached to necklace. She wears a headdress consisting of a tall cylindrical tiara. Eyes were inlaid and ears are pierced for rings.

Louvre. Bronze. Height: 0.165 m. TEL, vol. 2, pl. 100D, E. R. Dussaud, *L'art phénicien du IIe millénaire*, Paris, 1949, fig. 27. Bossert, *Altsyrien*, 581-582. Photograph Archives Photographiques.

467. This nude female figurine, made in a double mold, may have served as an emblem of the goddess of fecundity. She wears a high headdress, decorated with ribbing, and holds her breasts with her hands. The genital region is emphasized by incisions which form a triangle.

Oriental Institute. Megiddo, tomb 26B. Terra cotta. Height: about 0.15 m. Middle Bronze to Late Bronze II (2000-1200). H. G. May, *Material Remains of the Megiddo Cult, OIP*, 26, Chicago, 1935, pl. 31, no. 598, pp. 27, 29, 30. Photograph courtesy of the Oriental Institute.

468. Two deities, each holding a spear, stand on either side of a hieroglyphic inscription '-*s-t(a)r-t*= 'Astart. The figure to the right represents 'Astart, who wears the high Egyptian tiara with feather on each side and streamers which are attached at the back. Opposite stands a god, wearing a horned headdress and brandishing a scimitar in his right hand.

Palestine Archaeological Museum, 35.4442. Bethel, excavation of 1934. Frit. About 1300 (Albright in *BASOR*, no. 56, p. 1). *BASOR*, no. 56, December 1934, fig. 1, pp. 7-8. B. Parker, "Cylinder Seals from Palestine," *Iraq*, vol. 11, 1949, pl. 26, no. 180, p. 40. Photograph courtesy PAM.

469. Figurines and plaques of the nude female figure

have been found in almost every major excavation in Palestine, ranging in date from the Middle Bronze to the Iron II periods. For a listing of 294 examples and a discussion of the possible use of these objects see James B. Pritchard, *Palestinian Figurines in Relation to Certain Goddesses Known through Literature, American Oriental Series*, vol. 24, New Haven, 1943, referred to as *PF*. The objects are described below, beginning at the top and going from left to right.

1. Palestine Archaeological Museum 1.8998. Tell Beit Mirsim, stratum C (1500-1230). Height: about 0.092. Arms are extended and hold papyrus stalks; heavy wig with ends extending to breasts. *PF*, no. 12, fig. 1.

2. PAM, P. 7. Provenience unknown. Nude figure with Hathor headdress, wearing necklace and bracelets, and holding lotus blossoms in her upraised hands.

3. PAM, P. 1088. Gezer. Height: 0.075. Similar to No. 467. R. A. S. Macalister, *The Excavation of Gezer*, vol. 3, London, 1912, pl. 220, no. 6.

4. PAM, P. 20. Provenience unknown. Height: 0.082 m. Female figure, wearing high, ribbed headdress, locks ending in curls, and necklace; with her hands she supports her breasts.

5. PAM, P. 1798. Beth-shan, level IX. Fourteenth century. Figurine with head missing; breasts and genital region indicated; arms support the breasts, almost encircling them; entire figure decorated with hatches. *PF*, no. 285.

6. PAM, P. 43. Gezer. The left hand of the nude figure holds the breast; right hand is placed over the abdomen; headdress consists of a tiara, from which two locks hang down to the shoulders. *PF*, no. 101, fig. 8.

7. PAM, P. 44. Gezer. Plaque with arms to the side. *PF*, no. 129.

8. PAM, P. 435. Provenience unknown. Pillar figurine, consisting of a torso of a nude female mounted on a bell-shaped base; arms support prominent breasts.

9. PAM, 36.44. Megiddo, stratum II. Seventh century. Upper part of a figurine holding a disc by the left arm, perhaps intended for a tambourine or hand drum. *PF*, no. 166.

10. PAM, 36.958. Megiddo, stratum V. Eleventh century. Nude female figure holding disc over left breast; feet are indicated; genital region and abdomen enlarged, suggesting pregnancy. *PF*, no. 168, fig. 16.

11. PAM, 1.3839. Beth-shan, stratum IX. Fourteenth century. Figurine of nude woman holding a sucking child in her left arm. *PF*, no. 185.

12. PAM, 36.926. Megiddo, stratum IV. Tenth to eighth centuries. Upper part of figurine of woman holding over her left breast a disc, which is pierced with small holes; suggestions of a back veil. *PF*, no. 165.

Photograph JBP.

470. A nude goddess, with Hathor hairdress, stands upon the back of a lion and holds in her left hand lotus blossoms and in her right, what may represent a serpent. To the right stands a woman, perhaps a worshiper, wearing a heavy wig and holding an *ankh* sign in her left hand. The phallus may be the remains of an earlier figure of Min, or a later addition. To the left stands the figure of Seth, wearing a tall crown ending in a streamer (see No. 555), and holding a scepter. The stela bears no inscription.

Cairo. Limestone. New Kingdom (1550-1090). W. Max Müller, *Egyptological Researches*, Washington, 1906, vol. 1, pl. 41

(right), p. 32. *AOB*, 272. J. Leibovitch, *Ancient Egypt*, Cairo, 1938, fig. 138 (right). Photograph courtesy of the Cairo Museum.

471. Standing on the back of a lion is the nude female figure of the goddess "Qadesh, the beloved of Ptah." She wears a heavy wig ending in two curls at her breasts and surmounted by the Hathor crown, on the top of which is a crescent and disc. In each hand she holds a serpent. Circles are incised about the field of the relief.

Berlin, Äg. 21626. Limestone. Height: 0.28 m. Nineteenth Dynasty (1350-1200). G. Röder, *Ägypter und Hethiter, AO*, vol. 20, Leipzig, 1919, p. 63, fig. 26. *AOB*, 276. Photograph Fremdvölker, 653A.

472. The nude goddess, presumably Qadesh, stands upon the back of a lion holding a serpent in one hand and a stylized lotus blossom in the other; on her head she wears a crown of feathers or of vegetation. Before her, but on a lower level, stands a female worshiper before an offering stand with gifts.

Cairo. Limestone. W. Max Müller, *Egyptological Researches*, vol. 1, Washington, 1906, pl. 41 (left), p. 32. *AOB*, 271. J. Leibovitch, *Ancient Egypt*, Cairo, 1938, fig. 138 (left). Photograph courtesy of the Cairo Museum.

473. On the upper part of the stela is the triad of Qadesh (labeled here as '*knt*), Min, and Resheph. To the left is the ithyphallic Min, wearing the high feathered headdress of Amon, and holding with his upraised right hand the flail; behind him is a shrine (?) containing plants. In the center is the goddess, either nude or clothed in a sheer garment, standing on the back of a lion; in her right hand she holds lotus blossoms and in her left, serpents. To the right is the god Resheph, standing, as does also Min, on a pylon, and holding a spear and an *ankh* sign; he wears a heavy beard and wig, encircled by a fillet with a projection in the form of an antelope head in front. Below are three figures who present offerings to the goddess Anat, who is seated on her throne. She is shown clothed in a long garment, wearing the white crown, to which are attached the plumes of Maat, holding in her right hand a lance and shield, and brandishing a club or axe with her upraised left hand. For the view that this and similar stelae, on which are portrayed Syrian gods and goddesses, were dedicated by Syrian workmen who had migrated to Egypt and continued there their devotion to the deities of their homeland, see C. Boreux, "La stèle C. 86 du Musée du Louvre et les stèles similaires," *Mélanges . . . Dussaud*, vol. 2, Paris, 1939, pp. 673-687. See also *ANET*, 250.

British Museum, 646 (191). Limestone. Height: 0.749 m. Nineteenth Dynasty (1350-1200). British Museum, *A General Introductory Guide to the Egyptian Collections in the British Museum*, London, 1930, fig. 205. *AOB*, 270. Photograph courtesy BM.

474. The goddess Qadesh stands with feet extending in opposite directions upon the back of a lion and holds a serpent in one hand and lotus blossoms in the other. Her hairdress is in the fashion of Hathor and is surmounted by a crescent holding a disc. To the left is the god Min,

who wears the high feathered crown of Amon and holds the flail in his right hand; behind is a stand with symbols of vegetation. To the right is Resheph, wearing the white crown and holding a spear by one hand and an *ankh* sign in the other. Inscription: "Qadesh, lady of the sky and mistress of all the gods."

Louvre, C. 86. Limestone. Height: 0.315 m. New Kingdom (1550-1090). C. Boreux, "La stèle C. 86 du Musée du Louvre et les stèles similaires," *Mélanges . . . Dussaud*, vol. 2, Paris, 1939, plate after p. 696, pp. 673-687. Photograph Archives Photographiques.

475. To the left, stands a goddess, clothed in a long flowing garment and holding a scepter in her left hand and an *ankh* sign in her right. Her headdress consists of a high conical crown flanked by two feathers, horns below, and a streamer attached to the back. A woman stands at right holding a lotus before the face of the goddess.

University Museum, 29-107-949. Beisan excavations of 1925, great court of temple of "Amenophis III." Limestone. Height: 0.372. Thirteenth century (city-level VII). A. Rowe, *The Topography and History of Beth-shan*, Philadelphia, 1930, pl. 48, no. 2, pp. 19-21. Photograph courtesy UM.

476. The Asiatic war-god Resheph, clothed in a kilt decorated with tassels and held by two shoulder straps, wears a conical crown with the gazelle emblem in front and streamers hanging down from the top. He holds the shield and spear in his left hand and brandishes the scalloped axe with his right. The inscription to the right mentions the name of the god; to the left is the name of the man making the dedication. Cf. I Chron. 7:25.

Oriental Institute, 10569. Limestone. New Kingdom (1550-1090). J. A. Wilson, *The Burden of Egypt*, Chicago, 1951, fig. 28b. W. K. Simpson, *BMMA*, vol. 10, 1952, pp. 185-186. Photograph courtesy of the Oriental Institute.

477. "The lady of Byblos" sits upon a throne with her feet on a footstool, holding a papyrus scepter in her left hand, and her right hand upraised. She is clothed in a long garment and is represented with the headdress of the Egyptian goddess Hathor. Before her is the figure of Yeḥawmilk, king of Byblos, who is clothed in a shawl over a long garment, and wears a conical headdress with streamer at the back; his right hand is upraised in a gesture of respect, while his left holds a bowl, which he offers to the goddess. Above the two figures is the winged sun-disc. For other references to the "lady of Byblos" see J. B. Pritchard, *Palestinian Figurines*, New Haven, 1943, pp. 70-71.

Louvre, Collection de Clercq. Byblos, 1869. Limestone. Height of stela: 1.13 m. Fifth century, or early fourth. *CIS*, part 1, vol. 1, Paris, 1881, no. 1, pl. 1. *AOB*, 516. M. Dunand, "Encore la stèle de Yehavmilk roi de Byblos," *Bulletin du Musée de Beyrouth*, vol. 5, 1941, pp. 57-85. Photograph JBP.

478. Nude female figure, with long hair, or wig, which falls down beyond the shoulders, raises the right hand and holds the *was* scepter in her left. The feet and head are shown in profile, but the body is seen from a three-quarters view.

Palestine Archaeological Museum. Beisan excavations. Gold. City-level IX (fourteenth century). A. Rowe, *The Four Canaanite Temples of Beth-shan*, Philadelphia, 1940, pl. 68A, no. 5. Photograph courtesy PAM.

479. A nude female figure, probably a Syrian goddess, wearing only a necklace and earrings, sits astride a horse, grasping reins (or mane) with the left hand and brandishing a weapon with the right.

Berlin, Äg. 21826. Thebes. Pottery. Height: 0.095 m. Nineteenth Dynasty (1350-1200). Schäfer-Andrae, 398, 4. *AOB*, 274. Photograph courtesy of Staatliche Museen.

480. The seated goddess extends her right hand as if to receive an offering and once held in the other, to judge from a vertical hole, an emblem. She has a prominent nose and well-formed mouth, and the eyes, from which the inlays are now missing, are large and almost round. The headdress consists of a folded turban which is raised into a point in front and then wound about the head above the ears, and crossed at the back of the head. The long garment is represented as of thick material on which a lozenge pattern is incised. At the bottom is a rolled edge or cord. About the upper part of the body is wound a heavy cord, which is arranged around the neck and brought around under the breasts and again about the waist. Were it not for the absence of any indication of a head or a tail this decoration might be interpreted as a serpent. For suggestion that this is a Hurrian goddess, perhaps Hepa, see C. F. A. Schaeffer, *Ugaritica I*, Paris, 1939, pp. 139-143; and for contrary opinion see R. Dussaud, *L'art phénicien du IIe millénaire*, Paris, 1949, p. 61.

Louvre, AO 19397. Ras Shamra, 1937, sanctuary south of the residence, level II. Copper. Height: 0.248 m. Nineteenth-seventeenth centuries, according to excavator. *Syria*, vol. 19, 1938, pl. 34, 3, pp. 321-323. C. F. A. Schaeffer, *Ugaritica I*, Paris, 1939, pls. 28-30, pp. 128-131. See W. F. Albright, *BASOR*, no. 77, 1940, p. 25, who dates it to about the seventeenth century. Photograph courtesy of C. F. A. Schaeffer.

481. Figure of a god wearing a high crown (similar to white crown of Upper Egypt). A gold ring is around his right arm, which is extended upward as he brandishes a weapon (now lost). The left hand is extended forward, perhaps to grasp a lance or a staff.

Louvre. Minet el-Beida. Bronze; headdress and head covered with gold, body with silver. Height: 0.179 m. Fifteenth-fourteenth century, according to excavator. *Syria*, vol. 10, 1929, pl. 53, p. 288. C. F. A. Schaeffer, *Ugaritica I*, Paris, 1939, pl. 25. TEL, vol. 2, p. 101F, G. Photograph Archives Photographiques.

482. Standing side by side within a jar were found two silver statuettes, thought to have been intended for deities. The god (to the left) stands on a pedestal, with arms extending forward in a symmetrical gesture. The head is crudely represented, with a beaklike nose and two slots over the eyes, perhaps for the insertion of horns. About his neck is a gold band or torque; his kilt is also of gold and is held by a broad gold belt. Breasts are suggested by the two projections high on the chest; between them is an incised cross. The goddess is smaller

but is represented in a similar fashion. She too wears the torque of gold; about her waist is a broad belt of gold. Her hair is done into a chignon on the top of her head.

Louvre and Aleppo. Ras Shamra, excavation of 1932, level II. Silver and gold. Height of larger figure: 0.28 m.; height of smaller: 0.16 m. 2000-1800, according to excavator (*Ugaritica II*, p. 73). *Syria*, vol. 14, 1933, pl. 17. C. F. A. Schaeffer, *Ugaritica II*, Paris, 1949, pls. 17-19, pp. 71-80. Photograph Archives Photographiques.

483. An elongated male figure of a god stands on a pedestal (not shown) with arms extending forward in a symmetrical fashion. The phallus, which appears, may originally have been covered by a kilt as in No. 482. The eyes were once inlaid; the hair is represented by a chevron-like design and is done up on the top of the head and pierced with a hole.

Louvre, AO 20118. Bronze, covered with silver. A. Parrot suggest date between 1660 and 1400, on basis of style and features (*Syria*, vol. 29, 1952, p. 50). A. Parrot, *Syria*, vol. 29, 1952, pl. 1, pp. 44-51. Photograph JBP.

484. A bronze figure of a Syrian god, originally covered with gold or silver foil, stands with upraised right hand and extended left hand in a gesture similar to that shown in No. 481. The kilt and the headdress show strong Egyptian influence.

British Museum, 25096. Vicinity of Tyre. Bronze. Height: 0.114 m. R. D. Barnett, *British Museum Quarterly*, vol. 9, 1934, pl. 13, 3, p. 46. Photograph courtesy BM.

485. In the upper left of this badly broken stela is the figure of a god, holding a scepter (*was*) in his left hand. He wears a high conical cap, from the top of which a streamer hangs down his back. Before him are an offering stand and a lotus blossom. The offerer, Maimi, stands with upraised hands before the god. The inscription has been read: "To Seth of Ṣapuna in favor of the royal scribe and keeper of the house of silver, Mami (or Maimi)" (A. Rowe, *Syria*, vol. 12, 1931, p. 10).

Louvre. Ras Shamra. Red sandstone. Beginning of Nineteenth Dynasty (1350-1200), according to excavator. *Syria*, vol. 12, 1931, pl. 6, pp. 10-11. C. F. A. Schaeffer, *Ugaritica I*, Paris, 1939, fig. 30. Photograph from *Syria*, vol. 12, 1931, pl. 6, courtesy of Librairie Orientaliste Paul Geuthner, Paris.

486. A god stands with one foot on the head and the other upon the upturned tail of a lion and holds with his left hand a small lion by the feet (see No. 615) and brandishes a throw stick or curved sword with his other hand. He is beardless and is dressed in a garment which covers the upper part of his body and extends below the waist as a kilt, with a back flap which hangs down behind. The headdress consists of high crown (like the white crown of Upper Egypt) flanked by two feathers and having the uraeus in front. From the top of the crown there hangs a streamer, which reaches to the shoulder (see Nos. 485, 487). At the bottom of the stela are represented mountains; at the top are the winged sun-disc and the crescent holding a disc.

Louvre, Collection de Clercq. 'Amrit. Limestone. Height: 1.80 m. Not later than sixth-fifth century (*BASOR*, no. 87, p. 30). Collection de Clercq, *Catalogue, Antiquités assyriennes*, vol. 2, Paris, 1903, pl. 36, pp. 234-252. *AOB*, 307. Contenau, *Man.*, vol. 3, fig. 895. Photograph JBP.

487. To the left of the upper register is seated Mekal, god of Beth-shan, upon a throne, holding the *was* scepter in his left hand, and an *ankh* symbol in his right. He is bearded, wears an ornamented collar, and has a headdress of a conical cap, from which two horns protrude in front, and to which two streamers are attached, one to the top and the other from the bottom of the headdress. Before the enthroned god are the architect Amen-em-Opet and his son. The lower register of the stela gives the inscription of dedication, and shows a flower, an offering stand, and parts of the figures of the father and his son. See *ANET*, 249.

Palestine Archaeological Museum, S 982. Beisan excavations, 1927, city-level IX, temple of Mekal. Limestone. Height: 0.283 m. Fourteenth century. A. Rowe, *The Topography and History of Beth-shan*, Philadelphia, 1930, pl. 33, pp. 14-15. L. H. Vincent, "Le Ba'al cananéen de Beisan et sa parèdre," *RB*, vol. 37, 1928, pp. 512-543. A. Rowe, *The Four Canaanite Temples of Beth-shan*, Philadelphia, 1940, frontispiece (drawing). Photograph courtesy PAM.

488. To the left is a god, clothed in a kilt, wearing the crown of Upper and Lower Egypt, and holding a *was* scepter. To the right is a goddess, wearing a long garment and a headdress composed of the high crown and feathers, and holding an *ankh* sign in her right hand. Between the two deities is a suppliant of equal size, standing with upraised hands before the god. The headdress, profile of the face, and the beard are similar to the features of the Shasu-Bedouin on No. 326. W. F. Albright, *AP*, p. 79, suggests a date toward the end of the third millennium for the illegible inscription at the top, and the twelfth or eleventh century for the relief.

'Amman, Jordan Archaeological Museum. Balu'ah. Black basalt. Height: 1.83 m. G. Horsfield and L. H. Vincent, "Une stèle égypto-moabite au Balou'a," *RB*, vol. 41, 1932, pls. 11, 12, pp. 417-444. Étienne Drioton, "À propos de la stèle du Balou'a," *RB*, vol. 42, 1933, pp. 353-365. J. W. Crowfoot, "An Expedition to Balu'ah," *PEFQS*, April 1934, pl. 1, pp. 76-84. Photograph courtesy of the Palestine Archaeological Museum.

489. A god clothed in a kilt and wearing sandals; about the waist is a belt, into which a dagger is attached diagonally. The right hand clutches some object, perhaps an emblem or weapon, which rests upon his right shoulder; the left hand holds a *was* scepter. A horn projects from the front of the head; and about the neck are traces of a torque. The face seems to be beardless. Before the face of the god is a rectangular object, perhaps a place for a cartouche, to which is attached an *ankh* sign. For suggested identification with Mot, see C. F. A. Schaeffer, *Ugaritica II*, Paris, 1949, pp. 99-106.

Aleppo, National Museum. Ras Shamra, sanctuary to the west of the great temple, found in 1932-1933. Dated: 2000-1800, by excavator. C. F. A. Schaeffer, *Fondation Piot*, vol. 34, 1934, p. 14, fig. 4. C. F. A. Schaeffer, *Ugaritica II*, Paris, 1949, pl. 22 (right), pp. 93-95. Photograph JBP.

490. The so-called "Baal au foudre" stands on what appear to be mountains, brandishes a club in his right hand, and holds in his left a lance with point resting on the ground and the upper part extending upward in the form of a tree or stylized lightning. The god wears a pointed cap, from which emerge two horns. He is bearded, has shaved upper lip, and wears his hair in two long locks ending in curls which hang down below the shoulders. His only article of clothing is a plain kilt of striped material, held in place by a belt, to which a sheathed dagger is attached. No shoes are represented. Between the left leg of the god and the lance, there is a small human figure, clothed in a typical Syrian garment and standing on a pedestal, which may represent a deity or a person under the protection of the god.

Louvre, AO 15775. Ras Shamra, sanctuary to the west of the great temple, found in 1932. Limestone. Height: 1.42 m.; width: 0.47-0.50 m.; thickness: 0.28 m. Dated to 1900-1750, according to excavator; Albright would place between 1650-1500 (*BASOR*, no. 118, 1950, p. 31). C. F. A. Schaeffer, *Syria*, vol. 14, 1933, pl. 16, pp. 122-123. C. F. A. Schaeffer, *Ugaritica II*, Paris, 1949, pls. 23, 24, pp. 121-130. C. F. A. Schaeffer, "La stèle du 'Ba'al au foudre' de Ras-Shamra," Fondation Piot, vol. 34, 1934, pp. 1-18, pl. 1. *Syria*, vol. 16, 1935, pp. 410-411. Photograph JBP.

491. The god is clothed in a horizontally decorated kilt, held in place by a belt, to which a dagger is attached. His right hand grasps a scepter, like that held by Osiris on Egyptian monuments (*heqa*). With his left hand he holds a lance with point turned upward. The headdress, from the front of which emerges a single horn, is very high and appears to be a stylized tree or a plume of feathers. The god is beardless; hair cut short; about the neck there is a torque. Thonged sandals which have slightly upturned toes are represented.

Louvre, AO 13174. Ras Shamra, found in 1930. Limestone. Height: about 1.00 m. Dated 2000-1800 by excavator. C. F. A. Schaeffer, *Syria*, vol. 12, 1931, pl. 8, no. 2, pp. 11-14. C. F. A. Schaeffer, *Ugaritica II*, Paris, 1949, pl. 22 (center), pp. 90-93; 95-99 for suggestion that this divinity is to be identified with Aliyan Baal. Photograph JBP.

492. The stela contains a female figure, holding in her right hand an object which resembles an *ankh* sign, and with her left a lance with upturned point. She is clothed in a long garment reaching almost to her ankles and wears thonged sandals. Over the garment is spread a stylized wing of a bird. The representation is not unlike that found on certain Egyptian divinities protected by the wings of a falcon and suggests the reference to certain descriptions of Anath in the Ugaritic texts (*ANET*, 152-153).

Aleppo, National Museum. Ras Shamra, found in 1930. Limestone. Height: 0.93 m. Dated 2000-1800, by excavator. C. F. A. Schaeffer, *Syria*, vol. 12, 1931, pl. 8, no. 1, pp. 11-14. C. F. A. Schaeffer, *Ugaritica II*, Paris, 1949, pl. 22 (left), pp. 89-90. Photograph JBP.

493. A suppliant stands making an offering to a bearded deity, who wears a long Syrian robe and is barefoot. The headdress of the god is a high crown with horns emerging from the base; he wears his hair in a lock down his back. His right hand holds an object which may represent an incense burner; his left is upraised in a gesture of benediction. He is seated on an elaborate lion-footed throne and rests his feet on a footstool. The beardless suppliant is more simply clad in a long garment fastened by a belt about his waist. He wears a tiara with the uraeus in front. His left hand holds a vase; his right, a scepter-like object with an animal's head. Spanning the entire scene is the winged disc with an eight-pointed star in the middle. On the basis of the texts found at Ras Shamra, it has been suggested that the deity is the god El and that the figure making the offering is the king or chief priest of Ugarit; but since the stela is uninscribed these identifications are only conjectural.

Aleppo, National Museum. Ras Shamra, found in 1936. Serpentine stone. Height: 0.47 m. Schaeffer, in 1937, dated it to the thirteenth century. C. F. A. Schaeffer, *Syria*, vol. 18, 1937, pl. 17, pp. 128-134, fig. 1 on p. 129. G. Contenau, *Man.*, vol. 4, fig. 1307, pp. 2300-2301. Photograph courtesy of C. F. A. Schaeffer.

494. Beardless male figure, clothed in a kilt and wearing a high conical headdress flanked by feathers (?), brandishes a weapon in his upraised right hand and carries a shield in his left.

Oriental Institute, A 18331. Megiddo, stratum VB. Bronze. Height: 0.108 m. Stratum V is dated to 1050-1000 by excavators. The Megiddo Expedition, *Megiddo II, OIP*, 62, Chicago, 1948, pl. 239, no. 31. Photograph courtesy of the Oriental Institute.

495. A seated deity, wearing high conical headdress, is clothed in a long, heavily bordered garment which reaches below the knees. About the neck is a ring of silver.

Oriental Institute, A 18355. Megiddo, strata IX-VII. Bronze. Height: 0.105 m. 1550-1150 as dates for strata IX-VII, according to excavators. The Megiddo Expedition, *Megiddo II, OIP*, 62, Chicago, 1948, pl. 235, no. 23. Photograph courtesy of the Oriental Institute.

496. A beardless male figure, clothed in a kilt, stands with a sword in his upraised right hand and a shield in his left. Cf. No. 481.

Palestine Archaeological Museum. Megiddo, tomb 4. Bronze. Height: about 0.13 m. Late Bronze II (1350-1200), according to excavator. H. G. May, *Material Remains of the Megiddo Cult, OIP*, 26, Chicago, 1935, pl. 34, no. 357, pp. 33-34. Photograph courtesy of the Oriental Institute.

497. A seated figure of a god with arms extended forward, covered with gold. He wears a conical headdress, earrings (only one preserved), and a long garment which reaches to the ankles. Facial features are indicated by black inlay.

Oriental Institute, 18316. Megiddo, stratum VII or VI. Bronze covered with gold. Height: about 0.256 m. From between 1350 and 1100. The Megiddo Expedition, *Megiddo II, OIP*, 62, Chicago, 1948, pl. 238, no. 30. Photograph courtesy of the Oriental Institute.

498. The god is shown facing left and holding up his right hand in benediction. He wears a high headdress,

from the front of which emerge two curved horns. The beard and back hair are full and elaborately curled.

Istanbul, Museum of the Ancient Orient, 7786. Umm-Shershuḥ, near Tell Bise in Syria. Basalt. Height: 0.66 m. Bossert, *Altsyrien*, 487. M. Lidzbarski, *Ephemeris für semitische Epigraphik*, vol. 3, Giessen, 1915, p. 167, fig. 7. M. Ebert, ed., *Reallexikon der Vorgeschichte*, vol. 7, Berlin, 1926, pl. 164a. Photograph JBP.

499. The god Milqart, mentioned in the Aramaic inscription on the lower part of the stela, stands grasping in his left hand a battle-axe with curved blade which rests upon his shoulder, and holding a small object (perhaps an *ankh*) in his right. He wears a conical cap, long beard, hair falling down his back in strands, and a kilt, to the front of which are attached two uraei. The artist has attempted to represent either the fringes of an Assyrian garment over the kilt (Dunand), or a composite bow attached to the belt (Albright). For the inscription, which mentions a Bar-Hadad who was king of Aram, see references listed below.

Aleppo, National Museum. Village of Breij, 7 km. north of Aleppo. Basalt. Height: 1.15 m. Ninth century (Albright: about 850). M. Dunand, "Stèle araméenne dédiée à Melqart," *Bulletin du Musée de Beyrouth*, vol. 3, 1939, pl. 13, pp. 65-76. W. F. Albright, *BASOR*, no. 87, 1942, pp. 23-29. G. Levi Della Vida and W. F. Albright, *BASOR*, no. 90, 1943, pp. 30-34. M. Dunand, *Bulletin du Musée de Beyrouth*, vol. 6, 1942-1943, pp. 41-45. Photograph JBP.

500. A deity, clothed in a long, fringed garment and shoes with upturned toes, stands on the back of a bull moving to the right. He is bearded and has long hair, over which is a cap with streamers. In his left hand he holds a three-pronged thunderbolt and reins which guide the bull. The right hand holds a leaf or cone. The face and the back of the stela are covered with Hittite hieroglyphs, from which may be read the name of Kamanas, king (or governor) or Carchemish.

Aleppo, National Museum, 2459. Found in open field at Jekke, 22 km. to the east of Azaz, which lies 25 km. to the north of Aleppo. Gray volcanic basalt. Height: 1.62 m. Eighth or seventh century (see R. D. Barnett, *Iraq*, vol. 10, 1948, pp. 128, 136). M. Dunand, *Bulletin du Musée de Beyrouth*, vol. 4, 1940, pp. 85-92. R. D. Barnett, "Hittite Hieroglyphic Texts at Aleppo," *Iraq*, vol. 10, 1948, pl. 19, pp. 122-137. Photograph JBP.

501. Standing as if in motion is the god of the storm, perhaps Adad, on the back of a bull. He is clothed with a robe, over which has been thrown a mantle extending over the left shoulder. He is bearded, has long hair which falls in a mass upon his shoulder, and has a horned headdress which is surmounted by a large disc with star. In each hand the god holds a double three-pronged fork, representing lightning. See No. 537 for similar representation.

Louvre. Arslan Tash. Basalt. Height: 1.35 m. Tiglath-pileser III (744-727). F. Thureau-Dangin, *et al.*, *Arslan-Tash*, Paris, 1931, pl. 2, no. 1, pp. 65-66. TEL, vol. 1, pl. 300. Contenau, *Man.*, vol. 4, fig. 1251. Photograph JBP.

MESOPOTAMIAN AND ANATOLIAN

502. This tall vase from Warka, which has been reconstructed from fifteen fragments, is decorated with three bands of relief. In the upper register (left) a nude server presents a basket of fruit or vegetables to a figure intended to represent either the goddess Inanna or her priestess. She is clothed in a long garment without a belt and draped over her shoulders so as to leave her right arm free. Her long hair hangs down her back, and upon her head she wears a horned headdress. Behind her, extending the full measure of the register, are two symbols of the gatepost-with-streamer, an emblem associated with Inanna (E. D. van Buren, *Symbols of the Gods*, Rome, 1945, pp. 43-44). Behind the symbols (middle) are two horned rams, the second represented by a duplicate outline of the first. On the back of each is shown a small human figure mounted on a platform. The first is beardless, wears long hair hanging down the back, is clothed in a long garment, and holds in his hands an object or symbol; the second figure is similar but smaller in size and clasps his hands before his face. Extending from the back of the pedestal of the second figure is the gatepost-with-streamer symbol of Inanna. To the right of the two rams is a representation of various offerings. Above, are two vases, similar in shape to the one on which the reliefs appear, a gazelle and a lion, and two smaller vessels, possibly containing bread. In the lower part of the register are two baskets full of fruit or vegetables, a bull's head, a quiver (?), and two square unidentifiable objects. Beyond the offering display (right) is a human figure, beardless, wearing long hair and a kilt, who holds in his hands the girdle belonging to what was probably the principal figure of the procession. Only the foot and a part of the skirt of this figure can be seen. In the second register is a line of nude porters of offerings, each with head and face shaved. The third register is divided into two parts: the upper is a row of animals, ewes alternating with rams, or sheep and goats; below is a register of plants and stalks of grain. At the very bottom of the vase itself is a wavy line, possibly intended for a representation of a stream of water.

Baghdad, Iraq Museum, 19606. Warka, 1933-1934. Alabaster. Height, after restoration, 1.10 m. Jemdet Nasr Period (around 3000), although F. Basmachi (*Sumer*, vol. 3, 1947, pp. 118-127) seeks to prove date as latter part of Uruk Period. E. Heinrich, *Kleinfunde aus den archaischen Tempelschichten in Uruk*, Berlin, 1936, pls. 2, 3, 38 (drawing), pp. 15-16. Contenau, *Man.*, vol. 4, fig. 1073, pp. 1977-1982. E. D. van Buren, *AfO*, vol. 13, 1939, pp. 32 ff. Photograph of cast in Berlin courtesy of Staatliche Museen.

503. This troughlike stone vessel has on its side a relief of a reed hut with the symbol of the gatepost-with-streamer, associated with Inanna (No. 502). From each of the two doors emerges a lamb.

British Museum, 120000. Said to have come from Warka. Alabastrine limestone. Length: 0.965 m.; height: 0.152 m.; width: 0.355 m. *British Museum Quarterly*, vol. 3, 1929, pl. 22, pp. 40-41. Photograph courtesy BM.

504. Nine examples of the more than 300 intact "eye-idols" found in the Eye-Temple platform or its precincts at Brak. It is estimated by the excavator that there were originally at least 20,000 of these objects. The eye-idol consists of an oblong body, short neck, and two eyes with indication of eyebrows. The eyes were originally filled up with black or green paint (center one in top row has been repainted). These objects have been interpreted by M. E. L. Mallowan as "abstract symbols of some divinity" (*Iraq*, vol. 9, 1947, p. 153).

British Museum. Tell Brak. Alabaster, terra cotta (3), and limestone (6). Height of one at upper left: 0.05 m. Early Jemdet Nasr period (around 3000). M. E. L. Mallowan, "Excavations at Brak and Chagar Bazar," *Iraq*, vol. 9, 1947, pl. 25, pp. 33-36, 150-154. Photograph courtesy BM.

505. The seated goddess holds in her right hand a bunch of date blossoms. Her full hair hangs in locks before and behind her shoulders. From her shoulders grow three stalks with buds at the ends, a feature which suggests the patronage of vegetation. On her head she wears a horned crown decorated with palms or stalks of vegetation and a small object which supports a crescent in the center. The identification with Nina, the date-goddess has been suggested.

Berlin, VA 7248. Basalt. Height: 0.25 m. Entemena of Lagash (middle third millennium). *AOB*, 247. C. Zervos, *L'art de la Mésopotamie*, Paris, 1935, p. 98. Photograph courtesy of Staatliche Museen.

506. This female figure, found at Mari, wears a high crown, splayed toward the top, over her full hair which extends at the sides in two large buns. The eyes are of shell, set in bitumen. The figure is covered by a long robe, fringed at the bottom, which extends over the left shoulder, but leaves the right arm and shoulder free. The hands are joined in front over the breast. It is possible that this figure with the high (polos) headdress, so unlike the usual headdress of women of the period, may have been intended for a representation of a goddess.

Aleppo, National Museum. Mari, 1933-1934, temple of Ishtar. White alabaster. Height: 0.23 m. Same context as Nos. 21, 24. Middle third millennium. *Syria*, vol. 16, 1935, pl. 10, no. 1, pp. 27-28. A. Parrot, "Sur quelques statuettes de Mari," *Fondation Piot*, vol. 35, 1935-1936, pp. 1-6, pl. 1. Photograph JBP.

507. The goddess is shown seated on a throne resting on water and supported by geese, with hands joined before the breast, and clothed in a long, flounced garment with a short tiered cape. Over her hair, part of which is bound in back into a chignon, is a flat-topped cap. The drilled holes at the sides suggest that some decoration completed the headdress. The nose was of a separate piece and has been lost; eyes were once inlaid. Cf. No. 601.

Baghdad. Ur, 1925-1926, U.6779. Diorite. Height: 0.29 m. Ur III (about 2060-1955) on basis of style. *AJ*, vol. 6, 1926, pl. 51a,b. *MJ*, vol. 18, 1927, pp. 230-231. Photograph courtesy of the Iraq Museum.

508. The goddess Ningal is seated on an inscribed throne, with her hands clasped before her breast. She wears a long, flounced garment, over which is a short cape of the same material. Her long hair flows down in two curled locks in front. She wears a simple diadem, which, to judge from the copper nails, was once surmounted by a miter. In the inscription is mentioned Enannatum, high priest, son of Ishme-Dagan, king of Isin.

University Museum, CBS 16229. Diorite; part of base, skirt, elbows, right shoulder and lower part of head restored. Height: 0.24 m. Isin period (about 1960-1700). *AJ*, vol. 6, 1926, pl. 52a, p. 376. *MJ*, vol. 18, 1927, p. 224. Photograph courtesy UM.

509. A sitting figure of a woman holding her breasts with her hands. The legs are crudely formed; head is missing. Bands of brown paint decorated the neck, arms, and breasts.

University Museum, 38-13-500. Gawra, 1937-1938, stratum XVII. Terra cotta. Height: 0.083 m. Obeid period (fourth millennium). A. J. Tobler, *Excavations at Tepe Gawra*, vol. 2, Philadelphia, 1950, pl. 81b. Photograph courtesy UM.

510. Figurines with nude female bodies, but with reptilian heads with slanting eyes, wearing high bitumen crowns. Breasts and genital regions are prominently displayed. The shoulders are broad; hands hold the waist. Clay spots are represented on shoulders.

University Museum, 31-16-733 (left), 31-16-734 (right). Ur, 1929-1930. Clay, bitumen wig. Heights: 0.165 m. and 0.143 m. Obeid period (fourth millennium). *AJ*, vol. 10, 1930, pl. 48c, d. Photograph courtesy UM.

511. An inscribed libation vase, decorated with entwined serpents and a pair of dragons. To the left is the head of one of the two serpents of the caduceus and a portion of the entwined bodies. To the right is one of the pair of composite creatures, each of which stands upright on his hind legs and holds a staff with his forefeet. The creature has a serpent's head, crowned by a low crown, from which two horns emerge at the top, and the mane extends to the shoulders; wings and claws suggest an eagle; the body is spotted by incisions; the tail is long and ends with a sharp point (the sting of a scorpion?). The dedicatory inscription is to Ningizzida by Gudea of Lagash (G. A. Barton, *The Royal Inscriptions of Sumer and Akkad*, New Haven, 1929, pp. 260-261). The symbol of the entwined serpents has been taken as the symbol of Ningizzida (H. Frankfort, *Cylinder Seals*, London, 1939, p. 119); for another view see E. D. van Buren, *Symbols of the Gods*, Rome, 1945, pp. 40-42.

Louvre, AO 190. Tello. Dark green steatite. Height: 0.23 m. Gudea (beginning of twenty-first century). E. de Sarzec, *Découvertes en Chaldée*, Paris, 1884-1912, pl. 44, 2a, b, c. A. Parrot, *Tello*, Paris, 1948, pl. 21, pp. 198-199. TEL, vol. 1, p. 224. *AOB*, 367. H. Frankfort, "Gods and Myths on Sargonid Seals," *Iraq*, vol. 1, 1934, fig. 1, pp. 2-29. E. D. van Buren, "The God Ningizzida," *Iraq*, vol. 1, 1934, pp. 60-89. E. D. van Buren, "Entwined Serpents," *AfO*, vol. 10, 1935, pp. 53-65, figs. 1-12. Photograph Archives Photographiques.

512. On the corner of a plaque is the goddess Ninsun, who is identified by the inscription to the left. She is

dressed in a flounced garment, wears a collar and a tiara consisting of a simple band around her hair, which hangs down her back. The throne has a back and the arm ends in an animal's head. Ninsun was the mother of Gilgamesh (*ANET*, 76).

Louvre. Black steatite. Height: 0.14 m. Neo-Sumerian period (end of third millennium). TEL, vol. 1, p. 243C. Contenau, *Man.*, vol. 2, fig. 532. AOB, 251. Photograph Archives Photographiques.

513. To the left of this scene from the upper part of a stela is Gudea, draped in a fringed shawl and holding a palm branch. He is led by a deity, probably Ningizzida. The latter wears a long, flounced robe reaching to his ankles, but leaving his right arm and shoulder free, a horned miter with a knob at the top, and a long beard, curled at the end. From the shoulders emerge the heads of serpents, which wear a crown consisting of two horns curving upward and inward and surmounted by two small feathers or horns. Ningizzida is preceded by another deity, dressed similarly. He stands with a staff in his left hand and with his right hand folded over the left. The central figure of the scene, the deity to whom Gudea is presented, sat upon a throne carved with the head of a lion (but not a protome, serving as the arm of the throne), and probably held a vase from which water flowed. Behind the throne is another bearded deity, who stands with folded hands in an attitude of respect.

Berlin, VA 2796. Probably from Tello. Gray limestone. Height: about 0.70 m. Gudea (beginning of twenty-first century). A. Parrot, *Tello*, Paris, 1948, pl. 20b, pp. 184-185. Schäfer-Andrae, 502. AOB, 47. E. D. van Buren, "The God Ningizzida," *Iraq*, vol. 1, 1934, p. 72. Photograph Foto Marburg.

514. To the right a bearded god sits enthroned, wearing a long, flounced robe, a miter of four horns over a stepped cap. Long hair is tied into a chignon at the back. His right arm, on which he wears a bracelet, extends toward the worshiper the ring and the rod. Before the god is a fragment of what may represent the top of an incense burner. The worshiper is smaller and stands with clasped hands before the god. He is bearded and wears a long plain garment with a fitted stole. His hair falls down before and behind his shoulder in long locks. His headdress is either a helmet-like cap or consists of hair which has been cut into this unusual shape. At the top of the stela is the eight-pointed star within a disc. The scene is similar to that on the top of the Hammurabi stela (No. 515).

Louvre. Susa. Basalt. Height: 0.67 m. First part of second millennium. TEL, vol. 1, p. 260. Contenau, *Man.*, vol. 2, fig. 607, pp. 852-854. Photograph Giraudon, Paris.

515. The god Shamash, clothed in a long, flounced garment which leaves free the right arm and shoulder, sits enthroned, with his feet resting on a triple-staged platform decorated with semicircles which may represent mountains. He wears the horned miter, consisting of four pairs of horns and a peak. He also wears a long beard and a chignon. Rays or flames are coming from his shoulders. He extends with his right hand the ring and

the rod to the worshiper, who stands before him. The worshiper, to judge from the text of the code inscribed below, is Hammurabi, king of Babylon. He is bearded, clothed in a long flowing garment, and wears a headdress similar in form to that worn by Gudea (Nos. 430, 431). About his neck is a necklace. Over his left arm is folded a part of his garment; his right is raised to the height of his lips in a gesture of supplication. See No. 246 for entire stela.

Louvre. Susa. Diorite. Height of relief: about 0.65 m. Hammurabi (1728-1686). V. Scheil, *Mémoires, Délégation en Perse*, vol. 4, Paris, 1902, pl. 3. AOB, 318. Photograph Giraudon, Paris.

516. The upper part of a life-sized statue of a goddess holding a vase drilled with a hole for the flow of water from the base of the statue. The goddess wears a headdress of a single pair of horns. Her hair falls down on the shoulders and is tied behind in a heavy chignon. She wears a tight-fitting robe which extends to the ground, leaving only a triangular opening to display the feet. The robe is decorated with representations of streams in which fish are swimming. She wears three bracelets on each arm and a six-strand necklace of stones of various sizes. See representation of goddess with flowing vase in No. 610. While the identification of the goddess is not certain, the single horns would suggest a deity of inferior rank.

Aleppo, National Museum, 1659. Mari, palace. Limestone. Height of statue: about 1.50 m. First half of second millennium. *Syria*, vol. 18, 1937, pl. 13, pp. 78-80. For an earlier study of this type of symbolism see: E. D. van Buren, *The Flowing Vase and the God with Streams of Water*, Berlin, 1933. Photograph JBP.

517. This fragment of an inscribed statue, dedicated by [Ia]smaḫ-Addu, viceroy of Mari, to Shamash, is of a bearded figure, clothed in a skirt, on which are represented mountains. The figure is nude above the waist; the skirt is held by a belt. The hands are crossed in front of the breast. The symbolism suggests the connection with the familiar scenes of Shamash arising from the mountain as shown in Nos. 683, 685.

Aleppo, National Museum, 1329. Mari, brought by Lt. Cabane to Museum in August 1933. Gray limestone. Height: 1.09 m. First part of second millennium. F. Thureau-Dangin, "La statue Cabane," *Mélanges . . . Dussaud*, vol. 1, Paris, 1939, pl. opp. p. 158, pp. 157-159. Inscription: RA, vol. 31, 1934, p. 144. Photograph JBP.

Boundary-stones

Symbols of Babylonian gods appear on the so-called "boundary-stones" (*kudurru*). These monuments, which appear first in Mesopotamia in the Kassite period, may originally have served for marking boundaries in a field, but seem later to have been legal records dealing with landed property. The emblems of the gods were of those deities invoked in the texts which were inscribed on the stones. E. D. van Buren, *Symbols of the Gods in Mesopotamian Art*, Rome, 1945, is a convenient handbook on the interpretations of these symbols. Other studies are: Franz X. Steinmetzer, *Die babylonischen Kudurru (Grenzsteine) als Urkundenform*, Paderborn, 1922. L. W. King, *Babylonian Boundary-Stones and Memorial-Tablets in the British Museum*, London, 1912. For a later example of boundary-stones see No. 454.

518. Under the symbols of the sun-disc (Shamash), crescent (Sin), and the eight-pointed star (Ishtar) is the seated goddess Nana, who receives the king Meli-Shipak and his daughter Hunnubat-Nana. The goddess is seated on a lion-footed platform and is clothed in a long, flounced garment and a conical headdress decorated with feathers at the top (see Elamite headdress). Her hair is caught into a chignon at the back of her neck. Before her is the bearded king, clothed in a long, fringed robe and wearing an ovoid cap over his long hair, which falls down his back in curled strands. His right hand is upraised in a gesture of respect. The smaller figure, unfortunately mutilated, is evidently a representation of the king's daughter, who is being presented to the goddess. She wears a long robe, over which a shawl is draped, and carries what appears to be a lyre. Between the king and the goddess is a cylindrical stand on which is a conelike object. Inscription on the back.

Louvre. Susa. Diorite. Height: 0.90 m. Meli-Shipak (twelfth century). TEL, vol. 1, p. 264. V. Scheil, *Mémoires, Délégation en Perse*, vol. 10, Paris, 1908, pl. 13, no. 1. Contenau, *Man.*, vol. 2, fig. 622, pp. 897-899. F. X. Steinmetzer, *Die babylonischen Kudurru (Grenzsteine) as Urkundenform*, Paderborn, 1922, pp. 70-71. Photograph TEL, vol. 1, p. 264.

519. The inscription (not shown) on this stone describes the military services which Ritti-Marduk rendered to Nebuchadnezzar and sets forth the terms of the charter granted to Ritti-Marduk by the king. At the end are imprecations in the names of various gods upon violators of the charter or any who injure the record. The symbols (listed from left to right and from top to bottom; in parentheses are references to divisions in E. D. van Buren, *Symbols of the Gods*, Rome, 1945, pp. 190-191, and the names of the deities with which they are generally connected) are as follows: 1. Eight-pointed star inscribed on a disc (E5b, Inanna-Ishtar). 2. Crescent (E1a, Sin). 3. Sun-disc (E7, Shamash). 4-6. Horned cap mounted on base representing façade of a temple, or throne (F1, Anu, Enlil, Ea). 7. *marru* (or spear point) on shrine, beside which is a horned dragon *Tiamat* (A2, Marduk). 8. Wedge (stylus) on shrine base, with horned dragon at side (I4a, Nabu). 9. Shrine with band (?) symbol. 10. Eagle-headed scepter (K3, Ninurta). *Nergal?* 11. Double-lion-headed mace (M7). 12. Horse's head set on a base within a double arch (B5). 13. Bird on a rod (B1). 14. Goddess (Gula) seated on a throne, wearing feather-like crown to conical headdress; dog lying beside her. 15. Scorpion-man, with conical headdress, bow and arrow, body of scorpion, and legs and feet of bird. 16. Double lightning-forks supported by young bull (E3b, Adad). 17. Tortoise. 18. Scorpion. 19. Lamp on pedestal (I3, Nusku). 20. Serpent (along left side, with *Nergal?* head at center of top).

British Museum, 90858. At or near Abu Habbah, 1882. Limestone. Height: 0.65 m. Nebuchadnezzar I (twelfth century). L. W. King, *Babylonian Boundary-Stones and Memorial-Tablets in the British Museum*, London, 1912, pls. 90-91, pp. 29-36. F. X. Steinmetzer, *Die babylonischen Kudurru (Grenzsteine) als Urkundenform*, Paderborn, 1922, pp. 12-14. British Museum, *A*

Guide to the Babylonian and Assyrian Antiquities, London, 1922, pl. 25, pp. 66-67. Photograph courtesy BM.

520. The text on the back of this boundary-stone deals with a grant made to Marduk-apal-iddin, son of the king, and ends with a list of gods invoked for cursing any who do not respect the terms of the grant. Shown here are twenty-four symbols which are divided into five registers. Below are listed the symbols, from left to right and from top to bottom (references in parentheses are to divisions in E. D. van Buren, *Symbols of the Gods*, Rome, 1945, pp. 190-191, and to the names of the deities with which the symbols are generally connected; for an earlier discussion of the meaning of these emblems see F. X. Steinmetzer, *Die babylonischen Kudurru (Grenzsteine) als Urkundenform*, Paderborn, 1922, pp. 115-208). 1. Crescent (E1a, Sin). 2. Eight-pointed star (E5b, Ishtar). 3. Sun-disc (E7, Shamash). 4-5. Horned cap mounted on base (façade of temple or throne) (F1, Anu and Enlil). 6. Ram-headed scepter mounted on base, with goat-fish at side (K4, Ea). 7. *Omega*-shaped symbol, over knife (?), and base (F2, "swaddling-bands," emblem of Ninhursag). 8. Mace with two lions' heads, supported by a winged dragon with head of a lion (M7). 9. Eagle-headed scepter (K3, Ninurta). 10. Bird, with head turned backward. 11. Lion-headed scepter. 12. Lion-griffin. 13. *marru* (or spear point) mounted on base, with dragon (A2, Marduk). 14. Wedge (stylus) and support mounted on base, with dragon (I4a, Nabu). 15. Bust of Gula mounted on base, with dog (cf. No. 519). 16. Double lightning-fork on base, with young bull (E3b, Adad). 17. Stylus supported by base, with ram (I4a, Nabu). 18. Plow (A3). 19. Lamp (I3, Nusku). 20. Bird, walking. 21. Bird on rod (B1). 22. Base supporting bundle (grain?). 23. Scorpion. 24. Serpent.

Louvre. Susa. Black limestone. Height: 0.68 m. Meli-Shipak (twelfth century). J. de Morgan, *Mémoires, Délégation en Perse*, vol. 1, Paris, 1900, pl. 16. TEL, vol. 1, p. 265. Contenau, *Man.*, vol. 1, fig. 117; vol. 2, p. 897. F. X. Steinmetzer, *Die babylonischen Kudurru (Grenzsteine) als Urkundenform*, Paderborn, 1922, pp. 52-54. Photograph JBP.

521. The reverse of the *kudurru* has four registers of emblems (listed from left to right and from top to bottom; references in parentheses are to divisions in E. D. van Buren, *Symbols of the Gods*, Rome, 1945, pp. 190-191 and names of deities with which the symbols are usually associated). 1-2. Cap of horns mounted on base, which may represent a throne or the façade of a temple (F1, Anu and Enlil). 3. Destroyed. 4. Base, without emblem. 5. *marru*, or spear point (A2, Marduk). 6. Mace with two lions' heads (M7). 7. Eagle-headed scepter (K3, Ninurta). 8. Lion-headed scepter. 9. Bird perched on post with bifurcated top (B1). 10. Double lightning-fork upon the back of a bull (E3b, Adad).

Louvre. Susa. Black limestone. Height: 0.50 m. Nazi-Maruttash II (1320-1295). J. de Morgan, *Mémoires, Délégation en Perse*, vol. 1, Paris, 1900, pl. 15, pp. 170-172. F. X. Steinmetzer, *Die babylonischen Kudurru (Grenzsteine) als Urkundenform*, Paderborn, 1922, pp. 50-52. *AOB*, 317. Photograph JBP.

522. Identified by an inscription on the face of this stela is the figure of Ishtar of Arbela standing on a lion moving to the right. She is clothed in a short garment over which is a mantle, and is armed with a sword and a quiver. A nimbus extends from her shoulders. Her headdress consists of a high conical crown, the top being decorated by vertical incisions and a star-disc at the top. Her right hand is extended in a gesture of benediction; her right holds a leash and a lotus (?).

Louvre, AO 11503. Til-Barsib (Tell 'Ahmar). Reddish breccia. Height: 1.21 m. Eighth century. F. Thureau-Dangin, M. Dunand, *Til-Barsib*, Paris, 1936, pl. 14, no. 1, pp. 156-157. Contenau, *Man.*, vol. 4, fig. 1245, p. 2218. Photograph JBP.

523. Marduk, identified by an accompanying inscription, wears a high conical crown, decorated with circles and a band of feathers at the top, a long-sleeved robe, decorated above the waist with rosettes. He is full bearded and wears his hair in a bun at the back of his neck. Suspended from his shoulders by a band or chain are three discs which almost cover the skirt of his garment. In his right hand Marduk holds what may be a curved sword; in his left he holds the rod and ring. Beside him lies a horned demon. On the plinth a stream of water is represented by wavy lines. In the text is mentioned the *kunukku*, a word which may refer to the lapis object itself.

Berlin. Babylon. Lapis lazuli. Height of figure: about 0.10 m. Mardukzakirshumi (middle of ninth century). R. Koldewey, *Die Tempel von Babylon und Borsippa, WVDOG*, 15, Leipzig, 1911, fig. 74 (photograph), p. 48. F. H. Weissbach, *Babylonische Miscellen, WVDOG*, 4, Leipzig, 1903, p. 16, fig. 1, pl. 6, no. 2 (text). *AOB*, 314. Contenau, *Man.*, vol. 1, fig. 137. Photograph from F. H. Weissbach, p. 16, fig. 1.

524. On the sculptured rock at Zohab, in the Zagros mountain region to the east of the Diyala, is an inscribed relief celebrating the victory of Anubanini, king of the Lullu(bians) (for inscription see G. A. Barton, *The Royal Inscriptions of Sumer and Akkad*, New Haven, 1929, pp. 150-151). In the middle of the upper register stands Inanna or Ishtar, clothed in a long, flounced garment, horned crown, and beaded collar. From her shoulders emerge shoots with buds at the ends. Her left hand holds a rope tied to a ring in the lip of a nude prisoner, followed by a second. Her right hand is extended toward the king, Anubanini, who stands before her with one foot on the body of another nude prisoner. He is clothed in a kilt, cape, sandals, and a turban headdress. In his right hand he holds a curved stick; in his left hand may be a bow. He wears a long beard which reaches down below his neck. The lower register is carved with the figures of nude prisoners, bearded and wearing what may be fur caps, preceded by a figure with long hair and a feathered crown. The remainder of the register contains the inscription.

Zohab. Period of Naram-Sin (first half of twenty-third century). J. de Morgan, *Mission scientifique en Perse*, vol. 4, pt. 1, Paris, 1896, p. 161. E. Meyer, *Sumerier und Semiten in Babylonien*, Berlin, 1906, p. 25. *AOB*, 254. Contenau, *Man.*, vol. 2, fig. 541, pp. 763-765. N. C. Debevoise, "The Rock Reliefs of Ancient Iran," *JNES*, vol. 1, 1942, p. 81, fig. 2 (drawing). Photograph from E. Meyer, *loc. cit.*

525. The goddess Ishtar is seated on a throne placed on a dais. From her shoulders sprout the mace, a curved pole with globes placed at alternating points near the top (perhaps a bough indicating fertility), and the axe with a curved blade. She wears a multiple-horned headdress and long hair which hangs down her shoulders in wavy locks curled at the ends and is clad in a long, flounced garment which leaves her right arm and shoulder bare. The throne is decorated with crossed lions. Ishtar raises her hand in a welcoming gesture to the two female worshipers, of whom the first pours a libation into an offering stand, while the other carries a pail, perhaps containing more of the liquid to be offered. The two worshipers are identically clad in robes made of a rectangular piece of fringed material. Each has her hair tied in a bun at the back by a ribbon which seems to be wound three times around the bun; the uncurled ends of the hair protrude at the back (for similar figures see *Corpus*, 250). Behind the goddess Ishtar stands a minor goddess dressed in a long, pleated robe and wearing a headdress of a single pair of horns. She grasps her left wrist with her right hand in a peculiar gesture. Her hair falls down her back in a single wavy lock curled at the end.

New York, private collection. Nephrite. Length: 0.043. Akkadian period (about 2360-2180). Photograph courtesy of E. Borowski.

526. Ishtar, goddess of war, placing one foot on a lion, which she holds by a leash, resting her hand on a lion-scimitar, represented with wings and weapons growing from her shoulders. She wears a multiple-horned miter, long hair flowing over her wings and falling down in two curls on either side of her face, and a many-tiered, flounced robe. At her right are a star and a female worshiper (or minor goddess) raising her hand in a gesture of adoration.

Oriental Institute, A 27903. Iraq, provenience unknown. Black stone. Height: 0.042 m.; diameter: 0.025 m. Akkadian period (about 2360-2180). H. A. Groenewegen-Frankfort, *Arrest and Movement*, Chicago, 1951, pl. 63c. For description see E. Porada, *JCS*, vol. 4, 1950, p. 156. Photograph courtesy of the Oriental Institute.

527. To the left stands the god of vegetation holding in his left hand stalks of grain and in his right a bunch of grapes, while around his waist are other clusters attached to the vine. The god is clothed in a short-sleeved shirt, a kilt with spiral decoration at the corners, and shoes with upturned points. He is bearded, has long hair which falls down behind the ears in spirals, and wears a crown extending upward to a peak and decorated with two rows of horns. Before the god is the smaller figure of a bearded worshiper (a king), who wears a long robe of patterned material and a fringed cape, and shoes with upturned pointed toes. He wears a headdress with rounded top which fits tightly over his elaborately curled hair.

Ivriz (southeastern Anatolia). Relief on live rock. Eighth century. Schäfer-Andrae, 602. Bossert, *Altanatolien*, 796. *AOB*, 343. I. J. Gelb, *Hittite Hieroglyphic Monuments, OIP*, 45, Chicago, 1939, pl. 46, p. 15. Photograph of cast in Museum of Ancient Orient, Istanbul, through courtesy of the Museum.

528. The central figure is bearded and wears a cap of heavy material rounded at the top and a skirt, on which may be representations of mountains. In each hand he holds a branch which ends in three conelike objects, possibly intended for bunches of grapes (see No. 527). From the hips emerge two additional branches of the same type. Two goats stand with their hind legs on the ends of the lower branches and nibble at the ends of those held over the shoulders. At each side of the central figure stand two smaller female figures, each holding two vases from which water flows in streams over their shoulders and down to the ground. They wear skirts decorated with wavy lines, suggesting flowing water. While the three figures are without the usual horned miters belonging to deities, it is possible that the central figure represents the god of the mountains who makes possible the vines from which the goats eat, and that the two smaller figures are goddesses who provide from their flowing vases the moisture necessary for vegetation.

Berlin, VA Ass. 1358. Ashur. Alabaster. Height: 1.36 m. First half of second millennium, on basis of style. W. Andrae, *Kultrelief aus dem Brunnen des Asurtempels zu Assur, WVDOG*, 53, Leipzig, 1931, pl. 1, pp. 1-11. Contenau, *Man.*, vol. 1, fig. 138. Photograph courtesy of Staatliche Museen.

529. A relief on the upper part of a stone tablet engraved with the record of Nabuaplaiddin's endowment of the sun temple at Sippar. The stone tablet was found in a clay box along with two impressions in clay of the relief. The scene, which is labeled by three inscriptions, represents the presentation of Nabuapaliddin to the enthroned Shamash. To the left is a goddess (Aya is mentioned in the text), who stands with upraised hands sponsoring the king. The next figure is that of the king, who wears a conical headdress and raises his right hand in supplication to the god. Leading him is a third figure (Nabunadinshumi is mentioned in the text of the tablet), who stands before an altar supported by ropes and on which is a large sun-disc. The bodies of attendant deities spring from the roof of the shrine and their hands hold the ropes which extend downward to the altar. Within the shrine sits the enthroned Shamash holding the ring and rod in his right hand. He is bearded, clothed in a long, flounced garment, and is crowned by a multiple-horned miter. His throne bears the design of two bullmen who support the pillars at each side. Within the shrine are the emblems of the crescent (Sin), sun-disc (Shamash), and the eight-pointed star (Ishtar), their identifications appearing in the inscription over the top of the shrine. Below the entire scene are wavy lines in which four stars are set, a representation of the heavenly ocean (*apsû*).

British Museum. 91000. Abu Habbah, 1881. Stone. Width of scene: 0.18 m. Nabuapaliddin (middle of ninth century). L. W. King, *Babylonian Boundary-Stones and Memorial-Tablets in the British Museum*, London, 1912, pl. 98, pp. 120-127. *AOB*, 322. Schäfer-Andrae, 518. Photograph courtesy BM.

530. The statue of a bearded figure fits into a socket consisting of two lions and a dwarfed man squatting between them. An abnormally large head is set down into the shoulders of the body, the mouth well below the line of the shoulders. The beard and hair are elaborately curled; the upper lip is shaved; and there is no headdress except a narrow band or fillet, which is apparent only at the forehead. The figure is clothed in a short-sleeved robe which reaches to the ankles. To a broad belt around the waist is attached a long tassel at the front; a sword is thrust through the belt. The right hand originally held a staff, the lower part of which is still visible along the skirt. Although the figure does not wear a horned miter the lion base suggests that a god is intended (E. Akurgal, *Späthethitische Bildkunst*, Ankara, 1949, p. 149, considers that it is the weather-god who is represented).

Istanbul, Museum of the Ancient Orient. Zinjirli. Height of statue: 3 m.; base: 0.72 m. Ninth century. F. von Luschan, *Ausgrabungen in Sendschirli*, vol. 4, Berlin, 1911, fig. 265, pp. 362-369. Schäfer-Andrae, 588. *AOB*, 345. Bossert, *Altanatolien*, 901-904. Photograph courtesy of Turkish Information Office, New York.

531. Fragments of a stela showing the weather-god standing on the back of a bull. Most of the detail above the knees of the god has been restored from No. 532. The god wears shoes with pointed, upturned toes. The bull is shown with horns and with his tail hanging between his legs. Below is a frieze of twisted design.

Aleppo, National Museum. Til-Barsib (Tell 'Ahmar). Basalt. Height: 3 m. Found out of context, but dated to eleventh or twelfth century by excavators. F. Thureau-Dangin and M. Dunand, *Til-Barsib*, Paris, 1936, pl. 3, pp. 135-136. Photograph JBP.

532. A broken stela, inscribed with Hittite hieroglyphs, shows the weather-god standing beneath a winged sun-disc and crescent. He is clothed in a short-sleeved shirt and kilt with wide fringe, and a wide belt, to which is attached a long dagger. His headdress consists of a conical cap, which has two pairs of horns at different stages, and a ball-like projection at the top. The god wears a long beard of curled locks; his hair hangs down his back in locks which end in spirals. In his left hand he holds the triple-pronged lightning; with his right he brandishes an axe. For comparable representations see R. Koldewey, *Die Hettitische Inschrift, WVDOG*, 1, Leipzig, 1900, pl. 1 (from Babylon); F. von Luschan, *Ausgrabungen in Sendschirli*, vol. 3, Berlin, 1902, pl. 41 (Zinjirli).

Louvre. Til-Barsib (Tell 'Ahmar). Basalt. Height: 2.06 m. Found out of datable context, but dated to eleventh or twelfth century by excavators. F. Thureau-Dangin and M. Dunand, *Til-Barsib*, Paris, 1936, pl. 1, pp. 134-135. Contenau, *Man.*, vol. 2, fig. 705. Photograph JBP.

533. To the left is the figure of Ishtar, identified by an inscription beside her. She wears a long garment, the skirt of which is covered in front by three shields which are bound around her by bands. She has a high crown and her hair hangs in a mass to her shoulders with strands hanging down below. She holds in her left hand a ring and a bow to which a star is attached; her right hand is raised in a gesture of greeting. Before her stands the bearded figure of Adad, also identified by an inscription, wearing a dress similar to that of Ishtar, a conical crown topped with a row of feathers. His left hand holds the lightning bolts; his right, bolts and a ring. Both of these divine figures and the third divine figure to the extreme right stand on pedestals decorated with conventionalized mountains. At a lower level and before Adad stands a figure dressed as an Assyrian king (perhaps Shamash-resh-usur, governor of Suhi and Mari, mentioned in the accompanying text). In the upper part of the relief are emblems of the gods (from left to right): *marru* (or spear point) emblem of Marduk, the wedge or stylus (Nabu), the winged sun-disc (mutilated), and the crescent (Sin).

Istanbul, Museum of the Ancient Orient, 7815. Babylon. Limestone. Height of fragment: 1.18 m.; width: 1.32 m. Perhaps eighth century. F. H. Weissbach, *Babylonische Miscellen, WVDOG*, 4, Leipzig, 1903, frontispiece. *AOB*, 330. Contenau, *Man.*, vol. 3, fig. 823, pp. 1302-1303. Photograph JBP.

534. A god standing on the back of a winged lion with head of a bull. He wears a short Assyrian garment, over which is a long double robe, and is fully armed, with sword, quiver, and mace. He wears a long beard, hair to his shoulders, and a horned miter with cylindrical top decorated with a band of feathers. Behind his head is a winged sun-disc; before his face a crescent and disc, seven circles (Pleiades), and an eight-pointed star (Ishtar).

Berlin, VA 8750. Ashur. Limestone. Height: about 0.50 m. About time of Sennacherib (704-681). W. Andrae, *Das wiedererstandene Assur*, Leipzig, 1938, pl. 22b. *AOB*, 331. Photograph courtesy of Staatliche Museen.

535. A bearded Assyrian, clothed in a long, fringed garment and fringed shawl, stands before a god, who stands on a pedestal. The god is clothed in a long, multicolored garment and wears a horned headdress with a row of feathers circling the top. Above, is a standard consisting of a lotus-like base on which is mounted an eight-rayed disc. W. Andrae (*Das wiedererstandene Assur*, Leipzig, 1938, frontispiece, p. 50) identifies the figure as Shamash. The god holds in his left hand a staff and a ring (perhaps consisting of a string of beads); his right hand is upraised to receive the worshiper. To the right of the divine headdress are three additional emblems: the winged sun-disc, the crescent, and the eight-pointed star. A locust over the head of the worshiper would suggest either a prayer for the deliverance from locusts or thanksgiving for a past deliverance from the plague.

Berlin, VA 897. Ashur. Brick orthostat, with colored enamel painting on one side. Height: 0.56 m. Latter part of eighth century. W. Andrae, *Coloured Ceramics from Ashur*, London, 1925, pl. 10, pp. 29-31. *AOB*, 334. Schäfer-Andrae, pl. 32. Photograph courtesy of Staatliche Museen.

536. Within a disc decorated with tongues of flames is the figure of a god with spread wings and a drawn bow. The lower part of his body spreads out into the tail of a bird. The entire emblem, which has been associated with Ashur (E. D. van Buren, *Symbols of the Gods*, Rome, 1945, pp. 95-96), is placed in stylized rain clouds and over a chariot scene, of which only the head of the charioteer and the upper part of a horse's head remain.

British Museum, 115706. Ashur. Fragment of brick, with colored glaze on one side. Height: 0.28 m. Tukulti-Ninurta II (890-884). W. Andrae, *Coloured Ceramics from Ashur*, London, 1925, pl. 8, p. 27. *AOB*, 333. W. Andrae, *Das Wiedererstandene Assur*, Leipzig, 1938, pl. 22a. Photograph courtesy of Staatliche Museen.

537. One of the four panels carved in live rock at Maltaya, about 70 km. north of Mosul. At each end of this panel (II or B) is a figure of the Assyrian king, clothed in a long garment and a high headdress with spike top, and holding a mace in his left hand, while his right is upraised in a gesture of supplication. Depicted are seven deities, each mounted on an animal or animals moving toward the left. While the absence of inscriptions makes it impossible to identify with certainty the deities on the relief, the identifications suggested by Thureau-Dangin (see reference below) are given here with the identifications of Bachmann in parentheses where he differs from Thureau-Dangin. The deities are numbered from left to right: 1. A god, wearing a long garment, a headdress consisting of seven pairs of horns over a cylindrical cap surmounted by a peak in the form of a blossom, or cone, stands on a <u>dragon</u> and a horned lion, and holds in his right hand a curved weapon ending in a feline head and in his left a rod and ring. He, like all the gods, wears a sword at his side. His hair hangs down his back in a long lock. Because of his place at the head of the procession he is identified as Ashur. 2. A goddess, wearing a headdress similar to that of the first figure, sits upon a throne borne by a lion, and holds with her left hand a ring. The throne is supported by a pedestal and footstool decorated with a griffin, a scorpion-bird man, and a human figure standing with crossed hands. The side of the throne itself displays three views of a king shown in profile, between which are two composite creatures composed of the upper part of a man and the lower part of an animal. The back of the throne is decorated with five shields or globes. The goddess has been identified as Ninlil (or the Ishtar of Nineveh). 3. A god dressed and equipped like the first deity, except for a crown with only five pairs of horns and a peak in the form of an astral disc, stands upon a horned lion. He has been identified with Enlil (Bachmann, Sin). 4. A god, dressed and equipped like no. 3, except that he holds his right hand upraised in a gesture of welcome, stands upon the back of a dragon. He has been identified with Sin (Bachmann, Nabu or Anu). 5. A god, represented in the same manner as 4, stands upon a harnessed horse, and has been identified as Shamash (see II Kings 23:11). 6. A god, dressed like 5, holds forks of lightning in both hands, and stands upon a horned lion and a bull. The

emblems he holds in his hands would suggest Adad as a probable identification. 7. A goddess, dressed in long robe and wearing the conical headdress with five pairs of horns and astral disc at top, stands with right hand upraised and the left holding a ring, upon the back of a lion. She has been identified with Ishtar (Bachmann, Ishtar of Arbela).

Maltaya (not to be confused with Malatya in Anatolia). Length: 6 m.; height: 1.85 m. One of the Sargonids and possibly Sennacherib (704-681). V. Place, *Ninive et l'Assyrie*, vol. 3, Paris, 1867, pl. 45 (lower). F. Thureau-Dangin, "Les sculptures rupestres de Maltaï," *RA*, vol. 21, 1924, pp. 185-197. W. Bachmann, *Felsreliefs in Assyrien*, WVDOG, 52, Leipzig, 1927, pl. 27 (photographs), pp. 24-26. *AOB*, 335. Photograph from *RA*, vol. 21, 1924, p. 187.

538. This part of a larger scene depicting the capture of a hostile city shows squads of Assyrian soldiers carrying away the statues of the gods of the city. Each of the four statues is carried by four helmeted soldiers. To the left is a god wearing four horns and holding forked lightning, symbol of Adad, and an axe. Before him is a diminutive figure almost hidden by the screen beside the throne on which he stands. The two figures to the right are of enthroned goddesses, each crowned by a conical, horned headdress topped by an astral disc. The goddess shown with face in profile holds a ring in each hand; the goddess to the right holds a ring in her left hand and a goblet (?) in her right hand.

British Museum, 118934 (contains upper part only). Nimrud. Gypsum. Width: 2.34 m. Tiglath-pileser III (744-727). *AOB*, 336. Contenau, *Man.*, vol. 1, figs. 150-151. See A. Salonen, "Prozessionswagen der babylonischen Götter," *Studia Orientalia*, vol. 13, 1946. Photograph from A. H. Layard, *The Monuments of Nineveh*, London, 1849, pl. 65.

539. Parts of three figures from a line of twelve gods represented in identical manner. Each wears a high, ribbed cap with a horn protruding at the forehead, rings in the ears, a garment with a short skirt held by a belt at the waist, and shoes with upturned toes. Each holds a sickle-sword in his right hand. The identity of the gods is not known.

Yazilikaya (two miles east of Boghazköy). Height: about 0.80 m. K. Bittel, R. Naumann, H. Otto, *Yazilikaya*, WVDOG, 61, Leipzig, 1941, pl. 27, 2, pp. 97-98. Bossert, *Altanatolien*, 543. Photograph courtesy Turkish Information Office, New York.

540. Basalt head of a god who wears a tiara consisting of a pointed cap with four pairs of horns.

Louvre. Jabbul, southeast of Aleppo. Basalt. Height: 0.35 m. Middle of second millennium. TEL, vol. 1, p. 286B. Bossert, *Altsyrien*, 434. Photograph Archives Photographiques.

541. On this sculpture in live rock at Yazilikaya, shown with cast of reconstruction, right, is a god standing with his left arm around a Hittite king and carrying a smaller figure on his right hand. The god wears a high pointed cap decorated with ribs and half circles, a garment with short skirt, a belt, from which protrudes the handle of a sword, and shoes with upturned toes. In his protection is a king, wearing a cap with rounded top, a long

robe, and shoes with upturned toes. The king carries in his left hand the curved staff. Over the king is his cartouche, identifying him with one of the kings bearing the name of Tudhaliyas (perhaps the Fourth, belonging to the middle of the thirteenth century, *WVDOG*, 61, p. 145). Both god and king are beardless.

Cast in Staatliche Museen, Berlin. Yazilikaya (two miles east of Boghazköy), relief 81. Height of god: 1.64 m. Perhaps middle of thirteenth century. K. Bittel, R. Naumann, H. Otto, *Yazilikaya*, *WVDOG*, 61, Leipzig, 1941, frontispiece, pl. 28, 1, pp. 98-101. Schäfer-Andrae, pl. 35. *AOB*, 342. Photograph courtesy of Staatliche Museen, Berlin.

EGYPTIAN

The selection of representations of Egyptian gods and goddesses in the following plates cannot do justice to the wealth of material from which this limited choice was made. An attempt has been made to represent the principal deities mentioned in the texts translated in *Ancient Near Eastern Texts*, and to suggest by the choices the wide range of materials— bas-relief on stone, bronze, wood, painting, ivory, gold, etc. —which the Egyptians used for representing their gods and goddesses. The endeavor has also been made to vary the representation of the deities so as to indicate the fluidity of the Egyptian artists in their use of animal and human forms for the gods. Attention should be called to the drawings of Étienne Drioton in No. 573, where a selection of distinctive features associated with the more important Egyptian deities is readily accessible. Other representations of the gods of Egypt are scattered throughout the volume and can be found by consulting the index.

542. A vignette on a copy of the "Book of the Dead" shows the sky-goddess Nut as a nude woman arched as the heavens over the earth. She is supported by the upraised arms of the air-god Shu, who is represented in human form, with the symbol for "year" crowning his headdress. At his feet lies the earth-god Geb, with his left arm stretched out along the ground. A ram-headed god stands on each side supporting one of Shu's arms. Watching are several gods and the deceased owner of the papyrus.

British Museum, 10554, 87. Deir el-Bahri. Papyrus. Height: about 0.40 m.; length of entire roll: about 37.5 m. Tenth century. E. A. W. Budge, *The Greenfield Papyrus in the British Museum*, London, 1912, pls. 105-107, pp. 79-81. Photograph courtesy BM.

543. The goddess Nut is represented nude within the sarcophagus of Ankh-nes-Nefer-ib-Re, daughter of Psamtik II. The disc below her mouth represents the sun, which was believed to enter her mouth at sunset; the disc at the genital region is also the sun, born from her body at daybreak. The third disc between her legs may again represent the sun in its course.

British Museum, 32 (811). Thebes, near the Ramesseum. Black marble. Length of sarcophagus: 2.59 m. Twenty-sixth Dynasty (663-525). British Museum, *A General Introductory Guide to the Egyptian Collections in the British Museum*, London, 1930, p. 198. E. A. W. Budge, *Egyptian Sculptures in the British Museum*, London, 1914, pl. 46. E. A. W. Budge, *The Sarcophagus of Ānchnesrāneferāb*, London, 1885, for publication of text of sarcophagus. Photograph courtesy BM.

544. The goddess Isis wears a circular crown studded with uraei and surmounted by a pair of horns containing a disc; the uraeus extends from the front of her heavy wig. Between the wings which extend from her hips stands Osiris, in mummy form, wearing the *atef*-crown. He wears a ceremonial beard and holds the flail and crook. The statue was dedicated to Isis by Sheshonk, a high official at Thebes.

British Museum, 1162 (964). Karnak, temple of Osiris. Granite. Height: 0.81 m. Thirtieth Dynasty (fourth century). E. A. W. Budge, *Egyptian Sculptures in the British Museum*, London, 1914, pl. 48. British Museum, *A General Introductory Guide to the Egyptian Collections in the British Museum*, London, 1930, fig. 100. Photograph courtesy BM.

545. The goddess Isis, seated upon her throne, and wearing an elaborate wig, covered with vulture head-dress, and crowned with eight uraei supporting another uraeus and the horned moon-disc. Similarly crowned uraei flank the vulture's beak on her forehead. Seti I is seated on her lap and holds a crook, which rests upon his shoulder, and perhaps an emblematic staff in his other hand. His feet rest upon a footstool decorated with the emblem of the union of Upper and Lower Egypt. See No. 422 for another representation of the king and a goddess.

Abydos, inner hypostyle hall, wall between the sanctuaries of Amon and Osiris. Seti I (1318-1301). G. Jéquier, *L'architecture et la décoration dans l'ancienne Égypte, Les temples ramessides et saïtes*, Paris, n.d., pl. 14. J. Capart, *Le temple de Séti Ier*, Brussels, 1912, pl. 11. Porter and Moss, *Bibliography*, vol. 6, p. 9. Photograph courtesy of A. Gaddis, Luxor.

546. Shu, dressed in a kilt and wearing wig and ceremonial beard, is shown kneeling with raised arms.

Brooklyn Museum, 37.953. Blue-green glazed faïence. Height: 0.063 m. Twenty-sixth Dynasty (663-525) or later. Photograph courtesy Br. M.

547. On a capital the goddess Hathor is represented as a woman, with cow's ears, heavy wig with two locks falling down in front and ending in curls. At the top of the capital are uraei.

British Museum, 1107. Bubastis, temple of Osorkon II. Red granite. Height: 1.98 m. Twenty-second Dynasty (945-745). British Museum, *A General Introductory Guide to the Egyptian Collections in the British Museum*, London, 1930, p. 378. Photograph courtesy BM.

548. A jackal, representing the god Anubis, lies on the top of a funerary chest. The animal is carved from wood and covered with a varnish of black resin, except for the inside of the ears and the ribbon around the neck, which are gilded. The eyes are of gold inlay. The chest is of gilded wood, decorated with the emblems of Osiris and Isis.

Cairo Museum. Thebes, tomb of Tut-ankh-Amon, object no. 261. Wood. Height: 1.10 m. Tut-ankh-Amon (1361-1352). TEL, Cairo, p. 125. P. Fox, *Tutankhamun's Treasure*, London, 1951, pl. 39. Photograph courtesy of the Metropolitan Museum of Art, New York.

549. The god Ptah sits enthroned within his shrine as the king kneels before him with an offering of cloth. The god is clothed in a long, tight-fitting garment, decorated with a broad collar and wears on his head a plain cap, which seems to be connected with the chin strap that holds the ceremonial beard. With both hands the god grasps the composite scepter made of the *was*, the *ankh*, and the *djed* pillar. Around his neck he wears a pectoral; from the back of his neck there hangs a tassel.

Abydos, chapel of Ptah, south wall, eastern section. Seti I (1318-1301). A. M. Calverley, *The Temple of King Sethos I at Abydos*, vol. 2, London, 1935, pl. 27 lower left (drawing). Photograph courtesy of the Metropolitan Museum of Art, New York.

550. A gold statuette of Amon, in which can be seen the features of King Thut-mose III. He wears a high crown (the plumes have been broken off) and carries a curved sword in his right hand and an *ankh* sign in his left. He is clothed in the royal kilt and wears a ceremonial beard attached to his chin.

New York, Metropolitan Museum of Art, 26.7.1412. Purchased, but said to have come from Thebes. Gold. Height: 0.175 m. Eighteenth Dynasty, perhaps Thut-mose III (1490-1436). N. E. Scott, *Egyptian Statuettes*, New York, 1946, no. 16. Burlington Fine Arts Club, *Catalogue of an Exhibition of Ancient Egyptian Art*, London, 1922, p. 106, no. 11, pl. 16. C. Aldred, *New Kingdom Art in Ancient Egypt*, London, 1951, no. 35. Photograph courtesy MMA.

551. This detail from a lintel depicting the *sed* festival of Sen-Usert III shows the god Amon holding a vessel from which spring the *was* and the *ankh* emblems. He wears the royal kilt and a headdress consisting of a tight-fitting cap, to which are attached two tall feathers and a streamer. An animal's tail, attached to the waist, hangs almost to the ground. He wears the ceremonial beard bound to his chin.

Cairo Museum. Medamud. Limestone. Height: about 0.75 m. Sen-Usert III (1880-1840). F. Bisson de la Roque, *Rapport sur les fouilles de Médamoud* (1929), *Fouilles de l'institut français d'archéologie orientale du Caire*, 7, Cairo, 1930, pl. 4, pp. 81-82. Photograph Foto Marburg.

552. The god Amon, dressed in the royal kilt and broad collar and wearing the headdress of a cylindrical cap surmounted by two feathers, stands with his left hand to his side and his right raised to hold a staff or scepter, which, together with the ceremonial beard once worn by the god, is now missing. A fragmentary inscription on the base tells of the dedication of the statuette to the god Amon by one of his priests.

Brooklyn Museum, 37.4. Said to have been found at Minya, near Thebes. Bronze. Height: 0.338 m. Eighteenth to Twenty-sixth Dynasty (1550-525). Albright Art Gallery, *Master Bronzes Selected from Museums and Collections in America*, Buffalo, N.Y., 1937, no. 45. Also mentioned in G. Roeder, *Ägyptische Bronzewerke*, Glückstadt, 1937, p. 7, ¶30. Photograph courtesy Br. M.

553. A human figure with animal head, wearing a royal kilt, stands with right arm raised as though brandishing a weapon, while the right extends forward as though

clutching a prisoner. Conforming to the usual representation of Seth, there had once been ears attached to the base of the crown; these, however, have been replaced by the horns of a ram, thus making the statue into the figure of Khnum. The headdress worn is that of the crowns of Upper and Lower Egypt.

Copenhagen, Collection égyptienne, Æ. I. N. 614. Bronze. Height: 0.70 m. Nineteenth-Twentieth Dynasty (1320-1090). M. Mogensen, *La collection égyptienne, La Glyptothèque Ny Carlsberg*, Copenhagen, 1930, no. A99, pl. 24, pp. 26-27. Photograph courtesy of La Glyptothèque Ny Carlsberg, Copenhagen.

554. Bronze statuette of the ithyphallic god Min. For other representations of Min see Nos. 473-474.

New York, Metropolitan Museum of Art, 10.184.2. Bronze. Perhaps Ptolemaic (332-30). Photograph courtesy MMA.

555. "Seth of Ramses-beloved-of-Amon" is clothed in a kilt held by two crossed shoulder straps, decorated with discs. About his neck is a broad collar; two bracelets are represented on each forearm and each upper arm. The headdress is a conical tiara, with two horns in front, a disc between the horns and the ear, and a long streamer which extends from the top of the tiara almost to the ground. The right hand holds an *ankh*; the left a *was* scepter. A ceremonial beard is attached to the chin. For similar representations see Nos. 485, 487. Translation of text of stela in *ANET*, 252-253.

Cairo Museum. Tanis, temple of San, 1863. Granite. Height of entire stela: 2.20 m.; the relief occupies about one-third of the face. About 1330. P. Montet, "La stèle de l'an 400 retrouvée," *Kemi*, vol. 4, 1931, pl. 14, pp. 191-215, where previous publications and comparative material are listed. Photograph from *Kemi*, courtesy Librairie Orientaliste Paul Geuthner.

556. Osiris is represented as a standing, mummiform figure, holding scepter and flail. He wears the *atef*-crown which is supported on twisted ram's horns. On the forehead is a uraeus with tail running up along the crown. The eyes, the broad collar, and the feathers of the crown are inlaid with gold, as was also possibly the ceremonial beard.

Brooklyn Museum, 08.480.27. Bronze. Height: 0.191 m. Perhaps Twenty-sixth Dynasty (663-525). Photograph courtesy Br. M.

557. The god Osiris, with mummiform body, *atef*-crown, ceremonial beard, broad collar, stands beside the *djed* pillar holding the flail and the crook.

Thebes, valley of the kings, tomb of Hor-em-heb (57). Paint on stone. Height: about 1.80 m. T. M. Davis, *The Tombs of Harmhabi and Touatânkhamanou*, London, 1912, pls. 63, 64. M. Gorce and R. Mortier, eds. *Histoire générale des religions*, vol. I, Paris, 1948, p. 216. Photograph courtesy of the Metropolitan Museum of Art, New York.

558. The goddess Sekhmet, with human body and lioness head, is seated on a throne. The headdress consists of a heavy wig surmounted by a uraeus and a disc. She wears a long skirt held by a belt and bands which extend over her breasts (decorated with rosettes) to her shoulders. Her costume also includes the broad collar, anklets, and bracelets. Her left hand holds the *ankh* sign.

Metropolitan Museum of Art, 15.8.3. Karnak, gift 1915. Diorite. Height: 2.13 m. Amen-hotep III (1413-1377). *BMMA*, vol. 14, 1919, October, pt. ii, fig. 14. N. E. Scott, *Egyptian Statues*, New York, 1945, no. 15. Photograph courtesy MMA.

559. The goddess Mut stands on an inscribed base, with arms to the sides, wearing a vulture headdress with double crown.

Brooklyn Museum, 08.480.45. Purchased. Bronze. Height: 0.181 m. Twenty-sixth Dynasty to Late Dynastic (663-332). Mentioned by G. Roeder, *Ägyptische Bronzewerke*, Hamburg, 1937, §124. Photograph courtesy Br. M.

560. The goddess Neith, clad in a long, close-fitting garment, strides forward on a base, which is inscribed on three sides. She is crowned with the red crown of Lower Egypt, from the top of which the curled wire has been broken away. Her right arm is straight at her side and once held an attribute, which is now missing. Her left arm is bent forward to hold a staff or spear. The eyes are inlaid with gold.

Brooklyn Museum, 37.357L. Bronze. Height: 0.274 m. Ptolemaic Period (332-30). Photograph courtesy Br. M.

561. The goddess Maat, dressed in a cloak which conceals all details of her body, is shown in squatting posture on the top of a square pillar. Her headdress consists of a wig, bound by a fillet which is tied in the back with a loop and two ends, and the high feather, the emblem of "truth."

Brooklyn Museum, 37.561. Bronze. Height: 0.094 m. Photograph courtesy Br. M.

562. The painted wooden figure of the goddess Nephthys, sister of Isis, on an oblong plinth. She wears a blue wig, a high headdress, painted yellow, and a green garment, bound under her exposed breasts. The right arm is raised; her left rests on her thigh.

Brooklyn Museum, 11.681. Wood. Height: 0.346 m. Probably Late Dynastic to Ptolemaic Period (525-30). Photograph courtesy Br. M.

563. The upper part of a statue of Khonsu, the moon-god of Thebes, represented as a child with the side lock. He wears the uraeus, the ceremonial beard, and a heavy necklace over his broad collar. In his hands he grasps the composite scepter, composed of the *was*, the *ankh*, and the *djed* pillar. Upon his right shoulder is the flail; and over his left the crook or scepter. The features of the face are those of the Amarna Period, suggesting the dating.

Cairo Museum, 38488. Karnak, temple of Khonsu. Granite. Height of entire statue: 2.52 m. Shortly after the Amarna Period (about 1380-1362). G. Daressy, *Statues de divinités*, vol. I, *Cat. gén.*, Cairo, 1905-1906, no. 38488, pl. 28. *AOB*, 306. Schäfer-Andrae, 356. Photograph from Schäfer-Andrae, 356, courtesy Verlag Ullstein, Berlin.

564. The hawk, representing the god Horus, wears the

crown of Upper and Lower Egypt and a broad collar engraved on its chest. The eyes are inlaid with gold rims.

Brooklyn Museum, 05.394. Bronze. Height: 0.288 m. Twenty-sixth Dynasty to Ptolemaic Period (663-30). Albright Art Gallery, *Master Bronzes Selected from Museums and Collections in America*, Buffalo, N.Y., 1937, no. 50. Photograph courtesy Br. M.

565. The god Horus, with falcon head and double crown, stands on a stepped base, with left arm and leg advanced.

Brooklyn Museum, 08.480.47. Bronze. Height: 0.149 m. Late Dynastic to Ptolemaic Period (525-30). Photograph courtesy Br. M.

566. The infant Horus, wearing an *atef*-crown—the normal form of the top being changed so as to support the disc above—composed of spreading ram's horns, and crowned uraei, sits upon a lotus blossom as he raises the forefinger of his left hand to his lips. He wears the side lock and holds a flail in his right hand. The plaque had been decorated with colored insets and gold foil, some of which was still in place when found. The entire piece was an ivory inset, which may have formed the center piece to the back of a throne.

Palestine Archaeological Museum, 33.2574. Samaria, section Qc, 1932. Ivory. Height: 0.061 m. Ninth century. J. W. and Grace M. Crowfoot, *Early Ivories from Samaria*, London, 1938, pl. 1, 1, p. 12. Photograph courtesy of PAM.

567. The god Horus is represented in human form with a hawk head. The elaborate composite crown consists of the white crown flanked by two feathers, resting upon two ram's horns. In the center are two bull's horns with disc between. Four uraei emerge from the ram's horns; the outer pair wear the crowns of Upper and Lower Egypt respectively.

Abydos, chapel of Horus, south wall, western section. Seti I (1318-1301). A. M. Calverley, *The Temple of King Sethos I at Abydos*, vol. 1, London, 1933, pl. 32B. Photograph from publication, courtesy of Egypt Exploration Society.

568. Ta-weret is represented as a composite creature: feet and hands are lion's claws, body is that of a woman with elongated breasts, and the head is that of a hippopotamus (or crocodile). She wears a heavy wig, cylindrical headdress, and rests her arms upon two amulets which project from the base.

Cairo Museum, 39145. Karnak. Black basalt. Height: 0.96 m. Twenty-sixth Dynasty (663-525). G. Daressy, *Statues de divinités*, vol. 1, *Cat. gén.*, Cairo, 1906, no. 39145, *AOB*, 269. Schäfer-Andrae, pl. 22. Photograph Foto Marburg.

569. The ram-headed Khnum sits upon his throne before a potter's wheel, on which he fashions the prince Amen-hotep III and his *ka*. The goddess Hathor is seated opposite and extends with her left hand the *ankh* sign, the emblem of life.

Luxor. A. J. Gayet, *Le temple de Louxor, Mémoires, Mission archéologique française au Caire*, vol. 15, Paris, 1894, pl. 63 (71), figs. 202-203. Also reproduced in M. Gorce and R. Mortier, eds.,

Histoire générale des religions, vol. 1, Paris, 1948, p. 257. *AOB*, 303. Photograph from publication.

570. The bull Apis wears a disc between his horns and a uraeus. A collar encircles the neck; the body is decorated with representations of a winged scarab, a flying vulture, and a carpet ornamented with fringes.

Copenhagen, Collection égyptienne, Æ. I. N. 616. Bronze. Height: 0.13 m. Saïte Period (663-525). M. Mogensen, *La collection égyptienne, La Glyptothèque Ny Carlsberg*, Copenhagen, 1930, no. A415, p. 58, pl. 56. Photograph courtesy of La Glyptothèque Ny Carlsberg, Copenhagen.

571. A long, narrow box is surmounted by a slightly undulated body of a cobra with a human head, which wears the double crown. The representation is of the god Atum and the box probably served as a container for a mummified serpent.

Brooklyn Museum, 36.624. Bronze. Height: 0.153 m. Late Dynastic to Ptolemaic Period (525-30). See G. Daressy, *Statues de divinités*, vol. 1, *Cat. gén.*, Cairo, 1906, nos. 38702-38704. Photograph courtesy Br. M.

572. Seti I, wearing the blue crown and streamers, kneels before the seated figure of Thoth as he offers him a statuette of Maat. The ibis-headed Thoth is clothed in a broad collar and royal kilt and holds in his right hand a staff with a dog's (?) head and in his left an *ankh* sign.

Cincinnati, 1945.64. Probably from Abydos. White limestone with traces of polychromy. Height: 0.75 m. Seti I (1318-1301). Photograph courtesy of Cincinnati Art Museum, Cincinnati, Ohio.

573. 1. Amon or Amon-Re. 2. Anukis. 3. Anubis. 4. Bastet. 5. Shu. 6. Har-akhti. 7. Harsaphes. 8. Hathor. 9. Horus. 10. The Infant Horus (Harpocrates). 11. Isis. 12. Khnum. 13. Khonsu. 14. Montu. 15. Mut. 16. Nefer-tem. 17. Neith. 18. Nekhbet. 19. Nephthys. 20. Onuris. 21. Osiris. 22. Uto. 23. Ptah. 24. Satis. 25. Sebek. 26. Sekhmet. 27. Selqet. 28. Seth. 29. Sokaris. 30. Thoth.

Drawings by Étienne Drioton. Photograph from É. Drioton, "La religion égyptienne dans ses grandes lignes," *La revue du Caire*, no. 84, November 1945, pp. 16-17, courtesy of *La revue du Caire*, Cairo.

VII. *The Practice of Religion*

ALTARS AND SOCKETS

574. The frieze which decorated an altar or podium standing against the north wall of the "Eye-Temple" at Brak consisted of a band of gold foil at the top and bottom (about 0.02 m. wide), an upper band of carbonized blue limestone with hollowed circles in high relief (0.025 m. wide), a central band of white marble (0.012 m. wide), and a lower band of corrugated strips of green shale (0.0375 m. wide). The gold foil was nailed to a wood backing with gold-headed silver nails. It has been suggested that the hollowed circle decoration may have been in imitation of the common mosaic cone

decoration employed in building and that the fluted shale decoration may have been intended to imitate other architectural detail. See No. 504 for eye-idols.

British Museum, 127430. Tell Brak. Gold, limestone, marble, and shale. Height: about 0.115 m. Jemdet Nasr period (around 3000). M. E. L. Mallowan, "Excavations at Brak and Chagar Bazar," *Iraq*, vol. 9, 1947, pl. 3, pp. 32, 93-94. Photograph courtesy BM.

575. This small limestone altar, with four projections at the top, is one of a number of such objects found at Megiddo, some of which evidenced discoloration by fire at the top. Although it has been suggested that these objects served as house altars or as incense altars, and that the four projections at the top served to hold a bowl of incense, the exact function of the altars is as yet undetermined.

Palestine Archaeological Museum. Megiddo, locus R12, stratum IV?, near sacred area. Limestone. Height: 0.545 m. Tenth-ninth century. H. G. May, *Material Remains of the Megiddo Cult, OIP*, 26, Chicago, 1935, pl. 12, no. 2982, pp. 12-13. See also: H. M. Wiener, *The Altars of the Old Testament, Beigabe zur Orientalistischen Literatur-Zeitung*, Leipzig, 1927; review in *JPOS*, vol. 9, 1929, pp. 50-54. Photograph courtesy of the Oriental Institute.

576. An inscribed cult socket which shows Tukulti-Ninurta I (shown twice, once kneeling and again standing) before a cult socket on which is mounted a staff and oblong shield, the symbol of the fire-god Nusku. The king, dressed in a long, fringed robe, holds a mace in his left hand and raises his right hand and extends his index finger in the direction of the symbol of Nusku.

Berlin, VA 8146. Ashur. Gypsum. Height: 0.575 m. Tukulti-Ninurta I (about 1240). W. Andrae, *Die jüngeren Ischtar-Tempel in Assur, WVDOG*, 58, Leipzig, 1935, pl. 30, pp. 67-71. *AOB*, 484. D. Opitz, *AfO*, vol. 7, 1931, pp. 83-90. Photograph Foto Marburg.

577. In the center of this scene, carved on a cult socket, stands the king, bearded and bareheaded, extending his right hand in a gesture of adoration and holding a club in his left. At each side are posts surmounted by a crescent with tassels and an eight-rayed disc. Each standard is held by a wild man or guardian of the gate (see No. 615), who wears on his head the eight-rayed disc. The same symbol appears in each of the two curved projections at the top of the socket. The base is carved with a scene of human figures standing on representations of mountainous regions, but the detail is badly damaged.

Istanbul, Museum of the Ancient Orient, 7802. Ashur. Limestone. Height: 1.03 m. Thirteenth century, on analogy to No. 576. W. Andrae, *Die jüngeren Ischtar-Tempel in Assur, WVDOG*, 58, Leipzig, 1935, pl. 29, pp. 60-67. *AOB*, 485. Schäfer-Andrae, 526. Contenau, *Man.*, vol. 2, p. 1031, fig. 722. See E. D. van Buren, *Symbols of the Gods*, Rome, 1945, p. 93. Photograph courtesy of Staatliche Museen, Berlin.

578. A reconstructed model house of pottery bricks, some incised with geometric designs and human figures, and a stone foundation. This object may represent a Hurrian votive shrine.

University Museum, 32-20-414. Tell Billa, level III. Height: 0.185 m. Middle of second millennium. *BASOR*, no. 46, April 1932, p. 5, fig. 4. Photograph courtesy UM.

579. A square trough on four legs, with South Arabic inscription on the sides, probably served as an incense burner. Inscription: *lbny qsṭ*.

University Museum, 30-47-32. Limestone. Third to first century (W. F. Albright). Height: about 0.09 m. L. Legrain, *AJA*, vol. 38, 1934, p. 336, fig. 6. G. Ryckmans, "Inscriptions Sud-Arabes," *Le Muséon*, vol. 48, 1935, pl. 3, 137. Photograph courtesy UM.

580. A three-footed altar with circular top is carved in stone. Each of the three legs ends in a lion's foot. The altar rests upon a tripod base which has circular posts for legs. An inscription of Sargon II is incised around the edge of the top.

Istanbul, Museum of the Ancient Orient, 4784. Perhaps from Khorsabad. Stone. Height: 1.04 m. Sargon II (721-705). E. Nassouhi, "Les autels trépieds assyriens," *RA*, vol. 22, 1925, pp. 85-87. Cf. *AOB*, 439. Photograph JBP.

581. A square trough on four feet connected by rungs. The four faces are carved in low relief with South Arabic inscriptions. The top is decorated with the tooth pattern; double lines form a band at the ends of each side. Inscription: *rnd, ḥdk*.

University Museum, 30-47-31. Limestone. Height: about 0.08 m. Third to first century (W. F. Albright). G. Ryckmans, "Inscriptions Sud-Arabes," *Le Muséon*, vol. 48, 1935, pl. 4, 136. Photograph courtesy UM.

OTHER CULTIC OBJECTS

582. A pottery stand, with two handles and a pair of windows on each side, is decorated with red lines and adorned with two crudely fashioned female figures on the front. Each holds her breast with her right hand and covers the genital region with the left (see No. 469, no. 6).

Palestine Archaeological Museum, 36.1997. Megiddo. Pottery, yellow ware with red line decoration. Height: 0.371 m. Stratum VI (1150-1100). H. G. May, *Material Remains of the Megiddo Cult, OIP*, 26, Chicago, 1935, pl. 20, no. P 6055, pp. 20-23. See H. Frankfort, *Studies in Early Pottery of the Near East I, Royal Anthropological Institute, Occasional Papers*, No. 6, London, 1924, pp. 127-130, and fig. 13. Photograph courtesy PAM.

583. A pottery stand, with bell-like bottom and two windows, is decorated by two plain bands and a row of projections which have been interpreted as lotus leaves. The bowl, which fits into the stand by a projection at the bottom, is decorated by a row of projecting tabs similar to those on the stand. The bowl and the stand were fastened together by a pin through pierced holes. Within the basin of the bowl there was evidence of discoloration by fire.

Oriental Institute, A 20830. Megiddo. Pottery. Height of stand with bowl: 0.67 m. Stratum VI (1150-1100). H. G. May, *Material Remains of the Megiddo Cult, OIP*, 26, Chicago, 1935, pl. 20, no. P 6056, pp. 20-23. Photograph courtesy of the Oriental Institute.

584. Tall, roughly cylindrical pottery stand has two loop-handles and many apertures, arranged in four rows. At the level of the lowest apertures is a row of five animal-paws which extend outward as projecting tabs. A necklace of hard, well-cut stones was found inside the stand.

Palestine Archaeological Museum, 36.575. Ai, area D, room 65, 1934 excavations. Pottery, pinkish buff ware. Height: 0.80 m. 1200-1050, according to excavator. J. Marquet-Krause, *Les fouilles de 'Ay (et-Tell) 1933-1935*, Paris, 1949, pl. 64 bis (top), pl. 74, no. 1052 (for drawing), p. 23. *Syria*, vol. 16, 1935, p. 340, fig. 6. Photograph courtesy PAM.

585. This cylindrical cult object has a bell-shaped open base, two loop-handles, on which sit birds. Between the handles are four triangular apertures, in which birds are perched. Four serpents wind their way to the upper row of openings. Below is a second row of triangular apertures, in each of which is represented a bird.

University Museum, 29-103-830. Beth-shan. Pottery: brown ware with drab surface, over exterior of which is light red wash. Height: 0.545 m. Beth-shan V (eleventh century). A. Rowe, *The Four Canaanite Temples of Beth-shan*, Philadelphia, 1940, pl. 14, no. 3, pl. 57A, nos. 3, 4. Photograph courtesy UM.

586. This model of a shrine has a row of oblong openings at the sides and a row of circular apertures (perhaps pigeon-holes) above. At each corner stands a female sphinx, wearing her hair in two long coils on either side of the face and over the ears. The crown of the headdress is a narrow tiara with vertical bands. The body is that of a lion. In the middle of the side wall is a male sphinx, wearing a conical headdress. Trace of discoloration by smoke was observed on the inside face of the part of the walls projecting above the roof.

Palestine Archaeological Museum. Megiddo, stratum IV?, in sacred area. Pottery: yellow and gray ware, with light red wash, which is closely burnished. Height: about 0.41 m. Probably belonging to stratum IV (1000-800). H. G. May, *Material Remains of the Megiddo Cult*, OIP, 26, Chicago, 1935, pl. 13, pp. 13-17. Photograph courtesy of the Oriental Institute.

587. Bronze openwork stand with square base and round top, which has on each side the scene of a worshiper or priest presenting a gift to, or standing in an attitude of adoration before, a seated deity. The deity wears a long dress, in contrast to the short dress of the worshiper.

Palestine Archaeological Museum. Megiddo, M 1342. Bronze. Height: about 0.10 m. Stratum V? (1050-1000). H. G. May, *Material Remains of the Megiddo Cult*, OIP, 26, Chicago, 1935, pl. 18, pp. 19-20. Photograph courtesy of the Oriental Institute.

588. A stand consisting of a circular top, from which hang pendants in the form of pomegranates, and three legs which rest upon a three-footed base. For example from Cyprus see Bossert, *Altsyrien, 283*. Belonged to same hoard of bronze as axes of No. 261.

Louvre. Ras Shamra. Bronze. Height: 0.121 m. Fifteenth-fourteenth century (Louvre catalogue). *Syria*, vol. 10, 1929, pl. 60, no. 1. Photograph from *Syria*, vol. 10, 1929, pl. 60, no. 1, courtesy of Librairie Orientaliste Paul Geuthner, Paris.

589. The kernos ring consists of a hollow ring base on which are mounted a gazelle head, two amphorae (one now broken away), two pomegranates, two doves, and one cup. Each of these objects is hollow, communicating with the hollow base. Although their heads are now broken off, the doves were so placed as to appear to drink from the cup. Cf. Cant. 4:12-13.

Oriental Institute, A 11835. Megiddo. Pottery: burnt umber ware, closely burnished surface. Diameter: about 0.22 m. Stratum VI (1150-1100). H. G. May, *Material Remains of the Megiddo Cult*, OIP, 26, Chicago, 1935, pl. 16, P 2282, pp. 17-18. Photograph courtesy of the Oriental Institute.

590. A rectangular shrine model, oblong in plan, consists of two stages and a rounded top, ornamented with three birds now broken away. On the upper stage of each long side is a nude human figure holding two birds, standing in an open door and looking outward. On the long sides of the lower stage are two windows with a serpent winding up between them. On each stage of the short sides is a rectangular opening or window. The rounded top suggests that the object may have served as a support for a bowl containing offerings or incense.

University Museum, 29-103-807. Beth-shan. Pottery: brown ware, drab-red surface. Height: 0.50 m. Beth-shan V (eleventh century). A. Rowe, *The Four Canaanite Temples of Beth-shan*, Philadelphia, 1940, pl. 17, no. 1, pl. 56A, no. 2, pl. 57A, nos. 1, 2, p. 62. Photograph courtesy UM.

591. This elaborately decorated clay house consists of two stages, the upper being smaller than the lower. In each stage are cut oblong and triangular apertures. On the sides are represented serpents which wind upward. Also represented are crudely molded birds, on the upper beams of the structure.

Berlin, VA 8143. Ashur, S 22546. Clay. Height: 0.90 m. Ashur, level H-G (middle third millennium). W. Andrae, *Die archaischen Ischtar-Tempel in Assur*, WVDOG, 39, Leipzig, 1922, pl. 14, pp. 36-37. *AOB*, 442-443. Contenau, *Man.*, vol. 1, fig. 158. Photograph courtesy of the Staatliche Museen.

592. The bowl of this incense spoon is but the continuation of a lion's lower jaw, at the outer rim of which the lion's lower incisors project as two small cones. To the back of the lion's head projects the broken end of a pipe, originally longer, which communicated through the throat with the ladle. The back of the spoon is decorated with an intricate pattern of volutes and palmettes.

Palestine Archaeological Museum, 32.2739. Tell Beit Mirsim, no. 2165, from dump, excavation of 1932. Steatite. Length: about 0.12 m. Ninth century. W. F. Albright, *The Excavation of Tell Beit Mirsim, Vol. III, The Iron Age*, AASOR, 21-22, New Haven, 1943, pl. 59a, b, par. 42. *BASOR*, no. 47, 1932, fig. 11, p. 16. See for comparative material: St. Przeworski, "Les encensoirs de la Syrie du nord et leurs prototypes égyptiens," *Syria*, vol. 11, 1930, pp. 133-145. Photograph courtesy PAM.

593. On this clay figurine of a bound prisoner is written a curse upon enemies of Egypt. The figurine was broken in an act which was intended to make effective upon the enemy the inscribed curse. For description of this magic

and a translation of some execration texts see *ANET*, 328-329. Cf. Jer. 19:10-11.

Brussels. Sakkarah. Pottery. Height: about 0.33 m. Latter part of Twelfth or the Thirteenth Dynasty (around the eighteenth century). G. Posener, *Princes et pays d'Asie et de Nubie*, Brussels, 1940, frontispiece. Photograph courtesy of the Musées Royaux d'Art et d'Histoire.

594. A model liver made of clay, divided into some fifty sections, is inscribed with omens and magical formulae for the use of diviners. See B. Meissner, *Babylonien und Assyrien*, vol. 2, Heidelberg, 1925, pp. 268 ff. for discussion of liver divination. See Ezek. 21:26.

British Museum, 92668. Clay. 0.133 m. by 0.083 m. First Dynasty of Babylon (about 1830-1530). British Museum, *Cuneiform Texts from Babylonian Tablets, &c. in the British Museum*, part 6, London, 1898, pl. 1. *AOB*, 486. British Museum, *A Guide to the Babylonian and Assyrian Antiquities*, London, 1922, p. 119. Photograph courtesy BM.

595. Roughly modeled liver, but without inscriptions usually found on Mesopotamian examples.

Palestine Archaeological Museum, 36.1889. Megiddo, level VII, eastern temple. Pottery: light, reddish buff ware, with white and gray grits. Length: about 0.10 m. Megiddo VII (1350-1150). The Megiddo Expedition, *Megiddo II, OIP*, 62, Chicago, 1948, pl. 255, no. 1. Photograph courtesy PAM.

596. A semicircular offering table carved from a slab of limestone. The front rim is decorated by a lioness head; shoulders and forelegs are roughly incised on the adjacent rims; extending outward at the two rear corners are the heads (the right one is broken away) of two lion cubs, whose two pairs of hind legs stretch out to form the channel of a spout to the rear.

Palestine Archaeological Museum, I.8987. Tell Beit Mirsim, débris of stratum C, excavation of 1930. Limestone. 0.279 m. by 0.293 m. Thirteenth century, according to excavator. W. F. Albright, *The Excavation of Tell Beit Mirsim, Vol. II, The Bronze Age, AASOR*, vol. 17, New Haven, 1938, pl. 24a, pars. 75-76. Photograph courtesy PAM.

PRIESTS, OFFERINGS, AND RITUALS

597. A priest, completely nude and shaved, pours a libation from a spouted vessel into a vase, from which grow a plant and bunches of dates. Before the vase is seated a goddess, with large head shown in full face. Her hair falls down her shoulders in four braids, two behind and two in front. She wears a crown of horns (?) and feathers; from each of her shoulders spring three stalks. See No. 505 for similar representation. The entire scene is represented as taking place on a stylized mountain. In the center of the limestone plaque is a square opening, possibly for attachment to a wall.

Louvre, AO 276. Tello. Limestone. Height: 0.17 m. Early Dynastic period (first half third millennium). E. de Sarzec, *Découvertes en Chaldée*, Paris, 1884-1912, p. 209. A. Parrot, *Tello*, Paris, 1948, fig. 22b, pp. 88-90. TEL, vol. 1, p. 198. *AOB*, 530. Photograph Archives Photographiques.

598. Standing before two posts, with ball-like tops, is a man clothed in a long skirt and wearing a headdress of two plumes or palms. His face is shaved, but hair from his neck is represented in the form of a beard which falls down his bare chest. His long hair is held in place by a fillet around his head. With one hand he grasps the post in front of him; the other hand is held at his waist. The inscription on the plaque mentions the name of the god Ningirsu and of his temple E-ninnu. It has been suggested that the two posts may represent the entrance to the temple.

Louvre, AO 221. Tello. White limestone. Height: 0.18 m. Early Dynastic period (first half third millennium). E. de Sarzec, *Découvertes in Chaldée*, Paris, 1884-1912, pl. 1 bis, a, b. A. Parrot, *Tello*, Paris, 1948, fig. 17a, p. 70. Contenau, *Man.*, vol. 1, fig. 321, pp. 453-454. Photograph JBP.

599. Dudu, priest of the god Ningirsu, wearing a flounced skirt, stands facing right holding a staff. To the left is an eagle with spread wings, seizing with its claws the backs of two lions, which turn their heads upward to bite the eagle's wings—the emblem of Lagash. In a panel to the left is a recumbent calf. Below is a braid decoration.

Louvre, AO 2354. Tello. Bituminous material. Height: 0.25 m. Early Dynastic period (first half of third millennium). E. de Sarzec, *Découvertes en Chaldée*, Paris, 1884-1912, pl. 5 bis, fig. 2, pp. 204-209. Fondation Piot, vol. 1, 1894, pl. 2. TEL, vol. 1, p. 208. A. Parrot, *Tello*, Paris, 1948, pl. 7a, fig. 22e, pp. 87-88. Photograph TEL.

600. In the upper register of the offering plaque is a duplicate scene of a nude and shaven priest offering a libation from a spouted jug to a seated god. The god, clothed in a long robe and wearing a vegetation crown on his head, is seated on his throne with folded hands. His face is shaved, except for a long chin-beard which extends over his chest; he wears long hair, part of which is caught up in a bun. In the lower register are a sheep and a goat driven by two shaven men, each dressed in a long skirt. One bears a container (perhaps for milk) on his head; the other carries a stick for driving the animals. The archaic inscription identifies the suppliant as "Ur-Enlil, the chief merchant."

Istanbul, 1944. Nippur. Slate. Height: 0.19 m. H. V. Hilprecht, *The Babylonian Expedition, Series A: Cuneiform Texts*, Philadelphia, 1896, vol. 1, pt. 2, pl. XVI, no. 37. *AOB*, 531. Contenau, *Man.*, vol. 1, fig. 338. *MJ*, vol. 15, 1924, p. 169. Photograph courtesy of Museum of the Ancient Orient, Istanbul, and E. Porada.

601. A goddess (perhaps Nina), attired in a fleecelike garment and wearing a tiara of three pairs of horns, is seated on a goose and holds a bowl in her left hand and a fish in her right. Behind her a mitered figure with long beard and long hair, wearing a kilt and holding a stick in his left hand, conducts a worshiper who carries a horned animal, perhaps a kid or a young gazelle. The worshiper is clad in a kilt like that worn by his deity, but is shaved and without headdress. Before the goddess is an offering table, flaming brazier, or vase with branches protruding. Beyond is a curious object, which has been variously interpreted as a tripod supporting an offering table and as a nude woman seated, possibly in

the pangs of childbirth. Cf. No. 507 for a goddess supported by geese.

University Museum, L-29-346. Nippur, 1899-1900. Limestone. Height: 0.04 m. Sargonid (about 2360-2180) or earlier. *MJ*, vol. 20, 1929, pp. 231-232, pl. 8B. *University Museum Bulletin*, vol. 9, 1941, no. 1, pp. 10-14. E. Meyer, *Sumerier und Semiten in Babylonien*, Berlin, 1906, pp. 98-99. Photograph courtesy UM.

602. In the fragment from the upper register of a festival scene are the feet of a person seated on a chair, and of an attendant. Below, to the left, is a server who holds two cups before another who plunges an object into a large jar. Behind him is a third person holding a jar with pointed vase.

Louvre, Susa. Limestone. Width: 0.13 m. Early Dynastic period (first half third millennium). Contenau, *Man.*, vol. 1, fig. 317. TEL, vol. 1, p. 177. Photograph JBP.

603. In the upper register, a nude priest pours from a spouted vessel an oblation to a seated god, who wears a horned miter and holds a vessel in his hands. Behind the priest are three smaller figures, clothed in long garments. Below, the nude priest makes a similar offering before the door of a temple flanked by two gateposts without streamers. Following the priest is a woman, distinguishable by her long locks which fall down before her shoulders, and two attendants, the first of whom carries an animal for the offering in his arms.

British Museum, 118561. Ur, 6831. Limestone. Height: 0.22 m. Middle third millennium. *MJ*, vol. 17, 1926, p. 258. *AJ*, vol. 6, 1926, pl. 53A. Contenau, *Man.*, vol. 1, fig. 356, p. 486. Photograph courtesy of the University Museum.

604. Upper register: to the right sits a bearded and long-haired figure receiving a cup from an attendant and holding a branch (?) in his left hand. Following the cupbearer is a bearded musician with a harp. To the left is a seated female figure with an attendant before her and a maidservant behind. She sits upon a high stool with her feet upon a footstool, and holds a cup and branch. The male attendant holds a jar in a netlike support and a rounded object with massive long handle. Middle register: to the right is an animal, followed by three porters carrying food and drink for the festival pictured above. Lower register: in this panel there once appeared (to judge from fragment found at Ur, No. 163) a chariot drawn by four asses. Frankfort (in publication cited below) sees the representation as that of the celebration of an annually recurring festival, rather than as the celebration of a victory (as on the Ur Standard, Nos. 303-304).

Baghdad, Iraq Museum. Khafajah, Temple Oval III, "house D," room IX. Limestone. Height: 0.32 m. Early Dynastic III (middle third millennium). H. Frankfort, *Sculpture of the Third Millennium B.C. from Tell Asmar and Khafajah*, OIP, 44, Chicago, 1939, pl. 107, pp. 43-48. Contenau, *Man.*, vol. 4, fig. 1111, pp. 2017-2018. Photograph courtesy of the Oriental Institute.

605. A nude, clean-shaven priest faces right as he holds up a libation vase in front of a pillar mounted on a tripod of bulls' legs. In his right hand he holds some object,

perhaps a cup. To each side of the post there hangs a cord with a loop at the end.

British Museum, 120850. Ur, 7900. Shell. Height: 0.075 m. Early Dynastic III (middle third millennium) or later. C. L. Woolley, *The Royal Cemetery*, London, 1934, pl. 102b, pp. 282, 525. Photograph courtesy of the University Museum.

606. On an inscribed calcite disc is this panel showing the priestess Enheduanna, daughter of Sargon, in a long, flounced garment, with her attendants, making an offering. The priestess stands with upraised hand, wearing her hair in long locks, three of which hang down before her shoulder. A turban-like band is wound around the top of her head. Before her is a shaven priest, who pours a libation from a spouted jar into a receptacle which stands before an altar shaped like a staged tower. Following the priestess are two figures, one carrying a bucket and the other, a whisk (?).

University Museum, CBS 16665. Ur, 6612. Calcite. Width: 0.265 m. Sargon of Akkad (second half of twenty-fourth century). *AJ*, vol. 6, 1926, pl. 54b, pp. 376-377. *MJ*, vol. 18, 1927, pp. 237-240. Photograph courtesy UM.

607. A fragment of plaster on a wall of the palace at Mari shows a bearded attendant, wearing a high mobcap, and leading a bull by a rope attached to a ring in his nose. The tip of the one horn of the bull which has been preserved is sheathed, perhaps with gold; he wears a pendant of the same material.

Aleppo. Mari, third campaign, 1935-1936. Length: 0.55 m.; height: 0.40 m. Colors of paint: black, white, and shades of red. First half of second millennium. *Syria*, vol. 18, 1937, pl. 37, no. 2, fig. 5, pp. 330-332. Photograph courtesy of the National Museum.

608. Two male figures, clothed in Syrian costume, stand on opposite sides of a table, with hands extended so that the tips of the fingers touch. The figure to the right wears a conical hat. The table, which probably has tripod base, holds four tablet-like objects arranged in two piles. At the upper part of the stela there are two lotus blossoms.

Aleppo, National Museum. Ras Shamra, 1935. Limestone. Fourteenth century, according to excavator. *Syria*, vol. 17, 1936, pl. 14, pp. 115-119. Photograph JBP.

609. In this reconstruction of a wall painting Sargon II is shown holding a mace and extending his finger in a gesture of supplication before his god, who stands on a pedestal and holds the emblems of authority, the rod and ring. Behind the king is an officer, who stands with folded hands. The inner border of the scene is decorated with alternating rosettes and winged genii. The painting was found in the house of a high official of the king (K, room 12).

Khorsabad. Wall painting in black, red, and blue. Height of central figure: about 3 m. Sargon II (721-705). G. Loud and C. B. Altman, *Khorsabad*, pt. 2, OIP, 40, Chicago, 1938, pl. 89. Photograph courtesy of the Oriental Institute.

610. This is the central part of a larger scene, referred to as "the investiture of the king," on the palace wall

at Mari. In the center of the upper register stands the goddess Ishtar, her right foot on a lion, holding a curved sword in her left hand and the rod and ring in the right. Weapons spring from her shoulders. Before her stands a bearded king, who touches the rod and ring, the emblems of authority. Both the king and the goddess are accompanied by an attendant goddess, who stands with upraised hands. To the right is a god, with his hand across his breast. The lower register depicts two goddesses holding vases, from which flow free streams of water, filled with fish. The upper scene has been interpreted as the investiture of the king, held in the palace itself, where the statue of Ishtar was brought for the purpose (A. Parrot, *Studia Mariana*, Leiden, 1950, pp. 37-40), or as a representation of an annual festival (A. Haldar, *Orientalia Suecana*, vol. 1, 1952, pp. 51-65. H. Frankfort, *Bibliotheca Orientalis*, vol. 8, 1951, pp. 181-183).

Mari, third campaign, 1935-1936. Wall painting. Height of figures in upper register: about 0.35 m. First part of second millennium. *Syria*, vol. 18, 1937, pl. 39, fig. 8, pp. 335-346. Marie-Thérèse Barrelet, "Une peinture de la cour 106 du palais de Mari," *Studia Mariana*, ed. by A. Parrot, Leiden, 1950, pl. 1, pp. 9-35. Photograph from A. Parrot, *Studia Mariana*, Leiden, 1950, p. 16.

611. A bearded figure, perhaps a king (Sulumeli?), wearing a long robe, horned headdress with streamers, and shoes with upturned toes, pours a libation to four deities, who stand in line before him. The worshiper is followed by a small attendant, who holds a bull. The first and third deities are bearded and similarly attired in kilts and conical headdresses decorated with rows of horns (cf. No. 541), and are fully armed. The second and the fourth are beardless and wear long, pleated garments; each holds a hammer in the right hand and carries an axe over the left shoulder. The second figure is equipped with wings.

Ankara, Hittite Museum, 12253. Malatya (relief D). Limestone. Height: 0.47 m.; length: 1.26 m. Dated by E. Akurgal on stylistic grounds to 1050-900 (*Späthethitische Bildkunst*, Ankara, 1949, p. 141, where references are given to later dating by Bossert). L. Delaporte, *Malatya: Arslantepe, I*, Paris, 1940, pl. 20, 1. E. Akurgal, *Späthethitische Bildkunst*, Ankara, 1949, pl. 2. Bossert, *Altanatolien*, 770. Photograph courtesy of E. Akurgal, Ankara.

612. Top of a statuette of a man, wearing a full beard arranged in four rows and curled at the ends, a headband, and a capelike garment which covers both shoulders. The upper lip is shaven. Held firmly by both hands is a small animal, perhaps intended for sacrifice.

Aleppo. Mari, fifth campaign, 1937, on esplanade of the ziggurat. Gypsum. Height: 0.23 m. First part of second millennium, and nearer to the Ur III period than to the time of Zimrilim, according to excavator. *Syria*, vol. 20, 1939, pl. 7, fig. 8, pp. 11-14. A. Parrot, "Le 'Bon Pasteur,' à propos d'une statue de Mari," *Mélanges ... Dussaud*, vol. 1, Paris, 1939, pp. 171-182. Photograph courtesy of the National Museum.

613. A man with tonsured head, long beard, but shaved upper lip, and wearing a robe which leaves the right shoulder and arm free, holds a small animal by the feet. The eyes are inlaid with shell and bitumen; the nose has been repaired in antiquity.

Aleppo. Mari, first campaign, 1933-1934. Gypsum. Height: 0.58 m. Originally assigned by the excavator to the pre-Sargonid period, but later (*Mélanges ... Dussaud*, vol. 1, Paris, 1939, p. 172, fn. 2) lowered. *Syria*, vol. 16, 1935, pl. 21, no. 2, p. 6. Photograph courtesy of the National Museum.

614. A bearded human figure, perhaps a priest, dressed in an Assyrian fringed mantle, and equipped with wings, holds a branch of vegetation (a palm or ear of grain) in his raised right hand and a goat in his left. The figure is represented as wearing a headband with rosette, earrings, necklace, arm bands and bracelets with rosettes.

British Museum, Nimrud Gallery 18. Nimrud, palace of Ashurnasirpal II. Alabaster. Height: 2.26 m. Ashurnasirpal II (883-859). C. J. Gadd, *The Assyrian Sculptures*, London, 1934, pl. 14. E. A. W. Budge, *Assyrian Sculptures in the British Museum*, London, 1914, pl. 27. *AOB*, 382. Photograph courtesy BM.

615. The colossal human figure, dressed in a garment of the Assyrian style, is shown with long hair, which extends in ringlets to his shoulders, and with an elaborately curled beard, which covers his chest. In his right hand he holds what seems to be a curved weapon and in his left the foot of a small lion which he clutches to his side. Although this carving has been frequently referred to as the figure of "Gilgamesh" the identification is far from certain.

Louvre. Khorsabad. Alabaster. Height: 4.70 m. Sargon II (721-705). P. E. Botta, *Monument de Ninive*, vol. 1, Paris, 1849, pl. 47. TEL, vol. 1, p. 304. *AOB*, 605. E. Pottier, *Les antiquités assyriennes*, Paris, 1924, no. 17, pl. 8. Photograph TEL.

616. On the smaller block, a horned bull stands on a paneled pedestal with projecting cornice. To the right of the larger block is an altar, probably round in shape, decorated with lateral bands and in the upper part with herringbone design. Before the altar are two human figures. The first, who may represent the priest-king, is clothed in a long robe and a tight-fitting cap, and holds a staff with curved end in hand, while he raises the other toward the top of the altar. He is followed by a female figure, probably the queen and chief priestess, who wears a pleated skirt and hair done in a pigtail down her back. She seems to be holding a staff.

Ankara, Hittite Museum, 44. Alaça Hüyük. Granite. Width of larger block: about 1 m.; width of smaller block: about 0.30 m. Fifteenth century (Bossert, *Altanatolien*, p. 53). Th. Macridy-Bey, *La porte des sphinx à Euyuk*, Berlin, 1908, fig. 17. J. Garstang, *The Hittite Empire*, London, 1929, pl. 29, pp. 134-135. Contenau, *Man.*, vol. 2, fig. 673, pp. 973-974. Photograph from A. Götze, *Kleinasien*, Munich, 1933, fig. 9, courtesy of C. H. Beck'sche Verlagsbuchhandlung, Munich.

617. A human figure with eagle head and wings holds a bucket with its left hand and a cone with its right. The genius is dressed in a garment which is similar to that worn by the king Ashurnasirpal II. The emblems of the cone and the bucket are frequently associated with

the "sacred tree," and must be intended to convey here something of the same suggestion.

British Museum, Nimrud Gallery 40. Nimrud. Gypsum. Height: 2.18 m. Ashurnasirpal II (883-859). British Museum, *A Guide to the Babylonian and Assyrian Antiquities*, London, 1922, pl. 16. E. A. W. Budge, *Assyrian Sculptures in the British Museum*, London, 1914, pl. 46. Photograph courtesy BM.

618. Three almost identical figures, each clad in a kilt and short-sleeved shirt, carry sacrificial animals (gazelles?) over their shoulders.

Ankara, Hittite Museum, 78. Carchemish, processional entry, no. 9. Basalt. Height: 1 m. Ninth-eighth century(?). C. L. Woolley, *Carchemish, Part II*, London, 1921, pl. B23b. E. Akurgal, *Späthethitische Bildkunst*, Ankara, 1949, pl. 16. Bossert, *Altanatolien*, no. 844. Photograph courtesy of the British Museum.

619. This bronze model *ṣit šamši* has been interpreted as a representation of the ritual of the dawn. Two entirely nude persons squat; one holds out his hands while another holds a vase of purification water for the ablution. At the ends of the tray are representations of stepped temples. Altars of sacrifice, libation bowls or jars holding water, sacred trees, and other cultic objects make up the equipment.

Louvre. Susa. Bronze. Length: 0.60 m.; width: 0.40 m. Shilhak-Inshushinak (twelfth century). J. de Morgan, *Mémoires, Délégation en Perse*, vol. 12, Paris, 1911, pp. 143-151. TEL, vol. 1, p. 279A. Contenau, *Man.*, vol. 2, fig. 635, pp. 920-922. *AOB*, 468. See A. Parrot, *La tour de Babel*, Neuchatel and Paris, 1953, p. 120. Photograph TEL.

620. One of two similar statues found in the temple of Nabu at Nimrud has a dedication to Nabu by Bel-tarsi-iluma, governor of Calah, "for the life of Adad-nirari, king of Assyria, his lord, and Sammuramat, the queen, his lady" (Luckenbill, *AR*, vol. 1, §§744-745). The bearded figure wears the horned miter and stands with folded hands, ready to serve. Once identified as Nabu, this statue has recently been considered as a divine servant (C. J. Gadd, *The Stones of Assyria*, London, 1936, pp. 150-151).

British Museum, 118889. Nimrud, found by Rassam in 1854, in temple of Nabu. Coarse limestone. Height: 1.77 m. Adadnirari III (810-783). British Museum, *Assyrian Sculptures in the British Museum from Shalmaneser III to Sennacherib*, London, 1938, pl. 3. H. R. Hall, *Babylonian and Assyrian Sculpture in the British Museum*, Paris and Brussels, 1928, pl. 24, 2. Photograph courtesy BM.

621. A bearded human figure, wearing a horned miter with a single row of horns and a long garment with fringed edge, stands holding a box. Similarity to No. 620 suggests that this too may have been intended to portray a divine servant or attendant.

Aleppo, National Museum. Arslan Tash. Height: 1.73 m. Tiglath-pileser III (744-727). F. Thureau-Dangin, *et al., Arslan-Tash*, Paris, 1931, pl. 1, p. 66. Contenau, *Man.*, vol. 4, fig. 1250. Photograph JBP.

622. A worshiper, wearing a turbaned headdress, kneels upon a base and holds his right hand to the level of his face with forefinger extended. At the end of the base is a small basin; at the side is a ram and an inscription which mentions the name of the god Amurru, to whom the object is dedicated.

Louvre, AO 15704. Presented to Louvre, thought to have come from Larsa. Bronze, hands and face covered with gold leaf. Height: 0.196 m. Hammurabi (1728-1686). R. Dussaud, "Ex-voto au dieu Amourrou pour la vie de Hammourabi," Fondation Piot, vol. 33, 1933, pls. 1, 2, pp. 1-10. Contenau, *Man.*, vol. 4, fig. 1175. TEL, vol. 1, p. 261B. Photograph Archives Photographiques.

623. Two beardless attendants carry an elaborately decorated table. It has claw feet and sits upon a base with conelike legs. The side panel contains two bearded human figures who support with their hands the upper frame.

Baghdad, Iraq Museum, 18630. Khorsabad. G. Loud, *Khorsabad*, pt. 1, *OIP*, 38, Chicago, 1936, fig. 42. Photograph courtesy of the Oriental Institute.

624. At the left is the holy place of a temple set on a hill and protected by two towers. Within, a priest-king stands before the seated figure of the god. In front of the temple are the table, on which are piled offerings, an incense burner, and a large bowl on a stand. The king stands, bearded and wearing the royal headdress, holding an undetermined offering, and he is followed by an attendant bearing a bowl. The figure at the extreme right is holding a steer by the horns. This obelisk has generally been attributed to Ashurnasirpal II, but it has been proposed recently to assign it to an earlier Ashurnasirpal.

British Museum, 118807. Kuyunjik, found by Rassam in 1853. Limestone. Height of entire obelisk: about 3.5 m. Ashurnasirpal I (?) (middle of eleventh century). *AOB*, 533. C. J. Gadd, *The Assyrian Sculptures*, London, 1934, pp. 9-10. Photograph courtesy BM.

625. In the field of this register of bronze band I of the gates of Balawat (but not shown in photograph) is the inscription of Shalmaneser III: "I set up an image on the shore of the sea of Nairi (Lake Van); I offered sacrifices to my gods" (Luckenbill, *AR*, vol. 1, §614). To the left, a soldier throws the legs of an ox into a lake, where they are seized by a monster. Another soldier drags the head of the sacrificial animal toward the water. In the center is the king's image carved in the rock, represented as standing on a mountain. Before the image are two royal standards, an offering table, an incense stand, and a vessel on its stand. The king, wearing a conical headdress with small peak, is accompanied by a priest who pours out a libation.

British Museum. "Tell Balawat." Bronze. Height of register: about 0.08 m. Shalmaneser III (858-824). L. W. King, *Bronze Reliefs from the Gates of Shalmaneser*, London, 1915, pl. 1, pp. 21-22. *AOB*, 534. Photograph courtesy BM.

626. King Ashurbanipal is shown wearing the royal headdress, holding a bow and arrows in his left hand and in his right a shallow bowl, from which he pours a libation over the four dead lions at his feet. He is accompanied by two pages, who hold fly-whisks and doubled

napkins. In front of the king are an offering table with cover and offering, an incense stand, and two musicians playing lyres with plectra. For translation of inscription see Luckenbill, *AR*, vol. 2, §1021.

British Museum, 124886. Kuyunjik. Alabastrine limestone. Height: 0.559 m. Ashurbanipal (668-633). H. R. Hall, *Babylonian and Assyrian Sculpture in the British Museum*, Paris and Brussels, 1928, pl. 52, 3. C. J. Gadd, *The Assyrian Sculptures*, London, 1934, pl. 12, p. 73. *AOB*, 535. Photograph courtesy BM.

627. To the left is a priest standing before an incense stand, as though placing something upon it. An offering table with claw feet supports four spherical objects. To the right is a four-staged tower, or ziggurat (?). Over the scene is an eight-pointed star.

Berlin, VA 5362. Ashur. Red marble. Height: 0.042 m.; diameter: 0.016 m. Last quarter of the second millennium. A. Moortgat, *Vorderasiatische Rollsiegel*, Berlin, 1940, no. 591. Photograph courtesy of Staatliche Museen.

628. In the center of this painting on a vessel is the winged sun-disc over a stylized palm tree. To the right is the offering table, of gold and lapis and covered with white cloth, bearing a small gold box, a gold dish containing a white object, and a white aspergillum laced round with yellow. A worshiper (broken away) places some incense (?) in the flaming incense stand. To the left of the scene are players of musical instruments, the first playing the double flute and the second a hand drum.

Berlin, VA 5043. Ashur. Painting on pottery. Height: 0.36 m. W. Andrae, *Coloured Ceramics from Ashur*, London, 1925, pl. 29. Photograph courtesy of Staatliche Museen.

629. To the left, a boy, who does not wear the lock of hair usually shown on children, stands while he is being circumcised, as his hands are held firmly by an assistant. The operator, who is labeled a "mortuary priest," performs the operation with a rounded object, perhaps a flint knife (cf. Exod. 4:25), and says: "Hold on to him; do not let him faint." The assistant answers: "I shall act to thy pleasure." In the scene to the right, the patient braces himself by placing his hand on the head of the operator and says: "*Rub off what is (there) thoroughly.*" The operator answers: "I shall make (it) heal." The legend to the scene is "Circumcision." See *ANET*, 326, fn. 2, for translations.

Sakkarah, tomb of Ankh-ma-Hor. Sixth Dynasty (2350-2000). Wresz., vol. 3, pl. 26. *AOB*, 158 (drawing). Photograph courtesy of the Service des Antiquités, Cairo.

FUNERARY SCENES AND OBJECTS

630. To the right of the funerary stela sits an elaborately dressed woman (perhaps a queen), holding a cup and a blossom, before an offering table. She wears a tight-fitting cap with streamers hanging down at the back, a long pleated garment ending in a fringe just above the ankles, pinned with a fibula just over the left breast. She is adorned with necklaces, bracelets, and ankle bands. Upon the bull-footed table are various of-

ferings of food, over which a server waves a fly-whisk. Above the scene is the stylized sun-disc.

Berlin, VA 2995. Zinjirli. Dolerite. Height of relief: 1.34 m. Eighth century. F. von Luschan, *Ausgrabungen in Sendschirli*, vol. 4, Berlin, 1911, pl. 54, pp. 325 ff. Schäfer-Andrae, 593. Bossert, *Altanatolien*, 953. Discussion of this type of representation: E. Akurgal, *Späthethitische Bildkunst*, Ankara, 1949, pp. 119-125. Photograph courtesy of Staatliche Museen.

631. Two woman, clothed with long, fringed garments and high cylindrical caps, sit on chairs, with their feet on footstools, before a small offering table, on which there are three cakelike objects and a cup. The figure to the left holds a cup in her left hand and a pomegranate in her right. The woman to the right holds a mirror and a pomegranate (or spindle). The inscription is in hieroglyphic Hittite.

Istanbul, Museum of the Ancient Orient, 7694. Marash. Basalt. Height: 1.24 m. J. Garstang, *The Hittite Empire*, London, 1929, pp. 224-225, fig. 18. E. Akurgal, *Späthethitische Bildkunst*, Ankara, 1949, pp. 119-121. Photograph JBP.

632. To the left sits a bearded figure holding in his right hand a cup, and in his left stalks of grain. To the right are two women, the first holding a mirror and a pomegranate, and the second sitting on a stool and holding a pomegranate in her left hand. Between the men and the two women is a table piled with offerings. The scene has been interpreted as an offering to the dead, who is represented by the male figure.

Istanbul, Museum of the Ancient Orient, 7785. Marash. Eighth century (?). M. Ebert, *Reallexikon der Vorgeschichte*, vol. 7, Berlin, 1926, pl. 164b. E. Akurgal, *Späthethitische Bildkunst*, Ankara, 1949, fig. 18, pl. 41. Bossert, *Altsyrien*, 499. Photograph JBP.

633. To the left sits a bearded male figure holding a staff in his right hand and drinking from a cup held in his left. Opposite sits a woman holding two flowers (?) and drinking from a cup held by the right hand. Between the couple is an offering table with bull's feet, piled high with offerings of bread and a fish.

Istanbul, Museum of the Ancient Orient, 7778. Zinjirli. Ninth-eighth century (?). F. von Luschan, *Ausgrabungen in Sendschirli*, vol. 3, Berlin, 1902, fig. 105, pl. 37. E. Akurgal, *Späthethitische Bildkunst*, Ankara, 1949, pl. 22a. Bossert, *Altanatolien*, 911. Photograph JBP.

634. To the extreme right of the upper register is the sorrowing widow of the deceased. Behind her, servants sorrowfully prepare booths for the passage of the funeral procession. Below, to the right are two sons of the deceased, the first of whom is standing beside the coffin. Following them are Hor-em-heb, later to become king, and the viziers of Upper and Lower Egypt; the first is characterized by his title, the viziers are identifiable by their garments. A line of mourners constitute the end of the row.

Berlin, Äg. 12411. Memphis. Limestone. Height: about 0.52 m. Nineteenth Dynasty (1350-1200). A. Erman, *ÄZ*, vol. 33, 1895, pl. 1, pp. 18-24. Porter and Moss, *Bibliography*, vol. 3, p. 197. Schäfer-Andrae, 387. *AOB*, 196. Photograph Foto Marburg.

635. On a funerary stela the priest Agbar is shown seated before an offering table with food, drinking from a cup which he holds to his lips. Before the table is an attendant with fly-whisk. The priest is dressed in a long robe which leaves his right arm and shoulder free. For inscription see G. A. Cooke, *A Text-Book of North-Semitic Inscriptions*, Oxford, 1903, pp. 189-191. See also No. 280 for other stela from Nerab.

Louvre. Nerab, southeast of Aleppo. Basalt. Height: 0.95 m. First half of sixth century. Contenau, *Man.*, vol. 3, fig. 852, p. 1367. Bossert, *Altsyrien*, 492. G. Contenau, *Les antiquités orientales, monuments hittites, assyriens, phéniciens, perses, judaïques, chypriotes, araméens*, Paris, n.d. pl. 27. Photograph Archives Photographiques.

636. In the upper register of this Sabaean grave stela is a figure seated before a table, and holding a cup which has been taken from the offering. An attendant stands before the offering table, while another figure stands to the left. Below are two camels and a rider. For inscription see *CIS*, pt. 4, vol. 2, pl. 13, no. 445.

Louvre, AO 1029. Alabaster. Height: 0.55 m. Second or third century A.D. (W. F. Albright). Bossert, *Altsyrien*, 1302. TEL, vol. 2, p. 128. J. H. Mordtmann, Jr., *ZDMG*, vol. 32, 1878, pp. 200-203. J. G. Février, *La religion des Palmyréniens*, Paris, 1931, p. 27. Photograph Giraudon, Paris.

637. While this composition is in the style of the cultic and funerary representations, it may well be a purely secular representation of a person at a banquet (E. Akurgal, *Späthethitische Bildkunst*, Ankara, 1949, p. 121, fn. 206). To the left of a table sits a bearded figure, holding a cup, and attended by a servant with a fly-whisk. To the right is another attendant and a musician, who plays upon a stringed instrument.

Ankara, Hittite Museum, 123. Carchemish. Limestone. Height: 1.35 m. Second half of eighth century. C. L. Woolley, *Carchemish, Part II*, London, 1921, pl. B30b. Bossert, *Altanatolien*, 833 (who dates to tenth? century). Discussion in E. Akurgal, *Späthethitische Bildkunst*, Ankara, 1949, pp. 119-121. L. Woolley, *Carchemish III*, London, 1952, p. 248, suggests a date as early as the eighteenth century. Photograph courtesy of the British Museum.

638. A group of women and girls stand with raised hands mourning for the deceased. One small girl is shown nude; some wear a long flowing garment which extends from the waist downward, leaving the breasts bare; others wear garments which cover the shoulders and flow downward to the feet. Indication of tears can be seen on the faces.

Thebes, tomb of Ra-mose (55). Ra-mose was a high official under Amen-hotep IV (1380-1362). Schäfer-Andrae, 380, 2. Wresz., vol. 1, pl. 8a. See M. Werbrouck, *Les pleureuses dans l'Égypte ancienne*, Brussels, 1938, pp. 37-39, pl. 12. Photograph courtesy of A. Gaddis, Luxor.

639. In this vignette from the papyrus of Hu-nefer, Anubis leads the deceased toward the judgment balance, where his heart is being weighed against Maat by Anubis. Standing under the balance is the composite creature, the devourer. Thoth, the recorder, writes the results of the judgment, as Horus presents the deceased before the shrine of Osiris.

British Museum, 9901, sheet 3, left. New Kingdom (1550-1090). E. Naville, *Das ägyptische Todtenbuch*, vol. 1, Berlin, 1886, pl. 136 (top). E. A. W. Budge, *The Book of the Dead: Facsimiles of the Papyrus of Hunefer...*, London, 1899, pl. 4. Photograph courtesy BM.

640. In a vignette from the papyrus of Hu-nefer is shown the ceremony of the "opening the mouth," a ritual designed to give the deceased a new body in the other world and to establish communion between the living and the dead. The mummy is held by Anubis as a priest touches the mouth of the mummy with a ram-headed instrument called "great of magic," holding an adze in the other hand. Another priest presents four vases of water. Behind them is the lector, who pours out a libation and burns incense.

British Museum, 9901, sheet 5, left. Height of register: about 0.23 m. New Kingdom (1550-1090). E. Naville, *Das ägyptische Todtenbuch*, vol. 1, Berlin, 1886, pl. 2. British Museum, *A General Introductory Guide to the Egyptian Collections in the British Museum*, London, 1930, p. 86, fig. 32 (drawing). E. A. W. Budge, *The Book of the Dead: Facsimiles of the Papyrus of Hunefer...*, London, 1899, pl. 7. Photograph courtesy BM.

641. A clay sarcophagus has a lid on which are represented the face and crossed arms of the deceased. On the head is represented a headdress decorated with vertical lines.

Palestine Archaeological Museum. Beth-shan, great northern cemetery. Pottery. Height: 1.85 m.; maximum diameter: 0.70 m. Fifteenth to twelfth century, according to excavator; Iron I (twelfth to tenth century), according to W. F. Albright, *AP*, p. 106. A. Rowe, *The Topography and History of Beth-shan*, Philadelphia, 1930, pl. 37, p. 39. Photograph courtesy of the University Museum.

642. Scenes from the process of mummification, including the application of hot resin, bandaging of the mummy, the decoration of the mask, and the use of other objects connected with embalming.

Thebes, tomb of Amen-em-Opet (41). Beginning of Nineteenth Dynasty (1350-1200). W. R. Dawson, "Making a Mummy," *JEA*, vol. 13, 1927, pl. 18, pp. 40-49. I. Rosellini, *I Monumenti dell'Egitto e della Nubia, Monumenti Civili*, Pisa, 1834, pl. 126 [1-6]. Photograph from Rosellini.

643. Basalt sarcophagus of Shamshi-Adad V, with lid equipped with loop-handles to facilitate moving, and two knobs for fastening the lid securely to the body of the sarcophagus.

Berlin, VA Ass. 2282. Ashur. Basalt. Length: 2.49 m. Shamshi-Adad V (823-811). W. Andrae, *Das wiedererstandene Assur*, Leipzig, 1938, pl. 66b, pp. 139-140. Photograph courtesy of Staatliche Museen.

MONSTERS, DEMONS, AND AMULETS

644. A composite creature consisting of a lion, wings, and an added human head. The head wears a high conical cap with two horns. A double braided lock falls down in back to the shoulders.

Ankara. Carchemish. Basalt. Height: 1.30 m. Ninth century, according to Bossert (*Altanatolien*, 852). D. G. Hogarth, *Car-*

chemish, Part I, London, 1914, pl. B14a. E. Akurgal, *Späthethitische Bildkunst*, Ankara, 1949, pl. 12b (for human head), 14b. Photograph courtesy of the British Museum.

645. Two identical creatures, composed of human body and bird head and wings, stand with upraised hands, facing each other.

Ankara. Carchemish. Basalt. Height: 1.17 m. Ninth century, according to Bossert (*Altanatolien*, 847). E. Akurgal, *Späthethitische Bildkunst*, Ankara, 1949, fig. 50 (drawing of head). Photograph from D. G. Hogarth, *Carchemish, Part I*, London, 1914, pl. B12.

646. This figure was one of a pair which guarded the doorway to the palace of Ashurnasirpal at Nimrud. The body is that of a lion, to which are attached the wings and breast feathers of an eagle, and the head of a man, topped with a horned miter. That the figure was intended to be viewed from the front and the side is clear from the five legs portrayed. Around the loins of the creature is a broad band of several strands tied in a knot which leaves the tasselled ends hanging toward the back. These creatures, known as *lamassu* and as *šēdu*, were intended to serve as protective genii.

British Museum, 108801. Nimrud, palace of Ashurnasirpal. Limestone. Height: 3.50 m. Ashurnasirpal II (883-859). E. A. W. Budge, *Assyrian Sculptures in the British Museum*, London, 1914, pl. 4. C. J. Gadd, *The Assyrian Sculptures*, London, 1934, pp. 13-15, for discussion. *AOB*, 381. Photograph courtesy BM.

647. This creature is similar to No. 646, except that the body is that of a bull in general form, but decorated with the curly hair of a lion on the breast, flank, and hind quarters. The ears are bovine and fitted with earrings.

British Museum, 118872. Nimrud. Limestone. Height: 3.15 m. Ashurnasirpal II (883-859). E. A. W. Budge, *Assyrian Sculptures in the British Museum*, London, 1914, pl. 5. C. J. Gadd, *The Assyrian Sculptures*, London, 1934, pp. 13-15, for discussion. Photograph courtesy BM.

648. A column was supported by these two sphinxes. The lion's body has the wings of a bird and the head of a woman with long hair falling down before and behind her ears in ringlets.

Istanbul, Museum of the Ancient Orient, 7731. Zinjirli, Hilani III. Dolerite. Height: 0.96 m. Eighth century. F. von Luschan, *Ausgrabungen in Sendschirli*, vol. 2, Berlin, 1898, pl. 33 below, pp. 156 ff.; vol. 4, Berlin, 1911, pl. 66. *AOB*, 390. Bossert, *Altanatolien*, 900. Photograph JBP.

649. An ivory plaque of pierced work, with frame and tenons above and below for insertion in a panel. The beardless sphinx wears a double crown, a curling wig, and a patterned kilt. The creature has claw feet and is standing in a thicket of lotus plants.

Palestine Archaeological Museum, 33.2572. Samaria, 1932. Ivory. Height: 0.087 m. First half of ninth century, according to excavators. J. W. Crowfoot and Grace M. Crowfoot, *Early Ivories from Samaria*, London, 1938, pl. 5, 1, p. 20. Photograph courtesy PAM.

650. On a Syrian cylinder seal two seated sphinxes face each other, one at each side of a head of the Egyptian goddess Hathor, over which is a winged sun-disc. In the field are also the hare, an antelope head, and stars.

New York, Pierpont Morgan Library. Hematite. Height: 0.019 m.; diameter: 0.010 m. Fifteenth century. *Corpus*, no. 985. Photograph courtesy PML.

651. A winged deity, armed with a long straight sword and a sickle-sword and holding a lightning-fork in each hand, drives out a monster, having lion's head and body and the wings and claws of an eagle. Horns appear on the lion's head of this male monster. These slabs stood at the door of a temple.

British Museum, Nimrud Gallery, 28, 29. Nimrud. Limestone. Height: 2.36 m. Ashurnasirpal II (883-859). E. A. W. Budge, *Assyrian Sculptures in the British Museum*, London, 1914, pl. 37. *AOB*, 380. Photograph courtesy BM; inset from A. H. Layard, *A Second Series of the Monuments of Nineveh*, London, 1853, pl. 5.

652. Two bearded creatures with wings, face each other in a leaping pose. Each wears a peaked headdress with horns, suggestive of the Hittite style (Nos. 539, 541); the beard and hair are more in the Assyrian style. At the top of the panel and between the two figures is a crescent and rayed sun-disc. This thick block of basalt, found reused in a late Arab building at Aleppo, may have served as the base for a statue.

Aleppo, National Museum. Aleppo, citadel. Basalt. Height: 0.95 m.; width: 1.30 m.; thickness: 0.95 m. Eighth or ninth century, on grounds of style. *Syria*, vol. 12, 1931, p. 95. Bossert, *Altsyrien*, 494. Photograph JBP.

653. Two-bull men, each having the legs, tail and ears of a bull, and upper body and head of a man, stand upholding a stool on which rests an elaborate winged sun-disc; they are assisted by a smaller human figure standing between them. The bull-men wear a long beard, hair which hangs in curled locks to the shoulders, and a horned headdress; the upper lip is shaved. The smaller, human figure is bearded and wears a heavy, curled wig.

Aleppo, National Museum. Tell Halaf. Basalt. Height: 1.32 m. Ninth century (see No. 96). M. von Oppenheim, *Der Tell Halaf*, Berlin, 1931, pl. 8b. Bossert, *Altsyrien*, 451 center. Photograph JBP.

654. To the left is a bearded human figure, wearing a horned cap and wings from his shoulders and his hips. He holds a staff with both hands. In the center is a stylized tree. To the right is a beardless human figure, wearing a long, fringed robe, and high feathered headdress with horns. Wings emerge from the shoulders and from the hips.

Berlin, VA 8850, 8856, 8845. Tell Halaf. Basalt. Height: about 0.70 m. Ninth century (see No. 96). Photograph Foto Marburg.

655. A beardless figure, perhaps a woman, wears a long, fringed robe and six wings. Two spring from her shoulders, two from her hips, and two more emerge from her knees. With her hands she grasps two staves. On her head is an elaborate crown, perhaps intended to represent horns. Cf. Isa. 6:2 for reference to creatures with six wings.

Baltimore. Tell Halaf, 184B. Basalt. Height: about 0.70 m. Ninth century (see No. 65). M. von Oppenheim, *Tell Halaf*, London and New York, n.d., pl. 32B. Photograph courtesy of the Walters Art Gallery.

656. At each side of a stylized tree stands a winged female human figure wearing a miter of two pairs of horns. Each holds a chaplet in one hand as she raises the other toward the tree. This type of genii is to be distinguished from that which guards the entrances to temple and palace.

British Museum, Nimrud Gallery 37b. Nimrud. Limestone. Height: about 1 m. Ashurnasirpal II (883-859). E. A. W. Budge, *Assyrian Sculptures in the British Museum*, London, 1914, pl. 42, 2. A. H. Layard, *The Monuments of Nineveh*, London, 1849, pl. 7. See C. J. Gadd, *The Assyrian Sculptures*, London, 1934, pp. 52-53. Photograph courtesy BM.

657. A lion-headed demon (probably Lamashtu), with a dog and a pig hanging at her breasts and a serpent in each hand. At the sides are a lamp on a stand and a grotesque human head. On the reverse is a magical formula.

New York, Metropolitan Museum of Art, 86.11.2. Yellow alabaster. Width: 0.063 m. Period of Nebuchadnezzar II (605-562). *BMMA*, vol. 19, 1924, pp. 145-148, fig. 1. H. H. von der Osten, *AfO*, vol. 4, 1927, pp. 89-92. See G. Contenau, *La magie chez les Assyriens et les Babyloniens*, Paris, 1947, pp. 95-96, for discussion of the Lamashtu. Photograph courtesy MMA.

658. The figure of a demon (with lion body, eagle feet and wings, with tail and penis ending in serpent heads) is engraved on the back of this bronze plaque. His head and paws can be seen at the top of the side of the plaque shown here. The face of the plaque is divided into four registers depicting the exorcism of a demon from a sick man. In the upper register are the emblems of the major gods: Ashur (sun-disc), Ishtar (eight-pointed star), Sin (crescent), Ea (ram-headed scepter), Nabu (stylus), Marduk (*marru* or spear point), and the seven Pleiades. The second register is filled by a procession of seven demons clothed in long robes and with right hand raised in a menacing gesture. Each has the head of a different animal. The third register shows the exorcising scene. The sick man is lying upon a bed, at the ends of which stand two priests clothed in fishlike garments. To the left is a stand with a lamp (the emblem of Nusku); to the right, three genii, who are struggling. In the fourth register is a river with swimming fish and a boat, with animal-headed prow and stern, carrying an ass, on which is the demon Lamashtu (see description No. 657). To the left is a Pazuzu; while to the right is an assemblage of objects for the performance of the ritual.

Paris, Collection de Clercq. Bronze. Height, with head of monster: 0.135 m. Collection de Clercq, *Catalogue, Antiquités assyriennes*, vol. 2, Paris, 1903, pl. 34 (upper right), pp. 213-221. G. Contenau, *La magie chez les Assyriens et les Babyloniens*, Paris, 1947, pl. 8, pp. 228-230. *AOB*, 387. F. Thureau-Dangin, "Ritual et amulettes contre Labartu," *RA*, vol. 18, 1921, pp. 172 ff. Photograph from Collection de Clercq, *Catalogue*.

659. This inscribed statuette of the demon Pazuzu has the feet of an eagle, the body of a man, claws for hands, eagle wings, and a head which is misshapen and distorted. Inscription given by F. Thureau Dangin, *RA*, vol. 18, 1921, p. 190.

Louvre. Bronze. Height: 0.15 m. E. Pottier, *Catalogue des antiquités assyriennes*, Paris, 1924, no. 146. *AOB*, 383, G. Contenau, *La magie chez les Assyriens et les Babyloniens*, Paris, 1947, front cover, p. 99. Photograph Archives Photographiques.

660. The upper register of this broken amulet contains seven demons, each with a different animal's head. Right hands are raised in a brandishing gesture. In the second register at the center is the lion-headed, horned demon Lamashtu, holding a serpent in her hand and holding a dog at her breast. To the left is what remains of a bed on which the sick person lay; to the right, a smaller demon and a demonic head. In the field are other objects connected with exorcism. For the text of the reverse see F. Thureau-Dangin, *RA*, vol. 18, 1921, p. 197.

Louvre. AO 7088. Brown stone. Width: 0.07 m. F. Thureau-Dangin, "Rituel et amulettes contre Labartu," *RA*, vol. 18, 1921, pl. 1, no. 2, pp. 177-178. TEL, vol. 2, no. 143. Photograph TEL.

661. A grotesque head with bulging eyes and exaggerated mouth and teeth, which probably served as an amulet of the demon Pazuzu.

Collection E. Borowski. Bituminous stone. Height: 0.064 m. Second millennium. Photograph courtesy of E. Borowski.

662. On the obverse in the upper register is a sphinx with pointed helmet. Below is a she-wolf or jackal devouring a child, whose legs are seen hanging from the animal's mouth. The reverse (not shown) has the figure of a marching god, brandishing an axe in his right hand. The amulet contains a Phoenician incantation to assist women in childbirth.

Aleppo, National Museum, 1329. Arslan Tash, purchased. Soft gypsum. Height: 0.082 m. Sixth century (du Buisson); seventh century (Albright). Mesnil du Buisson, "Une tablette magique de la région du moyen Euphrate," *Mélanges . . . Dussaud*, vol. 1, Paris, 1939, pp. 421-434. T. H. Gaster, *Orientalia*, vol. 11, 1942, pp. 41-79. W. F. Albright, *BASOR*, no. 76, 1939, pp. 5-11. Photograph from *Mélanges . . . Dussaud*, pl. opp. p. 422 (left), courtesy of Librairie Orientaliste Paul Geuthner, Paris.

663. Openwork carving of the Egyptian Bes, fitted with tenons for insertion within a frame. The dwarf figure of Bes wears the feather or palm headdress, has long hair and beard, and wings which emerge from his shoulders. He is clothed in a kilt held by a sash tied around his waist, with ends which hang to the ground. The tongue is exaggerated. (See No. 664.)

Palestine Archaeological Museum, 38.781. Megiddo. Ivory. Height: about 0.10 m. 1350-1150, according to excavator. G. Loud, *The Megiddo Ivories, OIP*, 52, Chicago, 1939, pl. 8, no. 24. Photograph courtesy of the Oriental Institute.

664. A grotesque dwarf, with shaggy beard and prominent tongue, wears a feather headdress and is holding an infant Bes, two geese, and twelve monkeys. The figure is one of the forms of the Egyptian genius Bes, the

guardian of pregnant women against evil spirits, and the protector of children and of people asleep.

University Museum, E 14358. Green faïence. Height: 0.215 m. For type see G. Daressy, *Statues de divinités*, vol. 1, *Cat. gén.*, Cairo, 1906, no. 38728. Photograph courtesy UM.

665. The two ends of the handle and the clapper are in the form of a serpent's head; the dome bears representations of a tortoise and two lizards; on the sides are represented lion-headed demons standing with upraised right hands, a human figure, and a priest wearing a fish-skin and carrying a pail. The bell was probably used to drive out the evil spirits by sound.

Berlin, VA 2517. Bronze. Height: 0.30 m. Perhaps to about 700. B. Meissner, *Babylonien und Assyrien*, vol. 1, Heidelberg, 1920, pl.-fig. 142. G. Contenau, *La magie chez les Assyriens et les Babyloniens*, Paris, 1947, p. 230, fig. 9. *AOB*, 572. Photographs courtesy of Staatliche Museen.

666. This sphinx stood beside the inner doorway of Yerkapu at Boghazköy. Two locks fall down before the shoulders in the style of the Egyptian Hathor (No. 547); the headdress is the horned miter, a Mesopotamian feature. The tail of the sphinx is raised high and ends in a spiral (see No. 761).

Istanbul. Boghazköy, Yerkapu. New Kingdom of the Hittites. K. Bittel, *Boğazköy: Die Kleinfunde, WVDOG*, 60, Leipzig, 1937, pl. 5a, pp. 7-10. Contenau, *Man.*, vol. 2, fig. 668. Bossert, *Altanatolien*, 487. Photograph courtesy of the Museum of the Ancient Orient.

MYTH AND LEGEND

667-668. Each of these statues, found in the great death pit (PG/1237) at Ur, is of a he-goat standing on his hind legs, with his forelegs fastened to the branches of a tree against which the animal is reared. Both the animal and the post, which constitutes the trunk of the tree, stand on a pedestal of silver, with panels in shell, lapis, and red limestone. From the shoulder of the goat rises a support for something which has disappeared, perhaps a table top. While the dimensions of the goats differ slightly they originally constituted a pair, suggesting the heraldic motif of two animals beside a sacred tree (Nos. 464, 672). The legs and faces of the goats are of gold, as are the trees with their leaves and flowers and the covering for the supports rising from the shoulders of the animals. The bellies of the goats are silver (now disintegrated), the horns, eyes, and shoulder fleece are of lapis; the body fleece is of separate pieces of white shell. Wood constituted the cores of the statues and their supports, but has entirely perished.

(667) British Museum, 122200. Ur, great death pit. Height: 0.465 m. Early Dynastic III, twenty-fifth century. C. L. Woolley, *The Royal Cemetery*, London, 1934, pls. 87 (color), 88, pp. 264-266. Photograph courtesy BM.

(668) University Museum, 30-12-702. Ur, great death pit. Height: 0.51 m. Early Dynastic III, twenty-fifth century. C. L. Woolley, *The Royal Cemetery*, London, 1934, pl. 89, pp. 264-266. Photograph courtesy UM.

669. Seated under a tree, a cat armed with a long knife kills the serpent Apophis. See *ANET*, 6-7 for translation of a text dealing with the repulsing of the dragon.

Thebes, tomb of Inher-kha (299). Wall painting. Ramses IV (about 1164-1157). Photograph from M. Gorce and R. Mortier, eds., *Histoire générale des religions*, vol. 1, Paris, 1948, pl. opp. p. 240, courtesy Librairie Aristide Quillet, Paris.

670. To the left are two gods, wearing the high, horned tiara, and armed with spears, swords, and clubs. The god to the right engages the serpent-dragon. See *ANET*, 125-126 for the myth of Illuyankas.

Ankara, Hittite Museum. Malatya. Limestone. Height: 0.43 m. Eighth century (or earlier, see No. 611). L. Delaporte, *Malatya: Arslantepe, I*, Paris, 1940, pl. 22, 2. E. Herzfeld, *Archaeologische Mitteilungen aus Iran*, vol. 2, Berlin, 1930, pl. 12. Bossert, *Altanatolien*, 769. A. Götze, *Kleinasien*, Munich, 1933, fig. 13. Photograph from publication by Delaporte.

671. On this small shell plaque, pierced for suspension, is depicted the contest between a god and a seven-headed fiery monster. The god kneels before the monster, which has the body of a lion and seven serpent heads. From his back are represented tongues of fire. Cf. No. 691.

Collection E. Borowski. Provenience unknown. Shell. Height: about 0.04 m. Photograph courtesy of E. Borowski.

VIII. Myth, Legend, and Ritual on Cylinder Seals

With the exception of those illustrating some specific cultural or religious feature (Nos. 86, 97, 104, 158, 196, 222, 223, 224, 238, 239, 338, 468, 525, 526, 627, 650), the impressions of cylinder seals depicting myth, legend, and ritual have been placed in this section and arranged according to the general chronological periods to which they belong. These cylinder seals have been put into this separate section, rather than distributed among other objects dealing with deities and the practice of religion as known from artifacts, monuments, bas-reliefs, etc., because seal engraving was a distinctive medium with its own canons of style and specialized function (see No. 240 for the use of the cylinder seal).

The most comprehensive work on cylinder seals is H. Frankfort, *Cylinder Seals: a Documentary Essay on the Art and Religion of the Ancient Near East*, London, 1939 (abb.: Frankfort, *CS*). A popular essay on cylinder seals is E. Porada, *Mesopotamian Art in Cylinder Seals of the Pierpont Morgan Library*, New York, 1947. For a recent discussion of some of the symbols found on seals, as well as helpful references to her previous publications, see E. D. van Buren, *Symbols of the Gods in Mesopotamian Art*, Rome, 1945, and articles in recent issues of *Orientalia*.

Since Frankfort's general study the following publications of collections of seals in museums and from excavations have appeared: A. Moortgat, *Vorderasiatische Rollsiegel: ein Beitrag zur Geschichte der Steinschneidekunst*, Berlin, 1940; E. Porada, *Seal Impressions of Nuzi, AASOR*, 24, New Haven, 1947; E. Porada (in collaboration with Briggs Buchanan), *The Collection of the Pierpont Morgan Library, Corpus of Ancient Near Eastern Seals in North American Collections*, vol. 1 (Text and Plates), Washington, 1948 (abb.: *Corpus*); L. Legrain, *Seal Cylinders, Ur Excavations*, vol. 10, London, 1951.

URUK PERIOD

672. Center: a man, dressed in skirt of lozenge pattern, wearing beard and hair tied with a fillet, holds in each hand a branch from which grow eight-petaled flowers. Goats, standing to each side, nibble at the flowers. To the left: between two symbols of the gatepost-with-streamer is a sheep, standing above two tall stone vases with narrow circular bases (see No. 502). This symbol was probably derived from a feature of the reed architecture of the early inhabitants of Mesopotamia (see E. D. van Buren, *Symbols of the Gods in Mesopotamian Art*, Rome, 1945, pp. 43-44). The bearded man in the scene may be the ruler of the city—if we may judge from the role of the king in later times—who played an active part in the ritual (Frankfort, *CS*, p. 22). For another interpretation see A. Moortgat, *Tammuz*, Berlin, 1949, p. 30. For religious rites and ritual of this period see E. D. van Buren, *AfO*, vol. 13, 1939, pp. 32-45.

Berlin, VA 10537. Vicinity of Warka, acquired in 1915. Marble seal and bronze shaft surmounted by a bronze ram which served as a handle. Height: 0.054 m.; diameter: 0.045 m. Uruk period (end of fourth millennium). A. Moortgat, *Vorderasiatische Rollsiegel*, Berlin, 1940, no. 29. Frankfort, *CS*, pl. 3a. Photograph courtesy of Staatliche Museen.

673. Boat, with prow ending in a double blossom and a stern decorated by a single leaf (?) and streamers (?), is steered by two nude and clean-shaven men, one at each end of the boat. The central figure is of a bearded man (see No. 672), dressed in a long skirt of lozenge pattern, through which the body of the man is visible, suggesting that the material was thin or almost transparent. Behind the figure stands a rectangular trellislike object, perhaps cultic. Before the man, is a bull, on whose back is a stepped object—possibly an altar in the form of a temple tower or ziggurat—surmounted by two gatepost-with-streamer symbols, the sign of Inanna (see No. 672). A. Moortgat (*Vorderasiatische Rollsiegel*, Berlin, 1940, p. 87) suggests that the bearded figure is a priest. See also No. 104 for another cultic scene involving a boat on a seal from the Uruk period.

Berlin, VA 11040. Warka, "Sammelfund." Lapis lazuli seal with a bronze shaft ending in a silver calf, which serves as a handle for the seal. Height: 0.043 m.; diameter: 0.035 m. Uruk period (end of fourth millennium). E. Heinrich, *Kleinfunde aus ... Uruk*, Berlin, 1936, pl. 17. A Moortgat, *Vorderasiatische Rollsiegel*, Berlin, 1940, no. 30. Frankfort, *CS*, pl. 3e. Photograph courtesy Staatliche Museen.

674. A bearded figure, with long hair and skirt (transparent material of lozenge pattern) reaching to the ankles, lifts an animal-shaped vase to add it to the offering already assembled: two baskets of fruits, surrounded, perhaps, by portions of meat; two low tables (?); the counterpart of the animal-vase held by the man; and two tall vases. See the Warka vase (No. 502) for similar pairs of objects offered to the deity. Behind the bearded man stands a clean-shaven and long-haired servant clad in a short skirt of lozenge design and carrying a ewer. To the extreme right are two emblems of the gatepost-with-streamer, the symbol of Inanna. For interpretations of the central figure see No. 672.

Dresden, Staatliche Skulpturensammlung, ZV 2996. Uruk period (end of fourth millennium). *ZA*, NF, vol. 7, 1933, pl. 1, 1, p. 200. Frankfort, *CS*, pl. 5c. A. Moortgat, *Die Entstehung der sumerischen Hochkultur*, Leipzig, 1945, pl. 29c. Photograph from *ZA*, NF, vol. 7, 1933, pl. 1, 1.

EARLY DYNASTIC PERIODS

675. Horned (?) figure, seated before a shrine, is drinking through a tube from a jar, over which are globes (?) and a crescent. Beyond, a human figure is prevented from drinking by a lion, which in turn is attacked by a nude figure with upturned curls. Above the entire scene are two entwined serpents, or the caduceus form. The head of one serpent touches the shrine. E. D. van Buren (*Symbols of the Gods in Mesopotamian Art*, Rome, 1945, pp. 40-42) sees in the entwined serpents a symbol of fertility. Frankfort (*CS*, p. 71, note 1) interprets the scene as the god of fertility seated before his shrine.

New York, Pierpont Morgan Library. Lapis lazuli. Height: 0.025 m.; diameter: 0.012 m. Early Dynastic II (early third millennium). *Corpus*, no. 62. Photograph courtesy PML.

676. God seated in a boat, holding an oar. The prow consists of a human figure which manipulates a punting pole (see B. Landsberger, *Die Welt des Orients*, 1950, pp. 362-366). Before the boat is a feline creature, over which is a plow and a cup; behind, a crescent (above) and a bird-man with a stick. Frankfort (*CS*, pp. 67-68) suggests that it is the sun-god depicted in Early Dynastic seals of this type, and that the god steers with a paddle the boat which moves of its own accord.

New York, Pierpont Morgan Library. Pinkish marble. Height: 0.022 m.; diameter: 0.016 m. Early Dynastic III (middle third millennium). (ED II, according to H. Frankfort, *JNES*, vol. 7, 1948, p. 273.) *Corpus*, no. 126. Photograph courtesy PML.

677. Upper register: sun-god in a boat (see No. 676). Lower register: a figure, either a ruler of the city or a god, is seated, as if to preside over the work. A row of men carrying material move toward the temple tower, where two builders, one on either side, build up the tower.

Chicago. Kish. Shell. Height: 0.028 m.; diameter: 0.0135 m. Early Dynastic III (middle third millennium). E. Mackay, *Report on the Excavation of the "A" Cemetery at Kish, Mesopotamia*, pt. 1, Chicago, 1925, pl. 6, 17. Frankfort, *CS*, pl. 14k, p. 76. E. D. van Buren, "The Building of a Temple-Tower," *RA*, vol. 46, 1952, pp. 65-74. Photograph courtesy of the Chicago Natural History Museum.

678. To the left of the central scene, a leopard attacks a horned creature, which has been seized by a lion. The body of the latter is crossed with that of another lion fighting with a bull which is held by a bull-man. At the end of the scene are two horizontals with a scorpion above and two small crossed animals below. Contest scenes of human and superhuman beings with animals and monsters are common in Mesopotamian glyptic art, and are interpreted as representing the continual conflict which raged between man and the enemies of civilized life.

New York, Pierpont Morgan Library. White marble. Height: 0.041 m.; diameter: 0.025 m. Early Dynastic III (middle third millennium). *Corpus*, no. 75. Photograph courtesy PML.

679. Upper register: two men seated on stools, drink liquid, probably beer, through straws from a jar set on a stand between them. Three extra straws are represented. Another figure sits apart with cup in hand, attended by a server. Lower register: a group of musicians consisting of a flutist, a lyrist, two other musicians, and three dancers. The lyre, supported by two smaller figures, has a sound-box shaped like a bull, and five strings (see No. 193). The three dancers are clapping their hands to the music. Frankfort (*CS*, p. 77) associates the banquet scenes of the Early Dynastic period with the cult, and more specifically with the ceremonies of the ritual marriage (see No. 680, where the jar with drinking tubes is shown next to the couch for the ritual marriage). For a drinking scene on a Syrian cylinder, see No. 158. O. E. Ravn (*Acta Orientalia*, vol. 10, 1932, pp. 1-8) considers the scene of two people drinking through tubes as a banquet for the dead.

University Museum, 30-12-2. Ur, U.12374. Lapis lazuli. Height: 0.041 m.; diameter: 0.017 m. Early Dynastic III (middle third millennium). C. L. Woolley, *The Royal Cemetery*, London, 1934, pl. 194, no. 22, p. 338. Frankfort, *CS*, pl. 15a, pp. 77-78. Photograph courtesy of the British Museum.

680. The fleece-covered couch with animal-shaped legs supports two figures consummating the ritual marriage of the god and goddess during the New Year's festival. Below the bed is a scorpion (perhaps to represent Ishhara, the goddess of love, as Frankfort, *CS*, p. 75, suggests). The figure standing at the end of the couch may depict the officiating priest. For references to related materials, both graphic and literary, see H. Frankfort, "Gods and Myths on Sargonid Seals," *Iraq*, vol. 1, 1934, pp. 8-9.

Baghdad, Iraq Museum. Tell Asmar. Limestone. Height: 0.02 m.; diameter: 0.012 m. Early Dynastic III (middle third millennium). Frankfort, *CS*, pl. 15l. *Iraq*, vol. 1, 1934, pl. 1b. Contenau, *Man.*, vol. 4, fig. 1026. Photograph courtesy of the Oriental Institute.

AKKADIAN PERIOD

For the mythological themes of the seals of the Akkadian period see H. Frankfort, "Gods and Myths on Sargonid Seals," *Iraq*, vol. 1, 1934, pp. 2-29, a pioneer attempt at a disciplined interpretation of the scenes on Akkadian seals, although in part superseded by his *CS*. The seals from the Akkadian period mark a transition in the glyptic art from the symbolic to the seen and appear to tell a story. While these scenes have tempted scholars to make identifications with the literary remains, it must be emphasized that as yet there is a high degree of uncertainty in the interpretation of these scenes. It is important to note that motifs which appear for the first time in this period continue persistently into subsequent periods.

681. Two groups of three figures each: to the right, a bearded hero wearing a hat topped by a zigzag pattern, and a short kilt, grasps the foreleg of a bull which is attacked by a lion. To the left, a human-headed bull grasps the foreleg of a long-bearded bull. Another figure, a duplicate of the latter, has been added. Below the inscription are two crossed lions. The seal belonged to Adda, major-domo of Enheduanna, daughter of Sargon.

Baghdad, Iraq Museum, 4221. Ur, U.9178. Black and white granite with copper caps. Height: 0.037 m. Akkadian period (about 2360-2180). C. L. Woolley, *The Royal Cemetery*, London, 1934, pl. 212, no. 307. Frankfort, *CS*, pl. 16a. For inscription see C. J. Gadd, *Royal Inscriptions, Ur Excavations, Texts*, 1, London, 1928, no. 272. Photograph courtesy of the British Museum.

682. Bearded hero, nude except for a belt, holds flowing vase, whose water the water-buffalo drinks. This twice repeated scene appears above a border of mountains and water. Inscription: "Shar-kali-sharri, king of Akkad, Ibni-sharrum, the scribe, thy servant" (translation of I. J. Gelb in R. A. Martin, *Ancient Seals of the Near East*, Chicago, 1940, no. 5).

Paris, Collection de Clercq. Dark jasper. Height: 0.04 m.; diameter: 0.027 m. Akkadian period (about 2360-2180). Shar-kalisharri was fifth king of the Dynasty of Akkad. Collection de Clercq, *Catalogue méthodique et raisonné*, vol. 1, Paris, 1888, no. 46. Frankfort, *CS*, pl. 17c. Photograph JBP.

683. The sun-god (Shamash), holding a saw in his right hand, and with rays coming out from his shoulders, stands between two mountains and places one foot on the mountain to his right. At each side a divine attendant opens the wings of the gate. To the left, is a god holding behind him a mace. For listing of the frequently recurring scene of the sun-god's ascension see E. D. van Buren, *Symbols of the Gods in Mesopotamian Art*, Rome, 1945, pp. 179-181.

New York, Pierpont Morgan Library. Black serpentine. Height: 0.0405 m.; diameter: 0.028 m. Akkadian period (about 2360-2180). *Corpus*, no. 178. Photograph courtesy PML.

684. Ea, the god of wisdom and of water, sits enthroned within his shrine entirely surrounded by streams of water which meet at the four corners of the shrine. Before the shrine as a suppliant stands the sun-god climbing what may be an artificial mountain with temple—perhaps a ziggurat (*ziqqurrat*). Behind him stands another solar deity, also represented with rays emerging from the shoulders, and holding a saw. Either he stands on the back of a lion or between two wings; one foot is poised on the shoulder of a smaller divine figure. To the left of the lion a nude, bearded figure kneels, with one arm around a pole which ends in a standard. Frankfort suggests the likelihood that the crouching deity beside the lion is Ninurta (*CS*, pp. 102-103).

Baghdad, Iraq Museum 14577. Ur, 9750. Dark green steatite with copper caps. Height: 0.036 m.; diameter: 0.024 m. Akkadian period (about 2360-2180). C. L. Woolley, *The Royal Cemetery*, London, 1934, pl. 215, no. 364. Frankfort, *CS*, pl. 18k, pp. 102-103. Photograph courtesy of the British Museum.

685. From between two mountains rises the sun-god with rays springing from his shoulders and holding a saw in his left hand. To the right stands Ea, symbolized

by a stream of flowing water in which fish swim. He is followed by his two-headed minister. Above and to the left of Ea is a bird, perched on his hand, somehow connected with the drama of liberation. On the mountain of the sun-god stands a winged goddess, from whose shoulders grow branches ending in leaves or fruit—obviously a goddess of vegetation—and in whose hand is a bunch of dates (see No. 505). To the left of the goddess of vegetation a branch grows out of the mountain from which the sun-god is being liberated. The god to the extreme left of the scene holds a bow and is accompanied by a lion. According to Frankfort (*CS*, p. 107), this is probably Ninurta. The bull under the figure of Ea is taken by Frankfort as an associate of the sun-god and to refer specifically to the later Marduk, the "young bull of the sun."

British Museum, 89115. Green stone. Height: 0.038 m.; diameter 0.025 m. Akkadian period (about 2360-2180). Frankfort, *CS*, pl. 19a, pp. 105-108. Photograph courtesy BM.

686. The sun-god, holding a plow, sits in a boat with human prow (one leg showing). Before the boat is another deity, who holds by a leash a quadruped, about whose neck is a bucket. Above, a goddess is seated on a birdlike throne. Possibly the scene is intended to suggest some connection between the sun-god and the plowing and planting of seed (contained in the bucket). Other jars and vessels are found in the field. Frankfort (*CS*, pp. 109-110) interprets the boating scenes as referring to the sun's passing through the underworld at night. See B. Landsberger, *Die Welt des Orients*, 1950, pp. 362-366, for discussion of the boat-god Sirsir.

Baghdad, 11497. Height: about 0.036 m. Akkadian period (about 2360-2180). Frankfort, *CS*, pl. 19f. Photograph courtesy of the Iraq Museum.

687. Enthroned water-god Ea holds flowing vase, with crescent in the sky. Approaching are a two-faced god (also an attendant of Ea in No. 685), a god carrying a branch attached to a curved stick held over his shoulder, and a god carrying a mace from which is suspended a bird-man. This is one of several examples of the theme of the bird-man brought by his captors before Ea.

New York, Pierpont Morgan Library. Black serpentine. Height: 0.0325 m.; diameter: 0.0195 m. Akkadian period (about 2360-2180). *Corpus*, 198. Frankfort, *CS*, pl. 23d, pp. 133-135. See P. Amiet, "L'homme-oiseau dans l'art mésopotamien," *Orientalia*, vol. 21, 1952, pp. 149-167. Photograph courtesy PML.

688. Left to right: god with stalks of grain sprouting from his skirt and three stalks in his hands, a god with a plow, and a god with extended hands approach the principal deity enthroned on a heap of grain and holding stalks of grain in his right hand as others sprout from his shoulders.

New York, Pierpont Morgan Library. Black serpentine. Height: 0.035 m.; diameter: 0.025 m. Akkadian period (about 2360-2180). *Corpus*, 207. Photograph courtesy PML.

689. To the left, a worshiper pours a libation over an altar in the shape of a shrine (see No. 591 for example

found at Ashur). The weather-god is mounted in a four-wheeled chariot drawn by a lion-griffin, on which stands a goddess holding bundles of rain.

New York, Pierpont Morgan Library. Shell. Height: 0.0335 m.; diameter: 0.02 m. Akkadian period (about 2360-2180). *Corpus*, 220. Frankfort, *CS*, pl. 22a. Photograph courtesy PML.

690. To the left of the building, which is in the process of construction, a man hacks up the soil and makes it into mortar as another carries it in a basket on his head to the top of the tower, where a mason waits to receive it. On the opposite side of the building a worker pitches bricks to his companion at the top. In the center of the scene a god dispatches a victim with his mace, while another deity stands with upraised hands. Before the latter, in the upper register, is a man making bricks in a mold. Cf. *ANET*, 68, lines 49-58, as a possible reference to scene.

Private Collection. Akkadian period (about 2360-2180). *AfO*, vol. 6, 1930, pl. 3, 2. Frankfort, *CS*, pl. 22k, p. 131. Photograph from Frankfort, *CS*.

691. A seven-headed dragon is attacked in front by a god with attendant, and from behind by another god with a smaller follower. Three of the heads of the dragon are alive and fighting, while four heads hang limp and defeated. Flames are seen arising from the back of the dragon. For similar representation see Nos. 670, 671.

Baghdad, Iraq Museum. Tell Asmar, 32/738. Gray stone. Height: 0.032 m.; diameter: 0.022 m. Akkadian period (about 2360-2180). Frankfort, *CS*, pl. 23j, p. 122. Photograph courtesy of the Oriental Institute. *Asag (water)*

692. A serpent-god (but without horned cap) faces a goddess (?), who leads worshiper. Behind the chthonic deity is a gate, presumably his shrine.

New York, Pierpont Morgan Library. Black serpentine. Height: 0.03 m.; diameter: 0.016 m. Akkadian period (about 2360-2180). *Corpus*, 217. Photograph courtesy PML.

693. The water-god Ea sits within a frame representing his shrine, holding a vase from which water flows. Reaching into the shrine to touch the hand of the water-god stands a two-faced god. He is followed by a bearded hero, nude save for a belt, who stands holding a gatepost. A similar figure stands with gatepost behind the shrine. A worshiper, clad in a long garment, raises his left hand to his mouth. Inscription: "God Gu."

New York, Pierpont Morgan Library. Black serpentine with calcite vein. Height: 0.03 m.; diameter: 0.019 m. Akkadian period (about 2360-2180). *Corpus*, 202. Photograph courtesy PML.

694. Man astride an eagle in the sky, over two sitting sheep dogs. At each side stands a shepherd: the one at the left holds a whip and a pail; the one at the right rests on a stick, and is followed by a ram and three sheep. Above the group are a rectangle of criss-crossed design, two men, each on one knee, and a large vessel between them. In the sky is a crescent. At the sides of the eagle are a small vessel (?) and a large jar. The

scene was probably intended to suggest the myth of the shepherd Etana (*ANET*, 114-118).

New York, Pierpont Morgan Library. Black serpentine. Height: 0.0365 m.; diameter: 0.028 m. Akkadian period (about 2360-2180). *Corpus*, 236. Photograph courtesy PML.

695. Man is being carried by an eagle (here with lion's head) into the sky. Below the eagle is a kneeling figure with arms upraised, flanked by two dogs gazing upward. To the left is a man who holds his hand to his mouth in a gesture of amazement. Above him are the figures of a small seated deity and a man leaping. In the left half of the scene is a shepherd coming out of a gate with a goat and two sheep. Above him is another figure sitting before a large vessel, perhaps a churn (cf. Nos. 97-99). Several vessels and other objects are distributed in the field. For Etana myth see *ANET*, 114-118.

Berlin, VA 3456. Serpentine. Height: 0.0405 m.; diameter: 0.0269 m. Akkadian period (about 2360-2180). A. Moortgat, *Vorderasiatische Rollsiegel*, Berlin, 1940, no. 234. Photograph courtesy of Staatliche Museen.

696. To the left, a nude, bearded hero, with belt around his waist, is subduing a water-buffalo; to the right, a bull-man is fighting a lion. Between, is a stylized tree standing on a knoll. The scene is typical of the contest scenes of this period, where the stress is on the physical appearance of the superhuman heroes of the myths.

New York, Pierpont Morgan Library. Greenish-black serpentine. Height: 0.036 m.; diameter: 0.025 m. Akkadian period (about 2360-2180). *Corpus*, 159. Photograph courtesy PML.

697. Seated on a throne, the back of which ends in the head of a snake, indicating his ophidian aspect, is a god who holds a plow. Before him stands another god, who leads a worshiper carrying a lamb. Between the latter figures are a pick-axe, a dagger, and a club; above, is a star surrounded by globes, indicating smaller astral bodies. Behind the seated god are a weapon with curved blade, a mountain, on which a tree grows, and a mountain goat. The principal god is a deity of agriculture.

Berlin, VA 243. Serpentine. Height: 0.034 m.; diameter: 0.02 m. Akkadian period (about 2360-2180). A. Moortgat, *Vorderasiatische Rollsiegel*, Berlin, 1940, no. 204. Frankfort, *CS*, pl. 20d. Photograph courtesy of Staatliche Museen.

698. Enthroned goddess, with upraised mace, faces worshiper, who carries a kid and pours a libation over the flaming altar. Behind him are two identically clad female worshipers, one of whom carries a pail and the other supports an object on the palm of her hand. Behind the latter is a plant. A star accompanies the seated goddess; a crescent appears over the altar. For a discussion of the motif of a worshiper with a kid and listing of other examples see A. Parrot, "Le 'bon pasteur' à propos d'une statue de Mari," *Mélanges . . . Dussaud*, vol. I, Paris, 1939, pp. 171-182, esp. pp. 176-178.

New York, Pierpont Morgan Library. Black serpentine. Height: 0.037 m.; diameter: 0.025 m. Akkadian period (about 2360-2180). *Corpus*, 245. Photograph courtesy PML.

699. A god, holding a curved sword in his left hand and a mace, flanked by two branches ending in feline heads, in his right, stands with one foot resting upon the body of a human figure lying upon a mountain. Nine column of an inscription contain a dedication to Nergal, with whom the god has been identified.

Baghdad, 15218. Larsa. Steatite. Height: 0.042 m.; diameter: 0.027 m. Akkadian period (about 2360-2180). *Sumer*, vol. 7, 1951, pp. 66-68. E. D. van Buren, *Symbols of the Gods*, Rome, 1945, pp. 177-178. Photograph courtesy of the Iraq Museum.

UR III PERIOD AND LATER

700. A worshiper is being led by a goddess into the presence of an enthroned god. Before the god are a star-disc within a crescent, a staff, and a vase. Placed above a kneeling bull is a three-column inscription: "Ur-Nusku son of Kaka, merchant."

New York, Pierpont Morgan Library. Jasper. Height: 0.032 m.; diameter: 0.02 m. Ur III period (about 2060-1955). *Corpus*, 277. Photograph courtesy PML.

701. A worshiper is led by a minor goddess to an enthroned king, who holds a cup in his outstretched hand. Above is a star-disc in a crescent; between the worshiper and the goddess is a scorpion. This representation of the king as a god reflects the custom of the Akkadian, Ur III, and certain other periods to endow the kings with some of the attributes of divinity. Inscription: "Ibbi-Sin, mighty king, king of Ur, Ur-Sakkud . . . (is) your servant."

New York, Pierpont Morgan Library. Black steatite. Height: 0.025 m.; diameter: 0.0135 m. Ur III period (about 2060-1955). *Corpus*, 292. On the moot problem of deification of kings see H. Frankfort, *Kingship and the Gods*, Chicago, 1948, pp. 295 ff. For a recent denial of deification of kings in Ur III see T. Fish, *Bulletin of the John Rylands Library*, vol. 34, 1951, pp. 42-43. Photograph courtesy PML.

702. To the left a god stands with his foot on a gazelle, holding a crescent standard in his hand. Before him are a worshiper and a smaller seated figure of a goddess holding a curved staff—probably the consort of the god. The curved staff also appears in the field between the god and worshiper. The accompanying text names "Amurru, son of Anu," who has been identified with the figure of the god.

Paris, Bibliothèque Nationale. Hematite. Height: 0.021 m.; diameter: 0.011 m. First Dynasty of Babylon (1830-1530). L. Delaporte, *Catalogue des cylindres orientaux*, vol. 2, Paris, 1923, A.317. Frankfort, *CS*, pl. 28e, pp. 164-165. Photograph from Delaporte.

703. A nude female appears above a bull carrying a double-pronged lightning-fork; to the right stands a worshiper. The inscription bears the names of the deities Adad and Shala.

New York, Pierpont Morgan Library. Amethyst. Height: 0.018 m.; diameter: 0.0075 m. First Dynasty of Babylon (1830-1530). *Corpus*, 506. Photograph courtesy PML.

704. A suppliant goddess and a god with mace appear

before the war-goddess, who stands with her foot on a crouching lion. Over her shoulders are two quivers with arrows; in her right hand she holds the staff composed of a mace and two feline heads (see No. 699); in her left hand is the curved sword (?). The representation is probably intended for Ishtar (cf. Nos. 525, 526).

New York, Pierpont Morgan Library. Dark green jasper. Height: 0.0325 m.; diameter: 0.0195 m. First Dynasty of Babylon (1830-1530). *Corpus*, 371. Photograph courtesy PML.

705. Above, in the center, is a winged sun-disc supported by a post and flanked by two lions and two birds. Below is a winged human figure holding in each hand a lion by a hind leg. To each side is a nude human figure, wearing a trifoliate crown and a long lock of hair down the back, and holding an animal. To the upper left, another figure is in conflict with an animal; to the right, a long-robed figure stands with upraised hands. In the field are animals, a star, and a grotesque human head. Inscription (showing only the last of three lines): "Saushshattar, son of Parsashatar, king of Maitani."

Cambridge, Mass., Harvard Semitic Museum. Nuzi. Impression on clay tablet. Height: about 0.085 m. Fifteenth century. R. F. S. Starr, *Nuzi*, vol. 2, Cambridge, Mass., 1937, pl. 118, I. Frankfort, *CS*, pl. 42a. For text: R. H. Pfeiffer, *The Archives of Shilwateshub Son of the King, Excavations at Nuzi*, vol. 2, Cambridge, Mass., 1932, pl. 1. Photograph courtesy of Harvard Semitic Museum.

706. Hero, with bow and quiver over his back and curved sword in right hand, grasps an ostrich, which kicks at him. A worshiper with cupped hands stands before a sacred tree flanked by two fish-men with buckets. Above the tree is the winged sun-disc with human figure (cf. No. 536).

New York, Pierpont Morgan Library. Carnelian. Height: 0.037 m.; diameter: 0.017 m. Eighth-ninth century. *Corpus*, 773. Photograph courtesy PML.

IX. *Views and Plans of Excavations*

GENERAL

707. General view of the caves at Wadi el-Mugharah, on the western slope of Carmel, eighteen miles south of Haifa, at the close of excavations in 1934. Excavations of these prehistoric caves were carried on in seven seasons from 1929 to 1934. The cave to the left is Mugharet el-Wad; the opening with a stone wall in front is Mugharet ej-Jamal; the cave to the right, with dump in front, is Mugharet et-Tabūn.

Publication of results: D. A. E. Garrod and D. M. A. Bate, *The Stone Age of Mount Carmel: Excavations of the Wady el-Mughara*, vol. 1, Oxford, 1937; T. D. McCown and Sir Arthur Keith, *The Stone Age of Mount Carmel: The Fossil Human Remains from the Levalloiso-Mousterian*, vol. 2, Oxford, 1939. For popular presentation of results see C. C. McCown, *The Ladder of Progress in Palestine*, New York, 1943, pp. 23-53. Photograph courtesy of the Palestine Archaeological Museum.

708. Tell el-Mutesellim, the ancient Megiddo (Armageddon), was excavated by the Deutsche Orient-Gesellschaft, 1903-1905, and by the Oriental Institute of the University of Chicago, 1925-1939. The areas AA, BB, and CC are the trenches, each originally about 6 meters wide and 50-70 meters long, which were dug in the final seasons at Megiddo. CC was abandoned, AA and BB were expanded in area, and BB was carried down in the eastern portion to bedrock (stratum XX). Photograph of June, 1937.

Photograph courtesy of the Oriental Institute, from The Megiddo Expedition, *Megiddo II*, Text, *OIP*, 62, Chicago, 1948, frontispiece.

709. An air view of the mound of the ancient town of Byblos, on the shore of the Mediterranean, with the modern village nearby. From Byblos have come: the sarcophagus of Ahiram (Nos. 456-459), stela of Yehawmilk (No. 477), and bronze plaque (No. 287). Known also as Gebal (Josh. 13:5; Ezek. 27:9).

Photograph courtesy of M. Dunand.

710. Air view of the mound of ancient Susa, in Iran. This Elamite capital, excavated by the French Délégation en Perse (beginning in 1897 and continuing until 1939), has yielded many important Mesopotamian monuments, which had been carried away to Elam as trophies of war in ancient times, as well as other important materials from prehistoric to Arab times. Noteworthy are: stela of Hammurabi (Nos. 244, 246, 515), stela of victory of Naram-Sin (No. 309), *kudurru's* (Nos. 520-521), and Nos. 30, 144, 307, 602, 619. Susa is biblical Shushan (Neh. 1:1; Dan. 8:2; Esth. 1:2, 5, etc.). For brief history of exploration and excavation of Susa, see A. Parrot, *Archéologie mésopotamienne, Les étapes*, Paris, 1946, pp. 170-174.

Photograph from E. F. Schmidt, *Flights over Ancient Cities of Iran*, Chicago, 1940, pl. 55, courtesy of the Oriental Institute.

WALLS, GATES, AND FORTIFICATIONS

711. The city wall to the left measures almost 8 meters in width (originally it had been but 4-5 meters wide, but an additional buttress was added), stands to a height of more than 4 meters, and is greater in section than any other city wall found at Megiddo. No finished top surface was found; the faces are of rubble laid in horizontal courses. The wall belongs to stratum XVIII, which is dated to 3000-2500 by the excavators.

The Megiddo Expedition, *Megiddo II*, Text, *OIP*, 62, Chicago, 1948, fig. 153, pp. 64-70. Photograph courtesy of the Oriental Institute.

712. A series of rubble steps lead up, along the outside face of a mud-brick wall with battered stone foundation, to the city gate, which turns sharply to the left at an angle of ninety degrees. The gate itself is a single chamber entered from the widened upper part of the approach. This sharp turn of the entrance afforded the defenders of the city considerable advantage in an attack.

Drawing from The Megiddo Expedition, *Megiddo II*, Text, *OIP*, 62, Chicago, 1948, fig. 8. Gate belongs to stratum XIII, in area AA, dated by excavators to 1800-1750.

713. A Middle Bronze gateway at Shechem, measuring approximately 18 by 16 meters, was composed of three pairs of massive piers guarding the access to the city, which must have been had by a ramp leading up from the valley outside. Inside the wall is a Late Bronze temple constructed of massive walls (5.30 m. thick) and measuring 21 meters wide by 25 meters long. In the interior there had been two rows of columns, each row containing three columns.

Drawing from *ZDPV*, vol. 64, 1941, no. 1, pl. 1, courtesy of Otto Harrassowitz, Leipzig. See also *ZDPV*, vol. 49, 1926, pl. 33; Albright, *AP*, pp. 88-89, 104.

714. Plan of the fortifications at Jericho uncovered by the excavations of Sellin and Watzinger (1907-1909) and Garstang (1930-1936) as interpreted by Kathleen M. Kenyon after her excavation of 1952. The innermost structure is the Early Bronze city wall; the outer is the Middle Bronze fosse; between is part of the Middle Bronze glacis. A trench cutting all three of these represents the work of the 1952 season.

Drawing from *BASOR*, no. 127, October 1952, fig. 1, courtesy of Kathleen M. Kenyon.

715. A massive city wall, belonging to the Middle Bronze period at Jericho, was composed of a base of polygonal masonry, a bulging face on the outside, and a superstructure of mud-brick.

Photograph courtesy of the Palestine Archaeological Museum. E. Sellin and C. Watzinger, *Jericho*, *WVDOG*, 22, Leipzig, 1913, pl. 12a. See Watzinger, *Denk.*, pl. 26, fig. 57; Albright, *AP*, pl. 14, p. 88.

716-717. On the east side of Tell en-Nasbeh the wall coming from the south overlapped the wall from the north for a distance of 10 meters, leaving a gap of 9.15 meters between the two. Into the southern end of this space was built the gate to the city, leaving 4.50 meters outside as an extramural area. The gate itself (width of gate entrances: 4.25 m.) had two pairs of doorjambs, one behind the other, but only the outer pair was supplied with gates. On each of the outer jambs were sockets for the pivots of the two leaves of the gate. Stone benches were in place along the walls of the extramural space and in the two "guard rooms" lying between the two pairs of jambs. The gate stop, against which the gates pressed when closed, was still in place and can be seen in the photograph.

Photograph courtesy of the Palestine Institute, Berkeley. See C. C. McCown, *Tell en-Naṣbeh*, vol. 1, Berkeley, 1947, pp. 195-199. Plan courtesy Palestine Institute.

718. This wall was believed by the excavators to have been the foundation of the fortification around one of the main gates of Samaria in the ninth century. The stones are drafted, with margin on three sides, and headers alternate with a pair of stretchers.

Photograph courtesy of the Palestine Archaeological Museum. See J. W. Crowfoot, K. M. Kenyon, E. L. Sukenik, *The Buildings at Samaria*, London, 1942, pl. 32, 2, pp. 18-20.

719. An eleventh-century fortress at Tell el-Ful (belonging to the time of Saul), preserved only in one corner, consisted of two shells, each constructed of hammer-dressed masonry, laid in rough courses, the outer being about 1.50 m. thick, the inner about 1.20 m. Between the two were a series of long chambers, some filled with stones and earth, others empty, probably serving as storerooms connected by doorways with the interior.

Drawing from *BASOR*, no. 52, 1933, fig. 1. See W. F. Albright, *Excavations and Results at Tell el-Fûl (Gibeah of Saul)*, *AASOR*, vol. 4, New Haven, 1924; Albright, *AP*, pp. 120-122.

720. This Hellenistic round tower at Samaria, having a diameter of 13 meters, belongs to the same period (about 300) as the two towers found in the earlier excavations by the Harvard Expedition (but considered then to belong to the reign of Jeroboam II). Nineteen courses of the masonry are preserved at one point.

Photograph courtesy of the Palestine Archaeological Museum. See J. W. Crowfoot, K. M. Kenyon, E. L. Sukenik, *The Buildings at Samaria*, London, 1942, pl. 36, 2, pp. 24-26.

721. Doorjambs project about 1 meter into the passage between two flanking towers in line with the city wall, leaving a passageway of about 4.25 m. South of these towers are three pairs of evenly spaced piers, which formed additional doorways of the same width as the entrance. Between the piers are chambers approximately 3 by 5 meters. To judge from one door socket found just inside the northernmost passageway, double doors pivoted on the inner corners of the jambs and folded back into the adjacent side chambers. Well-formed pavement surrounding the other piers precluded the possibility that door sockets had been at these points also. While the excavators place this gateway in stratum IV (tenth-ninth centuries), W. F. Albright and G. E. Wright (*JAOS*, vol. 70, 1950, p. 59) consider it a part of IVB-VA (± 975-925, according to Wright). Similarity between this plan and the description in Ezek. 40:5-16 has been noted by C. G. Howie in *BASOR*, no. 117, 1950, pp. 13-19.

Drawing from The Megiddo Expedition, *Megiddo II*, Text, *OIP*, 62, Chicago, 1948, fig. 389 (right half); see pp. 46-57.

HOUSES

722. Although this clay object was probably intended to receive the bones of the deceased, it is shaped like a house and may represent the pile-dwellings of the Chalcolithic period in Palestine.

Palestine Archaeological Museum. Khudeirah, in the Plain of Sharon, 7 km. southeast of Caesarea. Clay. Height: 0.54 m. Chalcolithic period. E. L. Sukenik, *JPOS*, vol. 17, 1937, frontispiece, pp. 21-22, pl. 3. Albright, *AP*, fig. 11, pp. 68-69. Photograph courtesy PAM.

723. A large open court, measuring 11.70 by 6.20 meters, and equipped with a shallow basin nearly 2 meters in diameter, formed a part of a patrician house of six rooms at Tell Beit Mirsim. Quantities of storage jars were found in rooms 1 and 4, indicating that they may have been storerooms. It was thought by excavator that this building of stratum D may have been constructed in the late seventeenth century.

Drawing from W. F. Albright, *The Excavation of Tell Beit Mirsim, Vol. II, The Bronze Age, AASOR*, 17, New Haven, 1938, pl. 55; see pp. 35-39.

724. A Middle Bronze house at Tell Beit Mirsim consisted of long hall, with post supports, measuring 4.50 meters wide and probably 11.20 meters long, with three adjoining rooms. Walls, averaging 0.80 meter in thickness, were of mud-brick on stone substructure and could have supported a second story for living purposes. Stratum G (nineteenth century).

Drawing from W. F. Albright, *The Excavation of Tell Beit Mirsim, Vol. II, The Bronze Age, AASOR*, 17, New Haven, 1938, pl. 56; see pp. 20-22.

725. A group of poorly built houses at Tell en-Nasbeh from the Iron II period (ninth-early sixth centuries), excavated in 1927, illustrate the simplicity—even poverty—of the construction during this period. Cisterns (indicated by dotted lines) appear in several of the houses.

Drawing from C. C. McCown, *Tell en-Naṣbeh*, vol. 1, Berkeley, 1947, fig. 54 (upper); see pp. 215-217; courtesy of the Palestine Institute.

726. A tenth-century palace at Megiddo (stratum IVB), measuring 23 by 21.5 meters, was constructed of solid ashlar masonry (although most of the superstructure has been destroyed). The building had a projection along the northern end of the east face, consisting of a rubble platform edged by a row of roughly squared stones. Walls measured about 1.50 meters in thickness. W. F. Albright dates building to latter half of tenth century (*BA*, vol. 13, 1950, p. 42). On date see also G. E. Wright, *JAOS*, vol. 70, 1950, pp. 59-60.

Photograph courtesy of Oriental Institute. R. S. Lamon and G. M. Shipton, *Megiddo I, OIP*, 42, Chicago, 1939, fig. 21, pp. 17-24.

727. Characteristic of the many private houses of the period immediately before the Exile are these two from Tell Beit Mirsim A. A row of three or four stone pillars (sometimes interpreted as cultic objects) set along the axis of a large room may have served as support for the ceiling of part of the room, leaving the other part open to the sky. Well-preserved staircases led to a second story. The irregular shape of the houses was due to the necessity of fitting the plan into the surrounding buildings.

Drawing from W. F. Albright, *The Excavation of Tell Beit Mirsim, Vol. III, The Iron Age, AASOR*, vols. 21-22, New Haven, 1943, fig. 3; see pp. 49-55.

728. A Persian villa, excavated on the summit of the

mound at Tell ed-Duweir (Lachish), is dated to the late fifth or early fourth century (Albright, *AP*, p. 145). Rooms surround a large inner court, from which three steps lead up to the principal hall of the house. Further to the south is another large hall, from which entrances lead to smaller rooms to the three sides. To the west of the court is another hall, separated by columns from the court.

Drawing from C. Watzinger, *Denkmäler Palästinas*, vol. 2, Leipzig, 1935, pl. 1, fig. 17; see pp. 4-5. See also O. Tufnell, *Lachish III*, London, 1953, pl. 119; J. L. Starkey, *PEFQS*, 1933, pls. 3, 4, pp. 190-199.

TEMPLES AND OTHER PUBLIC BUILDINGS

729. At Megiddo a broad-room type of structure, about 4 meters wide, was found built against a thick mud-brick wall, which varied in width from 2.80 to 3.20 meters. Opposite the entrance and against the thick wall was an altar, originally rectangular and 0.55 meter high, but which had been covered over completely by the larger altar shown in the photograph. Within the structure are a number of flat stones set in the floor, but whose function is unknown. Structure dated by excavators to Chalcolithic period (3300-3000), but placed by G. E. Wright (*JAOS*, vol. 70, 1950, p. 57) and by W. F. Albright (*AP*, p. 76) in Early Bronze I (about 3000).

Photograph courtesy of the Oriental Institute. See The Megiddo Expedition, *Megiddo II*, Text, *OIP*, 62, Chicago, 1948, fig. 139, pp. 61-63.

730. Corner of a small shrine found at Ai. In an inner room (room with meter stick), was found an altar, which measures 1.70 by 0.70 meters, made of stone and plastered. Five flat stones, painted red, formed a small niche, in which was found a red goblet. Fragments of alabaster bowls were found in the vicinity of the altar. W. F. Albright (*AP*, p. 76) suggests a date of the twenty-sixth century.

Photograph courtesy of the Palestine Archaeological Museum. See J. Marquet-Krause, "La deuxième campagne de fouilles à Ay (1934)," *Syria*, vol. 16, 1935, pp. 329-336.

731. General view of structure III at Tell ed-Duweir (Lachish), looking southwest, with pit 176 in right foreground. The main room of the temple, measuring 10 by 10.4 meters, was built of rough stones. In the upper left-hand corner steps led to a platform of mud-brick with an altar directly in front of it. To the right are clay benches, possibly used for holding offerings, around which broken pottery was found in profusion. Dated by excavators to 1325-1223.

Photograph courtesy of the Palestine Archaeological Museum. See O. Tufnell, C. H. Inge, L. Harding, *Lachish II*, London, 1940, pl. 10, 2. *PEFQS*, October 1934, pl. 5, fig. 1.

732. General view of the southern temple of Beth-shan IX, measuring about 39 meters in length from south to north, called the temple of Mekal from the stela found there (No. 487). The walls are of mud-brick laid on stone foundations. Originally dated by excavator to the fifteenth century; now generally dated to fourteenth century (Albright, *AP*, p. 104).

Photograph courtesy of the Palestine Archaeological Museum. See A. Rowe, *The Topography and History of Beth-shan*, Philadelphia, 1930, pl. 16, 1, pp. 10-14.

733. This broad-room type of building at Ai, measuring 20 by 6.50 meters, built of regular courses of hammer-dressed masonry, has along its long axis four rectangular bases of cut stone, perhaps the supports for pillars. The structure has been called a palace and a temple (Albright, *AP*, p. 76, where it is dated to the twenty-sixth century).

Drawing from *BA*, vol. 7, 1944, p. 71. See J. Marquet-Krause, "La deuxième campagne de fouilles à Ay (1934)" *Syria*, vol. 16, 1935, pl. 50, pp. 327-329.

734. These three megaron-type buildings are of similar plan, consisting of an inner altar-room with entrance on the broad side and a columned porch across the front. The altar chambers are approximately 9 by 14 meters. The altar in the central temple is of mud-brick, while the temple to the left has an altar of stone, almost square (about 2.20 by 2.60 meters) and standing 1.05 meters high. To the back of the temple, at the left, is a great altar of stones and rubble, built earlier, but used during the time of the three temples. While excavators dated stratum XV to Middle Bronze I (1950-1850), others have placed strata XV-XIII in Middle Bronze IIA and dated the structures to the nineteenth-eighteenth centuries (G. E. Wright, *JAOS*, vol. 70, 1950, p. 58).

Drawing from The Megiddo Expedition, *Megiddo II*, Text, *OIP*, 62, Chicago, 1948, fig. 181; see pp. 78-84.

735. The temple in its earliest phase (left) measured 21.50 by 16.50 meters and contained but a single room with a niche. At each side of the doorway there are protruding wings or towers of different widths. The general plan and the thick walls are similar to those of the temple at Shechem (No. 713). The heavy walls may indicate a building of two or more stories. Excavators date strata VIII-VII to 1479-1150; W. F. Albright lowers strata VIII-VIIA to about 1400-1150 (*AP*, p. 103).

Drawing from The Megiddo Expedition, *Megiddo II*, Text, *OIP*, 62, Chicago, 1948, fig. 247; see pp. 102-104.

736. A temple, measuring about 19.50 by 11.22 meters, had walls of mud-brick, all of which, with the exception of the eastern wall, rest upon layers of undressed basalt stones, 0.60 to 0.80 meters in height. In this building was found the rectangular shrine model (No. 590). Dated by excavator to 1198-1167, but date should be lowered to eleventh century.

Photograph of model, courtesy University Museum. See A. Rowe, *The Four Canaanite Temples at Beth-shan*, Philadelphia, 1940, pls. 12, 55A, no. 2; pp. 31-32, and fig. 9 for suggested reconstruction.

737. This temple, built of brick walls resting in debris, is about 14.85 meters long, exclusive of anteroom, and from 13.25 to 14.20 meters wide. The entrance is through an anteroom into a large court, surrounded on three sides by a low bench. At the northern end was a brick altar and steps leading to an upper room, which contained an altar with sloping top. Opposite the anteroom is a storeroom, with door leading off the court. Floor was of hard clay, approximately 0.10 m. thick. City-level VII, dated by excavator to 1411-1314, has been lowered to the thirteenth century by others (Albright, *AP*, p. 104).

Photograph of model, courtesy University Museum. See A. Rowe, *The Four Canaanite Temples of Beth-shan*, Philadelphia, 1940, pls. 6, 43A, no. 2; pp. 6-10.

738. Almost identical in external plan to No. 737 is this temple built over the older one. Walls are of brick. Length, exclusive of anteroom, is 14.65 meters; width is from about 12.67 to 14.55 meters. The arrangements of the steps, and the altar in the altar-room are different. Beth-shan VI, dated by excavator to 1313-1198, should be lowered to the twelfth century.

Photograph of model, courtesy University Museum. See A. Rowe, *The Four Canaanite Temples of Beth-shan*, Philadelphia, 1940, pls. 8, 50A, no. 2; pp. 13-20.

739. An isometric plan, drawn by H. D. Hill, of the residence (to right) and the royal chapel at Tell Tainat in Syria, which suggests the form of the Solomonic temple in Jerusalem. Eighth century.

Photograph courtesy of the Oriental Institute. See *AJSL*, vol. 52, 1935, pp. 65-66; *Oriental Institute Bulletin*, no. 1, 1937, p. 13; *AJA*, vol. 41, 1937, p. 9, fig. 4.

740. Suggested plan of the temple of Solomon, based on the descriptions in the book of Kings as well as upon details suggested by archaeological discoveries.

Drawing courtesy Paul Leslie Garber. See C. Watzinger, *Denkmäler Palästinas*, vol. 1, Leipzig, 1933, fig. 39, pp. 89 ff.; G. E. Wright, *BA*, vol. 4, 1941, pp. 17-31; P. L. Garber, *BA*, vol. 14, 1951, pp. 2-24.

MISCELLANEOUS

741-742. The northern stable compound of Area C (stable 364), consisted of five units, each accommodating about 24 horses. In each unit was a center passage, about 2.50 meters wide, flanked on each side by rows of pillars serving as supports for the roof and as hitching-posts. Between the pillars were mangers; to each side of the central passageway were stalls for the horses. The capacity of this compound and those found in Area A was from between 450 and 480 horses. Stratum IV (1000-800, according to excavators; Wright, *JAOS*, vol. 70, 1950, pp. 59-60, suggests that the building of the stables took place in VA-IVB, which he dates to ± 975-925). See I Kings 9:15, 19, etc.

Photographs courtesy of the Oriental Institute. See R. S. Lamon and G. M. Shipton, *Megiddo I, OIP*, 42, Chicago, 1939, figs. 51, 53, pp. 41-47.

743. This storage pit, found in stratum III at Megiddo, and measuring about 7 meters deep and 11 meters in diameter at the top, had a capacity approximately of 12,800 bushels. At the sides were two winding stairs. Chaff and grain were found in the chinks between the rubble stones out of which its walls were built; it had not been plastered. Stratum dated by excavators to 780-650.

Photograph courtesy of the Oriental Institute. See R. S. Lamon and G. M. Shipton, *Megiddo I, OIP*, 42, Chicago, 1939, fig. 77, pp. 66-68.

744. The Siloam tunnel, identified as having been cut by Hezekiah (II Kings 20:20 and II Chron. 32:30) and containing an inscription in the rock wall (No. 238), found in 1880, was cut to bring water from a spring outside of the city of Jerusalem to a pool within. Width: 0.58-0.65 meters; height: mostly over 1.45 meters; length: 512.50 meters over an S-shaped route for a direct distance of 325 meters. See *ANET*, 321 for inscription.

Photograph courtesy of the Palestine Archaeological Museum. See *AOB*, 626-628 for plans; J. Simons, *Jerusalem in the Old Testament*, Leiden, 1952, pp. 178-192.

FROM NEIGHBORING AREAS

745. Three temples at Tepe Gawra, built of mud-brick, were arranged around a large open court, measuring 18 by 15 meters. The northern temple (slightly to the left of the center of the photograph) was the smallest but best preserved of the three, measuring 12.25 by 8.65 meters. The walls were decorated by recessed niches both inside and outside. Stone foundations seen in the main court belong to the earlier (XIV) level. Gawra XIII, belonging to the Obeid period (fourth millennium).

Photograph courtesy of the University Museum. See A. J. Tobler, *Excavations at Tepe Gawra*, vol. 2, Philadelphia, 1950, pl. 39b, pp. 30-37.

746. A section of the southwest wall of the ziggurat of Ur-Nammu of the Third Dynasty at Ur. The casing of this wall is of burnt bricks set in bitumen mortar. Buttresses about 2.60 m. in width project outward 0.45 m. at intervals.

Photograph courtesy of the University Museum. See L. Woolley, *The Ziggurat and its Surroundings*, London, 1939, pl. 50b, pp. 98 ff.

747. A characteristic of temple architecture in Mesopotamia is the ziggurat (*ziqqurrat*), or temple tower, probably the feature known as the "tower" of Babel in Gen. 11:1-9. The steps leading to the top of the famous ziggurat at Ur can be seen from this aerial photograph.

Photograph courtesy of the University Museum. See L. Woolley, *The Ziggurat and its Surroundings*, London, 1939, pl. 41. H. J. Lenzen, *Die Entwicklung der Zikurrat*, Leipzig, 1941. A. Parrot, *Ziggurats et tour de Babel*, Paris, 1949. A. Parrot, *La tour de Babel*, Neuchatel and Paris, 1953.

748. A general plan of the city of Ur (Gen. 11:28, 31) during the Larsa period (1960-1700), showing the outline of the city walls, the temple area, with its ziggurat, and the residential area.

Photograph from *MJ*, vol. 22, 1931, pl. 28. See also *AJ*, vol. 11, 1931, pl. 46.

749. Held in the lap of Gudea (Statue B) is an architectural plan of a building or town. The plan is roughly rectangular in shape, has six openings in the walls, which are represented as crenelated or with projecting towers. To the left, in the shorter side, is pictured what may be an "altar" with two horns. While the plan cannot be identified with certainty, the obvious purpose was to show Gudea as an architect. See Nos. 430, 431 for statues of Gudea.

Photograph Archives Photographiques. Beginning twenty-first century. See E. de Sarzec, *Découvertes in Chaldée*, Paris, 1884-1912, pl. 15, 1. A. Parrot, *Tello*, Paris, 1948, pl. 14d.

750. A door socket appears in a stone which is carved in the form of a bound enemy, as though crushed under the weight of the door which fitted into his back.

University Museum, E 3959. Hierakonpolis (Kom el-Ahmar). Black sandstone. Length: about 0.775 m. First Dynasty (about 3000). J. E. Quibell, *Hierakonpolis*, pt. 1, London, 1900, pl. 3. *University Museum Bulletin*, vol. 15, 1950, fig. 14. Photograph courtesy UM.

751. A door socket inscribed with the name of King Sharkalisharri was found at Nippur. See No. 682.

University Museum, B 8751. Nippur. Diorite. Height: 0.415 m.; width: 0.75 m. Fifth king of Dynasty of Akkad (about 2360-2180). H. V. Hilprecht, *Old Babylonian Inscriptions Chiefly from Nippur*, Philadelphia, 1893, pl. 2, photographic pl. 1. Photograph courtesy UM.

752-753. Types of Mesopotamian houses, with suggested connections with buildings in other areas, drawn by Valentine Müller in *JAOS*, vol. 60, 1940, pp. 179-180. For explanatory text see V. Müller, "Types of Mesopotamian Houses," *JAOS*, vol. 60, 1940, pp. 151-180.

754. The Temple Oval at Khafajah covered an area of more than three-quarters of an acre and was founded on a bed of sand more than 8 meters thick. The reconstruction shown is of the complex of the first building period (Early Dynastic II, early third millennium).

Photograph courtesy of the Oriental Institute. See P. Delougaz, *The Temple Oval at Khafājah*, OIP, 53, Chicago, 1940, frontispiece.

755. A temple at Ashur consisted of two ziggurats (each measuring at its base 36.6 by 35.1 meters), one dedicated to Anu, the other to Adad, two cellae between the ziggurats, and an open court. Although the work may have been begun by Ashurreshishi, the temple is thought to have been the work of his son Tiglath-pileser I (1114-1076), whose prisms have been found in the temple.

Drawing from W. Andrae, *Das wiedererstandene Assur*, Leipzig, 1938, fig. 55, courtesy of J. C. Hinrichs Verlag, Leipzig; see pp. 130-133.

756. This temple of Sinsharishkun at Ashur, consisting of two grand courts and three cellae, represented the last testimony to Assyrian architecture at the close of the seventh century. It was dedicated to Ishtar, Nebo, and another deity, perhaps Tashmet, wife of Nebo.

Drawing from W. Andrae, *Die jüngeren Ischtar-Tempel in Assur*, WVDOG, 58, Leipzig, 1935, pl. 8a, courtesy of the Deutsche Orient-Gesellschaft. See also W. Andrae, *Das wiedererstandene Assur*, Leipzig, 1938, fig. 68, pp. 159-163; A. Parrot, *Archéologie mésopotamienne, Les étapes*, Paris, 1946, p. 228.

757. The mound of Kuyunjik, the site of ancient Nineveh, on the Tigris just opposite Mosul, produced much of the Assyrian sculpture in the British Museum, as well as tablets which have formed the nucleus of the sources for a knowledge of ancient Mesopotamia.

Drawing from R. C. Thompson, "The Buildings of Quyunjiq, the Larger Mound of Nineveh," *Iraq*, vol. 1, 1934, fig. 1, courtesy of the British School of Archaeology in Iraq; see pp. 95-104. See also A. Parrot, *Archéologie mésopotamienne, Les étapes*, Paris, 1946, pp. 412-419 for summary of recent excavations.

758. A century after the brilliant discoveries of Layard at Nimrud (biblical Calah, Gen. 10:11, 12), the British returned to Nimrud for further excavations. The plan of the northwest palace, drawn by R. W. Hamilton in 1950, shows the southeast wing, discovered in that year, in relation to the palace, which had been discovered by Layard.

Drawing from M. E. L. Mallowan, "Excavations at Nimrud, 1949-1950," *Iraq*, vol. 12, 1950, pl. 27, courtesy of the British School of Archaeology in Iraq; see pp. 147-183.

759. The palace of Sargon II (721-705) at Khorsabad, excavated by V. Place in the 1850's and by the Oriental Institute in the 1930's, was built on a terrace from 14 to 18 meters high. Place distinguished in this large structure 31 courts, 209 rooms, a ziggurat, and a temple.

Drawing from V. Place, *Ninive et l'Assyrie*, vol. 3, plates, Paris, 1867, pl. 18 bis. See A. Parrot, *Archéologie mésopotamienne, Les étapes*, Paris, 1946, pp. 61-76, 424-431.

760. The Ishtar gate at Babylon, belonging to the time of Nebuchadnezzar II (605-562), originally contained 13 rows of animals—rows of bulls alternating with rows of serpent-dragons—estimated at a minimum number of 575. This reconstruction is in the Vorderasiatische Abteilung, Staatliche Museen, Berlin. See Nos. 761, 762 for details.

Photograph Foto Marburg. Height: about 15 m. See R. Koldewey, *Das Ischtar-Tor in Babylon*, WVDOG, 32, Leipzig, 1918, pl. 9; AOB, 373. For account of excavations see R. Koldewey, *The Excavations at Babylon*, London, 1914.

761. This composite creature, with head of serpent, body of a lion, and hind feet of an eagle, served as decoration for the Ishtar gate at Babylon (No. 760).

Detroit, Institute of Arts, 31.25. Babylon. Glazed tile. Height about 1 m. Nebuchadnezzar II (605-562). J. Pijoán, *Summa Artis*, vol. 2, Madrid, 1931, fig. 264. See also Schäfer-Andrae, 521. Photograph courtesy of the Detroit Institute of Arts.

762. The procession street at Babylon, which runs from the Ishtar gate (No. 760), was lined on each side with lions of enameled bricks. It is estimated that there were originally 120 of these lions lining the walls. Ground is turquoise; mane, shoulders, and tip of tail are yellow with black markings; back and legs, white; tongue, yellow.

Boston, Museum of Fine Arts, 31.898. Babylon. Height about: 1 m. Nebuchadnezzar II (605-562). *BMFA*, vol. 30, 1932, p. 88. See Schäfer-Andrae, pl. 29; AOB, 375. Photograph courtesy MFA.

763. To the right and to the back of this model, now in Baghdad, made by W. Struck of a section of Babylon along the Euphrates, can be seen the Etemenanki, the tower of Babylon. To the left is the principal temple of Marduk, the Esagila ("temple with raised head," cf. Gen. 11:4). See *ANET*, index under "Esagila."

Photograph courtesy of Staatliche Museen, Berlin. See F. Wetzel and F. H. Weissbach, *Das Hauptheiligtum des Marduk in Babylon, Esagila und Etemenanki*, WVDOG, 59, Leipzig, 1938, pl. 17b.

764. A tomb for King Djoser (about 2700) at Sakkarah, made into the form of a step pyramid, rising to a height of 62 meters and covering an area of about 109 by 124 meters.

Photograph courtesy of B. V. Bothmer. See I. E. S. Edwards, *The Pyramids of Egypt*, West Drayton, 1947, pp. 45-66, for description and discussion.

765. A sphinx, the body of a lion and the head of King Khaf-Re (Chephren), is the guardian of the necropolis of Giza with its three great pyramids, two of which are shown here (to the right, the pyramid of Khufu or Cheops; to the left, the pyramid of Khaf-Re).

Photograph courtesy of Trans World Airline. See I. E. S. Edwards, *The Pyramids of Egypt*, West Drayton, 1947, pp. 85-132, for descriptions. See also AOB, 37.

766. The apadana, or audience hall, at Persepolis, begun by Darius (521-486) and completed by Xerxes (485-465), excavated by E. E. Herzfeld from 1931-1934 for the Oriental Institute, and later by E. F. Schmidt. See Nos. 11, 28 for details.

Photograph courtesy of the Oriental Institute. See E. F. Schmidt, *Persepolis I*, OIP, 68, Chicago, 1953, pl. 16B; A. T. Olmstead, *History of the Persian Empire*, Chicago, 1948, pl. 37 (upper). For description of work at Persepolis see A. Godard, "Les travaux de Persépolis," *Archaeologica Orientalia in Memoriam Ernst Herzfeld*, edited by G. C. Miles, New York, 1952, pp. 119-128.

767. Susian and Persian guards along the outer flight of the north wing of the eastern stairway of the apadana at Persepolis. See No. 30. Time of Xerxes (485-465).

Photograph courtesy of the Oriental Institute. See E. F. Schmidt, *Persepolis I*, OIP, 68, Chicago, 1953, pl. 50; A. T. Olmstead, *History of the Persian Empire*, Chicago, 1948, pl. 31.

768. The tomb of Cyrus at Pasargadae is set on six steps of irregular height and is in the form of a plain house with sharply gabled roof. A double door, in an opening measuring 0.79 by 1.37 meters, leads to a windowless chamber.

Pasargadae (Murghāb). Limestone blocks tied together by iron cramps. Base: 14.63 by 13.41 meters. Cyrus (557-529). *AOB*, 155. A. T. Olmstead, *History of the Persian Empire*, Chicago, 1948, pl. 10 (upper), pp. 65-66. See E. F. Schmidt, *Persepolis I, OIP*, 68, Chicago, 1953, p. 24, for description. Photograph courtesy of the Oriental Institute.

769. The royal tombs carved out of living rock at Naqsh-i-Rustam, near Persepolis, seen from left to right, are those of Darius II (423-404), Artaxerxes I (464-424), Darius I (521-486).

Photograph courtesy of the Oriental Institute. See E. F. Schmidt, *The Treasury of Persepolis, OIC*, 21, Chicago, 1939, fig. 69.

Index

The following Index is to the names and subjects mentioned in the descriptive catalogue. Proper names are given in the simpler form (without diacritics); place names are indexed according to both ancient and modern forms. References to the main sections (indicated by quotation marks), as well as to subdivisions listed in the table of Contents, are given in italic type. While specific references to passages in the Old Testament are listed under "Bible," biblical names and subjects are placed alphabetically.

Abimilki, 245
Abi-shar, 3
Abu Habbah, Sippar, map IV, 519, 529
Abu Shahrein, Eridu, map IV
Abu Simbel, map I, 32, 339
Abusir, map I, 1, 41-42
Abydos, map I, 33, 44, 59, 293, 294, 340, 422, 545, 549, 567
Acre, map II
Adab, Bismaya, map IV
Adad, 501, 519-521, 533, 537, 538, 703, 755
Adad-nirari III, 444, 620
Adda, 681
Addatur, 427
Adini, 362
adornment, personal, 67-83
adze, 116, 306, 640
adzehead, ceremonial, 261
Agade, 251, 309, see also Akkad
Agbar, 635
agriculture, 84-96, 697
Ahiram, 286, 456-459
Ah-mose I, 233, 310
Ahuni, 362
Ahuramazda, 249
Ai, et-Tell, map II, 584, 730, 733
air-god, 542
Akh-en-Aton, 245, 398, 401-403, 405-408, 410-412
Akhet-Aton, 406
Akkad, 682, see also Agade
Akurgal, 427
Alaça Hüyük, map III, 616
Alalakh, Atchana, map III, 452
Aleppo, map III, 280, 499, 500, 540, 635, 652
Alexandria, map I
'Alhan Nahfan, 285
Alishar Hüyük, map III
alphabet: table, 286; Ugaritic, 263
alphabetic writing, 270-286
altar, 223, 320, 529, 574, 575, 580, 606, 616, 619, 673, 689, 698, 729-731, 734, 737, 738, 749
altar-piece, 405
altar-room, 734, 738
altars and sockets, 574-581
el-'Amarna, map I, see Tell el-Amarna
Amen-em-heb, 46
Amen-em-het, 122
Amen-em-het III, 385, 386
Amen-em-Opet, 487, 642
Amen-hotep II, 80, 389-392
Amen-hotep III, 4, 394-400, 569
Amen-hotep son of Hapu, 399
'Amman, map II, 64
'Ammyada' of Šukaymim, 66

Amon, 312, 313, 317, 321, 327, 342, 349, 419, 473, 474, 550-552, 573
Amon-Re, 321, 573
Amor, 7, 9, 346
amphora, 589
'Amrit, map III, 486
'Amrum 'Abyad Karr, 65
amulet, 568, 661, 662
amulets, monsters, demons, 644-666
Amurru (god), 622, 702
Amurru, land of, 324
Anani bar Azariah, 282
Anat, Anath, 473, 492
Anath-is-content, 328
Anikurra, 427
animal head, 370, 493
animal-paw, 584
animals, hunting, 182-190
animal-vase, 674
Anita, 427
ankh (hieroglyph for "life"), 41-42, 223, 320, 338, 400, 408, 470, 473-475, 487-489, 492, 499, 549-551, 555, 563, 569, 572
Ankhes-en-Amon, 415-417
Ankh-ma-Hor, 629
Ankh-nes-Nefer-ib-Re, 543
ankle band, 465, 630
anklet, 558
Anta, 311
antelope, 222, 351-355
antelope head, 473, 650
Anu, 519-521, 537, 702, 755
Anubanini, 524
Anubis, 548, 573, 639, 640
Anukis, 573
Anunpad, 427
apadana, 766, 767
Apis, 570
Apophis, 669
Apries, 425
apsû, 529
Aqhat, 264
Arab, 63, 375
Arabia, 170
Arabian peoples and dress, 63-66
Aram, 499
Aramaic alphabet, 286
Aramaic endorsement, 255
Aramaic inscription, 119, 280, 281, 499
Aramaic papyrus, 265, 282
Aramaic writing, 235
Aramean, 62
Araras, 461
archer, 362, 369
architectural plan, 749
Armageddon, 708
arm band, 422, 441, 455, 614

armor, 161, 176
arrow, 172, 179, 182-185, 311, 333, 338, 346, 351-355, 371, 390, 519, 626, 704
arrowhead, 176
arrow making, 122
Arslan Tash, map III, 39, 58, 173, 174, 501, 621, 662
Artaxerxes I, 769
Arvad, Erwad, map III
Arzawa, 345
Asasif, 206
Ashdod, Esdud, map II
Ashkelon, map II, 334
Ashtamaku, 365
Ashtaroth, 366
Ashtart, 131, see also Astarte
Ashur (god), 247, 364, 536, 537, 658
Ashur, Qal'at Sherqat, map IV, 119, 247, 528, 534-536, 576, 577, 591, 627, 628, 643, 755, 756
Ashurbanipal: 63, 167, 170, 184, 204, 424, 448-449, 450, 451, 626; army of, 10
Ashurnasirpal, 624
Ashurnasirpal II, 350, 439, 441, 617, 624, 646
Ashurreshishi, 755
Asiatic, 3, 44, 311, 313, 314-316, 318, 320, 341, 393
'asor, 203
aspergillum, 628
ass, 89, 163, 166, 186, 303-305, 604, 658
Assuan, map I
Assyrian, 114, 170, 235, 535, 537
'-s-t(a)r-t, 468
Astarte, 314-316
Astartu, 366
'Astawalus, 289
Atchana, Alalakh, map III, 452
atef-crown (an Egyptian composite crown), 544, 556, 557, 566
'Athlit, map II, 71
Aton, 408
Atum, 381, 571
awl, 141
axe: 91, 135, 163, 224, 300, 302, 303, 305, 309, 329, 334, 473, 525, 532, 538, 611, 662; scalloped, 476
axehead, ceremonial, 178
axle, 303
Aya, 529
Azaz, 500

Baal, 460, 490
Ba'alat, 270
Babel, 747
baboon, 266